A NEW VOYAGE TO CAROLINA

A *New*

VOYAGE

to

CAROLINA

by

JOHN LAWSON

Edited with an Introduction and Notes
by
HUGH TALMAGE LEFLER

THE UNIVERSITY OF NORTH CAROLINA PRESS
CHAPEL HILL

PREFACE

John Lawson's *A New Voyage to Carolina* has been reprinted many times and under various titles. This is the first time, however, that this famous book has been edited, annotated, and indexed. This edition is a true copy of the original 1709 London edition, containing the original map and plate, "The Beasts of Carolina." It also contains nine prints of John White's "American Drawings." These paintings illustrate so vividly descriptions of Indian life as given by Lawson more than a century later that the editor believes they will add something of interest to the present volume. Also included are the "Plan of Bath" and Von Graffenried's "Map of New Bern," because Lawson was co-founder of both these towns.

The capitalization and punctuation of the 1709 edition have been followed, and no changes have been made in the original spelling, where it is obvious what Lawson meant, e.g., "Pampticough" and "Chuwon," with the exception of rendering the old-style "s" in its modern form. On the other hand, where the spelling is so different from that of today, or where the word used by Lawson cannot be found in a standard dictionary, the editor has inserted the modern spelling in square brackets after the word used by Lawson. Where a word is obsolete or archaic the meaning of the word is inserted in square brackets, e.g., "Hogoo [relish]," and "Lilleloo [lolling or hanging the tongue out]." The editor has also translated Latin words and phrases.

In the case of spelling of the numerous Indian names used by Lawson in his "Journal," the editor has given in footnotes the generally accepted spelling of modern anthropologists and ethnologists. For the remainder of Lawson's book, he has indicated the modern spelling in square brackets.

CONTENTS

PREFACE   v

INTRODUCTION   xi
Lawson's Long Trail   xi
John Lawson's Career in North Carolina   xv
The Lawson Map   xxxix
Naturalist and Collector of Botanical Specimens   xl
Editions of Lawson's Book   xliv
Plagiarisms of Lawson   lii

A NEW VOYAGE TO CAROLINA   1

DEDICATION   3

PREFACE   5

INTRODUCTION   7

A JOURNAL   13

A DESCRIPTION OF NORTH CAROLINA   68
Of the Corn of Carolina   80
Of the Herbs of Carolina   83

THE PRESENT STATE OF CAROLINA   86

THE NATURAL HISTORY OF CAROLINA   96
Of the Vegetables of Carolina   96

The Beasts of Carolina   120
Insects of Carolina   131
Birds of Carolina   140
Fish of Carolina   155

AN ACCOUNT OF THE INDIANS OF NORTH
CAROLINA   172

APPENDIXES
The Second Charter   249
An Abstract of the Constitution of Carolina   264
Letters from John Lawson to James Petiver of
   London   267
John Lawson's Will   274

INDEX   279

ILLUSTRATIONS

Lawson's Long Trail	x
Plan of the Town and Port of Bath, 1769	xxiii
Plan of Bath, 1807	xxv
Plan of the Swiss Colony begun in 1710 by Von Graffenried	xxvii
Plan of the Town of New Bern	xxix
Capture of Lawson and Von Graffenried	xxxii
Torture of Lawson and Von Graffenried	xxxiii
Portrait of Baron Christopher von Graffenried	xxxv
Lawson's Map of the Carolinas	xxxviii
Title page of first German edition, 1712	xlv
Letter from President Madison to Governor Montfort Stokes	xlvi
Presentation inscription in the 1714 edition	xlvii
Title page of the second German edition, 1722	xlviii
Title page of an undated manuscript copy of the 1718 edition	xlix
Title page of the original 1709 edition	1
Indians around a fire	179
Indians dancing	181
Indian man and woman eating	183
Cooking in an earthen pot	183
Indian charnel house	186
Indian woman and young girl	191
Old Indian man	198
Indian elder or chief	199
Indian in body paint	202

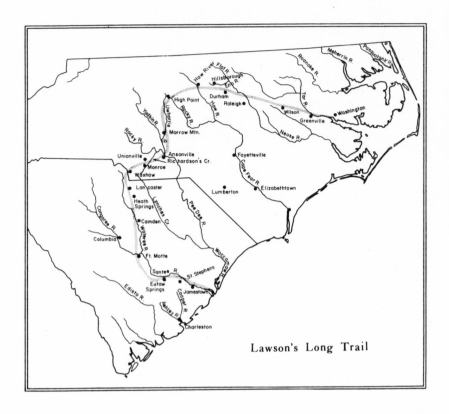

Lawson's Long Trail

INTRODUCTION

In 1700, John Lawson, a young man who was eager to travel, "accidentally met with a Gentleman" who had been to America and who assured him "that Carolina was the best country I could go to." [1] Accordingly, he booked passage for the New World on a ship then at anchor in the Thames. A few days later, on May 1, the vessel sailed from Cowes. After a stormy voyage lasting almost three months, it arrived off Sandy Hook and put into New York harbor. Lawson spent a fortnight in the city, where he was impressed by "the enterprising Dutch, the harbor, and the sturdy fortifications." [2] After taking on much needed supplies, the ship sailed for Charleston near the end of August, where it arrived after a two weeks' voyage. Lawson was impressed by the "thriving colony" which he considered "of more advantage to the Crown of Great Britain than any of the more northerly plantations (Virginia and Maryland excepted) ." [3]

Nothing is known of Lawson's sojourn in Charleston until December, 1700, when he was appointed by the Lords Proprietors to make a reconnaisance survey of the interior of Carolina. This was not an easy assignment. No one had been to the back country except a few Indian traders and Spaniards. Little was known about the natives of this area and their attitude towards the English. There were no adequate maps of the region and the only possible guides would be Indians encountered along the way. Equipment other than firearms and powder was scanty.

1. Lawson, *A New Voyage to Carolina* (1709) , "Introduction," p. xxv.
2. *Ibid.,* p. xxvi.
3. *Ibid.* Lawson commented on the trade of Charleston with Europe and with the West Indies. He also praised the education of the youth of the city.

On December 28, 1700, Lawson and five other Englishmen, three Indian men, and the Indian wife of the guide left Charleston in a "large Canoe," bound for the mouth of the Santee River.[4] The party passed Sullivan's, Bells, Dix, Bull's, and Racoon islands before they reached the mouth of the Santee on January 3. That night they stayed with a French Huguenot settler. Here their Indian guides deserted and Lawson managed to hire a Sewee guide, whom he called Scipio, for the trip up the Santee. Two days later, they reached the plantation of another Frenchman. The latter obtained a Negro who guided them to the Gallian plantation at a ferry where the party seems to have crossed to the south bank of the Santee. This plantation probably stood near present Jamestown. It was the last white habitation Lawson was to see for almost two months.

The Lawson party then proceeded westerly and finally reached the lodge of the king of the Santee Indians on January 9. This was probably near the present town of Eutaw Springs. While visiting the Santees, Lawson met the king, a "No-nosed Doctor," and a native seven feet tall, who was the most renowned hunter of the tribe. While here Scipio got gloriously drunk and Lawson left him among the Santees; shortly thereafter, he hired "Santee Jack" as guide.

Still traveling west and northwest along the Santee, the party reached the country of the Congarees near the present site of Fort Motte on January 15. Near the confluence of the Wateree and Congaree rivers, on the latter stream, they arrived at Congaree Town, located in present Richland County. Proceeding westerly and passing through land "strewn with marble," the party followed the Wateree River. About sixty miles from "Congaree Town," the party reached the Wateree Chickanee Indians or Waterees, located near the river of that name, not far from the present town of Great Falls. In this area, Lawson was impressed by water bubbling from springs, probably in the vicinity of present Health Springs. Leaving the Waterees, Lawson next visited the Waxhaws where, about January 19 to 21, he crossed into what is now North Carolina. Two days later, the party broke ice in a stream, probably a tributary of Lynch's River. Near the present town of Monroe, "Esaw" Indians were encountered on what is

4. The best description of "Lawson's Long Trail" is in Douglas L. Rights, *The American Indian in North Carolina* (Durham: Duke University Press, 1947), pp. 71–90.

probably a tributary of Rocky River. Moving east and north, Lawson passed villages of the Sugarees and, on January 22, spent the night with the chief of the Kadapahaws, or Catawbas, who lived on the Catawba River near the mouth of Sugar Creek, probably near present Unionville. The party remained with the Catawbas for three days and then resumed their journey over the famous Trading Path, which led northeast near the present locations of Charlotte, Concord, and Salisbury. After several days of delightful travel through a country Lawson called "delicious," the party arrived at Trading Ford on the Yadkin River. On the "pleasant Banks of Sapona River," there stood "the Indian Town and Fort." The backwater of High Rock Lake now covers the Yadkin River Valley, but in dry seasons the islands may be seen.[5] At the lower end of the islands is old Trading Ford. The Dukeville power station is located near the west end of the ford.

The Lawson party remained at "Sapona" until February 3. Then they proceeded eastward. Eight miles from Trading Ford, they "passed over a very pretty River called Rock River," which is present Abbott's Creek, near Lexington. The trail led near the present location of the settlements of Silver Hill and Cid. On February 5, the "Highwarrie," or Uwharrie River, was crossed and the party came to Keyauwee Town, which Lawson said was five miles northwest of the Uwharrie River.

The location of this town remained a mystery for more than a century, partly because Lawson's direction given as northwest is misleading and, besides, there is no stream of the size he described five miles west of the Uwharrie River. Archaeologists of the twentieth century have rediscovered the lost Keyauwee Town on Carraway Creek, and the site has been excavated by the Research Laboratories of Anthropology of The University of North Carolina at Chapel Hill.[6]

On February 8, most of Lawson's party decided to go directly to Virginia from Keyauwee Town, but Lawson and one of his group decided to continue their travels in North Carolina. His first day's

5. *Ibid.*, Plate 31, between pages 76 and 77, shows "The Famous Trading Ford on the Yadkin River near Salisbury," with an X marking the spot at which the Lawson party crossed.
6. *Ibid.*, Plate 33, between pages 76 and 77, shows "Burials at Keyauwee Village Site" and the "Keyauwee Village Site, Randolph County." Plate 34 is a photograph of "Shell Beads, Trade Beads, Shell Pins or Plugs, Shell Pendant, Animal Tooth, Trade Pipe and Broken Stem, and Paint Cup" at Keyauwee Site.

travel of twenty miles led across "two pretty Rivers, something bigger than Heighwaree," present Deep River and Polecat Creek. The crossing was a little north of present Randleman.

Lawson's trail then led across "three Great Rivers," Little and Big Alamance River and Haw River. Lawson crossed the latter at a ford near the present town of Swepsonville. He observed that the land in this area "is extraordinary Rich."

On February 12, Lawson reached Occaneechi [Occaneechee] Town, located near present Hillsborough.[7] Here he met an Indian, Enoe Will, who agreed to guide him to the English settlements in the coastal area. The next morning, Lawson's small party set out with their new guide, accompanied by several of his Indian friends. They left the Trading Path [8] and traveled eastward, crossing the Eno River at Occaneechi Town and proceeding about fourteen miles to the Indian village of Adshusheer, situated along a "Pretty Rivulet," northwest of the present city of Durham. Then proceeding southeasterly, they followed the western bank of the Neuse until they crossed to the northern bank at the falls [9] of that river on February 18. Two days later they reached the "hunting quarter" of five hundred Tuscarora Indians. Accompanied by some of these Indians, the party traveled through country densely settled with Indian towns. The party passed near the site of present Goldsboro, then turned north, crossed the Contentnea near Grifton and the Tar at present Greenville. On February 23, they arrived at the English settlements on "Pampticough River," in the vicinity of present Washington, "where, being well received by the inhabitants, and pleased with the goodness of the country, we all resolved to continue."

Here Lawson ended his "thousand miles travel" at the plantation of Richard Smith,[10] on Pamlico River, where he parted company forever with his devoted guide, Enoe Will. The trip was in

7. The name "Occaneechi Hills" still remains to designate the hills south of Eno River. The name has also been applied to a farm, a brand of flour, and to the Boy Scout Council of this area. Within recent years, the spelling of the county seat of Orange County has been changed from Hillsboro to Hillsborough.

8. *Ibid.*, Plate 43, between pages 92 and 93, indicates "The Trading Path to the Indians, Traced on a Map of Present Day North Carolina." See also Douglas L. Rights, "The Trading Path to the Indians," *North Carolina Historical Review* VIII (1931), 403.

9. Cliffs of the Neuse, in Wayne County, is now a state park.

10. Lawson's will, which was made in 1708, left most of his property to his "dearly beloved Hannah Smith." She may have been the daughter of this man. See footnote 67, p. xxxvii. Apparently Hannah Smith was Lawson's mistress, since there is no evidence of their marriage.

the neighborhood of 550 miles. The 1,000 miles, claimed by Lawson on the title page of his "Journal," must have been calculated as following the meanderings of rivers and creeks and to crookedness of the trail incident to travel on foot through wilderness country.

In fifty-nine days, and in the winter, Lawson had covered this great distance, following a horseshoe-shaped course from the South Carolina coast around through the Piedmont country and eastward to the North Carolina coast, with only the aid of Indian guides. During this period he managed to keep an extensive journal, make daily notes on the trip and the flora and fauna, and begin a small vocabulary of Indian words.

JOHN LAWSON'S CAREER IN NORTH CAROLINA

Little is known of the early life of John Lawson, traveler and explorer, surveyor, natural historian and collector of botanical specimens, humorist, founder of the two oldest towns in the state, and author of the only book to come out of proprietary North Carolina. Although the second edition of his book had the title *History of North Carolina*, it is not history at all in the usually accepted sense. Lawson's volume, which Moses Coit Tyler described as "an uncommonly strong and sprightly book," is one of the most valuable of the early volumes about North Carolina, and it is one of the best travel accounts of the early eighteenth-century colonies.

We have been unable to find when or where Lawson was born, who his parents were, or where he received his education. Stephen B. Weeks concluded—without proof—that he came from the Lawson's of Brough Hall of Yorkshire, England, and was probably "the son of that Lawson who was such a faithful adherent of the King in the civil war that he suffered sequestration of his estates under the Commonwealth, and that in 1665, during the Restoration, his estates were returned to him, and he received Knighthood for his loyalty." [11] The article on Lawson in the *Dictionary of American Biography* makes the same assumption.[12]

11. Stephen B. Weeks, "John Lawson," S. A. Ashe, ed., *Biographical History of North Carolina from Colonial Times to the Present* (Greensboro: C. L. Van Noppen, 1905–17), II, 212–18. This is the longest article on Lawson to appear before the publication of this volume. Hereinafter cited as Weeks, "John Lawson."

12. Allen Johnson, Dumas Malone, and others, eds., *Dictionary of American Biography* (New York: Charles Scribner's Sons, 1928–58), XI, 57–58. The article is by W. K. Boyd.

Lawson was certainly familiar with Yorkshire, and his book contains many references to towns, rivers, and various physical features of that county in northern England. It is unlikely, however, that he was one of the Lawsons of Brough Hall. Authorities in the British Museum say that "The Brough Hall Lawsons were baronets, and John Lawson does not appear in the genealogies of that family published in Burke's *Baronetage*." [13] The *British Dictionary of National Biography* states that Lawson was a Scotsman, as does *Appleton's Cyclopedia of American Biography* and several other encyclopedias.[14] It is likely that the writers of these articles have confused John Lawson with the family of the more famous scientist, Isaac Lawson, who was a Scot.

The editor of this volume is inclined to think that all of the above-mentioned articles are in error and that Lawson was from London. Raymond Phineas Stearns, the leading authority on James Petiver, one of the greatest promoters of natural science in his day, says: "In view of John Lawson's connection with James Petiver and of his obvious interest in and knowledge of medicine, botany, and natural history, it seems likely that he was the John Lawson referred to in the Court-Book of the London Society of Apothecaries under the date of February 1, 1675, 'John Lawson, son of Andrew Lawson, Citizen & Salter of London, examined, approved & bound to John Chandler for 8 years'." [15] Two years later, Chandler had died, and the Court, on May 1, 1677, turned Lawson over to James Hayes for the remaining six years. Whether he completed his apprenticeship is not known, and there is no further record of Lawson until his arrival in the colonies in 1700.

It is obvious from his book that Lawson was a man of education and training in the natural sciences. In his "Preface," he la-

13. Letter to the editor from the Department of Manuscripts, The British Museum, dated February 19, 1966.

14. Sir Leslie Stephen, Sir Sidney Lee, and others, eds., *The Dictionary of National Biography* (London: Oxford Press, 1885–1959), XI, 735–36. James G. Wilson, John Fiske, and others, eds. *Appleton's Cyclopedia of American Biography* (New York: D. Appleton and Company, 1888–1924), VII, 115. The *D.N.B.* and several other biographical sketches give "1712" as the date of his death, an obvious error.

15. Raymond Phineas Stearns, "James Petiver, Promoter of Natural Science, c. 1663–1718." *Proceedings of the American Antiquarian Society*, Vol. 62 (April 16, 1952—October 15, 1952), (Worcester, Mass., published by the Society, 1963), p. 335. Hereinafter cited as Stearns, "James Petiver." Stearns's quotation is from *Court Book of the London Society of Apothecaries*, 1 Sept., 1681—6 April, 1680, fols. 202, 220v.

mented the fact that many British travelers who went to America were "Persons of the meaner Sort, and generally, of a very slender Education," who, when they returned to England, were "uncapable of giving any reasonable Account of what they met withal in those remote Parts; though the Country abounds with Curiosities worthy a nice Observation." [16] Some writers have assumed that he was educated at either Oxford or Cambridge, but the records of these two great universities do not mention any "John Lawson" for the period of the late seventeenth century, obviously the time of Lawson's youth and early manhood.[17]

Francis Latham Harriss, in her "Foreword" to the 1937 edition of *Lawson's History of North Carolina,* says:

All we know of John Lawson indicates beyond doubt that he was a gentleman by birth [he signed himself "Gent."], that he was well educated, his tastes cultured, and that he possessed ample means to indulge them, and was free to choose the course of his life and steer it where he would. Being of a mind, as he tells us, to travel and see the world he started to journey with the human mass crowding toward Rome to witness the pageant of the Pope's Jubilee in the year 1700. But "he met a Gentleman, who had been Abroad, and was very well acquainted with the Way of Living in both Indies," and the course of his life was changed. The gentleman fired his imagination with the possibilities of adventure in the New World, so Lawson deserted the well known path across the old familiar world, to pit his youthful strength and ardor against the mystery and unknown hazards of the new.[18]

After the completion of his "thousand miles travel among the Indians of North Carolina and South Carolina," in the spring of 1701, and "after a brief sojourn on the Pamlico River," Lawson "built a House about Half a mile from an Indian town at the fork of Neus-River, where I dwelt by myself, excepting a young Indian

---

16. Lawson's "Preface," p. 5.
17. John Venn and J. A. Venn, comps. *Alumni Cantabrigienses: A Biographical List of All Known Students, Graduates and Holders of Office at the University of Cambridge, from the earliest times to 1900.* 10 vols. (Cambridge: at the University Press, 1922–1954). Joseph Foster, comp., *Alumni Oxonienses: The Members of the University of Oxford 1500–1714: Their Parentage, Birthplace, and Year of Birth, with a Record of their degrees.* 3 vols. (Oxford: James Parker & Co., 1891).
18. Francis Latham Harriss, ed., *Lawson's History of North Carolina* (Richmond: Garrett and Massie, Publishers, 1937), xi–xiii.

Fellow, and a Bull-Dog, that I had along with me." [19] This Indian town of Chatooka was the future site of New Bern. He said his cabin "stood on a pretty high Land and by a Creek-side." This creek still bears the name Lawson's Creek.

Apparently Lawson was engaged in surveying work from the beginning of his residence in North Carolina, first on his own, then as the deputy of Edward Moseley, Surveyor-General of the province. [20] The late Stephen B. Weeks wrote that "on April 28, 1708, Lawson was appointed by the Lords Proprietors to succeed Moseley in this position." [21] In his short article on Lawson, Weeks said: "This office demanded skill, courage, energy, integrity and some measure of learning; it conferred a high social rank, brought him into contact with the leading men in the province and was the best possible preparation for his account of the natural resources of the country." [22]

During the greater part of the decade Lawson lived in North Carolina, efforts to establish the Church of England and legal discriminations against Quakers and other "dissenters" kept the colony in a state of turmoil and confusion, finally culminating in "rebellion" in 1710. [23] Lawson seems to have kept out of political

19. Alonzo Dill, *Governor Tryon and His Palace* (Chapel Hill: The University of North Carolina Press, 1955) , p. 33. Hereinafter cited as Dill, *Tryon*.

20. Moseley was one of the largest landholders and one of the most prominent officials in Colonial North Carolina. He was a member of the Governor's Council, 1705-8, 1723-31, and 1734-49; Speaker of the Lower House, 1708-11, 1715-23, and 1731-34; Colonial Treasurer for the Province at Large, 1715-40; and Treasurer for the Southern District, 1740-49. He was also Surveyor General of the province for many years and Chief Justice in 1744. In 1733, he published "A New and Correct Map of the Province of North Carolina." As leader of the "popular party" for many years, he had many arguments with the governors, notably George Burrington, who once compared Moseley "to a Thief that hides himself in a house to rob it and fearing to be discovered, fires the house to make his escape in the smoak." At the time of his death, in 1749, Moseley owned over 35,000 acres of land.

21. It is not certain when Lawson became the official surveyor for the North Carolina region. On September 8, 1706, John Cartwright was surveyor for the colony. It is certain that Lawson was surveyor for that part of Carolina "north and east of Cape Fear" by the spring of 1709. Charles R. Holloman, a Raleigh attorney who has done extensive research on Lawson, says that "Landgrant records usually show the name of the Surveyor and even of the Chainbearers. I find not a one with his name on it as surveyor and infer from this that his surveying must have been almost, if not entirely, limited to work on the boundary line." Letter to the editor, July 11, 1966.

22. Weeks, "John Lawson," p. 214.

23. For an account of the "Cary Rebellion," see Hugh T. Lefler and A. R. Newsome, *North Carolina: The History of a Southern State* (rev. ed.; Chapel Hill: The University of North Carolina Press, 1963) , pp. 52-56. Hereinafter cited as Lefler-Newsome, *North Carolina*.

controversy during the "Cary Rebellion," though he favored William Glover, leader of the anti-Cary forces. While Lawson was in England seeing to the publication of his book, he probably discussed the troubled situation in North Carolina with one or more of the Lords Proprietors. On April 16, 1710, Thomas Pollock, one of North Carolina's largest land owners, a powerful political leader some years later and a close friend of Lawson, wrote that Frederick Jones said that Lawson "having been lately at his house, informed him that the Lords Proprietors are desirous of having Col Cary called to a strict account for their dues" and that Jones thought "it would be proper that some person should discourse Mr. Lawson in order to concert such proper methods as may put the government again on its proper foundation: to which he seems to think Mr. Lawson may be pursuaded to incline, both on the Lords Proprietors account and also on his own." [24] It is apparent that Pollock as well as the Lords Proprietors did not recognize Cary as governor. Yet, as President of the Council, he served as governor from 1708 to 1711. On May 27, 1710, Pollock wrote Lawson that he had removed to Virginia, "not being willing to live under a government I knew was altogether illegal." [25]

The "illegal government" and the "Cary Rebellion" came to an end in the early summer of 1711, when Cary fled to Virginia and Edward Hyde succeeded him as the first "Governor of North Carolina, independent of Carolina." At last the government was "again on its proper foundation." But three years of internal strife, plus a series of bad crop years, had left the colony so weakened, divided, and demoralized that it gave the Tuscarora Indians and their allies a glorious opportunity to launch a deadly attack against the whites in September, 1711. John Lawson was the first casualty.

Boundary Line Commissioner

Beginning many years before the Cary Rebellion, and lasting much longer, was the Virginia—North Carolina boundary dispute. This controversy began with the 1665 charter extension of the Carolina boundary 30 minutes north of the original 36 degrees provided for in the 1663 charter. The 36th parallel runs a little to the south of present Edenton, Durham, Greensboro, Win-

24. W. L. Saunders, ed., *The Colonial Records of North Carolina* (Raleigh: Printer to the State, 1886–90), I, 723–24. Hereinafter cited as *Colonial Records*.

25. *Ibid.*, pp. 727–28.

ston-Salem and due west, and if the Virginia contention had been
upheld that the 1665 extension was invalid, it would have given a
large block of territory to that colony. Virginia officials, from the
start, considered the 36th parallel as the "dividing line betwixt
Virginia and Carolina," and from 1681 to 1728 there was inter-
mittent controversy about land grants, quit rents, Indians, and
law enforcement in the disputed area. This region was the most
densely populated portion of North Carolina, and it was a matter
of great importance that the boundary be adjusted in that colony's favor. As early as 1681, the Lords Proprietors petitioned the
Crown for an official survey, but Virginia action prevented its
being made. In 1699, a royal order to survey the line went un-
heeded by Virginia, and Governor John Harvey of the North
Carolina region was informed by Virginia authorities that it was
"not convenient with us to treat with any person by you appointed." In 1705, the Virginia Council had a secret survey
made—to see how much land Virginia might lose by a proper
survey. Four years later, Queen Anne ordered the two colonies to
adjust the boundary.

About this time, probably on January 6, 1709, Lawson left for
England to see about the publication of his book. He was in Lon-
don on April 12, accompanied by Lyonell Reading, Luis Michel,
Richard Dereham, and Christopher Gale, the latter being the first
Chief Justice of North Carolina.

On July 21, 1709, while Lawson was still in England, the Lords
Proprietors appointed him and Edward Moseley "to be commissioners on the part of Carolina for surveying the lands in dispute"
with Virginia "and setting the boundaries as aforesaid." [26] The
Virginia commissioners, Philip Ludwell and Nathaniel Harrison,
set June 9, 1710 as the time for a meeting at Williamsburg "to
concert & adjust the method of proceeding in this affair." [27]
Shortly thereafter Lawson wrote Edward Jennings, President of
the Virginia Council, that he had not seen Mr. Moseley and that
he, Lawson, was then busy "in settling the Palatines" and could
not meet at the proposed time.[28] On July 18, the Virginia commissioners, writing from Williamsburg, suggested a meeting later
that month and agreed to meet elsewhere if Williamsburg was not
a convenient place.[29] Governor Alexander Spotswood wanted "to

26. *Ibid.*, p. 716.
27. *Ibid.*, p. 735.
28. *Ibid.*, p. 736.
29. *Ibid.*

have this affair expedited as much as possible,"[30] as did Governor Hyde of North Carolina. Moseley suggested August 21 as the time and Williamsburg as the place of meeting. On that date, the Virginia commissioners appeared at the appointed place, but Lawson and Moseley did not arrive until August 30.[31] The four commissioners met in the Conference Room of the Capitol, but the session ended without any agreement that the commissioners for both colonies "would proceed to take more Affidavits on both sides & then make a Tryal of the Latitude at both the contested places."[32] Nevertheless, the Virginia commissioners took more affidavits, but the Carolina commissioners did not. The Carolina representatives also "would allow no Instrument to be fitt for taking the Latitude except Mr. Lawson's, which they design to have some time or other, and then they expect we should meet again."[33] This delaying action on the part of the Carolina commissioners disgusted Ludwell and Harrison; it was even more exasperating to the Virginia Council.

On October 24 that body declared that *the Carolina commissioners are both of them persons engaged in Interest to obstruct it, for one of these Gentlemen* [Moseley] *has been for Several years last past Surveyor General of that Province & has acquired to himself great profit by Surveying Lands within the controverted bounds, and has taken up severall tracts of land in his owne name & sold the same to others for which he still stands obliged to obtain patents from the Government of Carolina. The other of them* [Lawson] *is at this time Surveyor Generall, & hath the same prospect of advantage by making future surveys within ye said Bounds—That the whole behaviour of the Carolina Commissioners hath tended visibly to no other end than to protract & Defeat the Settling this Affair: & particularly Mr. Moseley has used as many Shifts & excuses to disappoint all Conference with the Commissioners of Virginia as plainly show his Aversion to proceed in a business that tends so manifestly to his disadvantage.*[34]

---

30. *Ibid.*, pp. 737, 752.
31. *Ibid.*, p. 738.
32. *Ibid.*, p. 739.
33. *Ibid.*, p. 744.
34. *Ibid.*, p. 745. As early as March 1, 1710, the King in Council proposed that the Lords Proprietors be instructed to appoint two other persons "not having any personal Interest in, or claim to, any of the Land lying within the Boundary's in the room of Edward Moseley & John Lawson." Quoted in John Spencer Bassett, ed., *The Writings of "Colonel William Byrd of Westover in Virginia, Esq."* (New York: Doubleday & Page Co., 1901), p. 264. Hereinafter cited as Bassett, *William Byrd*.

No further conferences were held and the boundary line was not run at this time. Lawson, however, must have made some observations as to the proper boundary, for when the line was finally run in 1728, it was only "about half a mile to the Northward of the mouth of Nottoway River, which agreed to half a minute with the observations made formerly by Mr. Lawson. He had made the Latitude of the mouth of Nottoway River to be 36° 30' and our Line made it 36° 30½' which was but a small difference." [35] It is noteworthy that one of the four North Carolina commissioners in 1728 was Edward Moseley.[36]

Co-founder of Bath

John Lawson played a prominent role in the founding of North Carolina's two oldest towns, Bath and New Bern. Within a few years after his arrival in the province, he had acquired land in the Pamlico region along the banks of Old Town Creek (now Bath Creek). Other large landowners in the area of Bath County, which had been created in 1696, were Joel Martin, Simon Alderson, David Perkins, William Barrow, William Brice, Richard Collins, David Depre, Levi Truewhite, Robert Daniel, Nicholas Daw, John Burras, and Collingwood Ward.[37] Either in 1704 or 1705, Perkins transferred about sixty acres of his property to Lawson, Martin, and Alderson. On March 8, 1705, the town of Bath was incorporated by an act of the General Assembly, meeting at the house of John Hecklefield "with divers privileges & immunities therein granted which land was therein & thereby invested in the same John Lawson, Joel Martin, & Nicholas Daw to and for the uses aforesaid." [38] These three men were the first commissioners of the new town.

The first recorded sale of lots was on September 27, 1706; thirteen persons, including Lawson, are listed as purchasers. Herbert Paschal says "there can be little doubt that Lawson laid out

35. *Colonial Records,* II, 756.
36. See W. K. Boyd, ed., *William Byrd's Dividing Line Histories* (Raleigh: North Carolina Historical Commission, 1929).
37. Herbert R. Paschal, Jr., *A History of Colonial Bath* (Raleigh: Edwards & Broughton Company, 1955), p. 4. Hereinafter cited as Paschal, *Colonial Bath.* Lawson's name first appears in the Bath records as applicant for a land grant dated March 15, 1701.
38. *Ibid.,* p. 7.

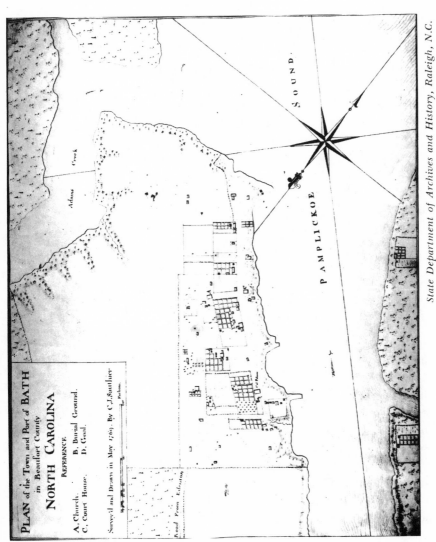

PLAN of the Town and Port of BATH
in Beaufort County
NORTH CAROLINA

REFERENCE

A. Church.   B. Burial Ground.
C. Court House.   D. Gaol.

Surveyed and Drawn in May 1769. By C.J. Sauthier

Adams Creek

SOUND

PAMPLICKOE

Road from Edenton

the town of Bath." [39] Apparently his plan called for seventy-one lots, each of which contained one acre and four poles. Lawson owned lots number 5 and 6. Lawson made his home at Bath, building on his two lots. His lots, and perhaps those of others, were enclosed by a fence.

Lawson was active in the political and economic life of the town and county. From January 1706/7 to August 1708, he served as Clerk of the Court and Public Register of "Pampticough Precinct." [40] In 1707 a "horse-mill" was erected by three of the town's leading citizens, Lawson, Chief Justice Christopher Gale, and Dr. Maurice Luellyn. These men "entered into an agreement that no owner would grind any grain but what was properly for his own family's use nor grant permission for anyone else to grind their grain at the mill without the consent of the owners." [41]

Co-founder of New Bern

The founding of Bath, the oldest town in North Carolina was the result of individual initiative. The founding of New Bern, second oldest town in the state, was the result of the promotional activity of a Swiss land company, headed by Baron Christoph von Graffenried (de Graffenried) and Franz Louis Michel. The Baron had long been interested in planting an American colony of persecuted Palatines and Swiss and had made extensive inquiries about mines, farm land, forest resources, and the best means of making a settlement. He had read Joshua Kocherthal's glowing account (1706) of Carolina where the "English live with the Indians there in complete friendship and good understanding, since they are mutually useful and agreeable," [42] and he had gone to London where he had talked with the Duke of Albemarle, who told him about "the beauty, goodness and riches of Carolina." About this

39. *Ibid.*, p. 8. By the end of October, at least twenty-five persons owned lots in Bath. Paschal gives all of their names, including Christopher Gale, Thomas Cary, John Porter, Joel Martin, and Nathaniel Wyersdale. On pages 26 and 27, Paschal reproduces the "Early Plan of Bath." The original of this map is now preserved in the John Gray Blount papers in the State Archives in Raleigh.

40. *Ibid.*, p. 8.

41. *Ibid.*, p. 10.

42. Joshua Kocherthal, *Das verlangte/ nicht erlangte Canaan bey den lustgräbern; oder Ausführliche beschreibung von der unglücklichen reise derer jüngsthin aus Teutschland nach dem engelländischen in America gelegenen Carolina und Pensylvanien wallenden pilgrim/ absonderlich dem einseitigen übelgeg-ründeten Kocherthalerischen.*

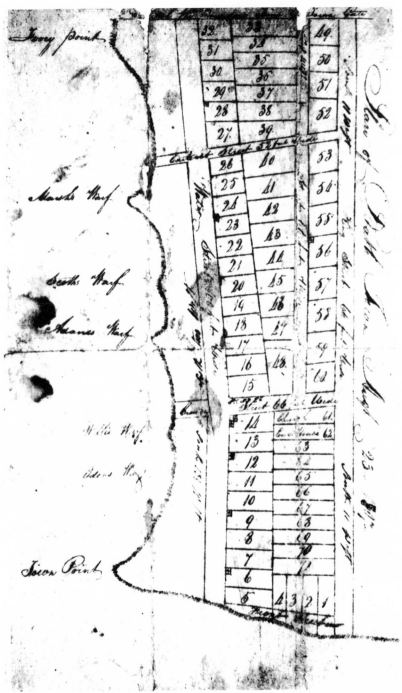

Plan of Bath, 1807, by Forbes and Hoyle

time, 1709, Parliament passed a law for the naturalization of foreign Protestants, with the result that an estimated 13,000 Palatines landed in England within the next two years. Most of these poor immigrants came to London, which was already burdened with its own poor and could hardly cope with the situation. Queen Anne and her advisers agreed with the views of Von Graffenried and a number of English capitalists that colonization was the solution, and she agreed to provide £5 10s each for the transportation of some six hundred "poor Palatines" to North Carolina "and for their comfortable settlement there." [43] After conferring with Lawson, then in London to arrange for the publication of his book, Von Graffenried decided to plant his colony in North Carolina. Accordingly, he purchased from the Lords Proprietors 17,500 acres of land, located along the Neuse and Trent rivers, for £175. He was also given a twelve-year option on 100,000 acres, and a "lease of all royal mines and minerals in Carolina" for thirty years.[44] Lawson also sold the company at least 1,250 acres of his holdings at the juncture of the two rivers.[45] He does not appear to have invested in the Baron's company.

In choosing settlers for his new colony, Von Graffenried selected only "young people, healthy, laborious and of all kinds of avocations and handicrafts in number about 650." [46] Tools, implements, and ships were all chosen with great care. The first group selected was placed under the supervision of "three persons, notables from Carolina, who happened then to be in London and who had lived already several years in Carolina." Two of these "notables" were John Lawson and Christopher Gale, Chief Justice of North Carolina. The Baron remained in London, awaiting the arrival of a Swiss group from Bern.

Lawson and the 650 Palatines sailed from Gravesend in Janu-

43. *Colonial Records*, I, 987. Dill, *Tryon*, pp. 35–36.
44. V. H. Todd and Julius Goebel, eds., *Christoph Von Graffenried's Account of the Founding of New Bern, with an Historical Introduction and an English Translation* (Raleigh: Edwards and Broughton Printing Co., 1920), p. 47. The Baron and his company were also given mining rights in Virginia, Maryland, and Pennsylvania. Hereinafter cited as Todd, *Von Graffenried's Account*.
45. *Ibid.*, 47. Todd says that Lawson had not sold all the land on the point between the two rivers to Von Graffenried, and "in order to further his own interests he had settled those under his charge on his own land to gain the benefit of any clearing they might do." Also see, Dill, *Tryon*, pp. 37–38. Von Graffenried complained that he had to pay three times for the site of the town—to the Lords Proprietors, to Lawson, and to the Indians of Chatooka.
46. *Colonial Records*, I, 908.

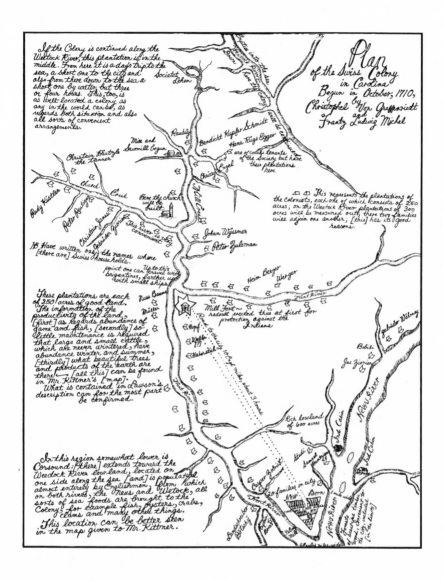

ary, 1710. After a stormy voyage of thirteen weeks, during which about one-half of the group died from "ship-fever" and other diseases, the transports reached Virginia, and as they entered the James River, a French privateer plundered one of the vessels and deprived the passengers of everything they had, including their clothes, in some cases.[47] The ships finally anchored at Hampton. The remnant of the original 650 set out overland and finally reached the Chowan River, where Thomas Pollock provided them "certain necessities" and furnished ships to carry them to their original destination.[48]

Von Graffenried had authorized Lawson to "lay out the triple-purchased land into the plan of a town," and the latter chose a point between the Neuse and Trent rivers. In his *Account of the Founding of New Bern,* the Baron explains his plan and the idea behind it.

Since in America they do not like to live crowded in order to enjoy a purer air, I, accordingly ordered the streets to be very broad and the houses well separated one from the other. I marked three acres of land for each family, for house, barn, garden, orchard, hemp field, poultry yard and other purposes. I divided the village like a cross and in the middle I intended a church. One of the principal streets extended from the bank of the River Neuse straight on into the forest and the other principal streets crossed it, running from the Trent River clear to the Neuse River. After that we planted stakes to mark the houses and to make the principal streets along and on the banks of the two rivers.[49]

The cruciform plan was suggested by the peninsula-like point of land. The "principal streets" survive as East and South Front. Among the first structures built—none of which survive—were Von Graffenried's lodging and a commissary, both very near the land peak between the rivers.[50] Lawson laid out most of the river front lots, and many were sold, but Thomas Pollock either mislaid or lost Lawson's plan of the town. On July 15, 1720, Pollock wrote that "I had a draught of the town of Mr. Lawson's drawing, with most of the river lots laid out, with the account which of them was taken up." [51]

47. *Ibid.,* 909; See also Todd, *Von Graffenried's Account,* p. 224.
48. *Ibid.,* pp. 909–10.
49. Dill, *Tryon,* pp. 38–39.
50. *Ibid.,* p. 39.
51. *Colonial Records,* II, 386.

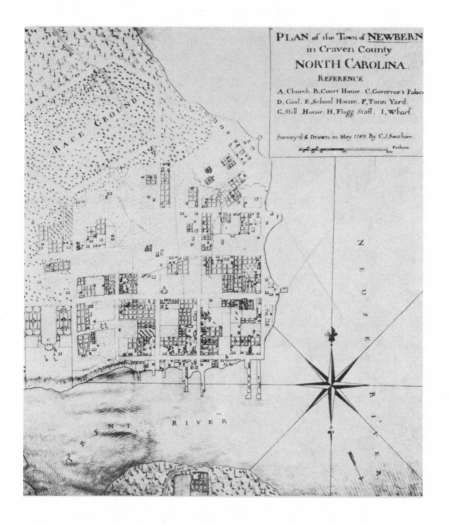

PLAN of the Town of NEWBERN
in Craven County
NORTH CAROLINA.

REFERENCE

A. Church. B. Court House. C. Governor's Palace
D. Goal. E. School House. F. Tann Yard.
G. Still House. H. Flagg Staff. I. Wharf.

Survey'd & Drawn in May 1769. By C. J. Sauthier.

When Von Graffenried arrived on September 10 with one hundred Swiss, he found the settlement in a wretched condition, "sickness, want, and desperation having reached their climax." Within a short time however, land was surveyed, forests cleared, houses built, and a water mill constructed for grinding grain. The Baron later wrote that "within eighteen months they managed to build houses and to make themselves so comfortable that they made more progress than the English inhabitants in several years." [52] He said: "There was a fine appearance of a happy state of things," when suddenly, in September, 1711, disaster struck and the colony was almost wiped out by the Tuscarora Indians.

In his book, Lawson declared that the Indians "are really better to us than we have been to them," but he added this significant and prophetic comment: "The Indians are very revengeful, and never forget an Injury done, till they have received Satisfaction." [53] Thomas Pollock declared that the Indians struck in 1711 "without any cause that we know of," though he later admitted that "our own divising hath been the cause of all our troubles." [54]

The Indians, and notably the numerous and powerful Tuscaroras, had many reasons for resentment against the whites: encroachments on their hunting grounds; kidnapping and enslaving

52. *Ibid.,* I, 913. Lawson was more pessimistic than the Baron. On December 30, 1701, he wrote James Petiver: "The Swiss gentlemen here arrived safe with their people. . . . What they will make of the Palatines I cannot guess, seeing they are the most sloathfull people I ever saw. Above half of them are dead of the spotted fever which took them in the ship, fluxes & the dropsy. When they are taken sick they go to bed & there lye until they dye or recover & cannot be persuaded to the contrary, although many of them were dispatched thereby. Above one half of them are dead, one reason & the chiefest was seeing they were twice as many as ought to have been on a healthful ship."

53. Lawson, *A New Voyage to Carolina* (1709), p. 212. Lawson wrote that the Indians "always give us Victuals at their Quarters, and take care we are armed against Hunger and Thirst: We do not do so by them, (generally speaking) but let them walk by our Doors Hungry and do not often relieve them. We look upon them with Scorn and Disdain, and think them little better than Beasts in Human shape." He also said that "we have furnished them with the Vice of Drunkeness, which is the open Road to all others, and daily cheat them in everything we sell, and esteem it a Gift of Christianity not to sell them so cheap as we do to the Christians, as we call ourselves." *Ibid.,* 256–57.

54. In a letter to Governor Alexander Spotswood of Virginia, dated April 30, 1713, Pollock said: "Our own divisions (chiefly occasioned by the Quakers and some other evil disposed persons) hath been the cause of all our troubles. *Colonial Records,* II, 40.

of their women and children; "sharp" practices of white traders; and, perhaps most important of all, the settlement of New Bern. Colonel William Byrd of Virginia maintained that white traders had abused the Indian women and mistreated the men "until the Indians grew weary and tired of the Tyranny and Injustice with which the whites treated them and resolved to endure the bondage no longer." [55] It is not surprising that Lawson, who laid out the town of New Bern and who was the chief surveyor in the colony, was the first victim of their wrath.

Lawson's Expedition up the Neuse and his Death

The following account of Lawson's ill fated voyage up the Neuse and his capture and execution by the Indians was related by Von Graffenried, who accompanied him on his final exploring expedition.[56]

One day, as the weather was very fine, and there was a good appearance that it would last, Surveyor General Lawson proposed to me to go up Neus River, hinting there were plenty of wild grapes which we could gather for refreshing ourselves. This statement, however, was not strong enough to prevail on me. A few days afterwards, he came back, giving better reasons. He remarked that we could see, in the meantime, whether the River may be navigated in its higher course, and that a new road to Virginia might be laid out there, the actual route being long and difficult,—and likewise visit the Upper Country. I had, indeed, been anxious for a long time to know and see by myself how far it is from here to the mountains.

I accordingly resolved to take the trip, and we took provisions for 15 days; I, however, asked Mr. Lawson whether there were any danger on account of the Indians, especially on account of those we did not know. He answered that there was no danger in that direction, as he had already taken that trip once, that surely there were no savages living on that branch of the River, that they used to be very far from it. But, in order to feel all the safer, we took with us two Indian neighbors, which we knew well, and to whom I had done much good with two negroes to row. One of the savages knew English, and we thought, as we had those two Indians with us, we had nothing to fear from the others; it had not rained for a long time, the River was not very high, and the current all the slower for it; the whole day we went up the river—by night we pitched our tents near the water, and early in the morning we proceeded further.

55. Quoted in Lefler-Newsome, *North Carolina,* p. 57.
56. *Colonial Records,* I, 925–27.

The Capture of Lawson and Von Graffenried

May your Lordship please to take notice that Surveyor General Lawson required my horses saying that we could go through the woods, to see where the road to Virginia might be begun most conveniently. At first I would not consent; at last, he asked for only one, which I granted. One of the Indians went on horseback by land, but he was compelled to cross the river at one place, what was our misfortune, for he came to the great village of Catechna. . . . There he was once asked what he was doing with that horse (they do not use horses in these parts) ; he answered that he was to bring it back to us, and that we were going up stream. This immediately alarmed the inhabitants of Catechna; they crowded together from the whole neighborhood, kept the horse, and told our Indian that he ought to warn us at once not to advance further in their country, that they would not allow it, and that we had to turn back, by the orders of the King who resided there. . . . I said that I did not like the looks of things altogether, and that we ought to turn back at once; but the Surveyor-General laughed at me. . . .

Such a number of Indians came out from the bushes, some even swimming across the river, and overtook us so suddenly, that is was impossible for us to defend ourselves, for fear of being killed on the spot, or cruelly mistreated. They, accordingly, took us prisoners, plundered our things, and led us away.

North Carolina Collection, The University of North Carolina at Chapel Hill

The Torture of Lawson and Von Graffenried

We had already made a good two day's journey, not far from another village called Coemtha. . . .

Mistaking Von Graffenried for Governor Hyde, the Tuscaroras were jubilant. They ran their white captives "all the night through the woods, across thickets and swamps till we arrived at about 3 o'clock in the morning at Catechna," a large Tuscarora town on Contentnea Creek, near the present site of Snow Hill.[57] The Tuscarora king, whom the whites called Hancock, appointed a young brave as prosecutor to represent the Indian people, and tried Lawson and Von Graffenried before a court of "forty Elders" whose dignity and solemnity drew the latter's respect.[58] Both white men were acquitted.

Unfortunately for Lawson, two kings and other leaders from tribes on the lower Neuse began to assemble at Cotechney. The Coree Indians accused him of offenses against them, and he had a heated quarrel with Cor Tom, their king.[59] This angered all of the

57. *Ibid.*, p. 927.
58. *Ibid.*, p. 928.
59. *Ibid.*, p. 929. Von Graffenried wrote that "though he made every effort to get Lawson to quit his quarreling, I could not succeed."

Indians and a council of war was held. Both white men were sentenced to death, "without being told what was the cause of such sudden change." [60] The Indians bound both prisoners and laid them on the ground before the Indian tribunal. The council of war delayed the Baron's execution and released him eventually, probably because he told them he was under the particular care and protection of "the great and powerful Queen of England" who "would avenge my blood" if any harm came to him.[61] There are many pages in Von Graffenried's narrative explaining how he escaped this death sentence and shifting all the blame and responsibility for Lawson's death upon the shoulders of Lawson himself.[62]

The concluding paragraph of the English translation of the French version of Von Graffenried's narrative reveals the Baron's unfavorable and unfair attitude toward Lawson and also to the Lords Proprietors:

If the Surveyor-General Lawson had not turned us aside from our first design [to plant a colony in Virginia], which was to establish ourselves here at the commencement, where we should have been more in security, better assisted and better supported, to all appearances we should not have failed in our enterprise. But the gentlemen would not have had the profits of surveying. But yet it would have been

60. *Ibid.,* p. 929.

61. *Ibid.,* pp. 931–32.

62. Von Graffenried, in the "French Version" of his account of the founding of New Bern, said: "The Surveyor-General has been punished with a terrible execution by the savages for his crimes and bad faith." Todd, *Von Graffenried's Account,* p. 375. For a contrary view, see Matt H. Allen, "John Lawson, Gentlemen," in an *Address to the North Carolina Society of Colonial Dames of America, 1900–1926* (Wilmington, n.d.), pp. 170–79. Allen says: "De Graffenried's own description of their capture, trial, and escape furnishes evidence of his treachery and of Lawson's bravery. . . . He represented himself as a King . . . If he had been a man and friend of Lawson's he would have made the same plea for Lawson and his negro as he did for himself; and his failure to make this plea convinces me that he desired Lawson's execution, hoping thereby to escape exposure by Lawson for his land stealing." Allen goes on to say: "After securing his freedom, he [Graffenried] left the Colonists, mortgaged their lands and embezzled their money, as appears from the petition of the Palatines in 1714 addressed to the King of England." This petition, signed by forty-two of the Palatines, declared: "Soon after De Graffenried was brought in, but did not stay long with us and carried off from our settlement all he could conveniently come at, promising to return with provisions and necessarys for the war, but he never returned nor made the least satisfaction for these things nor the money allowed us by her most Gracious Majesty of the Gentlemen of England (Lords Proprietors) with two hundred pounds which we put into interest at our departure from England."

*Oil portrait of Baron Christopher von Graffenried,
founder of New Bern*

better to be deprived of this profit than of his life which he miserably lost, as is seen (in the account). It is true that besides the fine speeches of Lawson, it was the first promises of the Lords Proprietors which tempted us to establish ourselves at first in North Carolina.[63]

Writing about Lawson's death, Von Graffenried said:

In the meantime, they executed that unfortunate Lawson; as to his death, I know nothing certain; some Indians told me, that he was threatened to have his throat cut, with the razor which was found in his pocket,—what also acknowledged the small negro, who was not executed,—but some said he was hung, some said he was burnt. The Indians kept that execution very secret. God have mercy upon the poor soul! [64]

A few months later, November 3, 1711, Christopher Gale wrote: "But the fate of Mr. Lawson (if our Indian information be true) was much more tragical, for we are informed that they stuck him full of fine small splinters of torch wood like hog's bristles and so set them gradually afire." [65] William Byrd, writing several decades later, said that Lawson "was waylaid and had his Throat cut from Ear to Ear." [66]

63. Todd, *Von Graffenried's Account*, p. 392.
64. *Colonial Records*, I, 933.
65. *Ibid.*, p. 826. Lawson gave a vivid account of Indian methods of punishment in his own book. He wrote:

"Their cruelty to their Prisoners of War is what they are seemingly guilty of an Error in, (I mean as to a natural failing) because they strive to invent the most Inhumane Butcheries for them that No Devils themselves could invent or hammer out of Hell; they esteeming Death no Punishment, but rather an Advantage to him, that is exported out of this into another World.

"Therefore they inflict on them Torments in which they prolong Life in that miserable state as long as they can, and never miss Skulping of them as they call it. Which is, to cut off the Skin from the Temples, and taking the whole Head of Hair along with it, as if it was a Night-Cap. Sometimes they take the Top of the Skull along with it; all which they preserve and carefully keep by them, for a Trophy of their Conquest over their Enemies. Others keep their Enemies Teeth which are taken in War, whilst others split the Pitch-Pine into Splinters, and stick them into the Prisoner's Body yet alive. Thus they light them which burn like so many Torches; and in this Manner they make him dance round a great Fire, every one buffeting and deriding him, till he expires, when every one strives to get a Bone or some Relick of this unfortunate Captive." See p. 207 of this volume.

66. Byrd wrote: "It was on that Provocation they [the Indians] resented their wrongs a little too severely upon Mr. Lawson, who under Colour of being Surveyor gen'l, had encroacht too much upon their Territories, at which they were so much enrag'd, that they waylaid him, and cut his Throat from Ear to Ear, but at the same time released the Baron de Graffenried,

An interesting and puzzling statement appears in the Foreword to the second German edition of Lawson's book, published at Hamburg in 1722 and obviously designed to encourage German migration to America. In translation it reads: "In this book, the kind reader has not to fear any inaccuracy. The reputable Mr. Lawson, still living in London, so is understood, grants to provide all the required information about his reports." Despite Von Graffenried's obvious animus toward Lawson, the editor accepts his version of Lawson's death in 1711. There is no known record of Lawson after that date, and the phrase "so is understood" is not at all convincing.

Lawson's will, which was written on August 12, 1708, left "to my Dearly beloved Hannah Smith, the house & Lott I now live in, to enjoy the same during her Natural life & also one third part of my Personale Estate in No. Carolina to her proper Use" and the remainder to be divided, share alike, between his "Daughter Isabella, of Bath Town and to the brother & sister (which her mother is w'th Child off at this present." [67] It is probable that Hannah, his mistress, was the daughter of Richard Smith, at whose plantation Lawson had stopped when he first came to North Carolina in 1701. His will was probated soon after his death. On September 12, 1712, "Upon petition of Hannah Smyth praying appraisors be appointed to appraise such part of the

---

whom they had Seized for Company, because it appeared plainly he had done them no wrong." Bassett, *William Byrd,* p. 228.

The Reverend John Urmstone, a disgruntled Anglican missionary, writing to the Secretary of the Society for the Propagation of the Gospel in Foreign Parts on June 12, 1715, said: "they [the Lords Proprietors] may and ought to be ashamed of their famous Country, they would have all men do as Lawson did write whole Volumes in praise of such a worthless place; he has had his reward." *Colonial Records,* II, 186.

67. J. Bryan Grimes, Comp., *North Carolina Wills and Inventories, Copied from Original and Recorded Wills and Inventories in the Office of Secretary of State* (Raleigh: Edwards & Broughton Printing Company, 1912), 280–81. This will, which is recorded in Will Book 2, page 98, is reprinted in the Appendixes of this volume, pp. 267–68. While other women in the colony were being prosecuted for having bastard children, apparently nothing of the kind happened to Hannah Smith whom Lawson openly lived with, had at least one illegitimate child by, and to whom he gave his own name as is evidenced by his deed of gift. Lawson also made Hannah Smith the executrix of his will.

When Lawson was killed he owned a "hair trunk" in which he had "several writings to him belonging." Apparently he had left these at the home of one William Kirk, a resident of Craven Precinct, who declined to deliver them to Hannah Smith. She may have recovered them from him, but no one has ever located these "several writings."

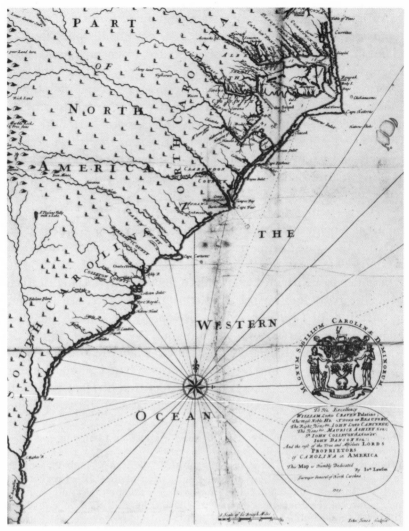

North Carolina Collection, The University of North Carolina at Chapel Hill

Lawson's Map of the Carolinas, from the 1709 edition

estate of John Lawson Dec'd as in this County of Albemarle," the
Council ordered that Thomas Boyd, Christopher Gale, and Tobias Knight "do appraise the said estate." [68] There can be no
doubt about Lawson's death in 1711.

THE LAWSON MAP

Size: 12 x 15. Scale: 1″ — ca.33 miles

On August 4, 1709, while Lawson was still in London, the
Lords Proprietors of Carolina, meeting at Craven House, agreed
to "subscribe Twenty pounds to Mr. Lawson for Maps of North
and South Carolina." [69] It is likely that Lawson had already prepared his "Map of Carolina," which appeared as the frontispiece
in his book, which was then in process of publication.

Numerous topographical similarities indicate that Lawson re-
lied to a great extent on *A New Map of Carolina* published about
1685 by three London map makers, John Thorton, Robert Mor-
den, and Philip Lee.[70] For the South Carolina area, Lawson omitted many details of physical features and settlements found on
this earlier map. Though the coastline on the Lawson map extends from below "St. Augustin" at 29°, the extreme southern
limit of Carolina under the 1665 charter, to "Chisapeake Bay" at
37°, which was 30 above the extreme northern limits of the province, very little of the South Carolina region except the coastal
area is given.[71] He does mention two rivers, "May" and "S.
Matheo," but fails to indicate their headwaters.

The North Carolina portion of the map is better, but it is still
far from satisfactory and does not contain any significant new
features about the interior or as many details as some of the
earlier maps. Such vague terms as "Hilly Land," "Rich Land,"
and "Marble Rocks & Free stones" throw some light on the physical features of the area, but the numerous hills that dot the whole

68. *Colonial Records,* I, 872.
69. *Colonial Records,* I, 717. This map is reproduced on page xxxviii of this
volume.
70. W. P. Cumming, *The Southeast in Early Maps, with an annotated
check list of printed and manuscript regional and local maps of Southeastern
North America during the Colonial Period* (Chapel Hill: The University of
North Carolina Press, 1962), pp. 163, 178. Hereinafter cited as Cumming,
Maps. Cumming describes the Lawson map but does not reproduce it. He
does reprint the Thorton-Morden-Lee map.
71. *Ibid.,* p. 178.

interior are unnamed. William P. Cumming, leading authority on maps of the Southeast, says that Lawson's "contribution to the cartographical knowledge" of North Carolina "is found in detailed names of creeks, rivers, and settlements in the vicinity of Pamlico Sound." The town of Bath, of which Lawson had been an incorporator, is named for the first time on a printed map, and the shape, soundings, and sand bars of Pamlico Sound are given.[72]

The Lawson map has been reproduced many times. In 1711, Johann Rudolff Ochs published at Berne a map, entitled *Die Provinz Nord und Sud Carolina,* which appeared in a guidebook for prospective Swiss settlers coming to America and especially to North Carolina.[73] This was based on Lawson's 1709 map. The legends, of course, are in German. The Lawson-Visscher map of 1712, which appeared in the first German edition of Lawson's book, published at Hamburg, is a copy of the Lawson map, but from a different plate.[74] The English edition of 1714 reproduces the original Lawson map, but a new map was made for the 1718 edition, printed after Lawson's death. Cumming says "it is a strange retrogression to the old errors of Lederer" [75] (London, 1672). The map in the German edition of 1722 is based on the 1709 Lawson map.[76] F. L. Hawks, *History of North Carolina,* Volume II (Fayetteville, 1859) contains a "Facsimile of a map of the inhabited parts of N. Carolina," drawn by George Schroeter of New York from the map in Lawson's 1709 edition. This facsimile of only the North Carolina coastal area is also found in S. A. Ashe, *History of North Carolina,* Volume I (Greensboro, 1908). The Lawson map is reproduced in all of the later editions of Lawson.

NATURALIST AND COLLECTOR OF BOTANICAL SPECIMENS

At no place in his book does Lawson give a reason for coming to America in 1700, except his desire to travel. There is reason to

72. *Ibid.*

73. At the same time, Ochs published a 120-page promotional tract based on Lawson's book. The full title of Ochs' book is given on page lii of this volume.

74. The full title of this book appears in the illustration on page xlv of this volume.

75. Cumming, *Maps,* p. 178.

76. The full title of this book appears in the illustration on page xlviii of this volume.

believe, however, that he was urged, or even hired, to make this trip by James Petiver, a London apothecary and the greatest collector of botanical specimens of his day. In a letter to Petiver from "Bath County on Pampicough River, North Carolina, April 12, 1701," soon after Lawson reached that area, he refers to "collections of Animals, Vegitables, etc" and says that he would "be very industrious in that Imploy I hope to your satisfaction & my own." [77] He also states that he will collect sea shells, butterflies, and "other Insects."

Petiver had several correspondents in the Carolinas, "the most knowledgeable" being John Lawson.[78] With the exception of the above-mentioned letter, all of the surviving letters of Lawson to Petiver were written in 1709 or later. (All of this correspondence is reprinted in the Appendix of this volume.) While in London in 1709, Lawson met Petiver and George London, Bishop Compton's gardener, and when he returned to North Carolina that winter, he was "armed with Petiver's many supplies and drugs, and Ray's tract on Banister's plants." [79]

On September 7, 1709, Petiver wrote his friend William London:

> I have lately obtained an Acquaintance with one Mr. Lawson Surveyor General of Carolina. He is a very cautious person & hath lately printed a Natural History of Carolina wherein he hath treated the Quadrupeds, Birds, Fishes, Reptiles & Vegitables, particularly the Trees, with a great deal of Judgment & accuracy. He suddenly designs

77. The original of this letter is in the Sloane Manuscripts #4063, f. 79, in the British Museum. Hereinafter cited as *Sloane*. It is reprinted in the Appendixes of this volume, page 259. For an excellent essay on Petiver, see Stearns, "James Petiver," p. 338. On page 338 of Stearns, it is recorded that Petiver sent Lawson a copy of John Banister, "Catalogus stirpum rariorum," which gave a kind of inventory of what plants were known up to that time. Petiver does not mention Lawson in "An Account of Animals and Shells sent from Carolina to Mr. James Petiver," published in the *Royal Society of London Philosophical Transactions,* Vol. 24 (May, 1705).

78. Edmund Berkeley and Dorothy Smith Berkeley, *John Clayton: Pioneer of American Botany* (Chapel Hill: The University of North Carolina Press, 1963), p. 49. Hereinafter cited as Berkeley, *John Clayton.*

79. Henry Compton, Bishop of London, who has been called the "Maecenas of botany," developed an outstanding botanical garden at Fulham Palace, his official residence. With the assistance of George London, his expert gardener, plants were sought all over the world. John Ray worked out a system of plant classification, which was widely used in his day. He published a number of books relating to botany and natural history. The third volume of his *Historia Plantarium,* published in 1704, was a significant work in botany and included plants collected by the Reverend John Banister in Virginia.

to return for Carolina & as he may be serviceable to you is very ambitious of being known to you. If therefore you will as soon as possibly you can appoint a time I will wait on you with him. He is very desirous of procuring what variety of Grapes & Plumbstones he can before his departure for which I doubt not but he will make you a suitable return from thence of whatever you desire from those parts.[80]

Before Lawson's departure for Carolina with the Palatines in midwinter of 1709–10, he consulted on numerous occasions with Petiver, "who gave him both encouragement, instructions, and supplies for further work in natural history and furnished him with drugs for use on his voyage and in the colonies." [81] On October 12 and 14, 1709, Petiver wrote George London asking him to send Lawson a copy of John Ray's tract on Banister's plants and also "a few pinns that your Insects may not fly away after you have once caught them." [82] He also requested that some "cholick root" and other drugs which Lawson had suggested be sent him. On November 9, Lawson replied from Portsmouth, England, thanking Petiver for his "kind present of Mr. Ray's book of Physick," declaring that the root was "excellent in the Collick" and that "a few drops" of Petiver's "Citron landanum" given to a "poor Patient" had given him "rest in a Delirium." He added that these were "choice remedies & fit for transportation to our parts." [83]

Lawson's delay in sailing for America gave Petiver an opportunity to send "4 Quires of Cholick root & 6 bottles of my Citron Laudanum," some papers of "universal purging powders," and "a Bill of the lowest ready Money prices, for the encouragement of those who practice with you or can otherwise dispose of them." [84]

Soon after Lawson's return to North Carolina, Petiver wrote requesting him to send "more physick," a *Hortus Siccus* of English plants, and some tracts on natural history,[85] but Lawson was so busy with the settlement of the Palatines at New Bern, that he failed to reply to Petiver until December 30, 1710. In this lengthy letter, he said that he had sent a collection of insects, plants, and animals to Petiver in the previous July and that he needed more

80. Stearns, "James Petiver," p. 337, quoting *Sloane*, #3337, fol. 56 v.
81. *Ibid.*, pp. 337–38, quoting *Sloane*, #3337, Vol. 63.
82. *Ibid.*, p. 338.
83. *Ibid.* quoting *Sloane*, #4064, Vols. 2, 4. The Lawson letter is reprinted in the Appendixes of this volume.
84. *Ibid.*, p. 339, quoting *Sloane*, #3337, Vols. 74, 75.
85. *Ibid.* quoting *Sloane*, #3337, Vol. 97v.

brown paper and more "preserving liquor." [86] Lawson declared that he had been unable to keep "an exact Dyary As you & I proposed until July last when I began & shall very strictly continue ye year 1711 from ye first of January with the weather & whatever happens worthy of Notice in this Collony." He said: "If God prolongs my dayes," his intention was "to make a strict collection" of all plants, beasts, birds, fishes, insects, fossils, and the like and that he "plans out a thorough investigation of the natural history of the region." [87] This work, of course never completed, would have covered "all phases of Carolina botany, agriculture, medicine, zoology, and paleontology." [88]

Lawson did not live to carry out his ambitious project, but only two months before his death in September, 1711, he sent Petiver "by our Governour's Lady one book of plants very Lovingly packt up" and expressed the hope that he would soon hear from his London friend.[89] Petiver received the plants in March, 1712, about the same time he heard of Lawson's death. On March 8, a depressed Petiver wrote his friend Jacob Bobart of Oxford: "The Death of these good Friends & the dilatory performances of many of my living ones quite disheartens me, so that nothing but the glimmerings of Peace & a South Sea Trade gives me hopes of a faint recovery." [90] Sometime later, Petiver acknowledged gifts from "my late curious Friend Mr. John Lawson." [91]

During the last year and a half of his life, Lawson sent collections of wild life to his friends Petiver and London. The plants were mostly trees collected in North Carolina in 1710 and in Virginia in 1711, "many with autograph tickets, some signed bearing notes on the specimens or indications of locality." In 1958, the Sloane Herbarium in the British Museum contained 337 specimens, thirty of which were from Carolina.[92] Prefixed to H.S. 242 is a list of "Lawson's Virginia trees" in Petiver's hand.

86. *Ibid.* The whole letter is reprinted in the Appendixes of this volume.
87. *Ibid.,* p. 340. See the letter in the Appendixes.
88. Berkeley, *John Clayton,* p. 49.
89. Stearns, "James Petiver," p. 342, quoting *Sloane,* #4064, Vol. 264.
90. *Ibid.,* p. 342, quoting *Sloane,* #3338, Vol. 37.
91. *Philosophical Transactions,* Nov.–Dec., 1715, XXIX, (London, 1715) 355.
92. *The Sloane Herbarium: An Annotated List of the Horti Sicci Composing it; with biographical accounts of the Principal Contributors, Based on Records Compiled by the late James Britten. With an Introduction by Spencer Savage.* Revised edition by J. E. Dandy (London: British Museum, 1958), p. 154.

In 1711, when Lawson and Moseley were meeting at Williamsburg with the Virginia boundary line commissioners, the great
Virginia botanist, John Clayton, was sent by Governor Alexander
Spotswood to arbitrate between Edward Hyde and Thomas Cary,
each claiming to be the legal governor of North Carolina, and
each being in Virginia then. Lawson met Clayton at this time.[93]
One can only speculate what this acquaintanceship might have
meant had it not been for Lawson's untimely death a few months
later.

EDITIONS OF LAWSON'S BOOK

John Stevens, *A New Collection of Voyages and Travels: with
    historical accounts of discoveries and conquests in all parts of
    the world. None of them ever before printed in English; being
    now first translated from the Spanish, Italian, French, Dutch,
    Portuguese and other languages. Adorned with cuts. For the
    month of December 1708. To be continued monthly.* London: J.
    Knapton [etc.] 1708–[10]. The first volume contains Lawson's
    "New Voyage to Carolina" iv, 258 pp.

*A New Voyage to Carolina; containing the exact description and
    natural history of that country; together with the present state
    thereof. And a Journal of a thousand miles travel'd thro' sev-
    eral nations of Indians. Giving a particular account of their
    customs, names, &c. By John Lawson, gent., surveyor-general of
    North Carolina.* London: printed in the year 1709. iv, 258 pp.
    [1]p. pl., map. 20 × 17½ cm. (In John Stevens, *A New Collec-
    tion of Voyages and Travels.* London, 1708, Vol. 1.)

*Allerneuste beschreibung der provintz Carolina in West-Indien.
    Samt einem Reise-Journal von mehr als Tausend Meilen
    unter allerhand Indianischen Nationen. Auch einer accuraten
    land-carte und andern kupfer-stichen. Aus dem englischen
    übersetzet durch M. Vischer.* Hamburg: T. Von Wierings
    Erben, 1712. viii, 365 [3] pp. front., fold. map. 17 cm. Transla-
    tion of Lawson's "A new voyage to Carolina," London, 1709, by
    "M" [i.e. Magister] Ludwig Friedrich Vischer.

*The history of Carolina; containing the exact description and
    natural history of that country; together with the present state
    thereof. And a journal of a thousand miles travel'd thro' several*

93. Berkeley, "James Petiver," p. 49. See also *Virginia Magazine of History
and Biography,* Vol. V (June, 1898), 15–17.

Allerneuste Beschreibung
der Provintz

CAROLINA

In

West-Indien.

Samt einem

Reise = Journal

von mehr als

Tausend Meilen

unter allerhand

Indianischen Nationen.

Auch einer

Accuraten Land=Carte und andern
Kupfer-Stichen.

Aus dem Englischen übersetzet durch
M. Vischer.

HAMBURG,
Bedruckt und verlegt/ durch seel. Thomas von Wierings Erben/
bey der Börse/im güldnen A, B, C. Anno 1712.
Sind auch zu Franckfurt und Leipzig/ bey Zacharias Herteln
zu bekommen.

Title page of the first German edition, 1712

Montpelier July 15 1831

Dear Sir

I observe in a Newspaper paragraph, referring to the late fire in Raleigh, a remark that nothing was saved from the Library, particularly Lawson's History of it; which had not been procured without difficulty. Happening to possess a copy of the work, I enclose it, with a request that it may be permitted to supply the loss; praying you to accept at the same time assurances of my great consideration & respect.

James Madison

Governour Stokes

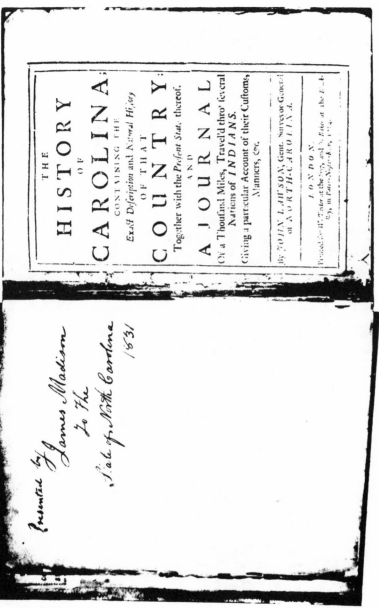

State Department of Archives and History, Raleigh, N.C.

Presentation inscription in the 1714 edition

Mr. LAWSON's
Allerneueste Beschreibung
der Groß-Britannischen Provintz

CAROLINA

in West-Indien.

Samt einem

Reise-JOURNAL
von mehr als Tausend Meilen
unter allerhand

Indianischen Nationen.
Auch accuraten Land-Charte
und Kupfer-Stichen.

Zweyte Aufflage/
mit einem curieusen Anhang
aller übrigen

Groß-Britannischen Colonien
in America vermehret.

HAMBURG,
Gedruckt und verlegt, durch seel. Thomas von Wierings Erben,
bey der Börse, im güldnen A, B, C. 1722.

Title page of the second German edition, 1722

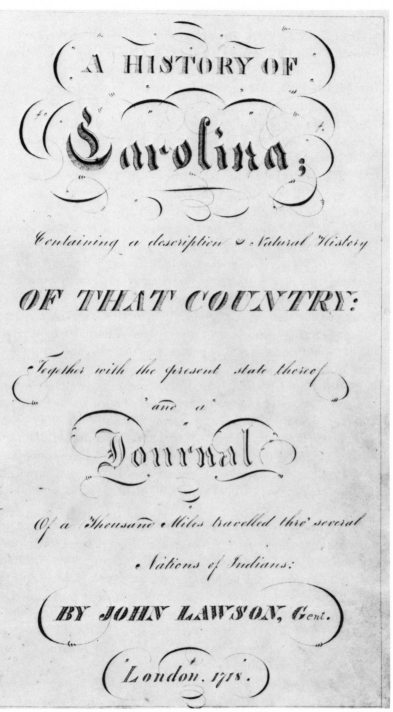

A HISTORY OF

Carolina;

Containing a description & Natural History

OF THAT COUNTRY:

Together with the present state thereof

and a

Journal

Of a Thousand Miles travelled thro' several

Nations of Indians:

BY JOHN LAWSON, Gent.

London, 1718.

Title page of an undated manuscript copy of the 1718 edition

nations of Indians. Giving a particular account of their customs, names, &c. By John Lawson, gent., surveyor-general of
North Carolina. London: Printed for W. Taylor and J. Baker,
1714. iv, 258 pp. 1 pl. fold. map. 21 × 16½ cm.

The history of Carolina; containing the exact description and
natural history of that country; together with the present state
thereof. And a journal of a thousand miles travel'd thro' several
nations of Indians. Giving a particular account of their customs, names, &c. By John Lawson, gent., surveyor-general of
North Carolina. London: Printed for T. Warner, 1718. iv,
258 pp. fold. map. 21½ cm. This edition is not so attractive as
the 1714 edition; the map is very small and poor.

Mr. Lawson's Allerneuste Beschreibung der Gross-Britannischen
Provintz Carolina in West-Indien. Samt einem Reise-Journal
von mehr als tausend meilen unter allerhand Indianischen Na-
tionen. Auch accuraten Land-Charte und Kupper-Stichen.
Zwente Aufflage mit enien curieusen Anhang aller übrigen
Gross-Britannischen Colonien in America vermehret. Hamburg: Gedruckt und verlegt, durch seel. Thomas von Wierings
Erben, den der Borse, un güldnen, A. B. C. 1722. xii, 396 [4]
pp. front., fold. map. 19 cm.

The history of Carolina; containing the exact description and
natural history of that country; together with the present state
thereof. And a journal of a thousand miles travel'd thro' several
nations of Indians. Giving a particular account of their customs, names &c. By John Lawson, gent., surveyor-general of
North Carolina. London: Printed for T. Warner, 1718. Raleigh, [O. H. Perry Co.] Printed by Strother & Marcom, 1860.
xviii, 410 pp. 19 cm.

History of North Carolina. By John Lawson . . . Being a reprint
of the copy now in the North Carolina State Library, presented by President James Madison, in the year 1831. Charlotte,
N.C.: Observer printing house, 1903. xvi, 172 pp., including fac-
sim. front. (fold. map). 23 × 18 cm. Compiler's preface signed:
Fred A. Olds. Extracts from Colonel William Byrd's History of
the dividing line between Virginia and North Carolina, pp.
145–71. Olds reprinted the Lawson map but not the "Beasts"
in this double-columned edition.

Lawson's History of North Carolina, containing the exact description and natural history of that country; together with the
present state thereof. And a journal of a thousand miles travel'd

thro' several nations of Indians, giving a particular account of their customs, names &c. By John Lawson, gent., surveyor-general of North Carolina. London: Printed for W. Taylor and J. Baker, 1714. Richmond, Va., Garrett and Massie, 1937. xxx, 260 pp. front. (map), plates. 23¼ cm. This edition was sponsored by the North Carolina Society of the Colonial Dames of America. Edited by Frances Latham Harris, recording secretary.

Lawson's History of North Carolina, containing the exact description and natural history of that country; together with the present state thereof. And a journal of a thousand miles travel'd thro' several nations of Indians, giving a particular account of their customs, names, &c. By John Lawson, gent., surveyor-general of North Carolina. London: Printed for W. Taylor and J. Baker, 1714. Richmond, Va., Garrett and Massie, 1937. xxviii, 260 pp. front. (map), plates. 23½ cm. This edition was sponsored by the North Carolina Society of the Colonial Dames of America. Edited by Frances Latham Harris, recording secretary. 2nd edition, 1951 [i.e. 1952].

Lawson's History of North Carolina, containing the exact description and natural history of that country; together with the present state thereof. And a journal of a thousand miles travel'd thro' several nations of Indians, giving a particular account of their customs, names, &c. By John Lawson, gent., surveyor-general of North Carolina. London: Printed for W. Taylor and J. Baker, 1714. Richmond, Va., Garrett and Massie, 1937. xxviii, 260 pp. front. (map), plates. 23½ cm. This edition, sponsored by the North Carolina Society of the Colonial Dames of America, was edited by Frances Latham Harris, recording secretary. 3rd. edition, 1960.

The North Carolina Collection of the University of North Carolina at Chapel Hill has an unusual volume transcribed from the 1718 edition of Lawson. This manuscript volume, "copied by Mr. Moore and presented by his father Mr. R. G. Moore to H. B. Croom," gives no date of transcription. A note on the first sheet reads:

This copy was made from the volume of Lawson's History which belonged to the Library of the State of North Carolina, and perished in the conflagration of the Capitol of the State in 1831.

It had been the property of E[dward] Moseley, and bore, on the title page, the following manuscript note "This author, the first public

employment he had, was to be my deputy, when I. E. Moseley was
Surveyor General of North Carolina."

Many writers have copied Lawson without giving proper credit
—or any credit at all. In 1711, the year of Lawson's untimely
death, Johann Rudolff Ochs published a 102-page promotional
tract at Bern, Switzerland, entitled, *Americanischer Wegeweiser,
oder, Kurtze und eigentliche Beschreibung der Englischen pro-
vintzen in Nord America sonderlich aber der Landschafft Carolina, mit Grossern Fleisz Zusammen getragen und an Tag gege-
ben.*

The best-known plagiarism of Lawson was John Brickell, *The
Natural History of North Carolina.*[94] *With an account of the
trade, manners, and customs of the Christian and Indian inhabitants. Illustrated with copper-plates, whereon are curiously en-
graved the map of the country, several strange beasts, birds, fishes,
snakes, insects, trees, and plants &c.* (Dublin, James Carson for
the author, 1737. viii, 408 pp. plates, folding map of North
Carolina; later editions Dublin, 1743, and Raleigh, 1911.)

Brickell practiced medicine in Edenton for many years. Part of
his book was probably written in Ireland. Critics have said that
his book was "almost a verbal transcript of Lawson" and that it
was a "slavish plagiarism." The Library of Congress card for
Brickell's book says that Lawson "was almost verbally copied,
without acknowledgment." These charges are only partially true.
Brickell did plagiarize Lawson extensively, but he included much
social and economic history not found in Lawson. His book is
probably the best account in print relating to diseases and medical practice in colonial North Carolina. His account of a visit to
"Cherokee Mountains" in February, 1730, is one of the most
interesting features of this volume, and, obviously, this is not a
plagiarism of Lawson.

When it came to natural history, the major theme of the book,
Brickell usually varied the language of Lawson and made numerous additions, particularly those relating to medicinal uses of

94. Percy G. Adams, *Travelers and Travel Liars* (Berkeley: University of
California Press, 1962) is an excellent study of plagiarisms of this period. See
also Adams, "John Lawson's Alter Ego—Dr. John Brickell," *North Carolina
Historical Review,* Vol. 34 (July, 1957), 326.

parts or products of birds. He was of Irish descent and, when Lawson used the word "England," Brickell substituted "Ireland." His list of birds includes a dozen or more not in Lawson and four kinds of vines not mentioned by the earlier writer. The book is better organized than Lawson, and it is considerably larger.

Less well-known than Brickell's plagiarism is a book that is usually listed in library catalogs and bibliographies as *William Byrd's Natural History of Virginia, or the Newly Discovered Eden* (Richmond, 1940). This book has a strange history indeed. In 1736, when Colonel William Byrd II of Virginia was trying to settle his "Land of Eden," along the Roanoke River near the North Carolina boundary with a colony of Swiss, he sold over 33,000 acres to a Swiss named Samuel Jenner for a price of £6,000. In 1737, Jenner published at Bern a 228-page book, written in German and called *Neu-gefundenes Eden*. Its title page claimed that it was "a Detailed Report on South and North Carolina, Pennsylvania, Maryland, and Virginia. Sketched through two journeys made to these Provinces [and based upon] a journal of travel and many letters." After the "Report" and Jenner's narrative of his visits in various parts of America, the author announced on page 96: "There follows now a short description of Virginia . . . a true report, which I have received from the president himself and have translated as well as I was able from English into German." "The president" referred to was William Byrd, but he was not president of the Council then. This book was edited and translated from the German by Richard Croom Beatty and William J. Mulloy and published under the title given at the beginning of this paragraph.[95]

Nowhere in Byrd's writings, and he was an excellent writer and something of a naturalist, is there the detailed knowledge of animals, plants, and fish that appears in *Neu-gefundenes Eden*. These facts came, with few exceptions, from Lawson's book.[96] The "translator," Jenner, followed Lawson's arrangement of the sections on natural history, though he omitted the section on "In-

95. *William Byrd's Natural History of Virginia, or the Newly Discovered Eden*. Edited and translated from a German version by R. C. Beatty and W. J. Mulloy (Richmond: The Dietz Press, 1940).

96. Percy G. Adams, "The Real Author of William Byrd's Natural History of Virginia," *American Literature*, Vol. 28 (1956–57), 211–20. Conway Zirkle commented on the close "paraphrasing" of Jenner's work and Lawson but did not pursue the matter closely. See *Virginia Magazine of History and Biography*, Vol. 67 (1959), 293.

sects," a category including nineteen varieties of snakes. This was not good promotional propaganda. He also discreetly omitted Lawson's story about a crop of peas being destroyed by birds. "Both Jenner and Lawson describe the same types of flora and fauna not only in the same way but in almost exactly the same sequence and with no important omissions." The "real author" of the *Natural History of Virginia* was Lawson, certainly not William Byrd.

A NEW VOYAGE TO CAROLINA;

CONTAINING THE

Exact Description and *Natural History*

OF THAT

COUNTRY:

Together with the *Present State* thereof.

AND

A JOURNAL

Of a Thousand Miles, Travel'd thro' several Nations of *INDIANS*.

Giving a particular Account of their Customs, Manners, *&c.*

By JOHN LAWSON, Gent. Surveyor-General of *North-Carolina*.

LONDON:

Printed in the Year 1709.

DEDICATION

To His Excellency
WILLIAM LORD CRAVEN, Palatine;
The most Noble, HENRY DUKE OF BEAUFORT;[1]
The Right Honble JOHN LORD CARTERET;
The Honble MAURICE ASHLEY, Esq;
Sir JOHN COLLETON, Baronet,
JOHN DANSON,[2] Esq;

And the rest of the True and Absolute
LORDS-PROPRIETORS
OF THE
Province of *Carolina* in *America.*

MY LORDS,

As Debts of Gratitude ought most punctually to be paid, so, where the Debtor is uncapable of Payment, Acknowledgments ought, at least, to be made. I cannot, in the least, pretend to retaliate *Your Lordships* Favours to me, but must farther intrude on that Goodness of which I have already had so good Experience, by laying these Sheets at *Your Lordships* Feet, where they beg Protection, as having nothing to recommend them, but Truth; a Gift which every Author may be Master of, if he will.

I here present *Your Lordships* with a Description of your own Country, for the most part, in her Natural Dress, and therefore less vitiated with Fraud and Luxury. A Country, whose Inhabit-

---

1. This was the original share of George Monck, Duke of Albemarle. It was acquired by Lord Granville in 1701. Six years later, this share was acquired by Henry Somerset, Duke of Beaufort. The name is perpetuated in both Carolinas.

2. This was the original William Berkeley share. It was acquired by Mary and John Danson in 1708.

ants may enjoy a Life of the greatest Ease and Satisfaction, and pass away their Hours in solid Contentment.

Those Charms of *Liberty* and *Right,* the Darlings of an *English* Nature, which *Your Lordships* grant and maintain, make you appear Noble Patrons in the Eyes of all Men, and we a happy People in a Foreign Country; which nothing less than Ingratitude and Baseness can make us disown.

As Heaven has been liberal in its Gifts, so are *Your Lordships* favourable Promoters of whatever may make us an easy People; which, I hope, *Your Lordships* will continue to us and our Posterity; and that we and they may always acknowledge such Favours, by banishing from among us every Principle which renders Men factious and unjust, which is the hearty Prayer of,

My Lords,
Your Lordships most obliged,
most humble,
and most devoted Servant,
John Lawson

PREFACE

TIS a great Misfortune, that most of our Travellers, who go to this vast Continent in America, are Persons of the meaner Sort, and generally of a very slender Education; who being hir'd by the Merchants, to trade amongst the Indians, in which Voyages they often spend several Years, are yet, at their Return, uncapable of giving any reasonable Account of what they met withal in those remote Parts; tho' the Country abounds with Curiosities worthy a nice Observation. In this Point, I think, the French outstrip us.

First, By their Numerous Clergy, their Missionaries being obedient to their Superiors in the highest Degree, and that Obedience being one great Article of their Vow, and strictly observ'd amongst all their Orders.

Secondly, They always send abroad some of their Gentlemen in Company of the Missionaries, who, upon their Arrival, are order'd out into the Wilderness, to make Discoveries, and to acquaint themselves with the Savages of America; and are oblig'd to keep a strict Journal of all the Passages they meet withal, in order to present the same not only to their Governors and Fathers, but likewise to their Friends and Relations in France; which is industriously spread about that Kingdom, to their Advantage. For their Monarch being a very good Judge of Mens Deserts, does not often let Money or Interest make Men of Parts give Place to others of less Worth. This breeds an Honourable Emulation amongst them to outdo one another, even in Fatigues, and Dangers; whereby they gain a good Correspondence with the Indians, and acquaint themselves with their Speech and Customs; and so make considerable Discoveries in a short time. Witness, their Journals from Canada, to the Missisipi, and its several Branches, where they have effected great Matters, in a few Years.

Having spent most of my Time, during my eight Years Abode

in Carolina, *in travelling; I not only survey'd the Sea-Coast and those Parts which are already inhabited by the Christians, but likewise view'd a spatious Tract of Land, lying betwixt the Inhabitants and the Ledges of Mountains, from whence our noblest Rivers have their Rise, running towards the Ocean, where they water as pleasant a Country as any in* Europe; *the Discovery of which being never yet made publick, I have, in the following Sheets, given you a faithful Account thereof, wherein I have laid down every thing with Impartiality, and Truth, which is indeed, the Duty of every* Author, *and preferable to a smooth Stile, accompany'd with Falsities and Hyperboles.*

Great Part of this pleasant and healthful Country is inhabited by none but Savages, who covet a Christian Neighbourhood, for the Advantage of Trade, and enjoy all the Comforts of Life, free from Care and Want.

But not to amuse my Readers any longer with the Encomium of Carolina, *I refer 'em to my* Journal, *and other more particular Description of that Country and its Inhabitants, which they will find after the* Natural History *thereof, in which I have been very exact, and for Method's sake, rang'd each Species under its distinct and proper Head.*

INTRODUCTION

N the Year 1700, when People flock'd from all Parts of the Christian World, to see the Solemnity of the Grand Jubilee at *Rome*,[3] my Intention, at that Time, being to travel, I accidentally met with a Gentleman, who had been Abroad, and was very well acquainted with the Ways of Living in both *Indies;* of whom, having made Enquiry concerning them, he assur'd me, that *Carolina* was the best Country I could go to; and, that there then lay a Ship in the *Thames,* in which I might have my Passage. I laid hold on this Opportunity, and was not long on Board, before we fell down the River, and sail'd to *Cowes*,[4] where, having taken in some Passengers, we proceeded on our Voyage, 'till we sprung a-leak, and were forc'd into the Islands of *Scilly*.[5] Here we spent about 10 Days in refitting; in which Time we had a great deal of Diversion in Fishing and Shooting on those rocky Islands. The Inhabitants were very courteous and civil, especially the Governor, to whose good Company and Favour, we were very much oblig'd. There is a Town[6] on one of these Islands, where is good Entertainment for those that happen to come in, though the Land is but mean, and Flesh-meat not Plenty. They have good Store of Rabbits, Quails, and Fish; and you see at the poor Peoples Doors great Heaps of Perriwinkle-shells, those Fish being a great Part of their Food. On the 1st Day

3. A great religious celebration, which since 1450, with three exceptions, has been held in Rome every twenty-five years. The most distinctive feature of the ceremonial of the Jubilee is the unwalling and final walling up of the "holy door" in each of the four great basilicas that the pilgrims are required to visit.

4. On the Isle of Wight, England.

5. A group of 140 islands in Cornwall County, England.

6. Hugh Town, largest town in the Scilly Isles.

of *May,* having a fair Wind at *East,* we put to Sea, and were on the Ocean (without speaking to any Vessel, except a Ketch [7] bound from *New England* to *Barbadoes,* laden with Horses, Fish, and Provisions) 'till the latter End of *July,* when the Winds hung so much *Southerly,* that we could not get to our Port, but put into *Sandyhook-bay,* and went up to *New York,* after a pinching Voyage, caus'd by our long Passage. We found at the Watering-Place, a *French* Man of War, who had on Board Men and Necessaries to make a Colony, and was intended for the *Messiasippi* River, there to settle.[8] The Country of *New-York* is very pleasant in Summer, but in the Winter very cold, as all the *Northern* Plantations are. Their chief Commodities are Provisions, Bread, Beer, Lumber, and Fish in abundance; all which are very good, and some Skins and Furrs are hence exported. The City is govern'd by a Mayor, (as in *England*) is seated on an Island, and lies very convenient for Trade and Defence, having a regular Fort, and well mounted with Guns. The Buildings are generally of a smaller Sort of *Flemish* Brick, and of the *Dutch* Fashion, (excepting some few Houses:) They are all very firm and good Work, and conveniently plac'd, as is likewise the Town, which gives a very pleasant Prospect of the neighbouring Islands and Rivers. A good Part of the Inhabitants are *Dutch,* in whose Hands this Colony once was.[9] After a Fortnight's Stay here, we put out from *Sandyhook,* and in 14 Days after, arriv'd at *Charles-Town,*[10] the Metropolis of *South Carolina,* which is scituate in 32, 45 *North* Latitude, and admits of large Ships to come over their Bar up to the Town, where is a very commodious Harbour, about 5 Miles distant from the Inlet, and stands on a Point very convenient for Trade, being seated between two pleasant and navigable Rivers.[11] The Town has very regular and fair Streets, in which are good Buildings of Brick and Wood, and since my coming thence, has had great Additions of beautiful, large Brick-buildings, besides a strong Fort, and regular Fortifications made to defend the Town. The Inhabitants, by

7. A fore-and-aft rigged vessel with mainmast and mizzenmast.

8. This effort of the French to colonize the Lower Mississippi Valley failed. New Orleans was not founded until 1718.

9. Dutch New Netherland became English New York in 1664.

10. Charleston, or Charles Town, as it was then spelled, was founded in 1670. It was located on a nine-acre tract on the west bank of the Ashley River just above Town Creek. In 1680, the settlers moved to the site of present Charleston.

11. Ashley and Cooper rivers.

their wise Management and Industry, have much improv'd the Country, which is in as thriving Circumstances at this Time, as any Colony on the Continent of *English America,* and is of more Advantage to the Crown of *Great Britain,* than any of the other more *Northerly* Plantations, (*Virginia* and *Maryland* excepted.) This Colony was at first planted by a genteel Sort of People, that were well acquainted with Trade, and had either Money or Parts, to make good Use of the Advantages that offer'd, as most of them have done, by raising themselves to great Estates, and considerable Places of Trust, and Posts of Honour, in this thriving Settlement. Since the first Planters, abundance of *French* and others have gone over, and rais'd themselves to considerable Fortunes.[12] They are very neat and exact in Packing and Shipping of their Commodities; which Method has got them so great a Character Abroad, that they generally come to a good Market with their Commodities; when oftentimes the Product of other Plantations, are forc'd to be sold at lower Prizes. They have a considerable Trade both to *Europe,* and the *West Indies,* whereby they become rich, and are supply'd with all Things necessary for Trade, and genteel Living, which several other Places fall short of. Their co-habiting in a Town, has drawn to them ingenious People of most Sciences, whereby they have Tutors amongst them that educate their Youth a-la-mode.

Their Roads, with great Industry, are made very good and pleasant. Near the Town is built a fair Parsonage-house, with necessary Offices, and the Minister has a very considerable Allowance from his Parish. There is likewise a *French* Church in Town,[13] of the Reform'd Religion, and several Meeting-houses for dissenting Congregations, who all enjoy at this Day an entire Liberty of their Worship; the Constitution of this Government, allowing all Parties of well-meaning Christians to enjoy a free Toleration, and possess the same Priviledges, so long as they appear to behave themselves peaceably and well: It being the Lords Proprietors Intent, that the Inhabitants of *Carolina* should be as free from Oppression, as any in the Universe; which doubt-

12. The first forty-five Huguenots arrived from England early in 1680. A 1713 report estimated the Huguenots as one-sixth of the colony's total population.

13. The church, still standing in the main part of Charleston, had regular services until recently. In early days, the Huguenots also had churches at Goose Creek, Eastern Branch of Cooper River, and Santee River.

less they will, if their own Differences amongst themselves do not occasion the contrary.

They have a well-disciplin'd *Militia;* their Horse are most Gentlemen, and well mounted, and the best in *America,* and may equalize any in other Parts: Their Officers, both Infantry and Cavalry, generally appear in scarlet Mountings, and as rich as in most Regiments belonging to the Crown, which shews the Richness and Grandeur of this Colony. They are a Fronteer, and prove such troublesome Neighbours to the *Spaniards,* that they have once laid their Town of St. *Augustine* in Ashes,[14] and drove away their Cattle; besides many Encounters and Engagements, in which they have defeated them, too tedious to relate here. What the *French* got by their Attempt against *South Carolina,* will hardly ever be rank'd amongst their Victories; their Admiral *Mouville* being glad to leave the Enterprize, and run away, after he had suffer'd all the Loss and Disgrace he was capable of receiving. They are absolute Masters over the *Indians,* and carry so strict a Hand over such as are within the Circle of their Trade, that none does the least Injury to any of the *English,* but he is presently sent for, and punish'd with Death, or otherwise, according to the Nature of the Fault. They have an entire Friendship with the neighbouring *Indians* of several Nations, which are a very warlike People, ever faithful to the *English,* and have prov'd themselves brave and true on all Occasions; and are a great Help and Strength to this Colony. The Chief of the savage Nations have heretofore groan'd under the *Spanish* Yoke, and having experienc'd their Cruelty, are become such mortal Enemies to that People, that they never give a *Spaniard* Quarter; but generally, when they take any Prisoners, (if the *English* be not near to prevent it) sculp them, that is, to take their Hair and Skin of their Heads, which they often flea away, whilst the Wretch is alive. Notwithstanding the *English* have us'd all their Endeavours, yet they could never bring them to leave this Barbarity to the *Spaniards;* who, as they alledge, use to murder them and their Relations, and make Slaves of them to build their Forts and Towns.

This Place is more plentiful in Money, than most, or indeed any of the Plantations on the Continent; besides, they build a considerable Number of Vessels of Cedar, and other Wood, with which they trade to *Cuirassau,*[15] and the *West Indies;* from one

14. This expedition captured the town, but it failed to capture Fort San Marcos.

15. Curacao, an island of 210 square miles, in the Dutch West Indies.

they bring Money, and from the other the Produce of their Islands, which yields a necessary Supply of both to the Colony. Their Stocks of Cattle are incredible, being from one to two thousand Head in one Man's Possession: These feed in the *Savannas,* and other Grounds, and need no Fodder in the Winter. Their Mutton and Veal is good, and their Pork is not inferior to any in *America.* As for Pitch and Tar, none of the Plantations are comparable for affording the vast Quantities of Naval Stores, as this Place does. There have been heretofore some Discoveries of rich Mines in the mountanous Part of this Country; but being remote from the present Settlement, and the Inhabitants not well vers'd in ordering Minerals, they have been laid aside 'till a more fit Opportunity happens. There are several noble Rivers, and spacious Tracts of rich Land in their Lordships Dominions, lying to the *Southward,* which are yet uninhabited, besides *Port Royal,* a rare Harbour and Inlet, having many Inhabitants thereon, which their Lordships have now made a Port for Trade. This will be a most advantageous Settlement, lying so commodiously for Ships coming from the Gulph,[16] and the Richness of the Land, which is reported to be there. These more *Southerly* Parts will afford Oranges, Limons, Limes, and many other Fruits, which the *Northerly* Plantations yield not.

The Merchants of *Carolina,* are fair, frank Traders. The Gentlemen seated in the Country, are very courteous, live very nobly in their Houses, and give very genteel Entertainment to all Strangers and others, that come to visit them. And since the Produce of *South* and *North Carolina* is the same, unless Silk,[17] which this Place produces great Quantities of, and very good, *North Carolina* having never made any Tryal thereof as yet, therefore I shall refer the natural Produce of this Country, to that Part which treats of *North Carolina,* whose Productions are much the same. The Christian Inhabitants of both Colonies pretty equal, but the Slaves of *South Carolina* are far more in Number than those in the *North.* I shall now proceed to relate my Journey thro' the Country, from this Settlement to the other, and then treat of the natural History of *Carolina,* with other remarkable Circumstances which I have met with, during my eight Years Abode in that Country.

16. Gulf of Mexico.
17. Efforts to produce silk in various English colonies were not very successful. Georgia, settled long after Lawson's death, seems to have produced more than any other colony.

JOURNAL

O F

A Thousand Miles Travel
among the Indians,
from South to North Carolina

N *December* the 28th, 1700, I began my Voyage (for *North Carolina*) from *Charles*-Town, being six *English*-men in Company, with three *Indian*-men, and one Woman, Wife to our *Indian*-Guide, having five Miles from the Town to the Breach we went down in a large Canoe, that we had provided for our Voyage thither, having the Tide of Ebb along with us; which was so far spent by that Time we got down, that we had not Water enough for our Craft to go over, although we drew but two Foot, or thereabouts. This Breach is a Passage through a Marsh lying to the *Northward* of *Sullivans* Island, the Pilot's having a Look out thereon, lying very commodious for Mariners (on that Coast) making a good Land-Mark in so level a Country, this Bar being difficult to hit, where an Observation hath been wanting for a Day or two; *North East* Winds bringing great Fogs, Mists, and Rains; which, towards the cool Months of *October,* *November,* and until the latter End of *March,* often appear in these Parts. There are three Pilots to attend, and conduct Ships over the Bar. The Harbour where the Vessels generally ride, is against the Town on *Cooper*'s River, lying within a Point which

parts that and *Ashley*-River, they being Land-lock'd almost on all Sides.

At 4 in the Afternoon, (at half Flood) we pass'd with our Canoe over the Breach, leaving *Sullivans* Island on our Starboard. The first Place we design'd for, was *Santee* River, on which there is a Colony of *French* Protestants,[1] allow'd and encourag'd by the Lords Proprietors. At Night we got to *Bell*'s-Island, a poor Spot of Land, being about ten Miles round, where liv'd (at that Time) a *Bermudian*,[2] being employ'd here with a Boy, to look after a Stock of Cattle and Hogs, by the Owner of this Island. One Side of the Roof of his House was thatch'd with Palmeto-leaves, the other open to the Heavens, thousands of Musketoes, and other trouble-some Insects, tormenting both Man and Beast inhabiting these Islands. The Palmeto-trees, whose Leaves growing only on the Top of the Tree, in the Shape of a Fan, and in a Cluster, like a Cabbage; this Tree in *Carolina*, when at its utmost Growth, is about forty or fifty Foot in Height, and two Foot through: It's worth mentioning, that the Growth of the Tree is not perceive-able in the Age of any Man, the Experiment having been often try'd in *Bermudas,* and elsewhere, which shews the slow Growth of this Vegitable, the Wood of it being porous and stringy, like some Canes; the Leaves thereof the *Bermudians* make Womens Hats, Bokeets,[3] Baskets, and pretty Dressing-boxes, a great deal being transported to *Pensilvania*, and other *Northern* Parts of *America*, (where they do not grow) for the same Manufacture. The People of *Carolina* make of the Fans of this Tree, Brooms very serviceable, to sweep their Houses withal.

We took up our Lodging this Night with the *Ber Mudian;* our Entertainment was very indifferent, there being no fresh Water to be had on the Island.

The next Morning we set away thro' the Marshes; about Noon we reach'd another Island, call'd *Dix*'s Island, much like to the former, tho' larger; there liv'd an honest *Scot*,[4] who gave us the best Reception his Dwelling afforded, being well provided of Oat-meal, and several other Effects he had found on that Coast;

1. The name "French Santee" appears on some of the early maps of the Carolina region.
2. Some Bermudians migrated to the southern English colonies, but the number was quite small.
3. Buckets.
4. There was a settlement of Scots at Stuart's town, a mile and a half south of present Beaufort. There was also a Scottish settlement at Port Royal.

which Goods belong'd to that unfortunate Vessel, the *Rising Sun*, a *Scotch* Man of War, lately arriv'd from the *Istmus* of *Darien*, and cast away near the Bar of *Ashley* River, the *September* before, Capt. *Gibson* of *Glasco*[5] then commanding her, who, with above an hundred Men then on Board her, were every Soul drown'd in that terrible Gust which then happen'd; most of the Corps being taken up, were carefully interr'd by Mr. *Graham*, their Lieutenant, who happily was on Shore during the Tempest.

After Dinner, we left our *Scotch* Landlord, and went that Night to the *North East* Point of the Island: It being dark ere we got there, our Canoe struck on a Sand near the Breakers, and were in great Danger of our Lives, but (by God's Blessing) got off safe to the Shore, where we lay all Night.

In the Morning we set forwards on our intended Voyage. About two a Clock we got to *Bulls* Island, which is about thirty Miles long, and hath a great Number of both Cattel and Hogs upon it; the Cattel being very wild, and the Hogs very lean. These two last Islands belong to one Colonel *Cary*,[6] an Inhabitant of *South Carolina*. Although it were Winter, yet we found such Swarms of Musketoes, and other troblesome Insects, that we got but little Rest that Night.

The next Day we intended for a small Island on the other Side of *Sewee-Bay*,[7] which joining to these Islands, Shipping might come to victual or careen; but there being such a Burden of those Flies, that few or none cares to settle there; so the Stock thereon are run wild. We were gotten about half Way to *Racoon*-Island, when there sprung up a tart Gale at *N.W.* which put us in some Danger of being cast away, the Bay being rough, and there running great Seas between the two Islands, which are better than four Leagues asunder, a strong Current of a Tide setting in and out, which made us turn Tail to it, and got our Canoe right before the Wind, and came safe into a Creek that is joining to the *North* End of *Bulls* Island. We sent our *Indians* to hunt, who brought us two Deers, which were very poor, and their Maws full of large Grubs.

On the Morrow we went and visited the *Eastermost* Side of this

5. Glasgow, Scotland, carried on a rather extensive trade with the southern English colonies.

6. Thomas Cary later served as governor of the North Carolina region during 1705–6 and again during 1708–11, when he was removed following the "Cary Rebellion."

7. A small bay, north of Sullivan's Island and west of Bull's Bay.

Island, it joining to the Ocean, having very fair sandy Beeches, pav'd with innumerable Sorts of curious pretty Shells, very pleasant to the Eye. Amongst the rest, we found the *Spanish* Oyster-Shell, whence come the Pearls. They are very large, and of a different Form from other Oysters; their Colour much resembles the Tortoise-Shell, when it is dress'd. There was left by the Tide several strange Species of a muciligmous slimy Substance, though living, and very aptly mov'd at their first Appearance; yet, being left on the dry Sand, (by the Beams of the Sun) soon exhale and vanish.

At our Return to our Quarters, the *Indians* had kill'd two more Deer, two wild Hogs, and three Racoons, all very lean, except the Racoons. We had great Store of Oysters, Conks, and Clanns, a large Sort of Cockles. These Parts being very well furnish'd with Shell-Fish, Turtle of several Sorts, but few or none of the green, with other Sorts of Salt-water Fish, and in the Season, good Plenty of Fowl, as Curleus, Gulls, Gannets, and Pellicans, besides Duck and Mallard, Geese, Swans, Teal, Widgeon, &c.

On *Thursday* Morning we left *Bulls* Island, and went thro' the Creeks, which lie between the Bay and the main Land. At Noon we went on Shore, and got our Dinner near a Plantation, on a Creek having the full Prospect of *Sewee*-Bay: We sent up to the House, but found none at Home, but a Negro, of whom our Messenger purchas'd some small Quantity of Tobacco and Rice. We came to a deserted *Indian* Residence, call'd *Avendaugh-bough,*[8] where we rested that Night.

The next Day we enter'd *Santee*-River's Mouth, where is fresh Water, occasion'd by the extraordinary Current that comes down continually. With hard Rowing, we got two Leagues up the River, lying all Night in a swampy Piece of Ground, the Weather being so cold all the Time, we were almost frozen ere Morning, leaving the Impressions of our Bodies on the wet Ground. We set forward very early in the Morning, to seek some better Quarters.

As we row'd up the River, we found the Land towards the Mouth, and for about sixteen Miles up it, scarce any Thing but Swamp and Percoarson,[9] affording vast Ciprus-Trees, of which the *French* make Canoes, that will carry fifty or sixty Barrels. After the Tree is moulded and dug, they saw them in two Pieces, and so put a Plank between, and a small Keel, to preserve them from the

8. Probably a Sewee village. The name seems to be preserved in Awendaw.
9. Pocosin or poquosin, a shrub bog.

Oyster-Banks, which are innumerable in the Creeks and Bays betwixt the *French* Settlement [10] and *Charles*-Town. They carry two Masts, and Bermudas Sails, which makes them very handy and fit for their Purpose; for although their River fetches its first Rise from the Mountains, and continues a Current some hundreds of Miles ere it disgorges it self, having no sound Bay or Sand-Banks betwixt the Mouth thereof, and the Ocean. Notwithstanding all this, with the vast Stream it affords at all Seasons, and the repeated Freshes it so often allarms the Inhabitants with, by laying under Water great Part of their Country, yet the Mouth is barr'd, affording not above four or five Foot Water at the Entrance. As we went up the River, we heard a great Noise, as if two Parties were engag'd against each other, seeming exactly like small Shot. When we approach'd nearer the Place, we found it to be some *Sewee Indians* firing the Canes Swamps, which drives out the Game, then taking their particular Stands, kill great Quantities of both Bear, Deer, Turkies, and what wild Creatures the Parts afford.

These *Sewees* have been formerly a large Nation,[11] though now very much decreas'd, since the *English* hath seated their Land, and all other Nations of *Indians* are observ'd to partake of the same Fate, where the *Europeans* come, the *Indians* being a People very apt to catch any Distemper they are afflicted withal; the Small-Pox has destroy'd many thousands of these Natives, who no sooner than they are attack'd with the violent Fevers, and the Burning which attends that Distemper, fling themselves over Head in the Water, in the very Extremity of the Disease; which shutting up the Pores, hinders a kindly Evacuation of the pestilential Matter, and drives it back; by which Means Death most commonly ensues; not but in other Distempers which are epidemical, you may find among 'em Practitioners [12] that have extraordinary Skill and Success in removing those morbifick Qualities which afflict 'em, not often going above 100 Yards from their Abode for their Remedies, some of their chiefest Physicians commonly carrying their Compliment of Drugs continually about them, which are Roots, Barks, Berries, Nuts, &c. that are strung

10. On the Santee River.

11. The Sewees were probably Siouan Indians. James Mooney estimated their population at 800 in 1600. In 1715, there were only fifty-seven of them. Lawson's description of the Sewee tribe constitutes all that we know of this interesting people.

12. Medicine men.

upon a Thread. So like a *Pomander,* the Physician wears them about his Neck. An *Indian* hath been often found to heal an *English*-man of a Malady, for the Value of a Match-Coat; which the ablest of our *English* Pretenders in *America,* after repeated Applications, have deserted the Patient as incurable; God having furnish'd every Country with specifick Remedies for their peculiar Diseases.

Rum, a Liquor now so much in Use with them, that they will part with the dearest Thing they have, to purchase it; and when they have got a little in their Heads, are the impatients Creatures living, 'till they have enough to make 'em quite drunk; and the most miserable Spectacles when they are so, some falling into the Fires, burn their Legs or Arms, contracting the Sinews, and become Cripples all ther Life-time; others from Precipices break their Bones and Joints, with abundance of Instances, yet none are so great to deter them from that accurs'd Practice of Drunkenness, though sensible how many of them (are by it) hurry'd into the other World before their Time, as themselves oftentimes will confess. The *Indians,* I was now speaking of, were not content with the common Enemies that lessen and destroy their Country-men, but invented an infallible Stratagem [13] to purge their Tribe, and reduce their Multitude into far less Numbers. Their Contrivance was thus, as a Trader amongst them inform'd me.

They seeing several Ships coming in, to bring the *English* Supplies from *Old England,* one chief Part of their Cargo being for a Trade with the *Indians,* some of the craftiest of them had observ'd, that the Ships came always in at one Place, which made them very confident that Way was the exact Road to *England;* and seeing so many Ships come thence, they believ'd it could not be far thither, esteeming the *English* that were among them, no better than Cheats, and thought, if they could carry the Skins and Furs they got, themselves to *England,* which were inhabited with a better Sort of People than those sent amongst them, that then they should purchase twenty times the Value for every Pelt they sold Abroad, in Consideration of what Rates they sold for at Home. The intended Barter was exceeding well approv'd of, and after a general Consultation of the ablest Heads amongst them, it

13. James C. Milling says, "We are also indebted to Lawson for the only account of an event which amounted to a national tragedy for the Sewee people." See his *Red Carolinians* (Chapel Hill: The University of North Carolina Press, 1940) , p. 208.

was, *Nemine Contradicente,*[14] agreed upon, immediately to make an Addition of their Fleet, by building more Canoes, and those to be of the best Sort, and biggest Size, as fit for their intended Discovery. Some *Indians* were employ'd about making the Canoes, others to hunting, every one to the Post he was most fit for, all Endeavours tending towards an able Fleet and Cargo for *Europe.* The Affair was carry'd on with a great deal of Secrecy and Expedition, so as in a small Time they had gotten a Navy, Loading, Provisions, and Hands ready to set Sail, leaving only the Old, Impotent, and Minors at Home, 'till their successful Return. The Wind presenting, they set up their Mat-Sails, and were scarce out of Sight, when there rose a Tempest, which it's suppos'd carry'd one Part of these *Indian* Merchants, by Way of the other World, whilst the others were taken up at Sea by an *English* Ship, and sold for Slaves to the Islands. The Remainder are better satisfy'd with their Imbecilities in such an Undertaking, nothing affronting them more, than to rehearse their Voyage to *England.*

There being a strong Current in *Santee*-River, caus'd us to make small Way with our Oars. With hard Rowing, we got that Night to Mons. *Eugee*'s [15] House, which stands about fifteen Miles up the River, being the first Christian dwelling we met withal in that Settlement, and were very courteously receiv'd by him and his Wife.

Many of the *French* follow a Trade with the *Indians,* living very conveniently for that Interest. There is about seventy Families seated on this River, who live as decently and happily, as any Planters in these *Southward* Parts of *America.* The *French* being a temperate industrious People, some of them bringing very little of Effects, yet by their Endeavours and mutual Assistance amongst themselves, (which is highly to be commended) have out-stript our *English,* who brought with 'em larger Fortunes, though (as it seems) less endeavour to manage their Talent to the best Advantage. 'Tis admirable to see what Time and Industry will (with God's Blessing) effect. *Carolina* affording many strange Revolutions in the Age of a Man, daily Instances presenting themselves to our View, of so many, from despicable Beginnings, which in a short Time arrive to very splended Conditions. Here Propriety hath a large Scope, there being no strict Laws to bind our Privileges. A Quest after Game, being as freely and peremptorily en-

14. Latin for "without a dissenting vote."
15. Lawson spelled Huger as it was pronounced.

joy'd by the meanest Planter, as he that is the highest in Dignity, or wealthiest in the Province. Deer, and other Game that are naturally wild, being not immur'd, or preserv'd within Boundaries, to satisfy the Appetite of the Rich alone. A poor Labourer, that is Master of his Gun, &c. hath as good a Claim to have continu'd Coarses of Delicacies crouded upon his Table, as he that is Master of a greater Purse.

We lay all that Night at Mons. *Eugee's*, and the next Morning set out farther, to go the Remainder of our Voyage by Land: At ten a Clock we pass'd over a narrow, deep Swamp, having left the three *Indian* Men and one Woman, that had pilotted the Canoe from *Ashly*-River, having hir'd a *Sewee-Indian*, a tall, lusty Fellow, who carry'd a Pack of our Cloaths, of great Weight; notwithstanding his Burden, we had much a-do to keep pace with him. At Noon we came up with several *French* Plantations, meeting with several Creeks by the Way, the *French* were very officious in assisting with their small Dories to pass over these Waters, (whom we met coming from their Church) being all of them very clean and decent in their Apparel; their Houses and Plantations suitable in Neatness and Contrivance. They are all of the Same Opinion with the Church of *Geneva*, there being no Difference amongst them concerning the *Punctilio's* of their Christian Faith; which Union hath propagated a happy and delightful Concord in all other Matters throughout the whole Neighbourhood; living amongst themselves as one Tribe, or Kindred, every one making it his Business to be assistant to the Wants of his Country-man, preserving his Estate and Reputation with the same Exactness and Concern as he does his own; all seeming to share in the Misfortunes, and rejoyce at the Advance, and Rise, of their Brethren.

Towards the Afternoon, we came to Mons. *L'Jandro*, where we got our Dinner; there coming some *French* Ladies whilst we were there, who were lately come from *England*, and Mons. *L'Grand*,[16] a worthy *Norman*, who hath been a great Sufferer in his Estate, by the Persecution in *France*, against those of the Protestant Religion: This Gentleman very kindly invited us to make our Stay with him all Night, but we being intended farther that Day, took our Leaves, returning Acknowledgments of their Favours.

About 4 in the Afternoon, we pass'd over a large *Ciprus* run in a small Canoe; the *French* Doctor sent his Negro to guide us over

16. Later spelled Legrand.

the Head of a large Swamp; so we got that Night to Mons. *Gallian*'s the elder, who lives in a very curious contriv'd House, built of Brick and Stone, which is gotten near that Place. Near here comes in the Road from *Charles-Town*, and the rest of the *English* Settlement, it being a very good Way by Land, and not above 36 Miles, altho' more than 100 by Water; and I think the most difficult Way I ever saw, occasion'd by Reason of the multitude of Creeks lying along the Main, keeping their Course thro' the Marshes, turning and winding like a Labyrinth, having the Tide of Ebb and Flood twenty Times in less than three Leagues going.

The next Morning very early, we ferry'd over a Creek that runs near the House; and, after an Hour's Travel in the Woods, we came to the River-side, where we stay'd for the *Indian*, who was our Guide, and was gone round by Water in a small Canoe, to meet us at that Place we rested at. He came after a small Time, and ferry'd us in that little Vessel over *Santee* River 4 Miles, and 84 Miles in the Woods, which the over-flowing of the Freshes, which then came down, had made a perfect Sea of, there running an incredible Current in the River, which had cast our small Craft, and us, away, had we not had this *Sewee Indian* with us; who are excellent Artists in managing these small Canoes.

Santee River, at this Time, (from the usual Depth of Water) was risen perpendicular 36 Foot, always making a Breach from her Banks, about this Season of the Year: The general Opinion of the Cause thereof, is suppos'd to proceed from the overflowing of fresh Water-Lakes that lie near the Head of this River,[17] and others, upon the same Continent: But my Opinion is, that these vast Inundations proceed from the great and repeated Quantities of Snow that falls upon the Mountains, which lie at so great a Distance from the Sea, therefore they have no Help of being dissolv'd by those saline, piercing Particles, as other adjacent Parts near the Ocean receive; and therefore lies and increases to a vast Bulk, until some mild *Southerly* Breezes coming on a sudden, continue to unlock these frozen Bodies, congeal'd by the *North-West* Wind, dissipating them in Liquids; and coming down with Impetuosity, fills those Branches that feed these Rivers, and causes this strange Deluge, which oft-times lays under Water the adjacent Parts on both Sides this Current, for several Miles distant

17. Lawson is in error here. The Santee is formed by the junction of the Congaree and Wateree rivers.

from her Banks; tho' the *French* and *Indians* affir'm'd to me, they never knew such an extraordinary Flood there before.

We all, by God's Blessing, and the Endeavours of our *Indian* Pilot, pass'd safe over the River, but was lost in the Woods, which seem'd like some great Lake, except here and there a Knowl of high Land, which appear'd above Water.

We intended for Mons. *Galliar's jun*, but was lost, none of us knowing the Way at that Time, altho the *Indian* was born in that Country, it having receiv'd so strange a *Metamorphosis*. We were in several Opinions concerning the right Way, the *Indian* and my self, suppos'd the House to bear one Way, the rest thought to the contrary, we differing, it was agreed on amongst us that one half should go with the *Indian* to find the House, and the other part to stay upon one of these dry Spots, until some of them return'd to us, and inform'd us where it lay.

My self and two more were left behind by Reason the Canoe would not carry us all; we had but one Gun amongst us, one Load of Ammunition and no Provision. Had our Men in the Canoe miscarry'd, we must (in all Probability) there have perish'd.

In about six Hours Time, from our Mens Departure, the *Indian* came back to us in the same Canoe he went in, being half drunk, which assur'd us they had found some Place of Refreshment. He took us three into the Canoe, telling us all was well: Padling our Vessel several Miles thro' the Woods, being often half full of Water; but at length we got safe to the Place we sought for, which prov'd to lie the same Way the *Indian* and I guess'd it did.

When we got to the House, we found our Comrades in the same Trim the *Indian* was in, and several of the *French* Inhabitants with them, who treated us very courteously, wondering at our undertaking such a Voyage, thro' a Country inhabited by none but Savages, and them of so different Nations and Tongues.

After we had refresh'd our selves, we parted from a very kind, loving, and affable People, who wish'd us a safe and prosperous Voyage.

Hearing of a Camp of *Santee Indians* not far of, we set out intending to take up our Quarters with them that Night. There being a deep Run of Water in the Way, one of our Company being top-heavy, and there being nothing but a small Pole for a Bridge, over a Creek, fell into the Water up to the Chin; my self laughing at the Accident, and not taking good Heed to my Steps, came to the same Misfortune: All our Bedding was wet. The

Wind being at *N.W.* it froze very hard, which prepar'd such a Night's Lodging for me, that I never desire to have the like again; the wet Bedding and freezing Air had so qualify'd our Bodies, that in the Morning when we awak'd, we were nigh frozen to Death, until we had recruited our selves before a large Fire of the *Indians.*

Tuesday Morning we set towards the *Congerees*,[18] leaving the *Indian* Guide *Scipio* drunk amongst the *Santee-Indians.* We went ten Miles out of our Way, to head a great Swamp, the Freshes having fill'd them all with such great Quantities of Water, that the usual Paths were render'd unpassable. We met in our Way with an *Indian* Hut, where we were entertain'd with a fat, boil'd Goose, Venison, Racoon, and ground Nuts. We made but little Stay; about Noon, we pass'd by several large Savannah's, wherein is curious Ranges for Cattel, being green all the Year; they were plentifully stor'd with Cranes, Geese, &c. and the adjacent Woods with great Flocks of Turkies. This Day we travell'd about 30 Miles, and lay all Night at a House which was built for the *Indian* Trade, the Master thereof we had parted with at the *French* Town, who gave us Leave to make use of his Mansion. Such Houses are common in these Parts, and especially where there is *Indian* Towns, and Plantations near at hand, which this Place is well furnish'd withal.

These *Santee-Indians* are a well-humour'd and affable People; and living near the *English*, are become very tractable. They make themselves Cribs after a very curious Manner, wherein they secure their Corn from Vermin; which are more frequent in these warm Climates, than Countries more distant from the Sun. These pretty Fabricks are commonly supported with eight Feet or Posts, about seven Foot high from the Ground, well daub'd within and without upon Laths, with Loom or Clay, which makes them tight, and fit to keep out the smallest Insect, there being a small Door at the gable End, which is made of the same Composition, and to be remov'd at Pleasure, being no bigger, than that a slender Man may creep in at, cementing the Door up with the same Earth, when they take Corn out of the Crib, and are going from Home, always finding their Granaries in the same Posture they left them;

18. The Congarees, located northwest of the Santee Indians, were probably Siouan. They were located along the river of that name, in the vicinity of present Columbia. Mooney estimated their population at eight hundred in 1600. According to a census taken in 1715, they had a total population of only forty.

Theft to each other being altogether unpractis'd, never receiving Spoils but from Foreigners.

Hereabouts the Ground is something higher than about *Charles*-Town, there being found some Quarries of brown free Stone, which I have seen made Use of for Building, and hath prov'd very durable and good. The Earth here is mix'd with white Gravel, which is rare, there being nothing like a Stone to be found, of the natural Produce, near to *Ashly*-River.

The next Day about Noon we came to the Side of a great Swamp, where we were forc'd to strip our selves to get over it, which, with much Difficulty, we effected. Hereabouts the late Gust of Wind, which happen'd in *September* last, had torn the large Ciprus-Trees and Timbers up by the Roots, they lying confusedly in their Branches, did block up the Way, making the Passage very difficult.

This Night we got to one *Scipio*'s Hutt, a famous Hunter: There was no Body at Home; but we having (in our Company) one that had us'd to trade amongst them, we made our selves welcome to what his Cabin afforded, (which is a Thing common) the *Indians* allowing it practicable to the *English* Traders, to take out of their Houses what they need in their Absence, in Lieu whereof they most commonly leave some small Gratuity of Tobacco, Paint, Beads, &c. We found great Store of *Indian* Peas, (a very good Pulse) Beans, Oyl, Thinkapin Nuts, Corn, barbacu'd Peaches, and Peach-Bread; which Peaches being made into a Quiddony,[19] and so made up into Loves like Barley-Cakes, these cut into thin Slices, and dissolv'd in Water, makes a very grateful Acid, and extraordinary beneficial in Fevers, as hath often been try'd, and approv'd on by our *English* Practitioners. The Wind being at *N.W.* with cold Weather, made us make a large Fire in the *Indian*'s Cabin; being very intent upon our Cookery, we set the Dwelling on Fire, and with much ado, put it out, tho' with the Loss of Part of the Roof.

The next Day we travell'd on our Way, and about Noon came up with a Settlement of *Santee Indians*,[20] there being Plantations

19. A thick fruit syrup or jelly, originally and properly one made from quinces.

20. The Santees, who were Siouan, were located along the middle course of the Santee River. Mooney estimated their population at one thousand in 1600. By 1715, their number had been reduced to fewer than ninety, located in two villages, at present Nelson's Ferry and Scott's Lake, in Clarendon County.

lying scattering here and there, for a great many Miles. They came out to meet us, being acquainted with one of our Company, and made us very welcome with fat barbacu'd Venison, which the Woman of the Cabin took and tore in Pieces with her Teeth, so put it into a Mortar, beating it to Rags, afterwards stews it with Water, and other Ingredients, which makes a very savoury Dish.

At these Cabins came to visit us the King of the *Santee* Nation. He brought with him their chief Doctor or Physician, who was warmly and neatly clad with a Match-Coat, made of Turkies Feathers, which makes a pretty Shew, seeming as if it was a Garment of the deepest silk Shag. This Doctor had the Misfortune to lose his Nose by the Pox, which Disease the *Indians* often get by the *English* Traders that use amongst them; not but the Natives of *America* have for many Ages (by their own Confession) been afflicted with a Distemper much like the *Lues Venerea*,²¹ which hath all the Symptoms of the Pox, being different in this only; for I never could learn, that this Country-Distemper, or Yawes, is begun or continu'd with a Gonorrhoea; yet is attended with nocturnal Pains in the Limbs, and commonly makes such a Progress, as to vent Part of the Matter by Botches, and several Ulcers in the Body, and other Parts; oftentimes Death ensuing. I have known mercurial Unguents and Remedies work a Cure, following the same Methods as in the Pox; several white People, but chiefly the *Criolo*'s,²² losing their Palates and Noses by this devouring Vulture.

It is epidemical, visiting these Parts of *America,* which is often occasion'd thro' the immoderate drinking of Rum, by those that commonly drink Water at other Times, cold Nights Lodging, and bad open Houses, and more chiefly by often wetting the Feet, and eating such Quantities of Pork as they do, which is a gross Food, and a great Propagator of such Juices as it often meets withal in human Bodies, once tainted with this Malady; which may differently (in some Respects) act its Tragedy; the Change being occasion'd by the Difference of Climates and Bodies, as in *Europe.* We being well enough assur'd that the Pox had its first Rise (known to us) in this new World, it being caught of the *Indian* Women, by the *Spanish* Soldiers that follow'd *Columbus* in one of his Expeditions to *America;* who after their Arrival in *Old Spain,* were hasten'd to the Relief of *Naples,* at that Time besieg'd by the

21. Syphilis.
22. Probably Creoles.

French. Provisions growing scarce, the useless People were turn'd out of the City, to lessen the Mouths; amongst these, the *Curtesans* [23] were one Part, who had frequently embrac'd the *Spaniards,* being well fraught with Riches by their new Discovery. The Leager Ladies [24] had no sooner lost their *Spanish* Dons, but found themselves as well entertain'd by the *French,* whose Camp they traded in, giving the Mounsieurs as large a Share of the pocky Spoils within their own Lines, as the *Spaniards* had, who took the Pains to bring it in their Breeches as far as from *America;* the large Supplies of Swines Flesh, which that Army was chiefly victuall'd withal, made it rage. The Siege was rais'd; the *French* and *Spaniards* retreating to *Flanders,*[25] which was a Parrade of all Nations; by which Means, this filthy Distemper crowded it self into most Nations of the known World.

Now to return to our Doctor, who in the Time of his Affliction withdrew himself (with one that labour'd under the same Distemper) into the Woods. These two perfected their Cures by proper Vegitables, &c. of which they have Plenty, and are well acquainted with their specifick Virtue.

I have seen such admirable Cures perform'd by these Savages, which would puzzle a great many graduate Practitioners to trace their Steps in Healing, with the same Expedition, Ease, and Success; using no racking Instruments in their Chirurgery, nor nice Rules of Diet and Physick, to verify the Saying, *qui Medice vivit, misere vivit.*[26] In Wounds which penetrate deep, and seem mortal, they order a spare Diet, with drinking Fountain-water; if they perceive a white Matter, or Pus to arise, they let the Patient more at large, and presently cure him.

After these two had perform'd their Cures at no easier Rate than the Expence of both their Noses, coming again amongst their old Acquaintance so disfigur'd, the *Indians* admir'd to see them metamorphos'd after that manner; enquir'd of them where they had been all that Time, and what were become of their Noses? They made Answer, That they had been conversing with the white Man above, (meaning God Almighty) how they were very kindly entertain'd by that Great Being; he being much pleas'd with their Ways, and had promis'd to make their Capacities equal

23. Courtesans were court mistresses.
24. Women attached to a camp.
25. Name formerly applied to Belgium and northern France.
26. "Who lives by medicine, lives miserably."

with the white People in making Guns, Ammunition, &c. in Retalliation of which, they had given him their Noses. The Verity of which, they yet hold, the *Indians* being an easy, credulous People, and most notoriously cheated by their Priests and Conjurers, both Trades meeting ever in one Person, and most commonly a Spice of Quackship added to the other two Ingredients, which renders that cunning Knave the Impostor to be more rely'd upon; thence a fitter Instrument to cheat these ignorant People; the Priest and Conjurers being never admitted to their Practice, 'till Years and the Experience of repeated Services hath wrought their Esteem amongst the Nations they belong to.

The *Santee* King, who was in Company with this Nonos'd Doctor, is the most absolute *Indian* Ruler in these Parts, although he is Head but of a small People, in Respect to some other Nations of *Indians,* that I have seen: He can put any of his People to Death that hath committed any Fault which he judges worthy of so great a Punishment. This Authority is rarely found amongst these Savages, for they act not (commonly) by a determinative Voice in their Laws, towards any one that hath committed Murder, or such other great Crime, but take this Method; him to whom the Injury was done, or if dead, the nearest of his Kindred prosecutes by Way of an actual Revenge, being himself, if Opportunity serves his Intent, both Judge and Executioner, performing so much Mischief on the Offender, or his nearest Relation, until such Time that he is fully satisfy'd: Yet this Revenge is not so infallible, but it may be bought off with Beads, Tobacco, and such like Commodities that are useful amongst them, though it were the most sable Villany that could be acted by Mankind.

Some that attended the King, presented me with an odoriferous, balsamick Root,[27] of a fragrant Smell and Taste, the Name I know not; they chew it in the Mouth, and by that simple Application, heal desperate Wounds both green and old; that small Quantity I had, was given inwardly to those troubl'd with the Belly-ach, which Remedy fail'd not to give present Help, the Pain leaving the Patient soon after they had taken the Root.

Near to these Cabins are several Tombs [28] made after the manner of these *Indians;* the largest and the chiefest of them was the Sepulchre of the late *Indian* King of the *Santees,* a Man of great Power, not only amongst his own Subjects, but dreaded by the

27. Probably sassafras.
28. One of John White's paintings depicts an Indian tomb. See p. 186.

neighbouring Nations for his great Valour and Conduct, having as large a Prerogative in his Way of Ruling, as the present King I now spoke of.

The manner of their Interment, is thus: A Mole or Pyramid of Earth is rais'd, the Mould thereof being work'd very smooth and even, sometimes higher or lower, according to the Dignity of the Person whose Monument it is. On the Top thereof is an Umbrella, made Ridge-ways, like the Roof of an House; this is supported by nine Stakes, or small Posts, the Grave being about six or eight Foot in Length, and four Foot in Breadth; about it is hung Gourds Feathers, and other such like Trophies, plac'd there by the dead Man's Relations, in Respect to him in the Grave. The other Part of the Funeral-Rites are thus, As soon as the Party is dead, they lay the Corps upon a Piece of Bark in the Sun, seasoning or embalming it with a small Root beaten to Powder, which looks as red as Vermilion; the same is mix'd with Bear's Oil, to beautify the Hair, and preserve their Heads from being lousy, it growing plentifully in these Parts of *America*. After the Carcass has laid a Day or two in the Sun, they remove and lay it upon Crotches cut on purpose for the Support thereof from the Earth; then they anoint it all over with the fore-mention'd Ingredients of the Powder of this Root, and Bear's Oil. When it is so done, they cover it very exactly over with Bark of the Pine or Cyprus Tree, to prevent any Rain to fall upon it, sweeping the Ground very clean all about it. Some of his nearest of Kin brings all the temporal Estate he was possess'd of at his Death, as Guns, Bows, and Arrows, Beads, Feathers, Match-coat, &c. This Relation is the chief Mourner, being clad in Moss, and a Stick in his Hand, keeping a mournful Ditty for three or four Days, his Face being black with the Smoak of Pitch, Pine, mingl'd with Bear's Oil. All the while he tells the dead Man's Relations, and the rest of the Spectators, who that dead Person was, and of the great Feats perform'd in his Life-time; all what he speaks, tending to the Praise of the Defunct. As soon as the Flesh grows mellow, and will cleave from the Bone, they get it off, and burn it, making all the Bones very clean, then anoint them with the Ingredients aforesaid, wrapping up the Skull (very carefully) in a Cloath artificially woven of Possums Hair. (These *Indians* make Girdles, Sashes, Garters, &c. after the same Manner.) The Bones they carefully preserve in a wooden Box, every Year oiling and cleansing them: By these Means preserve them for many Ages, that you may see an *Indian* in Possession of the Bones of his Grand-father, or some of his Relations of a larger Antiquity. They have other Sorts of Tombs; as where an *Indian* is slain, in that very Place they make a Heap of Stones, (or Sticks, where Stones are not to be found;) to this Memorial, every *Indian* that passes by, adds a Stone, to augment the Heap, in Respect to the deceas'd Hero.

We had a very large Swamp to pass over near the House, and would have hir'd our Landlord to have been our Guide, but he seem'd unwilling; so we press'd him no farther about it. He was the tallest *Indian* I ever saw, being seven Foot high, and a very strait compleat Person, esteem'd on by the King for his great Art in Hunting, always carrying with him an artificial Head to hunt withal: They are made of the Head of a Buck, the back Part of the Horns being scrapt and hollow, for Lightness of Carriage. The Skin is left to the setting on of the Shoulders, which is lin'd all round with small Hoops, and flat Sort of Laths, to hold it open for the Arm to go in. They have a Way to preserve the Eyes, as if living. The Hunter puts on a Match-coat made of Deer's Skin, with the Hair on, and a Piece of the white Part of a Deer's Skin, that grows on the Breast, which is fasten'd to the Neck-End of this stalking Head, so hangs down. In these Habiliments an *Indian* will go as near a Deer as he pleases, the exact Motions and Behaviour of a Deer being so well counter-feited by 'em, that several Times it hath been known for two Hunters to come up with a stalking Head together, and unknown to each other, so that they have kill'd an *Indian* instead of a Deer, which hath happen'd sometimes to be a Brother, or some dear Friend; for which Reason they allow not of that Sort of Practice, where the Nation is populous.

Within half a Mile of the House, we pass'd over a prodigious wide and deep Swamp, being forc'd to strip stark-naked; and much a-do to save our selves from drowning in this Fatiegue. We, with much a-do, got thro', going that Day about five Miles farther, and came to three more *Indian* Cabins, call'd in the *Indian* Tongue, *Hickerau*, by the *English* Traders, the *black House*,[29] being pleasantly seated on a high Bank, by a Branch of *Santee*-River. One of our Company, that had traded amongst these *Indians*, told us, That one of the Cabins was his Father's-in-Law; he call'd him so, by Reason the old Man had given him

29. A "black house" was a low windowless cottage.

a young *Indian* Girl, that was his Daughter, to lie with him, make Bread, and to be necessary in what she was capable to assist him in, during his Abode amongst them.

When we came thither first, there was no Body at Home, so the Son made bold to search his Father's Granary for Corn, and other Provisions. He brought us some *Indian* Maiz and Peas, which are of a reddish Colour, and eat well, yet colour the Liquor they are boil'd in, as if it were a *Lixivium* of red Tartar. After we had been about an Hour in the House, where was Millions of Fleas, the *Indian* Cabins being often fuller of such Vermin, than any Dog Kennel, the old Man came in to us, and seem'd very glad to see his Son-in-Law.

This *Indian* is a great Conjurer, as appears by the Sequel. The *Seretee* or *Santee Indians* were gone to War against the *Hooks* and *Backhooks* Nations,[30] living near the Mouth of *Win-yan*-River. Those that were left at Home, (which are commonly old People and Children) had heard no News a long Time of their Men at Arms. This Man, at the Entreaty of these People, (being held to be a great Sorcerer amongst 'em) went to know what Posture their fighting Men were in. His Exorcism was carry'd on thus: He dress'd himself in a clean white dress'd Deer-Skin; a great Fire being made in the Middle of the Plantation, the *Indians* sitting all round it, the Conjurer was blind-folded, then he surrounded the Fire several Times, I think thrice; leaving the Company, he went into the Woods, where he stay'd about half an Hour, returning to them, surrounded the Fire as before; leaving them, went the second Time into the Woods; at which Time there came a huge Swarm of Flies, very large, they flying about the Fire several Times, at last fell all into it, and were visibly confum'd. Immediately after the *Indian*-Conjurer made a huge Lilleloo,[31] and howling very frightfully, presently an *Indian* went and caught hold of him, leading him to the Fire. The old Wizard was so feeble and weak, being not able to stand alone, and all over in a Sweat, and as wet as if he had fallen into the River. After some Time he recover'd his Strength, assuring them, that their Men were near a River, and could not pass over it 'till so many Days, but would, in such a Time, return all in Safety, to their Nation. All which prov'd true at the *Indians*

30. Indians located near the mouth of Winyaw River. Lawson is the only writer who ever mentioned them by this name.

31. Making a face by lolling or hanging the tongue out.

Return, which was not long after. This Story the *English*-man, his Son-in-Law, affirm'd to me.

The old Man stay'd with us about two Hours, and told us we were welcome to stay there all Night, and take what his Cabin afforded; then leaving us, went into the Woods, to some Hunting-Quarter not far off.

The next Morning early we pursu'd our Voyage, finding the Land to improve it self in Pleasantness and Richness of Soil. When we had gone about ten Miles, one of our Company tir'd, being not able to travel any farther; so we went forward, leaving the poor dejected Traveller with Tears in his Eyes, to return to *Charles*-Town, and travel back again over so much bad Way, we having pass'd thro' the worst of our Journey, the Land here being high and dry, very few Swamps, and those dry, and a little Way through. We travell'd about twenty Miles, lying near a Savanna that was over-flown with Water; where we were very short of Victuals, but finding the Woods newly burnt, and on fire in many Places, which gave us great Hopes that *Indians* were not far of.

Next Morning very early, we waded thro' the Savanna, the Path lying there; and about ten a Clock came to a hunting Quarter, of a great many *Santees;* they made us all welcome; shewing a great deal of Joy at our coming, giving us barbacu'd Turkeys, Bear's Oil, and Venison.

Here we hir'd *Santee Jack* (a good Hunter, and a well-humour'd Fellow) to be our Pilot to the *Congeree Indians;* we gave him a Stroud-water-Blew,[32] to make his Wife an *Indian* Petticoat, who went with her Husband. After two Hours Refreshment, we went on, and got that Day about twenty Miles; we lay by a small swift Run of Water, which was pav'd at the Bottom with a Sort of Stone much like to Tripoli,[33] and so light, that I fancy'd it would precipitate in no Stream, but where it naturally grew. The Weather was very cold, the Winds holding *Northerly*. We made our selves as merry as we could, having a good Supper with the Scraps of the Venison we had given us by the *Indians*, having kill'd 3 Teal and a Possum; which Medly all together made a curious Ragoo.

This Day all of us had a Mind to have rested, but the *Indian* was much against it, alledging, That the Place we lay at, was

32. Stroud was a coarse blanket or garment, usually red or blue.
33. A friable, soft, schistose deposit of silica.

not good to hunt in; telling us, if we would go on, by Noon, he would bring us to a more convenient Place; so we mov'd forwards, and about twelve a Clock came to the most amazing Prospect I had seen since I had been in *Carolina;* we travell'd by a Swamp-side, which Swamp I believe to be no less than twenty Miles over, the other Side being as far as I could well discern, there appearing great Ridges of Mountains, bearing from us. *W. N. W.* One Alp with a Top like a Sugar-loaf, advanc'd its Head above all the rest very considerably; the Day was very serene, which gave us the Advantage of seeing a long Way; these Mountains were cloth'd all over with Trees, which seem'd to us to be very large Timbers.

At the Sight of this fair Prospect, we stay'd all Night; our *Indian* going about half an Hour before us, had provided three fat Turkeys e'er we got up to him.

The Swamp I now spoke of, is not a miry Bog, as others generally are, but you go down to it thro' a steep Bank, at the Foot of which, begins this Valley, where you may go dry for perhaps 200 Yards, then you meet with a small Brook, or Run of Water, about 2 or 3 Foot deep, then dry Land for such another Space, so another Brook, thus continuing. The Land in this Percoarson, or Valley, being extraordinary rich, and the Runs of Water well stor'd with Fowl. It is the Head of one of the Branches of *Santee*-River; but a farther Discovery Time would not permit; only one Thing is very remarkable, there growing all over this Swamp, a tall, lofty Bay-tree, but is not the same as in *England,* these being in their Verdure all the Winter long; which appears here, when you stand on the Ridge, (where our Path lay) as if it were one pleasant, green Field, and as even as a Bowling-green to the Eye of the Beholder; being hemm'd in on one Side with these Ledges of vast high Mountains.

Viewing the Land here, we found an extraordinary rich, black Mould, and some of a Copper-colour, both Sorts very good; the Land in some Places is much burthen'd with Iron, Stone, here being great Store of it, seemingly very good: The eviling [34] Springs, which are many in these Parts, issuing out of the Rocks, which Water we drank of, it colouring the Excrements of Travellers (by its chalybid Quality) as black as a Coal. When we were all asleep, in the Beginning of the Night, we were awaken'd with the dismall'st and most hideous Noise that ever pierc'd my Ears:

34. Lawson probably meant bubbling.

This sudden Surprizal incapacitated us of guessing what this threatning Noise might proceed from; but our *Indian* Pilot (who knew these Parts very well) acquainted us, that it was customary to hear such Musick along that Swamp-Side, there being endless Numbers of Panthers, Tygers,[35] Wolves, and other Beasts of Prey, which take this Swamp for their Abode in the Day, coming in whole Droves to hunt the Deer in the Night, making this frightful Ditty 'till Day appears, then all is still as in other Places.

The next Day it prov'd a small drisly Rain, which is rare, there happening not the tenth Part of Foggy-falling Weather towards these Mountains, as visits those Parts. Near the Sea-board, the *Indian* kill'd 15 Turkeys this Day; there coming out of the Swamp, (about Sun-rising) Flocks of these Fowl, containing several hundreds in a Gang, who feed upon the Acorns, it being most Oak that grow in these Woods. There are but very few Pines in those Quarters.

Early the next Morning, we set forward for the *Congeree-Indians*,[36] parting with that delicious Prospect. By the Way, our Guide kill'd more Turkeys, and two Polcats, which he eat, esteeming them before fat Turkeys. Some of the Turkeys which we eat, whilst we stay'd there, I believe, weigh'd no less than 40 Pounds.

The Land we pass'd over this Day, was most of it good, and the worst passable. At Night we kill'd a Possum, being cloy'd with Turkeys, made a Dish of that, which tasted much between young Pork and Veal; their Fat being as white as any I ever saw.

Our *Indian* having this Day kill'd good Store of Provision with his Gun, he always shot with a single Ball, missing but two Shoots in above forty; they being curious Artists in managing a Gun, to make it carry either Ball, or Shot, true. When they have bought a Piece, and find it to shoot any Ways crooked, they take the Barrel out of the Stock, cutting a Notch in a Tree, wherein they set it streight, sometimes shooting away above 100 Loads of Ammunition, before they bring the Gun to shoot according to their Mind. We took up our Quarters by a Fish-pond-side; the Pits in the Woods that stand full of Water, naturally breed Fish in them, in great Quantities. We cook'd our Supper, but having

35. There were no tigers in this region.
36. The Congaree village was located on the northeastern bank of the Congaree River below the junction of the Wateree.

neither Bread, or Salt, our fat Turkeys began to be loathsome to us, altho' we were never wanting of a good Appetite, yet a Continuance of one Diet, made us weary.

The next Morning, *Santee Jack* told us, we should reach the *Indian* Settlement betimes that Day; about Noon, we pass'd by several fair Savanna's, very rich and dry; seeing great Copses of many Acres that bore nothing but Bushes, about the Bigness of Box-trees; which (in the Season) afford great Quantities of small Black-berries, very pleasant Fruit, and much like to our Blues, or Huckle-berries, that grow on Heaths in *England*. Hard by the Savanna's we found the Town, where we halted; there was not above one Man left with the Women, the rest being gone a Hunting for a Feast. The Women were very busily engag'd in Gaming: The Name or Grounds of it, I could not learn, tho' I look'd on above two Hours. Their Arithmetick was kept with a Heap of *Indian* Grain. When their Play was ended, the King, or *Cassetta's* [37] Wife, invited us into her Cabin. The *Indian* Kings always entertaining Travellers, either *English,* or *Indian;* taking it as a great Affront, if they pass by their Cabins, and take up their Quarters at any other *Indian's* House. The Queen set Victuals before us, which good Compliment they use generally as soon as you come under their Roof.

The Town consists not of above a dozen Houses, they having other stragling Plantations up and down the Country, and are seated upon a small Branch of *Santee* River. Their Place hath curious dry Marshes, and Savanna's adjoining to it, and would prove an exceeding thriving Range for Cattle, and Hogs, provided the *English* were seated thereon. Besides, the Land is good for Plantations.

These *Indians* are a small People, having lost much of their former Numbers, by intestine Broils; but most by the Small-pox, which hath often visited them, sweeping away whole Towns; occasion'd by the immoderate Government of themselves in their Sickness; as I have mention'd before, treating of the *Sewees*. Neither do I know any Savages that have traded with the *English,* but what have been great Losers by this Distemper.

We found here good Store of Chinkapin-Nuts, which they gather in Winter great Quantities of, drying them; so keep these Nuts in great Baskets for their Use; likewise Hickerie-Nuts,

37. Chasetta or Cassetta was a title used for the King of the Congarees. See Milling, *Red Carolinians,* p. 213.

which they beat betwixt two great Stones, then sift them, so thicken their Venison-Broath therewith; the small Shells precipitating to the Bottom of the Pot, whilst the Kernel in Form of Flower, mixes it with the Liquor. Both these Nuts made into Meal, makes a curious Soop, either with clear Water, or in any Meat Broth.

From the Nation of *Indians,* until such Time as you come to the *Turkeiruros* [38] in *North Carolina,* you will see no long Moss upon the Trees; which Space of Ground contains above five hundred Miles. This seeming Miracle in *Nature,* is occasion'd by the Highness of the Land, it being dry and healthful; for tho' this moss bears a Seed in a Sort of a small Cod, yet it is generated in or near low swampy Grounds.

The *Congerees* are kind and affable to the *English,* the Queen being very kind, giving us what Rarities her Cabin afforded, as Loblolly [39] made with *Indian* Corn, and dry'd Peaches. These *Congerees* have abundance of Storks and Cranes in their Savannas. They take them before they can fly, and breed 'em as tame and familiar as a Dung-hill Fowl. They had a tame Crane at one of these Cabins, that was scarce less than six Foot in Height, his Head being round, with a shining natural Crimson Hue, which they all have. These are a very comely Sort of *Indians,* there being a strange Difference in the Proportion and Beauty of these Heathens. Altho' their Tribes or Nations border one upon another, yet you may discern as great an Alteration in their Features and Dispositions, as you can in their Speech, which generally proves quite different from each other, though their Nations be not above 10 or 20 Miles in Distance. The Women here being as handsome as most I have met withal, being several fine-finger'd Brounetto's amongst them. These Lasses stick not upon Hand long, for they marry when very young, as at 12 or 14 Years of Age. The *English* Traders are seldom without an *Indian* Female for his Bed-fellow, alledging these Reasons as sufficient to allow of such a Familiarity. First, They being remote from any white People, that it preserves their Friendship with the Heathens, they esteeming a white Man's Child much above

38. The Tuscaroras, the most numerous and warlike tribe or confederacy in eastern North Carolina, were Iroquoian. After the Tuscarora War of 1711–13, they removed to New York and became the Sixth Nation of the Iroquois Confederacy.

39. Thick gruel.

one of their getting, the *Indian* Mistress ever securing her white Friend Provisions whilst he stays amongst them. And lastly, This Correspondence makes them learn the *Indian* Tongue much the sooner, they being of the *French*-man's Opinion, how that an *English* Wife teaches her Husband more *English* in one Night, than a School-master can in a Week.

We saw at the *Cassetta*'s Cabin the strangest Spectacle of Antiquity I ever knew, it being an old *Indian* Squah, that, had I been to have guess'd at her Age by her Aspect, old *Parr*'s [40] Head (the *Welch Methusalem*) was a Face in Swadling-Clouts to hers. Her Skin hung in Reaves like a Bag of Tripe. By a fair Computation, one might have justly thought it would have contain'd three such Carcasses as hers then was. She had one of her Hands contracted by some Accident in the Fire, they sleeping always by it, and often fall into sad Disasters, especially in their drunken Moods. I made the strictest Enquiry that was possible, and by what I could gather, she was considerably above 100 Years old, notwithstanding she smoak'd Tobacco, and eat her Victuals, to all Appearance, as heartily as one of 18. One of our Company spoke some of their Language, and having not quite forgotten his former Intrigues with the *Indian* Lasses, would fain have been dealing with some of the young Female Fry; but they refus'd him, he having nothing that these Girls esteem'd. At Night we were laid in the King's Cabin, where the Queen and the old Squah pig'd in with us: The former was very much disfigur'd with Tettars, and very reserv'd, which disappointed our fellow Traveller in his Intrigues.

The Women smoak much Tobacco, (as most *Indians* do.) They have Pipes, whose Heads are cut out of Stone, and will hold an Ounce of Tobacco, and some much less. They have large wooden Spoons, as big as small Ladles, which they make little Use of, lading the Meat out of the Bowls with their Fingers.

In the Morning we rose before Day, having hir'd a Guide over Night to conduct us on our Way; but it was too soon for him to stir out, the *Indians* never setting forward 'till the Sun is an Hour or two high, and hath exhall'd the Dew from the Earth. The Queen got us a good Breakfast before we left her; she had a young Child, which was much afflicted with the Cholick; for

40. Thomas Parr, who was born in Winnington, Shropshire, about 1483 and lived until 1635. He was buried in the south transept of Westminster Abbey. The inscription on his tomb says that "he lived in the reigns of ten princes."

which Distemper she infus'd a Root in Water, which was held in a Goard; this she took into her Mouth, and spurted it into the Infant's, which gave it ease. After we had eaten, we set out (with our new Guide) for the *Wateree Indians.* We went over a great deal of indifferent Land this Day. Here begins to appear very good Marble,[41] which continues more and less for the Space of 500 Miles. We lay all Night by a Run of Water, as we always do, (if possible) for the Convenience of it. The Weather was very cold. We went this Day about 30 Miles from the *Congerees.*

In the Morning we made no Stay to get our Breakfast, but hasted on our Voyage, the Land increasing in Marble and Richness of Soil. At Noon we halted, getting our Dinner upon a Marble-Stone, that rose it self half a Foot above the Surface of the Earth, and might contain the Compass of a Quarter of an Acre of Land, being very even, there growing upon it in some Places a small red Berry, like a Salmon-Spawn, there boiling out of the main Rock curious Springs of as delicious Water, as ever I drank in any Parts I ever travell'd in.

These Parts likewise affords good free Stone, fit for Building, and of several Sorts. The Land here is pleasantly seated, with pretty little Hills and Valleys, the rising Sun at once shewing his glorious reflecting Rays on a great many of these little Mountains. We went this Day about 20 Miles, our Guide walking like a Horse, 'till we had sadl'd him with a good heavy Pack of some Part of our Cloaths and Bedding; by which Means we kept Pace with him.

This Night we lay by a Run-side, where I found a fine yellow Earth, the same with Bruxels-Sand, which Goldsmiths use to cast withal, giving a good Price in *England,* and other Parts. Here is likewise the true Blood-Stone, and considerable Quantities of Fullers-Earth, which I took a Proof of, by scouring great Spots out of Woollen, and it prov'd very good.

As we were on our Road this Morning, our *Indian* shot at a Tyger, that cross'd the Way, he being a great Distance from us. I believe he did him no Harm, because he sat on his Breech afterwards, and look'd upon us. I suppose he expected to have had a Spaniel Bitch, that I had with me, for his Breakfast, who run towards him, but in the Midway stopt her Career, and came sneaking back to us with her Tail betwixt her Legs.

We saw in the Path a great many Trees blown up by the Roots,

41. This was perhaps a fine quality of granite, not marble.

at the Bottom whereof stuck great Quantities of fine red Bole; I
believe nothing inferior to that of *Venice* or *Lemma.*[42] We found
some Holes in the Earth, which were full of a Water as black as
Ink. I thought that Tincture might proceed from some Mineral,
but had not Time to make a farther Discovery. About Noon we
pass'd over a pleasant stony Brook, whose Water was of a bluish
Cast, as it is for several hundreds of Miles towards the Heads of
the Rivers, I suppose occasion'd by the vast Quantities of Marble
lying in the Bowels of the Earth. The Springs that feed these
Rivulets, lick up some Potions of the Stones in the Brooks; which
Dissolution gives this Tincture, as appears in all, or most of the
Rivers and Brooks of this Country, whose rapid Streams are like
those in *Yorkshire,* and other *Northern* Counties of *England.* The
Indians talk of many Sorts of Fish which they afford, but we had
not Time to discover their Species.

I saw here had been some *Indian* Plantations formerly, there
being several pleasant Fields of clear'd Ground, and excellent
Soil, now well spread with fine bladed Grass, and Strawberry-
Vines.

The Mould here is excessive rich, and a Country very pleasing
to the Eye, had it the Convenience of a navigable River, as all
new Colonies (of Necessity) require. It would make a delightful
Settlement.

We went eight Miles farther, and came to the *Wateree Chickanee Indians.*[43] The Land holds good, there being not a Spot of
bad Land to be seen in several Days going.

The People of this Nation are likely tall Persons, and great
Pilferers, stealing from us any Thing they could lay their Hands
on, though very respectful in giving us what Victuals we wanted.
We lay in their Cabins all Night, being dark smoaky Holes, as
ever I saw any *Indians* dwell in. This Nation is much more populous than the *Congerees,* and their Neighbours, yet understand not
one anothers Speech. They are very poor in *English* Effects, several of them having no Guns, making Use of Bows and Arrows,
being a lazy idle People, a Quality incident to most *Indians,* but
none to that Degree as these, as I ever met withal.

42. Island of Lemnos in the Aegean Sea, on the west coast of Turkey.
Lemnian earth was a medical astringent sort of earth, of a fatty consistence
and reddish color.

43. The Wateree Indians were Siouan. They were located on the west bank
of the Wateree River, below the present Camden. Mooney estimated their
population at one thousand in 1600. There were no later enumerations.
Lawson is the only writer to use the term Chickanee.

Their Country is wholly free from Swamps and Quagmires, being high dry Land, and consequently healthful, producing large Corn-Stalks, and fair Grain.

Next Morning, we took off our Beards with a Razor, the *Indians* looking on with a great deal of Admiration. They told us, they had never seen the like before, and that our Knives cut far better than those that came amongst the *Indians*. They would fain have borrow'd our Razors, as they had our Knives, Scissors, and Tobacco-Tongs, the day before, being as ingenious at picking of Pockets, as any, I believe, the World affords; for they will steal with their Feet. Yesterday, one of our Company, not walking so fast as the rest, was left behind. He being out of Sight before we miss'd him, and not coming up to us, tho' we staid a considerable time on the Road for him, we stuck up Sticks in the Ground, and left other Tokens to direct him which way we were gone: But he came not to us that Night, which gave us Occasion to fear some of the Heathens had kill'd him, for his Cloaths, or the savage Beasts had devour'd him in the Wilderness, he having nothing about him to strike Fire withal. As we were debating which way we should send to know what was become of him, he overtook us, having a *Waxsaw Indian* [44] for his Guide. He told us, he had miss'd the Path, and got to another Nation of *Indians*, but 3 Miles off, who at that time held great Feasting. They had entertain'd him very respectfully, and sent that *Indian* to invite us amongst them, wondring that we would not take up our Quarters with them, but make our Abode with such a poor Sort of *Indians*, that were not capable of entertaining us according to our Deserts: We receiv'd the Messenger with a great many Ceremonies, acceptable to those sort of Creatures. Bidding our *Waterree* King adieu, we set forth towards the *Waxsaws*, going along clear'd Ground all the Way. Upon our Arrival, we were led into a very large and lightsome Cabin, the like I have not met withal. They laid Furs and Deer-Skins upon Cane Benches for us to sit or lie upon, bringing (immediately) stewed Peaches and green Corn, that is preserv'd in their Cabins before it is ripe, and sodden and boil'd when they use it, which is a pretty sort of Food, and a great Increaser of the Blood.

These *Indians* are of an extraordinary Stature, and call'd by their Neighbours flat Heads, which seems a very suitable Name

44. The Waxhaw Indians, also called Flatheads, were Siouan. They were located chiefly in the area of present Lancaster County, South Carolina, and Mecklenburg County, North Carolina.

for them. In their Infancy, their Nurses lay the Back-part of their Children's Heads on a Bag of Sand, (such as Engravers use to rest their Plates upon.) They use a Roll, which is placed upon the Babe's Forehead, it being laid with its Back on a flat Board, and swaddled hard down thereon, from one End of this Engine, to the other. This Method makes the Child's Body and Limbs as straight as an Arrow. There being some young *Indians* that are perhaps crookedly inclin'd, at their first coming into the World, who are made perfectly straight by this Method. I never saw an *Indian* of a mature Age, that was any ways crooked, except by Accident, and that way seldom, for they cure and prevent Deformities of the Limbs, and Body, very exactly. The Instrument I spoke of before, being a sort of a Press, that is let out and in, more or less, according to the Discretion of the Nurse, in which they make the Child's Head flat, it makes the Eyes stand a prodigious Way asunder, and the Hair hang over the Forehead like the Eves of a House, which seems very frightful: They being ask'd the Reason why they practis'd this Method, reply'd, the *Indian*'s Sight was much strengthened and quicker, thereby, to discern the Game in hunting at larger Distance, and so never miss'd of becoming expert Hunters, the Perfection of which they all aim at, as we do to become experienced Soldiers, learned School-Men, or Artists in Mechanicks: He that is a good Hunter never misses of being a Favourite amongst the Women; the prettiest Girls being always bestow'd upon the chiefest Sports-Men, and those of a grosser Mould, upon the useless *Lubbers*. Thus they have a Graduation amongst them, as well as other Nations. As for the Solemnity of Marriages amongst them, kept with so much Ceremony as divers Authors affirm, it never appear'd amongst those many Nations I have been withal, any otherwise than in the Manner I have mention'd hereafter.

The Girls at 12 or 13 Years of Age, as soon as Nature prompts them, freely bestow their Maidenheads on some Youth about the same Age, continuing her Favours on whom she most affects, changing her Mate very often, few or none of them being constant to one, till a greater Number of Years has made her capable of managing domestick Affairs, and she hath try'd the Vigour of most of the Nation she belongs to; Multiplicity of Gallants never being a Stain to a Female's Reputation, or the least Hindrance of her Advancement, but the more *Whorish*, the more *Honourable*, and they of all most coveted, by those of the first Rank, to make a Wife of. The *Flos Virginis*,[45] so much coveted by the *Europeans,* is never valued by these Savages. When a Man and Woman have gone through their Degrees, (there being a certain Graduation amongst them) and are allow'd to be House-Keepers, which is not till they arrive at such an Age, and have past the Ceremonies practis'd by their Nation, almost all Kingdoms differing in the Progress thereof, then it is that the Man makes his Addresses to some one of these thorough-paced Girls, or other, whom he likes best. When she is won, the Parents of both Parties, (with Advice of the King) agree about the Matter, making a Promise of their Daughter, to the Man, that requires her, it often happening that they converse and travel together, for several Moons before the Marriage is publish'd openly; After this, at the least Dislike the Man may turn her away, and take another; or if she disapproves of his Company, a Price is set upon her, and if the Man that seeks to get her, will pay the Fine to her Husband, she becomes free from Him: Likewise some of their War Captains, and great Men, very often will retain 3 or 4 Girls at a time for their own Use, when at the same time, he is so impotent and old, as to be incapable of making Use of one of them; so that he seldom misses of wearing greater Horns than the Game he kills. The Husband is never so enrag'd as to put his Adulteress to Death; if she is caught in the Fact, the Rival becomes Debtor to the cornuted Husband, in a certain Quantity of Trifles valuable amongst them, which he pays as soon as discharg'd, and then all Animosity is laid aside betwixt the Husband, and his Wife's Gallant. The Man proves often so good humour'd as to please his Neighbour and gratify his Wife's Inclinations, by letting her out for a Night or two, to the Embraces of some other, which perhaps she has a greater Liking to, tho' this is not commonly practis'd.

They set apart the youngest and prettiest Faces for trading Girls; these are remarkable by their Hair, having a particular Tonsure by which they are known, and distinguish'd from those engag'd to Husbands. They are mercenary, and whoever makes Use of them, first hires them, the greatest Share of the Gain going to the King's Purse, who is the chief Bawd, exercising his Perogative over all the Stews of his Nation, and his own Cabin (very often) being the chiefest Brothel-House. As they grow in Years, the hot Assaults of Love grow cooler; and then they commonly are

45. Latin term for virginity.

so staid, as to engage themselves with more Constancy to each other. I have seen several Couples amongst them, that have been so reserv'd, as to live together for many Years, faithful to each other, admitting none to their Beds but such as they own'd for their Wife or Husband: So continuing to their Life's end.

At our *Waxsaw* Landlord's Cabin, was a Woman employ'd in no other Business than Cookery; it being a House of great Resort. The Fire was surrounded with Roast-meat, or *Barbakues,* and the Pots continually boiling full of Meat, from Morning till Night. This She-Cook was the cleanliest I ever saw amongst the Heathens of *America,* washing her Hands before she undertook to do any Cookery; and repeated this unusual Decency very often in a day. She made us as White-Bread as any *English* could have done, and was full as neat, and expeditious, in her Affairs. It happen'd to be one of their great Feasts, when we were there: The first day that we came amongst them, arriv'd an Ambassador from the King of *Sapona,*[46] to treat with these *Indians* about some important Affairs. He was painted with Vermillion all over his Face, having a very large Cutlass stuck in his Girdle, and a Fusee in his Hand. At Night, the Revels began where this Foreign *Indian* was admitted; the King, and War Captain, inviting us to see their Masquerade: This Feast was held in Commemoration of the plentiful Harvest of Corn they had reap'd the Summer before, with an united Supplication for the like plentiful Produce the Year ensuing. These Revels are carried on in a House made for that purpose, it being done round with white Benches of fine Canes, joining along the Wall; and a place for the Door being left, which is so low, that a Man must stoop very much to enter therein. This Edifice resembles a large Hay-Rick; its Top being Pyramidal, and much bigger than their other Dwellings, and at the Building whereof, every one assists till it is finish'd. All their Dwelling-Houses are cover'd with Bark, but this differs very much; for, it is very artificially thatch'd with Sedge and Rushes: As soon as finish'd, they place some one of their chiefest Men to dwell therein, charging him with the diligent Preservation thereof, as a Prince commits the Charge and Government of a Fort or Castle, to some Subject he thinks worthy of that Trust. In these State-Houses is transacted all Publick and Private Business,

46. Siouan Indians who had moved south from the Rivanna region of Virginia before 1701. Lawson found them along the Yadkin River near the present site of Salisbury.

relating to the Affairs of the Government, as the Audience of Foreign Ambassadors from other *Indian* Rulers, Consultation of waging and making War, Proposals of their Trade with neighbouring *Indians*, or the *English*, who happen to come amongst them. In this Theater, the most Aged and Wisest meet, determining what to Act, and what may be most convenient to Omit, Old Age being held in as great Veneration amongst these Heathens, as amongst any People you shall meet withal in any Part of the World.

Whensoever an Aged Man is speaking, none ever interrupts him, (the contrary Practice the *English*, and other *Europeans*, too much use) the Company yielding a great deal of Attention to his Tale, with a continued Silence, and an exact Demeanour, during the Oration. Indeed, the *Indians* are a People that never interrupt one another in their Discourse; no Man so much as offering to open his Mouth, till the Speaker has utter'd his Intent: When an *English*-Man comes amongst them, perhaps every one is acquainted with him, yet, first, the King bids him Welcome, after him the War-Captain, so on gradually from High to Low; not one of all these speaking to the White Guest, till his Superiour has ended his Salutation. Amongst Women, it seems impossible to find a Scold; if they are provok'd, or affronted, by their Husbands, or some other, they resent the Indignity offer'd them in silent Tears, or by refusing their Meat. Would some of our *European* Daughters of Thunder [47] set these *Indians* for a Pattern, there might be more quiet Families found amongst them, occasion'd by that unruly Member, the Tongue.

Festination proceeds from the Devil, (*says a Learned* Doctor) a Passion the *Indians* seem wholly free from; they determining no Business of Moment, without a great deal of Deliberation and Wariness. None of their Affairs appear to be attended with Impetuosity, or Haste, being more content with the common Accidents incident to humane Nature, (as Losses, contrary Winds, bad Weather, and Poverty) than those of more civilized Countries.

Now, to return to our State-House, whither we were invited by the Grandees: As soon as we came into it, they plac'd our *Englishmen* near the King; it being my Fortune to sit next him, having his great General, or War-Captain, on my other Hand. The House is as dark as a Dungeon, and as hot as one of the *Dutch-*

47. Lawson probably meant talkative women.

Stoves in *Holland*. They had made a circular Fire of split Canes
in the middle of the House. It was one Man's Employment to add
more split Reeds to the one end as it consum'd at the other, there
being a small Vacancy left to supply it with Fewel. They brought
in great store of Loblolly, and other Medleys, made of *Indian*
Grain, stewed Peaches, Bear-Venison, &c. every one bringing
some Offering to enlarge the Banquet, according to his Degree
and Quality. When all the *Viands* were brought in, the first Figure began with kicking out the Dogs, which are seemingly Wolves,
made tame with starving and beating; they being the worst Dog-
Masters in the World; so that it is an infallible Cure for Sore-
Eyes, ever to see an *Indian*'s Dog fat. They are of a quite contrary
Disposition to Horses; some of their Kings having gotten, by
great chance, a Jade, stolen by some neighbouring *Indian*, and
transported farther into the Country, and sold; or bought sometimes of a *Christian*, that trades amongst them. These Creatures
they continually cram, and feed with Maiz, and what the Horse
will eat, till he is as fat as a Hog; never making any farther use
of him than to fetch a Deer home, that is killed somewhere near
the *Indian*'s Plantation.

After the Dogs had fled the Room, the Company was summon'd
by Beat of Drum; the Musick being made of a dress'd Deer's Skin,
tied hard upon an Earthen Porridge-Pot. Presently in came fine
Men dress'd up with Feathers, their Faces being covered with
Vizards made of Gourds; round their Ancles and Knees, were
hung Bells of several sorts, having Wooden Falchions in their
Hands, (such as Stage-Fencers commonly use;) in this Dress they
danced about an Hour, shewing many strange Gestures, and
brandishing their Wooden Weapons, as if they were going to fight
each other; oftentimes walking very nimbly round the Room,
without making the least Noise with their Bells, (a thing I much
admired at;) again, turning their Bodies, Arms and Legs, into
such frightful Postures, that you would have guess'd they had
been quite raving mad: At last, they cut two or three high Capers,
and left the Room. In their stead, came in a parcel of Women and
Girls, to the Number of Thirty odd; every one taking place according to her Degree of Stature, the tallest leading the Dance,
and the least of all being plac'd last; with these they made a circular Dance, like a Ring, representing the Shape of the Fire they
danced about: Many of these had great Horse-Bells about their

Legs, and small Hawk's Bells about their Necks. They had Musi-
cians, who were two Old Men, one of whom beat a Drum, while
the other rattled with a Gourd, that had Corn in it, to make a
Noise withal: To these Instruments, they both sung a mournful
Ditty; the Burthen of their Song was, in Remembrance of their
former Greatness, and Numbers of their Nation, the famous Ex-
ploits of their Renowned Ancestors, and all Actions of Moment
that had (in former Days) been perform'd by their Forefathers.
At these Festivals it is, that they give a Traditional Relation of
what hath pass'd amongst them, to the younger Fry. These verbal
Deliveries being always publish'd in their most Publick Assemblies, serve instead of our Traditional Notes, by the use of Letters. Some *Indians*, that I have met withal, have given me a very
curious Description of the great Deluge, the Immortality of the
Soul, with a pithy Account of the Reward of good and wicked
Deeds in the Life to come; having found, amongst some of them,
great Observers of Moral Rules, and the Law of Nature; indeed,
a worthy Foundation to build Christianity upon, were a true
Method found out, and practis'd, for the Performance thereof.

Their way of Dancing, is nothing but a sort of stamping Motion, much like the treading upon Founders Bellows. This Fe-
male-Gang held their Dance for above six Hours, being all of
them of a white Lather, like a Running Horse that has just come
in from his Race. My Landady was the Ringleader of the *Amazons*, who, when in her own House, behav'd herself very discreetly, and warily, in her Domestick Affairs; yet, Custom had
so infatuated her, as to almost break her Heart with Dancing
amongst such a confused Rabble. During this Dancing, the Spectators do not neglect their Business, in working the Loblolly-Pots,
and the other Meat that was brought thither; more or less of them
being continually Eating, whilst the others were Dancing. When
the Dancing was ended, every Youth that was so disposed, catch'd
hold of the Girl he liked best, and took her that Night for his
Bed-Fellow, making as short Courtship and expeditious Weddings, as the Foot-Guards us'd to do with the *Trulls* in *Salisbury-
Court*.

Next we shall treat of the Land hereabouts, which is a Marl as
red as Blood, and will lather like Soap. The Town stands on this
Land, which holds considerably farther in the Country, and is in
my Opinion, so durable that no Labour of Man, in one or two

Ages, could make it poor. I have formerly seen the like in *Leicestershire*, bordering upon *Rutland*.[48] Here were Corn-Stalks in their Fields as thick as the Small of a Man's Leg, and they are ordinarily to be seen.

We lay with these *Indians* one Night, there being by my Bed-side one of the largest Iron Pots I had ever seen in *America*, which I much wondred at, because I thought there might be no navigable Stream near that Place. I ask'd them, where they got that Pot? They laugh'd at my Demand, and would give me no Answer, which makes me guess it came from some Wreck, and that we were nearer the Ocean, or some great River, than I thought.

The next day about Noon, we accidentally met with a *Southward Indian*, amongst those that us'd to trade backwards and forwards, and spoke a little *English*, whom we hir'd to go with us to the *Esaw Indians*,[49] a very large Nation containing many thousand People. In the Afternoon we set forward, taking our Leaves of the *Wisack Indians*,[50] and leaving them some Trifles. On our Way, we met with several Towns of *Indians*, each Town having its Theater or State House, such Houses being found all along the Road, till you come to *Sapona*, and then no more of those Buildings, it being about 170 Miles. We reach'd 10 Miles this day, lying at another Town of the *Wisacks*. The Man of the House offer'd us Skins to sell, but they were too heavy Burdens for our long Voyage.

Next Morning we set out early, breaking the Ice we met withal, in the stony Runs, which were many. We pass'd by several Cottages, and about 8 of the Clock came to a pretty big Town, where we took up our Quarters, in one of their State Houses, the Men being all out, hunting in the Woods, and none but Women at home. Our Fellow Traveller of whom I spoke before at the *Congerees*, having a great Mind for an *Indian* Lass, for his Bed-Fellow that Night, spoke to our Guide, who soon got a Couple, reserving one for himself. That which fell to our Companion's Share, was a pretty young Girl. Tho' they could not understand one Word of what each other spoke, yet the Female *Indian*, being no Novice

48. A county in central England.
49. Also spelled Esau, Essaw, Essaugh, and Isaw. "Iswa" is the Catawba word for "river." The term was generally used to indicate a division or the whole of the Catawba proper and was used by some writers to include all the Siouan tribes in the Southeast.
50. Wisacky, a small tribe subject to the Ushery King.

at her Game, but understanding what she came thither for, acted her Part dexterously enough with her Cully, to make him sensible of what she wanted; which was to pay the Hire, before he rode the Hackney. He shew'd her all the Treasure he was possess'd of, as Beads, Red Cadis,[51] &c. which she lik'd very well, and permitted him to put them into his Pocket again, endearing him with all the Charms, which one of a better Education than Dame Nature had bestow'd upon her, could have made use of, to render her Consort a surer Captive. After they had us'd this Sort of Court-ship a small time, the Match was confirm'd by both Parties, with the Approbation of as many *Indian* Women, as came to the House, to celebrate our *Winchester*-Wedding.[52] Every one of the Bride-Maids were as great Whores, as Mrs. Bride, tho' not quite so handsome. Our happy Couple went to Bed together before us all, and with as little Blushing, as if they had been Man and Wife for 7 Years. The rest of the Company being weary with travelling, had more Mind to take their Rest, than add more Weddings to that hopeful one already consummated; so that tho' the other Virgins offer'd their Service to us, we gave them their Answer, and went to sleep. About an Hour before day, I awak'd, and saw somebody walking up and down the Room in a seemingly deep Melancholy. I call'd out to know who it was, and it prov'd to be Mr. Bridegroom, who in less than 12 Hours, was Batchelor, Hus-band, and Widdower, his dear Spouse having pick'd his Pocket of the Beads, Cadis, and what else should have gratified the *Indians* for the Victuals we receiv'd of them. However that did not serve her turn, but she had also got his Shooes away, which he had made the Night before, of a drest Buck-Skin. Thus dearly did our Spark already repent his new Bargain, walking bare-foot, in his Peni-tentials, like some poor Pilgrim to *Loretto*.[53]

After the *Indians* had laugh'd their Sides sore at the Figure Mr. Bridegroom made, with much ado, we muster'd up another Pair of Shooes, or *Moggisons,* and set forward on our intended Voyage, the Company (all the way) lifting up their Prayers for the new married Couple, whose Wedding had made away with that, which should have purchas'd our Food.

Relying wholly on Providence, we march'd on, now and then

51. A coarse cheap serge.
52. Probably a forced marriage.
53. Since the fifteenth century, and perhaps even earlier, Santa Casa di Loretto, the "Holy House" of Loretto, has been numbered among the most famous shrines in Italy.

paying our Respects to the new-married Man. The Land held rich and good; in many Places there were great Quantities of Marble. The Water was still of a wheyish Colour. About 10 of the Clock, we waded thro' a River,[54] (about the Bigness of *Derwent*, in *Yorkshire*) which I take to be one of the Branches of *Winjaw* River. We saw several Flocks of Pigeons, Field-Fares, and Thrushes, much like those of *Europe*. The *Indians* of these Parts use Sweating very much. If any Pain seize their Limbs, or Body, immediately they take Reeds, or small Wands, and bend them Umbrella-Fashion, covering them with Skins and Matchcoats: They have a large Fire not far off, wherein they heat Stones, or (where they are wanting) Bark, putting it into this Stove, which casts an extraordinary Heat: There is a Pot of Water in the *Bagnio*, in which is put a Bunch of an Herb, bearing a Silver Tassel, not much unlike the *Aurea Virga*.[55] With this Vegetable they rub the Head, Temples, and other Parts, which is reckon'd a Preserver of the Sight and Strengthener of the Brain. We went, this day, about 12 Miles, one of our Company being lame of his Knee. We pass'd over an exceeding rich Tract of Land, affording Plenty of great free Stones, and marble Rocks, and abounding in many pleasant and delightsome Rivulets. At Noon, we stay'd and refresh'd ourselves at a Cabin, where we met with one of their War-Captains, a Man of great Esteem among them. At his Departure from the Cabin, the Man of the House scratch'd this War-Captain on the Shoulder, which is look'd upon as a very great Compliment among them. The Captain went two or three Miles on our way, with us, to direct us in our Path. One of our Company gave him a Belt, which he took very kindly, bidding us call at his House, (which was in our Road) and stay till the lame Traveller was well, and speaking to the *Indian*, to order his Servant to make us welcome. Thus we parted, he being on his Journey to the *Congerees*, and *Savannas*, a famous, warlike, friendly Nation of *Indians*, living to the *South*-End of *Ashly* River. He had a Man-Slave with him, who was loaded with *European* Goods, his Wife and Daughter being in Company. He told us, at his Departure, that *James*[56] had sent Knots to all the *Indians* thereabouts, for every Town to send in 10 Skins, meaning Captain *Moor*,[57] then

---

54. Possibly the Catawba or one of its tributaries.
55. Golden rod.
56. Most likely James Moore.
57. Moore was governor of South Carolina during 1700–3 and again during 1719–21.

Governour of *South-Carolina*. The Towns being very thick hereabouts, at Night we took up our Quarters at one of the chief Mens
Houses, which was one of the Theaters I spoke of before. There
ran, hard-by this Town, a pleasant River, not very large, but, as
the *Indians* told us, well stor'd with Fish. We being now among
the powerful Nation of *Esaws*, our Landlord entertain'd us very
courteously, shewing us, that Night, a pair of Leather-Gloves,
which he had made; and comparing them with ours, they prov'd
to be very ingeniously done, considering it was the first Tryal.

In the Morning, he desired to see the lame Man's affected Part,
to the end he might do something, which (he believ'd) would
give him Ease. After he had viewed it accordingly, he pull'd out
an Instrument, somewhat like a Comb, which was made of a split
Reed, with 15 Teeth of Rattle-Snakes set at much the same distance, as in a large Horn-Comb: With these he scratch'd the place
where the Lameness chiefly lay, till the Blood came, bathing it,
both before and after Incision, with warm Water, spurted out of
his Mouth. This done, he ran into his Plantation, and got some
Sassafras Root, (which grows here in great plenty) dry'd it in the
Embers, scrap'd off the outward Rind, and having beat it betwixt
two Stones, apply'd it to the Part afflicted, binding it up well.
Thus, in a day or two, the Patient became sound. This day, we
pass'd through a great many Towns, and Settlements, that belong
to the *Sugeree-Indians,*[58] no barren Land being found amongst
them, but great plenty of Free-Stone, and good Timber. About
three in the Afternoon, we reach'd the *Kadapau*[59] King's House,
where we met with one *John Stewart*, a *Scot*, then an Inhabitant
of *James*-River in *Virginia*, who had traded there for many Years.
Being alone, and hearing that the *Sinnagers*[60] (*Indians* from *Canada*) were abroad in that Country, he durst not venture homewards, till he saw us, having heard that we were coming, above
20 days before. It is very odd, that News should fly so swiftly
among these People. Mr. *Stewart* had left *Virginia* ever since the
October before, and had lost a day of the Week, of which we
inform'd him. He had brought seven Horses along with him,
loaded with *English* Goods for the *Indians;* and having sold most

58. Sugar Creek in York County, South Carolina. Lawson was one of the
first writers to mention these Indians.

59. Probably Catawba, though they seem to have been a different tribe
from the "Esaws."

60. Senecas, who had from time immemorial raided the Catawba, a contrib-
uting factor to the rapid decline of the latter tribe.

of his Cargo, told us, if we would stay two Nights, he would go along with us. Company being very acceptable, we accepted the Proposal.

The next day, we were preparing for our Voyage, and baked some Bread to take along with us. Our Landlord was King of the *Kadapau Indians,* and always kept two or three trading Girls in his Cabin. Offering one of these to some of our Company, who refus'd his Kindness, his Majesty flew into a violent Passion, to be thus slighted, telling the *Englishmen,* they were good for nothing. Our old Gamester, particularly, hung his Ears at the Proposal, having too lately been a Loser by that sort of Merchandize. It was observable, that we did not see one Partridge from the *Waterrees* to this place, tho' my Spaniel-Bitch, which I had with me in this Voyage, had put up a great many before.

On *Saturday* Morning, we all set out for *Sapona,* killing, in these Creeks, several Ducks of a strange Kind, having a red Circle about their Eyes, like some Pigeons that I have seen, a Top-knot reaching from the Crown of their Heads, almost to the middle of their Backs, and abundance of Feathers of pretty Shades and Colours. They prov'd excellent Meat. Likewise, here is good store of Woodcocks, not so big as those in *England,* the Feathers of the Breast being of a Carnation-Colour, exceeding ours for Delicacy of Food. The Marble here is of different Colours, some or other of the Rocks representing most Mixtures, but chiefly the white having black and blue Veins in it, and some that are red. This day, we met with seven heaps of Stones, being the Monuments of seven *Indians,* that were slain in that place by the *Sinnagers,* or *Troquois.* Our *Indian* Guide added a Stone to each heap. We took up our Lodgings near a Brook-side, where the *Virginia* Man's Horses got away; and went back to the *Kadapau's.*

This day, one of our Company, with a *Sapona Indian,* who attended *Stewart,* went back for the Horses. In the mean time, we went to shoot Pigeons, which were so numerous in these Parts, that you might see many Millions in a Flock; they sometimes split off the Limbs of stout Oaks, and other Trees, upon which they roost o' Nights. You may find several *Indian* Towns, of not above 17 Houses, that have more than 100 Gallons of Pigeons Oil, or Fat; they using it with Pulse, or Bread, as we do Butter, and making the Ground as white as a Sheet with their Dung. The *Indians* take a Light, and go among them in the Night, and bring away some thousands, killing them with long Poles, as they roost in the

Trees. At this time of the Year, the Flocks, as they pass by, in great measure, obstruct the Light of the day.[61]

On *Monday,* we went about 25 Miles, travelling through a pleasant, dry Country, and took up our Lodgings by a Hill-side, that was one entire Rock, out of which gush'd out pleasant Fountains of well-tasted Water.

The next day, still passing along such Land as we had done for many days before, which was, Hills and Vallies, about 10 a Clock we reach'd the Top of one of these Mountains, which yielded us a fine Prospect of a very level Country, holding so, on all sides, farther than we could discern. When we came to travel through it, we found it very stiff and rich, being a sort of Marl. This Valley afforded as large Timber as any I ever met withal, especially of Chesnut Oaks, which render it an excellent Country for raising great Herds of Swine. Indeed, were it cultivated, we might have good hopes of as pleasant and fertile a Valley, as any our *English* in *America* can afford. At Night, we lay by a swift Current, where we saw plenty of Turkies, but pearch'd upon such lofty Oaks, that our Guns would not kill them, tho' we shot very often, and our Guns were very good. Some of our Company shot several times, at one Turkey, before he would fly away, the Pieces being loaded with large Goose-shot.

Next Morning, we got our Breakfasts; roasted Acorns being one of the Dishes. The *Indians* beat them into Meal, and thicken their Venison-Broth with them; and oftentimes make a palatable Soop. They are used instead of Bread, boiling them till the Oil swims on the top of the Water, which they preserve for use, eating the Acorns with Flesh-meat. We travell'd, this day, about 25 Miles, over pleasant *Savanna* Ground, high, and dry, having very few Trees upon it, and those standing at a great distance. The Land was very good, and free from Grubs or Underwood. A Man near *Sapona* may more easily clear 10 Acres of Ground, than in some places he can one; there being much loose Stone upon the Land, lying very convenient for making of dry Walls, or any other sort of durable Fence. This Country abounds likewise with curious bold Creeks, (navigable for small Craft) disgorging themselves into the main Rivers, that vent themselves into the Ocean. These Creeks are well stor'd with sundry sorts of Fish, and Fowl, and are very convenient for the Transportation of what Com-

61. This is one of the best accounts in print of the now extinct passenger pigeon.

modities this Place may produce. This Night, we had a great deal of Rain, with Thunder and Lightning.

Next Morning, it proving delicate. Weather, three of us separated ourselves from the Horses, and the rest of the Company, and went directly for *Sapona* Town. That day, we pass'd through a delicious Country, (none that I ever saw exceeds it.) We saw fine bladed Grass, six Foot high, along the Banks of these pleasant Rivulets: We pass'd by the Sepulchres of several slain *Indians.* Coming, that day, about 30 Miles, we reach'd the fertile and pleasant Banks of *Sapona* [62] River, whereon stands the *Indian* Town and Fort. Nor could all *Europe* afford a pleasanter Stream, were it inhabited by *Christians,* and cultivated by ingenious Hands. These *Indians* live in a clear Field, about a Mile square, which they would have sold me; because I talked sometimes of coming into those Parts to live. This most pleasant River may be something broader than the *Thames* at *Kingston,* keeping a continual pleasant warbling Noise, with its reverberating on the bright Marble Rocks. It is beautified with a numerous Train of Swans, and other sorts of Water-Fowl, not common, though extraordinary pleasing to the Eye. The forward Spring welcom'd us with her innumerable Train of small Choristers, which inhabit those fair Banks; the Hills redoubling, and adding Sweetness to their melodious Tunes by their shrill Echoes. One side of the River is hemm'd in with mountainy Ground, the other side proving as rich a Soil to the Eye of a knowing Person with us, as any this Western World can afford. We took up our Quarters at the King's Cabin, who was a good Friend to the *English,* and had lost one of his Eyes in their Vindication. Being upon his march towards the *Appallatche* Mountains, amongst a Nation of *Indians* in their Way, there happen'd a Difference, while they were measuring of Gunpowder; and the Powder, by accident, taking fire, blew out one of this King's Eyes, and did a great deal more mischief, upon the spot: Yet this *Sapona* King stood firmly to the *English* Man's Interest, with whom he was in Company, still siding with him against the *Indians.* They were intended for the *South Sea,* but were too much fatigued by the vast Ridge of Mountains, tho' they hit the right Passage; it being no less than five days Journey through a Ledge of Rocky Hills, and sandy Desarts. And which is yet worse, there is no Water, nor scarce a Bird to be seen, during your Passage over these barren Crags and

62. Yadkin River.

Valleys. The *Sapona* River proves to be the *West* Branch of *Cape-Fair*,[63] or *Clarendon* River, whose Inlet, with other Advantages, makes it appear as noble a River to plant a Colony in, as any I have met withal.

The *Saponas* had (about 10 days before we came thither) taken Five Prisoners of the *Sinnagers* or *Jennitos,* a Sort of People that range several thousands of Miles, making all Prey they lay their Hands on. These are fear'd by all the savage Nations I ever was among, the Westward *Indians* dreading their Approach. They are all forted in, and keep continual Spies and Out-Guards for their better Security. Those Captives they did intend to burn, few Prisoners of War escaping that Punishment. The Fire of Pitch-Pine being got ready, and a Feast appointed, which is solemnly kept at the time of their acting this Tragedy, the Sufferer has his Body stuck thick with Light-Wood-Splinters, which are lighted like so many Candles, the tortur'd Person dancing round a great Fire, till his Strength fails, and disables him from making them any farther Pastime. Most commonly, these Wretches behave themselves (in the Midst of their Tortures) with a great deal of Bravery and Resolution, esteeming it Satisfaction enough, to be assur'd, that the same Fate will befal some of their Tormentors, whensoever they fall into the Hands of their Nation. More of this you will have in the other Sheets.

The *Toteros*,[64] a neighbouring Nation, came down from the Westward Mountains, to the *Saponas,* desiring them to give them those Prisoners into their Hands, to the Intent they might send them back into their own Nation, being bound in Gratitude to be serviceable to the *Sinnagers,* since not long ago, those Northern-*Indians* had taken some of the *Toteros* Prisoners, and done them no Harm, but treated them civilly whilst among them, sending them, with Safety, back to their own People, and affirming, that it would be the best Method to preserve Peace on all Sides. At that time, these *Toteros, Saponas,* and the *Keyauwees,* 3 small Nations, were going to live together, by which they thought they should strengthen themselves, and become formidable to their Enemies. The Reasons offer'd by the *Toteros* being heard, the *Sapona* King, with the Consent of his Counsellors, deliver'd the *Sinnagers* up to the *Toteros,* to conduct them home.

63. Early maps called it "Cape Fear," as have all modern writers.
64. Tuteloes, or Toteloes, a Siouan tribe, located along the headwaters of the Yadkin River.

Friday Morning, the old King having shew'd us 2 of his Horses, that were as fat, as if they had belong'd to the *Dutch* Troopers, left us, and went to look after his Bever-Traps, there being abundance of those amphibious Animals in this River, and the Creeks adjoining. Taken with the Pleasantness of the Place, we walk'd along the River-side, where we found a very delightful Island, made by the River, and a Branch; there being several such Plots of Ground environ'd with this Silver Stream, which are fit Pastures for Sheep, and free from any offensive Vermin. Nor can any thing be desired by a contented Mind, as to a pleasant Situation, but what may here be found; Every Step presenting some new Object, which still adds Invitation to the Traveller in these Parts. Our *Indian* King and his Wife entertain'd us very respectfully.

On *Saturday,* the *Indians* brought in some Swans, and Geese, which we had our Share of. One of their Doctors took me to his Cabin, and shew'd me a great Quantity of medicinal Drugs, the Produce of those Parts; Relating their Qualities as to the Emunctories they work'd by, and what great Maladies he had heal'd by them. This Evening, came to us the Horses, with the Remainder of our Company, their *Indian* Guide (who was a Youth of this Nation) having kill'd, in their Way, a very fat Doe, Part of which they brought to us.

This day, the King sent out all his able Hunters, to kill Game for a great Feast, that was to be kept at their Departure, from the Town, which they offer'd to sell me for a small matter. That Piece of Ground, with a little Trouble, would make an *English-man* a most curious Settlement, containing above a Mile square of rich Land. This Evening, came down some *Toteros,* tall, likely Men, having great Plenty of Buffelos, Elks, and Bears, with other sort of Deer amongst them, which strong Food makes large, robust Bodies. Enquiring of them, if they never got any of the *Bezoar* Stone, and giving them a Description how it was found, the *Indians* told me, they had great plenty of it; and ask'd me, What use I could make of it? I answer'd them, That the white Men us'd it in Physick, and that I would buy some of them, if they would get it against I came that way again. Thereupon, one of them pull'd out a Leather-Pouch, wherein was some of it in Powder; he was a notable Hunter, and affirm'd to me, That that Powder, blown into the Eyes, strengthen'd the Sight and Brain exceedingly, that being the most common Use they made of it. I bought, for 2 or 3 Flints, a large Peach-Loaf, made up with a pleasant sort of Seed; and this did us a singular Kindness, in our Journey. Near the Town, within their clear'd Land, are several *Bagnios,* or Sweating-Houses, made of Stone, in Shape like a large Oven. These they make much Use of; especially, for any Pains in the Joints, got by Cold, or Travelling. At Night, as we lay in our Beds, there arose the most violent N. W. Wind I ever knew. The first Puff blew down all the *Palisadoes* that fortify'd the Town; and I thought it would have blown us all into the River, together with the Houses. Our one-ey'd King, who pretends much to the Art of Conjuration, ran out in the most violent Hurry, and in the Middle of the Town, fell to his Necromantick Practice; tho' I thought he would have been blown away or kill'd, before the *Devil* and he could have exchang'd half a dozen Words; but in two Minutes, the Wind was ceas'd, and it became as great a Calm, as ever I knew in my Life. As I much admir'd at that sudden Alteration, the old Man told me, the *Devil* was very angry, and had done thus, because they had not put the *Sinnagers* to Death.

On *Monday* Morning, our whole Company, with the Horses, set out from the *Sapona-Indian* Town, after having seen some of the Locust, which is gotten thereabouts, the same Sort that bears Honey. Going over several Creeks, very convenient for Water-Mills, about 8 Miles from the Town, we pass'd over a very pretty River, call'd Rocky River,[65] a fit Name, having a Ridge of high Mountains running from its Banks, to the Eastward; and disgorging itself into *Sapona*-River; so that there is a most pleasant and convenient Neck of Land, betwixt both Rivers, lying upon a Point, where many thousand Acres may be fenced in, without much Cost or Labour. You can scarce go a Mile, without meeting with one of these small swift Currents, here being no Swamps to be found, but pleasant, dry Roads all over the Country. The Way that we went this day, was as full of Stones, as any which *Craven,* in the West of *Yorkshire,* could afford, and having nothing but *Moggisons* on my Feet, I was so lam'd by this stony Way, that I thought I must have taken up some Stay in those Parts. We went, this day, not above 15 or 20 Miles. After we had supp'd, and all lay down to sleep, there came a Wolf close to the Fire-side, where we lay. My Spaniel soon discover'd him, at which, one of our Company fir'd a Gun at the Beast; but, I believe, there was a

65. If this is present Rocky River, Lawson was in error. It is a tributary of the Cape Fear, not of the Yadkin.

Mistake in the loading of it, for it did him no Harm. The Wolf stay'd till he had almost loaded again, but the Bitch making a great Noise, at last left us and went aside. We had no sooner laid down, but he approach'd us again, yet was more shy, so that we could not get a Shot at him.

Next day, we had 15 Miles farther to the *Keyauwees.* The Land is more mountainous, but extremely pleasant, and an excellent Place for the breeding Sheep, Goats, and Horses; or Mules, if the *English* were once brought to the Experience of the Usefulness of those Creatures. The Valleys are here very rich. At Noon, we pass'd over such another stony River, as that eight Miles from *Sapona.* This is call'd *Heighwaree,*[66] and affords as good blue Stone for Mill-Stones, as that from *Cologn,* good Rags, some Hones, and large Pebbles, in great abundance, besides Free-Stone of several Sorts, all very useful. I knew one of these Hones made use of by an Acquaintance of mine, and it prov'd rather better than any from *Old Spain,* or elsewhere. The Veins of Marble are very large and curious on this River, and the Banks thereof.

Five Miles from this River, to the N. W. stands the *Keyauwees* Town.[67] They are fortify'd in, with wooden Puncheons, like *Sapona,* being a People much of the same Number. Nature hath so fortify'd this Town, with Mountains, that were it a Seat of War, it might easily be made impregnable; having large Corn-Fields joining to their Cabins, and a *Savanna* near the Town, at the Foot of these Mountains, that is capable of keeping some hundred Heads of Cattle. And all this environ'd round with very high Mountains, so that no hard Wind ever troubles these Inhabitants. Those high Clifts have no Grass growing on them, and very few Trees, which are very short, and stand at a great Distance one from another. The Earth is of a red Colour, and seems to me to be wholly design'd by Nature for the Production of Minerals, being of too hot a Quality, to suffer any Verdure upon its Surface. These *Indians* make use of Lead-Ore, to paint their Faces withal, which they get in the neighbouring Mountains. As for the refining of Metals, the *Indians* are wholly ignorant of it, being content with the *Realgar.* But if it be my Chance, once more to visit these Hilly Parts, I shall make a longer Stay amongst them: For

66. Uwharrie or Uharie.
67. This Indian village was not far from present Asheboro and High Point. It was excavated in 1936 by Joffre Coe and the Research Laboratories of Anthropology of The University of North Carolina at Chapel Hill.

were a good Vein of Lead found out, and work'd by an ingenious Hand, it might be of no small Advantage to the Undertaker, there being great Convenience for smelting, either by Bellows or Reverberation; and the Working of these Mines might discover some that are much richer.

At the Top of one of these Mountains, is a Cave that 100 Men may fit very conveniently to dine in; whether natural, or artificial, I could not learn. There is a fine Bole between this Place, and the *Saps.*[68] These Valleys thus hemm'd in with Mountains, would (doubtless) prove a good place for propagating some sort of Fruits, that our Easterly Winds commonly blast. The Vine could not miss of thriving well here; but we of the Northern Climate are neither Artists, nor curious, in propagating that pleasant and profitable Vegetable. Near the Town, is such another Current, as *Heighwaree.* We being six in Company, divided ourselves into Two Parties; and it was my Lot to be at the House of *Keyauwees Jack,* who is King of that People. He is a *Congeree-Indian,* and ran away when he was a Boy. He got this Government by Marriage with the Queen; the Female Issue carrying the Heritage, for fear of Impostors; the Savages well knowing, how much Frailty possesses the *Indian* Women, betwixt the Garters and the Girdle.

The next day, having some occasion to write, the *Indian* King, who saw me, believ'd that he could write as well as I. Whereupon, I wrote a Word, and gave it him to copy, which he did with more Exactness, than any *European* could have done, that was illiterate. It was so well, that he who could read mine, might have done the same by his. Afterwards, he took great Delight in making Fishhooks of his own Invention, which would have been a good Piece for an Antiquary to have puzzled his Brains withal, in tracing out the Characters of all the Oriental Tongues. He sent for several *Indians* to his Cabin, to look at his Handy-work, and both he and they thought, I could read his Writing as well as I could my own. I had a Manual in my Pocket, that had King *David's* Picture in it, in one of his private Retirements. The *Indian* ask'd me, Who that Figure represented? I told him, It was the Picture of a good King, that liv'd according to the Rules of Morality, doing to all as he would be done by, ordering all his Life to the Service of the Creator of all things; and being now above us all, in Heaven, with God Almighty, who had rewarded him with all

68. Probably the Saponis. The Saponi village was excavated in 1938 by the group mentioned above.

the delightful Pleasures imaginable in the other World, for his Obedience to him in this; I concluded, with telling them, that we received nothing here below, as Food, Raiment, &c. but what came from that Omnipotent Being. They listned to my Discourse with a profound Silence, assuring me, that they believ'd what I said to be true. No Man living will ever be able to make these *Heathens* sensible of the Happiness of a future State, except he now and then mentions some lively carnal Representation, which may quicken their Apprehensions, and make them thirst after such a gainful Exchange; for, were the best Lecture that ever was preach'd by Man, given to an ignorant sort of People, in a more learned Style, than their mean Capacities are able to understand, the Intent would prove ineffectual, and the Hearers would be left in a greater Labyrinth than their Teacher found them in. But dispense the Precepts of our Faith according to the Pupil's Capacity, and there is nothing in our Religion, but what an indifferent Reason is, in some measure, able to comprehend; tho' a *New-England* Minister blames the *French* Jesuits for this way of Proceeding, as being quite contrary to a true Christian Practice, and affirms it to be no ready, or true Method, to establish a lively Representation of our Christian Belief amongst these Infidels.

All the *Indians* hereabouts carefully preserve the Bones of the Flesh they eat, and burn them, as being of Opinion, that if they omitted that Custom, the Game would leave their Country, and they should not be able to maintain themselves by their Hunting. Most of these *Indians* wear Mustachoes, or Whiskers, which is rare; by reason the *Indians* are a People that commonly pull the Hair of their Faces, and other Parts, up by the Roots, and suffer none to grow. Here is plenty of Chesnuts, which are rarely found in *Carolina*, and never near the Sea, or Salt-Water; tho' they are frequently in such Places in *Virginia*.

At the other House, where our Fellow-Travellers lay, they had provided a Dish, in great Fashion amongst the *Indians*, which was Two young Fawns, taken out of the Doe's Bellies, and boil'd in the same slimy Bags Nature had plac'd them in, and one of the Country-Hares, stew'd with the Guts in her Belly, and her Skin with the Hair on. This new-fashion'd Cookery wrought Abstinence in our Fellow-Travellers, which I somewhat wonder'd at, because one of them made nothing of eating *Allegators*, as heartily as if it had been Pork and Turneps. The *Indians* dress most things after the Wood-cock Fashion, never taking the Guts out. At the

House we lay at, there was very good Entertainment of Venison, Turkies, and Bears; and which is customary amongst the *Indians,* the Queen had a Daughter by a former Husband, who was the beautifullest *Indian* I ever saw, and had an Air of Majesty with her, quite contrary to the general Carriage of the *Indians.* She was very kind to the *English,* during our Abode, as well as her Father and Mother.

This Morning, most of our Company having some Inclination to go straight away for *Virginia,* when they left this Place; I and one more took our leaves of them, resolving (with God's Leave) to see *North-Carolina,* one of the *Indians* setting us in our way. The rest being indifferent which way they went, desired us, by all means, to leave a Letter for them, at the *Achonechy*-Town.[69] The *Indian* that put us in our Path, had been a Prisoner amongst the *Sinnagers;* but had out-run them, although they had cut his Toes, and half his Feet away, which is a Practice common amongst them. They first raise the Skin, then cut away half the Feet, and so wrap the Skin over the Stumps, and make a present Cure of the Wounds. This commonly disables them from making their Escape, they being not so good Travellers as before, and the Impression of their Half-Feet making it easy to trace them. However, this Fellow was got clear of them, but had little Heart to go far from home, and carry'd always a Case of Pistols in his Girdle, besides a Cutlass, and a Fuzee. Leaving the rest of our Company of the *Indian*-Town, we travell'd, that day, about 20 Miles, in very cold, frosty Weather; and pass'd over two pretty Rivers, something bigger than *Heighwaree,* but not quite so stony. We took these two Rivers to make one of the Northward Branches of *Cape-Fair* River, but afterwards found our Mistake.

The next day, we travell'd over very good Land, but full of Free-Stone, and Marble, which pinch'd our Feet severely. We took up our Quarters in a sort of *Savanna*-Ground, that had very few Trees in it. The Land was good, and had several Quarries of Stone, but not loose, as the others us'd to be.

Next Morning, we got our Breakfasts of Parch'd Corn, having nothing but that to subsist on for above 100 Miles. All the Pine-

---

69. Occaneechi, located near present Hillsborough. The name Occaneechi is associated particularly with the Occaneechi Trail or Trading Path, which extends southwest through North Carolina from the neighborhood of Petersburg, Virginia. Occaneechi Village was excavated by Coe and his assistants in 1938.

Trees were vanish'd, for we had seen none for two days. We pass'd through a delicate rich Soil this day; no great Hills, but pretty Risings, and Levels, which made a beautiful Country. We likewise pass'd over three Rivers this day; the first about the bigness of *Rocky* River, the other not much differing in Size. Then we made not the least Question, but we had pass'd over the North-West Branch of *Cape-Fair,* travelling that day above 30 Miles. We were much taken with the Fertility and Pleasantness of the Neck of Land between these two Branches, and no less pleas'd, that we had pass'd the River, which us'd to frighten Passengers from fording it. At last, determining to rest on the other side of a Hill, which we saw before us; when we were on the Top thereof, there appear'd to us such another delicious, rapid Stream, as that of *Sapona,* having large Stones, about the bigness of an ordinary House, lying up and down the River. As the Wind blew very cold at N. W. and we were very weary, and hungry, the Swiftness of the Current gave us some cause to fear; but, at last, we concluded to venture over that Night. Accordingly, we stripp'd, and with great Difficulty, (by God's Assistance) got safe to the North-side of the famous *Hau*-River, by some called *Reatkin;* [70] the *Indians* differing in the Names of Places, according to their several Nations. It is call'd *Hau*-River, from the *Sissipahau Indians,* [71] who dwell upon this Stream, which is one of the main Branches of *Cape-Fair,* there being rich Land enough to contain some Thousands of Families; for which Reason, I hope, in a short time, it will be planted. This River is much such another as *Sapona;* both seeming to run a vast way up the Country. Here is plenty of good Timber, and especially, of a Scaly-bark'd Oak; And as there is Stone enough in both Rivers, and the Land is extraordinary Rich, no Man that will be content within the Bounds of Reason, can have any grounds to dislike it. And they that are otherwise, are the best Neighbours, when farthest of.

As soon as it was day, we set out for the *Achonechy*-Town, it being, by Estimation, 20 Miles off, which, I believe, is pretty exact. We were got about half way, (meeting great Gangs of Turkies) when we saw, at a Distance, 30 loaded Horses, coming on the Road, with four or five Men, on other Jades, driving them. We charg'd our Piece, and went up to them: Enquiring, whence they came from? They told us, from *Virginia.* The leading Man's

70. The name "Reatkin" has led some writers to conclude that this was the Yadkin. It was the Haw River.

71. The Sissipahaw Indians were probably Siouan. Their principal settlement appears to have been about the present Saxapahaw on Haw River.

Name was *Massey*, who was born about *Leeds* in *Yorkshire*. He ask'd, from whence we came? We told him. Then he ask'd again, Whether we wanted any thing that he had? telling us, we should be welcome to it. We accepted of Two Wheaten Biskets, and a little Ammunition. He advised us, by all means, to strike down the Country for *Ronoack*, and not think of *Virginia*, because of the *Sinnagers*, of whom they were afraid, tho' so well arm'd, and numerous. They persuaded us also, to call upon one *Enoe Will*, as we went to *Adshusheer*,⁷² for that he would conduct us safe among the *English*, giving him the Character of a very faithful *Indian*, which we afterwards found true by Experience. The *Virginia*-Men asking our Opinion of the Country we were then in? we told them, it was a very pleasant one. They were all of the same Opinion, and affirm'd, That they had never seen 20 Miles of such extraordinary rich Land, lying all together, like that betwixt *Hau*-River and the *Achonechy* Town.⁷³ Having taken our Leaves of each other, we set forward; and the Country, thro' which we pass'd, was so delightful, that it gave us a great deal of Satisfaction. About Three a Clock, we reach'd the Town, and the *Indians* presently brought us good fat Bear, and Venison, which was very acceptable at that time. Their Cabins were hung with a good sort of Tapestry, as fat Bear, and barbakued or dried Venison; no *Indians* having greater Plenty of Provisions than these. The Savages do, indeed, still possess the Flower of *Carolina*, the *English* enjoying only the Fag-end of that fine Country. We had not been in the Town 2 Hours, when *Enoe-Will* came into the King's Cabin; which was our Quarters. We ask'd him, if he would conduct us to the *English*, and what he would have for his Pains; he answer'd, he would go along with us, and for what he was to have, he left that to our Discretion.

The next Morning, we set out, with *Enoe-Will*, towards *Adshusheer*, leaving the *Virginia* Path,⁷⁴ and striking more to the Eastward, for *Ronoack*.⁷⁵ Several *Indians* were in our Company belonging to *Will's* Nation, who are the *Shoccories*,⁷⁶ mixt with the *Enoe-Indians*, and those of the Nation of *Adshusheer*. *Enoe-*

72. The Eno Indians, probably Siouan, shared this town with the Shakori. The town was probably near Durham.

73. What came to be called "Haw Old Fields" constituted the largest area of fertile land in the region.

74. The Occaneechi Trail.

75. Lawson apparently meant Roanoke Island, North Carolina.

76. The Shakori a Siouan tribe, shared the town of Adshusheer with the Eno Indians. Mooney estimated their population at 1,500 to 1,600.

Will is their chief Man, and rules as far as the Banks of *Reatkin*. It was a sad stony Way to *Adshusheer*. We went over a small River by *Achonechy*, and in this 14 Miles, through several other Streams, which empty themselves into the Branches of *Cape-Fair*. The stony Way made me quite lame; so that I was an Hour or two behind the rest; but honest *Will* would not leave me, but bid me welcome when we came to his House, feasting us with hot Bread, and Bears-Oil; which is wholsome Food for Travellers. There runs a pretty Rivulet by this Town. Near the Plantation, I saw a prodigious overgrown Pine-Tree, having not seen any of that Sort of Timber for above 125 Miles: They brought us 2 Cocks, and pull'd their larger Feathers off, never plucking the lesser, but singeing them off. I took one of these Fowls in my Hand, to make it cleaner than the *Indian* had, pulling out his Guts and Liver, which I laid in a Bason; notwithstanding which, he kept such a Struggling for a considerable time, that I had much ado to hold him in my Hands. The *Indians* laugh'd at me, and told me, that *Enoe-Will* had taken a Cock of an *Indian* that was not at home, and the Fowl was design'd for another Use. I conjectur'd, that he was design'd for an Offering to their God, who, they say, hurts them, (which is the Devil.) In this Struggling, he bled afresh, and there issued out of his Body more Blood than commonly such Creatures afford. Notwithstanding all this, we cook'd him, and eat him; and if he was design'd for him, cheated the Devil. The *Indians* keep many Cocks, but seldom above one Hen, using very often such wicked Sacrifices, as I mistrusted this Fowl was design'd for.

Our Guide and Landlord *Enoe-Will* was of the best and most agreeable Temper that ever I met with in an *Indian,* being always ready to serve the *English,* not out of Gain, but real Affection; which makes him apprehensive of being poison'd by some wicked *Indians,* and was therefore very earnest with me, to promise him to revenge his Death, if it should so happen. He brought some of his chief Men into his Cabin, and 2 of them having a Drum, and a Rattle, sung by us, as we lay in Bed, and struck up their Musick to serenade and welcome us to their Town. And tho' at last, we fell asleep, yet they continu'd their Consort till Morning. These *Indians* are fortify'd in, as the former, and are much addicted to a Sport they call *Chenco,* which is carry'd on with a Staff and a Bowl made of Stone, which they trundle upon a smooth Place, like a Bowling-Green, made for that Purpose, as I have mention'd before.

Next Morning, we set out, with our Guide, and several other *Indians,* who intended to go to the *English,* and buy Rum. We design'd for a Nation about 40 Miles from *Adshusheer,* call'd the Lower Quarter: The first Night, we lay in a rich *Perkoson,* or low Ground, that was hard-by a Creek, and good dry Land.

The next day, we went over several Tracts of rich Land, but mix'd with Pines and other indifferent Soil. In our way, there stood a great Stone about the Size of a large Oven, and hollow; this the *Indians* took great Notice of, putting some Tobacco into the Concavity, and spitting after it. I ask'd them the Reason of their so doing, but they made me no Answer. In the Evening, we pass'd over a pleasant Rivulet, with a fine gravelly Bottom, having come over such another that Morning. On the other side of this River, we found the *Indian* Town, which was a Parcel of nasty smoaky Holes, much like the *Waterrees;* their Town having a great Swamp running directly through the Middle thereof. The Land here begins to abate of its Height, and has some few Swamps. Most of these *Indians* have but one Eye; but what Mischance or Quarrel has bereav'd them of the other I could not learn. They were not so free to us, as most of the other *Indians* had been; Victuals being somewhat scarce among them. However, we got enough to satisfy our Appetites. I saw, among these Men, very long Arrows, headed with Pieces of Glass, which they had broken from Bottles. They had shap'd them neatly, like the Head of a Dart; but which way they did it, I can't tell. We had not been at this Town above an Hour, when two of our Company, that had bought a Mare of *John Stewart,*[77] came up to us, having receiv'd a Letter by one of *Will's Indians,* who was very cautious, and asked a great many Questions, to certifie him of the Person, e'er he would deliver the Letter. They had left the Trader, and one that came from *South-Carolina* with us, to go to *Virginia;* these Two being resolved to go to *Carolina* with us.

This Day fell much Rain, so we staid at the *Indian* Town.

This Morning, we set out early, being four *English*-Men, besides several *Indians.* We went 10 Miles, and were then stopp'd by the Freshes of *Enoe*-River, which had rais'd it so high, that we could not pass over, till it was fallen. I enquir'd of my Guide, Where this River disgorg'd it self? He said, It was *Enoe*-River, and run into a Place call'd *Enoe*-Bay, near his Country, which he left

77. This Scottish merchant from Virginia was a long-time trader with the Indians of this region.

when he was a Boy; by which I perceiv'd, he was one of the *Cores* by Birth: This being a Branch of *Neus*-River.

This Day, our Fellow-Traveller's Mare ran away from him; wherefore, *Will* went back as far as the lower Quarter, and brought her back.

The next Day, early, came two *Tuskeruro Indians* to the other side of the River, but could not get over. They talk'd much to us, but we understood them not. In the Afternoon, *Will* came with the Mare, and had some Discourse with them; they told him, The *English*, to whom he was going, were very wicked People; and, That they threated the *Indians* for Hunting near their Plantations. These Two Fellows were going among the *Schoccores* and *Achonechy Indians,* to sell their Wooden Bowls and Ladles for Raw-Skins, which they make great Advantage of, hating that any of these Westward *Indians* should have any Commerce with the *English,* which would prove a Hinderance to their Gains. Their Stories deterr'd an Old *Indian* and his Son, from going any far-ther; but *Will* told us, Nothing they had said should frighten him, he believing them to be a couple of Hog-stealers; and that the *English* only sought Restitution of their Losses, by them; and that this was the only ground for their Report. *Will* had a Slave, a *Sissipahau-Indian* by Nation, who killed us several Turkies, and other Game, on which we feasted.

This River is near as large as *Reatkin;* the South-side having curious Tracts of good Land, the Banks high, and Stone-Quarries. The *Tuskeruros* being come to us, we ventur'd over the River, which we found to be a strong Current, and the Water about Breast-high. However, we all got safe to the North-Shore, which is but poor, white, sandy Land, and bears no Timber, but small shrubby Oaks. We went about 10 Miles, and sat down at the Falls of a large Creek, where lay mighty Rocks, the Water making a strange Noise, as if a great many Water-Mills were going at once. I take this to be the Falls of *Neus*-Creek,[78] called by the *Indians, Wee quo Whom.* We lay here all Night. My Guide *Will* desiring to see the Book that I had about me, I lent it him; and as he soon found the Picture of King *David,* he asked me several Questions concerning the Book, and Picture, which I resolv'd him, and in-vited him to become a Christian. He made me a very sharp Reply, assuring me, That he lov'd the *English* extraordinary well, and did believe their Ways to be very good for those that had already

78. Most likely "Falls of Neuse" River.

practis'd them, and had been brought up therein; But as for himself, he was too much in Years to think of a Change, esteeming it not proper for Old People to admit of such an Alteration. However, he told me, If I would take his Son *Jack,* who was then about 14 Years of Age, and teach him to talk in that Book, and make Paper speak, which they call our Way or Writing, he would wholly resign him to my Tuition; telling me, he was of Opinion, I was very well affected to the *Indians.*

The next Morning, we set out early, and I perceiv'd that these *Indians* were in some fear of Enemies; for they had an Old Man with them, who was very cunning and circumspect, wheresoever he saw any Marks of Footing, or of any Fire that had been made; going out of his Way, very often, to look for these Marks. We went, this day, above 30 Miles, over a very level Country, and most Pine Land, yet intermix'd with some Quantities of Marble; a good Range for Cattel, though very indifferent for Swine. We had now lost our rapid Streams, and were come to slow, dead Waters, of a brown Colour, proceeding from the *Swamps,* much like the Sluices in *Holland,* where the Track-*Scoots* go along. In the Afternoon, we met two *Tuskeruros,* who told us, That there was a Company of Hunters not far off, and if we walk'd stoutly, we might reach them that Night. But *Will* and He that own'd the Mare, being gone before, and the Old *Indian* tired, we rested, that Night, in the Woods, making a good light Fire, Wood being very plentiful in these Parts.

Next Day, about 10 a Clock, we struck out of the Way, by the Advice of our Old *Indian.* We had not gone past two Miles, e'er we met with about 500 *Tuskeruros* in one Hunting-Quarter. They had made themselves Streets of Houses, built with Pine-Bark, not with round Tops, as they commonly use, but Ridge-Fashion, after the manner of most other *Indians.* We got nothing amongst them but Corn, Flesh being not plentiful, by reason of the great Number of their People. For tho' they are expert Hunters, yet they are too populous for one Range; which makes Vension very scarce to what it is amongst other *Indians,* that are fewer; no Savages living so well for Plenty, as those near the Sea. I saw, amongst these, a Humpback'd *Indian,* which was the only crooked one I ever met withal. About two a Clock, we reach'd one of their Towns, in which there was no body left, but an Old Woman or two; the rest being gone to their Hunting-Quarters. We could find no Provision at that Place. We had a *Tus-*

keruro that came in company with us, from the lower Quarter, who took us to his Cabin, and gave us what it afforded, which was Corn-meat.

This Day, we pass'd through several Swamps, and going not above a dozen Miles, came to a Cabin, the Master whereof us'd to trade amongst the *English*. He told us, If we would stay Two Nights, he would conduct us safe to them, himself designing, at that time, to go and fetch some Rum; so we resolved to tarry for his Company. During our Stay, there happen'd to be a Young Woman troubled with Fits. The Doctor who was sent for to assist her, laid her on her Belly, and made a small Incision with Rattle-Snake-Teeth; then laying his Mouth to the Place, he suck'd out near a Quart of black conglutinated Blood, and *Serum*. Our Landlord gave us the Tail of a Bever, which was a choice Food. There happen'd also to be a Burial of one of their Dead, which Ceremony is much the same with that of the *Santees,* who make a great Feast at the Interment of their Corps. The small Runs of Water hereabout, afford great Plenty of Craw-Fish, full as large as those in *England,* and nothing inferior in Goodness.

Saturday Morning, our Patron, with *Enoe Will,* and his Servant, set out with us, for the *English*. In the Afternoon, we ferried over a River, (in a *Canoe*) called by the *Indians, Chattookau,*[79] which is the N. W. Branch of *Neus*-River. We lay in the *Swamp,* where some *Indians* invited us to go to their Quarters, which some of our Company accepted, but got nothing extraordinary, except a dozen Miles March out of their Way: The Country here is very thick of *Indian* Towns and Plantations.

We were forced to march, this day, for Want of Provisions. About 10 a Clock, we met an *Indian* that had got a parcel of Shad-Fish ready barbaku'd. We bought 24 of them, for a dress'd Doe-Skin, and so went on, through many *Swamps,* finding, this day, the long ragged Moss on the Trees, which we had not seen for above 600 Miles. In the Afternoon, we came upon the Banks of *Pampticough,* about 20 Miles above the *English* Plantations by Water, though not so far by Land. The *Indian* found a *Canoe,* which he had hidden, in which we all got over, and went about six Miles farther. We lay, that Night, under two or three Pieces of Bark, at the Foot of a large Oak. There fell abundance of Snow and Rain in the Night, with much Thunder and Lightning.

79. Indian village on the site of present New Bern. Lawson's map is the first to list this town.

Next Day, it clear'd up, and it being about 12 Miles to the *English,* about half-way we passed over a deep Creek, and came safe to Mr. *Richard Smith's,*[80] of *Pampticough*-River, in *North-Carolina;* where being well receiv'd by the Inhabitants, and pleas'd with the Goodness of the Country, we all resolv'd to continue.

80. Richard Smith, a large landowner, represented Bath County in the legislature of 1697. In his will, written in 1708, Lawson referred to his beloved Hannah Smith, probably Lawson's mistress. She was probably Richard Smith's daughter.

FINIS

A

DESCRIPTION

O F

North-Carolina

THE Province of *Carolina* is separated from *Virginia* by a due West-Line, which begins at *Currituck*-Inlet, in 36 Degrees, 30 Minutes, of Northern-Latitude, and extends indefinitely to the Westward, and thence to the Southward, as far as 29 Degrees; which is a vast Tract of Sea-Coast. But having already treated, as far as is necessary, concerning South-*Carolina*, I shall confine myself, in the ensuing Sheets, to give my Reader a Description of that Part of the Country only, which lies betwixt *Currituck* and *Cape-Fair,* and is almost 34 Deg. North. And this is commonly call'd *North Carolina.*

This Part of *Carolina* is faced with a Chain of Sand-Banks, which defends it from the Violence and Insults of the *Atlantick* Ocean; by which Barrier, a vast Sound is hemm'd in, which fronts the Mouths of the Navigable and Pleasant Rivers of this Fertile Country, and into which they disgorge themselves. Thro' the same are Inlets of several Depths of Water. Some of their Channels admit only of Sloops, Brigantines, small Barks, and Ketches; and such are *Currituck, Ronoak,* and up the Sound above *Hatteras:* Whilst others can receive Ships of Burden, as *Ocacock, Topsail*-Inlet, and *Cape-Fair;* as appears by my Chart.

The first Discovery and Settlement of this Country was by the Procurement of Sir *Walter Raleigh,* in Conjunction with some publick-spirited Gentlemen of that Age, under the Protection of Queen *Elizabeth;* for which Reason it was then named *Virginia,* being begun on that Part called *Ronoak*-Island, where the Ruins of a Fort [Fort Raleigh] are to be seen at this day, as well as some old *English* Coins which have been lately found; and a Brass-Gun, a Powder-Horn, and one small Quarter deck-Gun, made of Iron Staves, and hoop'd with the same Metal; which Method of making Guns might very probably be made use of in those Days, for the Convenience of Infant-Colonies.

A farther Confirmation of this we have from the *Hatteras Indians,* who either then lived on *Ronoak*-Island, or much frequented it. These tell us, that several of their Ancestors were white People, and could talk in a Book [read], as we do; the Truth of which is confirm'd by gray Eyes being found frequently amongst these *Indians,* and no others. They value themselves extremely for their Affinity to the *English,* and are ready to do them all friendly Offices. It is probable, that this Settlement miscarry'd for want of timely Supplies from *England;* or thro' the Treachery of the Natives, for we may reasonably suppose that the *English* were forced to cohabit with them, for Relief and Conversation; and that in process of Time, they conform'd themselves to the Manners of their *Indian* Relations. And thus we see, how apt Humane Nature is to degenerate.

I cannot forbear inserting here, a pleasant Story that passess for an uncontested Truth amongst the Inhabitants of this Place; which is, that the Ship which brought the first Colonies, does often appear amongst them, under Sail, in a gallant Posture, which they call Sir *Walter Raleigh*'s Ship; And the truth of this has been affirm'd to me, by Men of the best Credit in the Country.

A second Settlement of this Country was made about fifty Years ago, in that part we now call *Albemarl*-County, and chiefly in *Chuwon* Precinct, by several substantial Planters, from *Virginia,* and other Plantations; Who finding mild Winters, and a fertile Soil, beyond Expectation, producing every thing that was planted, to a prodigious Increase; their Cattle, Horses, Sheep, and Swine, breeding very fast, and passing the Winter, without any Assistance from the Planter; so that every thing seem'd to come by Nature, the Husbandman living almost void of Care, and free from those Fatigues which are absolutely requisite in Winter-Countries, for providing Fodder and other Necessaries; these Encouragements induc'd them to stand their Ground, altho' but a handful of People, seated at great Distances one from another, and amidst a vast number of *Indians* of different Nations, who were then in *Carolina*. Nevertheless, I say, the Fame of this new-discover'd Summer-Country spread thro' the neighbouring Colonies, and, in a few Years, drew a considerable Number of Families thereto, who all found Land enough to settle themselves in, (had they been many Thousands more) and that which was very good and commodiously seated, both for Profit and Pleasure. And indeed, most of the Plantations in *Carolina* naturally enjoy a noble Prospect of large and spacious Rivers, pleasant Savanna's, and fine Meadows, with their green Liveries, interwoven with beautiful Flowers, of most glorious Colours, which the several Seasons afford; hedg'd in with pleasant Groves of the ever-famous Tulip-tree, the stately Laurel, and Bays, equalizing the Oak in Bigness and Growth; Myrtles, Jessamines, Wood-bines, Honeysuckles, and several other fragrant Vines and Ever-greens, whose aspiring Branches shadow and interweave themselves with the loftiest Timbers, yielding a pleasant Prospect, Shade and Smell, proper Habitations for the Sweet-singing Birds, that melodiously entertain such as travel thro' the Woods of *Carolina*.

The Planters possessing all these Blessings, and the Produce of great Quantities of Wheat and *Indian* Corn, in which this Country is very fruitful, as likewise in Beef, Pork, Tallow, Hides, Deer-Skins, and Furs; for these Commodities the *New-England*-Men and *Bermudians* visited *Carolina* in their Barks and Sloops, and carry'd out what they made, bringing them, in Exchange, Rum, Sugar, Salt, Molosses, and some wearing Apparel, tho' the last at very extravagant Prices.

As the Land is very fruitful, so are the Planters kind and hospitable to all that come to visit them; there being very few House-keepers, but what live very nobly, and give away more Provisions to Coasters and Guests who come to see them, than they expend amongst their own Families.

Of the Inlets and Havens of this Country

The Bar of *Currituck* being the Northermost of this Country, presents itself first to be treated of. It lies in 36 deg. 30 min. and the Course over is S. W. by W. having not above seven or eight Foot on the Bar, tho' a good Harbour, when you are over, where you may ride safe, and deep enough; but this Part of the Sound is so full of Shoals, as not to suffer any thing to trade thro' it, that draws above three Foot Water, which renders it very incommodious. However, this affects but some part of the Country, and may be easily remedied, by carrying their Produce, in small Craft, down to the Vessels, which ride near the Inlet.

Ronoak Inlet has Ten Foot Water; the Course over the Bar is almost W. which leads you thro' the best of the Channel. This Bar, as well as *Currituck,* often shifts by the Violence of the N. E. Storms, both lying expos'd to those Winds. Notwithstanding which, a considerable Trade might be carry'd on, provided there was a Pilot to bring them in; for it lies convenient for a large Part of this Colony, whose Product would very easily allow of that Charge; Lat. 35 deg. 50 min.

The Inlet of *Hatteras* lies to the Westward of the Cape, round which is an excellent Harbour. When the Wind blows hard at N. or N. E. if you keep a small League from the Cape-Point, you will have 3, 4, and 5 Fathom, the outermost Shoals lying about 7 or 8 Leagues from Shoar. As you come into the Inlet, keep close to the South Breakers, till you are over the Bar, where you will have two Fathom at Low-Water. You may come to an Anchor in two Fathom and a Half when you are over, then steer over close aboard the North Shoar, where is four Fathom, close to a Point of March; then steer up the Sound a long League, till you bring the North Cape of the Inlet to bear S. S. E. half E. then steer W. N. W. the East-point of Bluff-Land at *Hatteras* bearing E. N. E. the Southermost large Hammock towards *Ocacock,* bearing S. S. W. half S. then you are in the Sound, over the Bar of Sand, whereon is but 6 Foot Water; then your Course to *Pampticough* is almost West. It flows on these three Bars S. E. by E. 1/4 E. about Eight of the Clock, unless there is a hard Gale of Wind at N. E. which will make it flow two hours longer; but as soon as the Wind is down, the Tides will have their natural Course: A hard Gale at N. or N. W. will make the Water ebb sometimes 24 hours, but still the Tide will ebb and flow, tho' not seen by the turning thereof, but may be seen by the Rising of the Water, and Falling of the same, Lat. 35° 20″.

Ocacock is the best Inlet and Harbour yet in this Country; and has 13 Foot at Low-water upon the Bar. There are two Channels; one is but narrow, and lies close aboard the South Cape; the other in the Middle, *viz.* between the Middle Ground, and the South Shoar, and is above half a Mile wide. The Bar itself is but half a Cable's Length over, and then you are in 7 or 8 Fathom Water; a good Harbour. The Course into the Sound is N. N. W. At High-water, and Neap-tides, here is 18 Foot Water. It lies S. W. from *Hatteras* Inlet. Lat. 35° 8″.

Topsail Inlet is above two Leagues to the Westward of *Cape Look-out*. You have a fair Channel over the Bar, and two Fathom thereon, and a good Harbour in five or six Fathom to come to an Anchor. Your Course over this Bar is almost N. W. Lat. 34° 44″.

As for the Inlet and River of *Cape Fair,* I cannot give you a better Information thereof, than has been already deliver'd by the Gentlemen, who were sent on purpose, from *Barbados,* to make a Discovery of that River, in the Year 1663. which is thus.

From *Tuesday* the 29th of *September,* to *Friday* the 2d of *October,* we rang'd along the Shoar from Lat. 32 deg. 20 min. to Lat. 33 deg. 11 min. but could discern no Entrance for our Ship, after we had pass'd to the Northward of 32 deg. 40 min. On *Saturday, Octob.* 3. a violent Storm overtook us, the Wind between North and East; which Easterly Winds and Foul Weather continu'd till *Monday* the 12th; by reason of which Storms and Foul Weather, we were forced to get off to Sea, to secure Ourselves and Ship, and were driven by the Rapidity of a strong Current to Cape *Hatteras* in Lat. 35 deg. 30 min. On *Monday* the 12th aforesaid, we came to an Anchor in seven Fathom at *Cape-Fair* Road, and took the Meridian Altitude of the Sun, and were in Latitude 33 deg. 43 min. The Wind continuing still easterly, and foul Weather, till *Thursday* the 15th and on *Friday* the 16th, the Wind being at N. W. we weigh'd and sail'd up *Cape-Fair*-River, some 4 or 5 Leagues, and came to an Anchor in 6 or 7 Fathom, at which time several *Indians* came on board, and brought us great Store of fresh Fish, large Mullets, young Bass, Shads, and several other Sorts of very good well-tasted Fish. On *Saturday* the 17th, we went down to the *Cape,* to see the *English* Cattle, but could not find 'em, tho' we rounded the *Cape:* And having an *Indian* Guide with us, here we rode till *Oct.* 24. The Wind being against us, we could not go up the River with our Ship; but went on shoar, and view'd the Land of those Quarters. On *Saturday,* we weigh'd, and sail'd up the River some 4 Leagues, or thereabouts. *Sunday* the 25th, we weigh'd again, and row'd up the River, it being calm, and got up some 14 Leagues from the Harbour's Mouth, where we mor'd our Ship. On *Monday Oct.* the 26th, we went down with the Yawl, to *Necoes,* an *Indian* Plantation, and view'd the Land there. On *Tuesday* the 27th, we row'd up the main River, with our Long-Boat, and 12 Men, some 10

Leagues, or thereabouts. On *Wednesday* the 28th, we row'd up about 8 or 10 Leagues more. *Thursday* the 29th, was foul Weather, with much Rain and Wind, which forc'd us to make Huts, and lie still. *Friday* the 30th, we proceeded up the main River, 7 or 8 Leagues. *Saturday* the 31st, we got up 3 or 4 Leagues more, and came to a Tree that lay cross the River; but because our Provisions were almost spent, we proceeded no farther, but return'd downward before Night, and on *Monday* the 2d of *November,* we came aboard our Ship. *Tuesday* the 3d, we lay still, to refresh ourselves. On *Wednesday* the 4th, we went 5 or 6 Leagues up the River, to search a Branch that run out of the main River towards the N. W. In which Branch we went up 5 or 6 Leagues; but not liking the Land, return'd on board that Night about Midnight, and call'd that Place *Swampy-Branch. Thursday, November* the 5th, we stay'd aboard. On *Friday* the 6th, we went up *Greens-River,* the Mouth of it being against the Place at which rode our Ship. On *Saturday* the 7th, we proceeded up the said River, some 14 or 15 Leagues in all, and found it ended in several small Branches; The Land, for the most part, being marshy and Swamps, we return'd towards our Ship, and got aboard it in the Night. *Sunday November* the 8th, we lay still, and on *Monday* the 9th, went again up the main River, being well stock'd with Provisions, and all things necessary, and proceeded upwards till *Thursday* noon, the 12th, at which time we came to a Place, where were two Islands in the Middle of the River; and by reason of the Crookedness of the River at that Place, several Trees lay cross both Branches, which stop'd the Passage of each Branch, so that we could proceed no farther with our Boat; but went up the River side by Land, some 3 or 4 Miles, and found the River wider and wider. So we return'd, leaving it, as far as we could see up a long Reach, running N. E. we judging ourselves near fifty Leagues North from the River's Mouth. In our Return, we view'd the Land on both Sides the River, and found as good Tracts of dry, well-wooded, pleasant, and delightful Ground, as we have seen any where in the World, with abundance of long thick Grass on it, the Land being very level, with steep Banks on both Sides the River, and in some Places very high, the Woods stor'd every where, and great Numbers of Deer and Turkies, we never going on Shoar, but we saw of each Sort; as also great Store of Partridges, Cranes, and Conies, in several Places; we likewise heard several Wolves howling in the Woods, and saw where they had torn a Deer in

Pieces. Also in the River we saw great Store of Ducks, Teal, Widgeon; and in the Woods, great Flocks of Parrakeeto's. The Timber that the Woods afford, for the most part, consists of Oaks of four or five Sorts, all differing in Leaves, but each bearing very good Acorns. We measur'd many of the Oaks in several Places, which we found to be, in Bigness, some Two, some Three, and others almost Four Fathom in Height, before you come to Boughs or Limbs; forty, fifty, sixty Foot, and some more; and those Oaks very common in the upper Parts of both Rivers; also a very tall large Tree of great Bigness, which some call *Cyprus*, the right Name we know not, growing in Swamps. Likewise Walnut, Birch, Beech, Maple, Ash, Bay, Willow, Alder, and Holly; in the lowermost Parts innumerable Pines, tall and good for Boards or Masts, growing, for the most part, in barren and sandy, but in some Places up the River, in good Ground, being mixt amongst Oaks and other Timbers. We saw Mulberry-Trees, Multitudes of Grape-Vines, and some Grapes which we eat of. We found a very large and good Tract of Land, on the N. W. Side of the River, thin of Timber, except here and there a very great Oak, and full of Grass, commonly as high as a Man's Middle, and in many Places to his Shoulders, where we saw many Deer, and Turkies; one Deer having very large Horns, and great Body, therefore call'd it *Stag-Park*. It being a very pleasant and delightful Place, we travell'd in it several Miles, but saw no End thereof. So we return'd to our Boat, and proceeded down the River, and came to another Place, some twenty five Leagues from the River's Mouth on the same Side, where we found a Place, no less delightful than the former; and as far as we could judge, both Tracts came into one. This lower Place we call'd *Rocky Point*, because we found many Rocks and Stones, of several Sizes, upon the Land, which is not common. We sent our Boat down the River before us; ourselves travelling by Land, many Miles. Indeed we were so much taken with the Pleasantness of the Country, that we travell'd into the Woods too far to recover our Boat and Company that Night. The next day being *Sunday,* we got to our Boat; and on *Monday* the 16th of *November,* proceeded down to a Place on the East-Side of the River, some 23 Leagues from the Harbour's Mouth, which we call'd *Turky-Quarters,* because we kill'd several Turkies thereabouts; we view'd the Land there, and found some Tracts of good Ground, and high, facing upon the River about one Mile inward, but backwards some two Miles, all Pine Land, but good Pasture Ground: We return'd to our Boat, and proceeded down some 2 or 3 Leagues, where we had formerly view'd, and found it a Tract of as good Land, as any we have seen, and had as good Timber on it. The Banks on the River being high, therefore we call'd it *High-Land-Point*. Having view'd that, we proceeded down the River, going on Shoar in several Places on both Sides, it being generally large Marshes, and many of them dry, that they may more fitly be call'd Meadows. The Wood-Land against them is, for the most part, Pine, and in some Places as barren, as ever we saw Land, but in other Places good Pasture-Ground. On *Tuesday, November* the 17th, we got aboard our Ship, riding against the Mouth of *Green*'s River, where our Men were providing Wood, and fitting the Ship for the Sea: In the interim, we took a View of the Country on both sides of the River there, finding some good Land, but more bad, and the best not comparable to that above. *Friday* the 20th was foul Weather; yet in the Afternoon we weigh'd, went down the River about two Leagues, and came to an Anchor against the Mouth of *Hilton*'s River, and took a View of the Land there on both sides, which appear'd to us much like that at *Green*'s River. *Monday* the 23d, we went, with our Long-Boat well victuall'd and mann'd, up *Hilton*'s River; and when we came three Leagues, or thereabouts, up the same, we found this and *Green*'s River to come into one, and so continu'd for four or five Leagues, which makes a great Island betwixt them. We proceeded still up the River, till they parted again, keeping up *Hilton*'s River on the Larboard side, and follow'd the said River five or six Leagues farther, where we found another large Branch of *Green*'s River to come into *Hilton*'s, which makes another great Island. On the Starboard side going up, we proceeded still up the River some four Leagues, and return'd, taking a View of the Land on both sides, and then judg'd ourselves to be from our Ship some 18 Leagues W. and by N. One League below this Place, came four *Indians* in a Canoe to us, and sold us several Baskets of Acorns, which we satisfy'd them for, and so left them; but one of them follow'd us on the Shoar some two or three Miles, till he came on the Top of a high Bank, facing on the River; and as we row'd underneath it, the Fellow shot an Arrow at us, which very narrowly miss'd one of our Men, and stuck in the upper edge of the Boat; but broke in pieces, leaving the Head behind. Hereupon, we presently made to the Shoar, and

went all up the Bank (except Four to guide the Boat) to look
for the *Indian*, but could not find him: At last, we heard some
sing, farther in the Woods, which we look'd upon as a Challenge
to us, to come and fight them. We went towards them with all
Speed; but before we came in Sight of them, heard two Guns
go off from our Boat; whereupon we retreated, as fast as we
could, to secure our Boat and Men. When we came to them, we
found all well, and demanded the Reason of their firing the Guns:
They told us, that an *Indian* came creeping along the Bank, as
they suppos'd, to shoot at them; and therefore they shot at him at
a great distance, with small Shot, but thought they did him no
Hurt; for they saw him run away. Presently after our Return to
the Boat, and while we were thus talking, came two *Indians* to
us, with their Bows and Arrows, crying *Bonny, Bonny*. We took
their Bows and Arrows from them, and gave them Beads, to
their Content; then we led them, by the Hand, to the Boat, and
shew'd them the Arrow-head sticking in her Side, and related
to them the whole Passage; which when they understood, both
of them shew'd a great Concern, and signify'd to us, by Signs, that
they knew nothing of it; so we let them go, and mark'd a Tree on
the Top of the Bank, calling the Place *Mount-Skerry*. We look'd
up the River, as far as we could discern, and saw that it widen'd,
and came running directly down the Country: So we return'd,
viewing the Land on both sides the River, and finding the Banks
steep in some places, but very high in others. The Bank-sides
are generally Clay, and as some of our Company did affirm, some
Marl. The Land and Timber up this River is no way inferiour
to the best in the other, which we call the main River. So far as
we could discern, this seem'd as fair, if not fairer, than the former,
and we think runs farther into the Country, because a strong
Current comes down, and a great deal more Drift-Wood. But,
to return to the Business of the Land and Timber: We saw several
Plots of Ground clear'd by the *Indians,* after their weak manner,
compass'd round with great Timber Trees, which they are no-wise
able to fell, and so keep the Sun from Corn-Fields very much; yet
nevertheless, we saw as large Corn-stalks, or larger, than we have
seen any where else: So we proceeded down the River, till we found
the Canoe the *Indian* was in, who shot at us. In the Morning, we
went on Shoar, and cut the same in pieces. The *Indians* perceiving
us coming towards them, ran away. Going to his Hutt, we pull'd it
down, broke his Pots, Platters, and Spoons, tore the Deer-Skins and

Matts in pieces, and took away a Basket of Acorns; and afterwards proceeded down the River 2 Leagues, or thereabouts, and came to another Place of *Indians*, bought Acorns and some Corn of them, and went downwards 2 Leagues more. At last, espying an *Indian* peeping over a high Bank, we held up a Gun at him; and calling to him, *Skerry*, presently several *Indians* came in Sight of us, and made great Signs of Friendship, saying *Bonny*, *Bonny*. Then running before us, they endeavour'd to persuade us to come on shoar; but we answer'd them with stern Countenances, and call'd out, *Skerry*, taking up our Guns, and threatning to shoot at them, but they still cry'd *Bonny*, *Bonny*: And when they saw they could not prevail, nor persuade us to come on shoar, two of them came off to us in a Canoe, one paddling with a great Cane, the other with his Hand. As soon as they overtook us, they laid hold of our Boat, sweating and blowing, and told us, it was *Bonny* on shoar, and at last persuaded us to go on shoar with them. As soon as we landed, several *Indians*, to the Number of near 40 lusty Men, came to us, all in a great Sweat, and told us *Bonny:* We shew'd 'em the Arrow-Head in the Boat-Side, and a Piece of the Canoe we had cut in Pieces: Whereupon, the chief Man amongst them made a long Speech, threw Beads into our Boat, which is a Sign of great Love and Friendship, and gave us to understand, that when he heard of the Affront which we had receiv'd, it caus'd him to cry; and that he and his Men were come to make Peace with us, assuring us, by Signs, that they would tye the Arms, and cut off the Head, of the Fellow who had done us that Wrong; And for a farther Testimony of their Love and Good-Will towards us, they presented us with two very handsome, proper, young *Indian* Women, the tallest that ever we saw in this Country; which we suppos'd to be the King's Daughters, or Persons of Distinction amongst them. Those young Women were so ready to come into our Boat; that one of them crowded in, and would hardly be persuaded to go out again. We presented the King with a Hatchet and several Beads, and made Presents of Beads also to the young Women, the chief Men, and the rest of the *Indians*, as far as our Beads would go. They promis'd us, in four Days, to come on board our Ship, and so departed from us. When we left the Place, which was soon after, we call'd it *Mount-Bonny*, because we had there concluded a firm Peace. Proceeding down the River 2 or 3 Leagues farther, we came to a Place where were

9 or 10 Canoes all together. We went ashoar there, and found several *Indians;* but most of them were the same which had made Peace with us before. We staid very little at that Place, but went directly down the River, and came to our Ship, before day. *Thursday* the 26th of *November,* the Wind being at South, we could not go down to the River's Mouth; but on *Friday* the 27th, we weigh'd at the Mouth of *Hilton's* River, and got down a League towards the Harbour's Mouth. On *Sunday* the 29th, we got down to *Crane-Island,* which is 4 Leagues or thereabouts, above the Entrance of the Harbour's Mouth. On *Tuesday* the 1st of *December,* we made a Purchase of the River and Land of *Cape-Fair,* of *Wat-Coosa,* and such other *Indians,* as appear'd to us to be the chief of those Parts. They brought us Store of fresh Fish aboard, as Mullets, Shads, and other sorts very good. This River is all fresh Water, fit to drink. Some 8 Leagues within the Mouth, the Tide runs up about 35 Leagues, but stops and rises a great deal farther up. It flows at the Harbour's Mouth, S. E. and N. W. 6 Foot at Neap-Tides, and 8 Foot at Spring-Tides. The Channel on the East side, by the *Cape*-Shoar, is the best, and lies close aboard the *Cape*-Land, being 3 Fathoms at high Water, in the shallowest Place in the Channel, just at the Entrance; But as soon as you are past that Place, half a Cables Length inward, you have 6 or 7 Fathoms, a fair turning Channel into the River, and so continuing 5 or 6 Leagues upwards. Afterwards the Channel is more difficult, in some Places 6 or 7 Fathoms, in others 4 or 5, and in others but 9 or 10 Foot, especially where the River is broad. When the River comes to part, and grows narrow, there it is all Channel from side to side, in most Places; tho' in some you shall have 5, 6, or 7 Fathoms, but generally 2 or 3, Sand and Oaze. We view'd the *Cape*-Land, and judg'd it to be little worth, the Woods of it being shrubby and low, and the Land sandy and barren; in some Places Grass and Rushes, in others nothing but clear Sand: A Place fitter to starve Cattle, in our Judgment, than to keep 'em alive; yet the *Indians,* as we understand, keep the *English* Cattle down there, and suffer them not to go off of the said *Cape,* (as we suppose) because the Country *Indians* shall have no Part with them; and therefore 'tis likely, they have fallen out about them, which shall have the greatest Share. They brought on board our Ship very good and fat Beef several times, which they sold us at a very reasonable Price; also fat and very large Swine, good and cheap; but they may

thank their Friends of *New-England,* who brought their Hogs to so fair a Market. Some of the *Indians* brought very good Salt aboard us, and made Signs, pointing to both sides of the River's Mouth, that there was great Store thereabouts. We saw up the River, several good Places for the setting up of Corn or Saw-Mills. In that time, as our Business call'd us up and down the River and Branches, we kill'd of wild Fowl, 4 Swans, 10 Geese, 29 Cranes, 10 Turkies, 40 Ducks and Mallards, 3 dozen of Parrakeeto's, and 6 dozen of other small Fowls, as Curlues and Plover, &c.

Whereas there was a Writing left in a Post, at the Point of *Cape-Fair* River, by those *New-England*-Men, that left Cattle with the *Indians* there, the Contents whereof tended not only to the Disparagement of the Land about the said River, but also to the great Discouragement of all such as should hereafter come into those Parts to settle: In answer to that scandalous Writing, We, whose Names are underwritten, do affirm, That we have seen, facing both sides the River and Branches of *Cape-Fair* aforesaid, as good Land, and as well timber'd, as any we have seen in any other Part of the World, sufficient to accommodate Thousands of our *English* Nation, and lying commodiously by the said River's Side.

On *Friday* the 4th of *December,* the Wind being fair, we put out to Sea, bound for *Barbados;* and, on the 6th of *February,* 1663¾, came to an Anchor in *Carlisle*-Bay; it having pleas'd God, after several apparent Dangers both by Sea and Land, to bring us all in Safety to our long-wish'd-for and much-desir'd Port, to render an Account of our Discovery; the Verity of which we do assert.

> *Anthony Long*
> *William Hilton* [81]
> *Peter Fabian*

Thus you have an Account of the Latitude, Soil, and Advantages of *Cape-Fair,* or *Clarendon*-River, which was settled in the Year 1661, or thereabouts; and had it not been for the irregular Practices of some of that Colony against the *Indians,*

81. William Hilton, commander of the *Adventure,* accompanied by Long and Fabian, sailed from Spikes Bay, Barbados, on August 10, 1663. This group explored the Carolina coast southward from Cape Fear to the thirty-first parallel. The next year Hilton published his *A Relation of a Discovery Lately made on the Coast of Florida.* See A. S. Salley, *Narratives of Early Carolina,* 1650–1780 (New York, 1911), pp. 37–61.

by sending away some of their Children, (as I have been told) under Pretence of instructing 'em in Learning, and the Principles of the Christian Religion; which so disgusted the *Indians*, that tho' they had then no Guns, yet they never gave over, till they had entirely rid themselves of the *English*, by their Bows and Arrows; with which they did not only take off themselves, but also their Stocks of Cattle; And this was so much the more ruinous to them, in that they could have no Assistance from South-*Carolina*, which was not then planted; and the other Plantations were but in their Infancy. Were it not for such ill Practices, I say, it might, in all Probability, have been, at this day, the best Settlement in their Lordships great Province of *Carolina*.

The Sound of *Albemarl*, with the Rivers and Creeks of that Country, afford a very rich and durable Soil. The Land, in most Places, lies indifferent low, (except in *Chuwon*, and high up the Rivers) but bears an incredible Burden of Timber; the Low-Grounds being cover'd with Beech; and the High-Land yielding lofty Oaks, Walnut-Trees, and other useful Timber. The Country, in some Plantations, has yearly produc'd *Indian* Corn, or some other Grain, ever since this Country was first seated, without the Trouble of Manuring or Dressing; and yet (to all appearance) it seems not to be, in the least, impoverish'd, neither do the Planters ever miss of a good Crop, unless a very unnatural Season visits them, which seldom happens.

Of the Corn of Carolina

The Wheat of this Place is very good, seldom yielding less than thirty fold, provided the Land is good where it is sown; Not but that there has been Sixty-six Increase for one measure sown in Piny-Land, which we account the meanest Sort. And I have been inform'd, by People of Credit, that Wheat which was planted in a very rich Piece of Land, brought a hundred and odd Pecks, for one. If our Planters, when they found such great Increase, would be so curious as to make nice Observations of the Soil, and other remarkable Accidents, they would soon be acquainted with the Nature of the Earth and Climate, and be better qualified to manage their Agriculture to more Certainty, and greater Advantage; whereby they might arrive to the Crops and Harvests of *Babylon*, and those other fruitful

Countries so much talk'd of. For I must confess, I never saw one Acre of Land manag'd as it ought to be in *Carolina*, since I knew it; and were they as negligent in their Husbandry in *Europe*, as they are in *Carolina*, their Land would produce nothing but Weeds and Straw.

They have try'd Rye, and it thrives very well; but having such Plenty of Maiz, they do not regard it, because it makes black Bread, unless very curiously handled.

Barley has been sowed in small quantities, and does better than can be expected; because that Grain requires the Ground to be very well work'd with repeated Ploughings, which our general Way of breaking the Earth with Hoes, can, by no means, perform, tho' in several Places we have a light, rich, deep, black Mould, which is the particular Soil in which Barley best thrives.

The naked Oats thrive extraordinary well; and the other would prove a very bold Grain; but the Plenty of other Grains makes them not much coveted.

The *Indian* Corn, or *Maiz*, proves the most useful Grain in the World; and had it not been for the Fruitfulness of this Species, it would have proved very difficult to have settled some of the Plantations in *America*. It is very nourishing, whether in Bread, sodden, or otherwise; And those poor Christian Servants in *Virginia, Maryland,* and the other northerly Plantations, that have been forced to live wholly upon it, do manifestly prove, that it is the most nourishing Grain, for a Man to subsist on, without any other Victuals. And this Assertion is made good by the *Negro*-Slaves, who, in many Places, eat nothing but this *Indian* Corn and Salt. Pigs and Poultry fed with this Grain, eat the sweetest of all others. It refuses no Grounds, unless the barren Sands, and when planted in good Ground, will repay the Planter seven or eight hundred fold; besides the Stalks bruis'd and boil'd, make very pleasant Beer, being sweet like the Sugar-Cane.

There are several sorts of Rice, some bearded, others not, besides the red and white; But the white Rice is the best. Yet there is a sort of perfum'd Rice in the *East-Indies*, which gives a curious Flavour, in the Dressing. And with this sort *America* is not yet acquainted; neither can I learn, that any of it has been brought over to *Europe;* the Rice of *Carolina* being esteem'd the best that comes to that Quarter of the World. It is of great Increase, yielding from eight hundred to a thousand-fold, and thrives best in wild Land, that has never been broken up before.

Buck-Wheat is of great Increase in *Carolina;* but we make no other use of it, than instead of Maiz, to feed Hogs and Poultry: And *Guinea* Corn, which thrives well here, serves for the same use.

Of the Pulse-kind, we have many sorts. The first is the Bushel-Bean, which is a spontaneous Product. They are so called, because they bring a Bushel of Beans for one that is planted. They are set in the Spring, round Arbours, or at the Feet of Poles, up which they will climb, and cover the Wattling, making a very pretty Shade to sit under. They continue flowering, budding, and ripening all the Summer long, till the Frost approaches, when they forbear their Fruit, and die. The Stalks they grow on, come to the Thickness of a Man's Thumb; and the Bean is white and mottled, with a purple Figure on each side it, like an Ear. They are very flat, and are eaten as the *Windsor*-Bean is, being an extraordinary well-relish'd Pulse, either by themselves, or with Meat.

We have the *Indian Rounceval,* or *Miraculous Pease,* so call'd from their long Pods, and great Increase. These are latter Pease, and require a pretty long Summer to ripen in. They are very good; and so are the *Bonavis, Calavancies, Nanticokes,* and abundance of other Pulse, too tedious here to name, which we found the *Indians* possess'd of, when first we settled in *America;* some of which sorts afford us two Crops in one Year; as the *Bonavis* and *Calavancies,* besides several others of that kind.

Now I am launch'd into a Discourse of the Pulse, I must acquaint you, that the *European* Bean planted here, will, in time, degenerate into a dwarfish sort, if not prevented by a yearly Supply of foreign Seed, and an extravagant rich Soil; yet these Pigmy-Beans are the sweetest of that kind I ever met withal.

As for all the sorts of *English* Pease that we have yet made tryal of, they thrive very well in *Carolina.* Particularly, the white and gray *Rouncival,* the common *Field-Pease,* and *Sickle-Pease* yield very well, and are of a good Relish. As for the other sorts, I have not seen any made tryal of as yet, but question not their coming to great Perfection with us.

The Kidney-Beans were here before the *English* came, being very plentiful in the *Indian* Corn-Fields.

The Garden-Roots that thrive well in *Carolina,* are Carrots, Leeks, Parsnips, Turneps, Potatoes, of several delicate sorts,

Ground Artichokes, Radishes, Horse-Radish, Beet, both sorts, Onions, Shallot, Garlick, Cives, [chives] and the Wild-Onions.

Of The Herbs of Carolina

The Sallads are the Lettice, Curl'd, Red, Cabbage, and *Savoy.* The Spinage round and prickly, Fennel, sweet and the common Sort, Samphire in the Marshes excellent, so is the Dock or Wild-Rhubarb, Rocket, Sorrel, *French* and *English,* Cresses of several Sorts, Purslain wild, and that of a larger Size which grows in the Gardens; for this Plant is never met withal in the *Indian* Plantations, and is, therefore, suppos'd to proceed from Cow-Dung, which Beast they keep not. Parsley two Sorts; Asparagus thrives to a Miracle, without hot Beds or dunging the Land, White-Cabbage from *European* or *New-England* Seed, for the People are negligent and unskilful, and don't take care to provide Seed of their own. The Colly-Flower we have not yet had an Opportunity to make Tryal of, nor has the Artichoke ever appear'd amongst us, that I can learn. Coleworts plain and curl'd, *Savoys;* besides the Water-Melons of several Sorts, very good, which should have gone amongst the Fruits. Of Musk-Melons we have very large and good, and several Sorts, as the Golden, Green, Guinea, and Orange. Cucumbers long, short, and prickly, all these from the Natural Ground, and great Increase, without any Helps of Dung or Reflection. Pompions yellow and very large, Burmillions, Cashaws, [cushaws, crook neck squash] an excellent Fruit boil'd; Squashes, Simnals [simling], Horns, and Gourds; besides many other Species, of less Value, too tedious to name.

Our Pot-herbs and others of use, which we already possess, are Angelica wild and tame, Balm, Bugloss, Borage, Burnet, Clary, Marigold, Pot-Marjoram, and other Marjorams, Summer and Winter Savory, Columbines, Tansey, Wormwood, Nep [catnip], Mallows several Sorts, Drage [dredge, a spice] red and white, Lambs Quarters, Thyme, Hyssop of a very large Growth, sweet Bazil, Rosemary, Lavender: The more Physical, are *Carduus Benedictus,* the Scurvy-grass of *America,* I never here met any of the *European* sort; *Tobacco* of many sorts, Dill, Carawa, Cummin, Anise, Coriander, all sorts of Plantain of *England,* and two sorts spontaneous, good Vulneraries; Elecampane, Comfrey, Nettle, the Seed from *England,* none Native; Monks Rhubarb, [species of dock, not garden rhubarb] Burdock, Asarum wild in the Woods, reckon'd one of the Snake-Roots; Poppies in the Garden, none wild yet discover'd; Wormseed, Feverfew, Rue, Ground-Ivy spontaneous, but very small and scarce, *Aurea virga,* four sorts of Snake-Roots, besides the common Species, which are great Antidotes against that Serpent's Bite, and are easily rais'd in the Garden; Mint; *James-Town*-Weed, so called from *Virginia,* the Seed it bears is very like that of an Onion; it is excellent for curing Burns, and asswaging Inflammations, but taken inwardly brings on a sort of drunken Madness. One of our Marsh-Weeds, like a Dock, has the same Effect, and possesses the Party with Fear and Watchings. The Red-Root whose Leaf is like Spear-Mint, is good for Thrushes and sore Mouths; Camomil, but it must be kept in the Shade, otherwise it will not thrive; Housleek first from *England;* Vervin; Night-Shade, several kinds; Harts-Tongue; Yarrow abundance, Mullein the same, both of the Country; Sarsaparilla, and abundance more I could name, yet not the hundredth part of what remains, a Catalogue of which is a Work of many Years, and without any other Subject, would swell to a large Volume, and requires the Abilities of a skilful Botanist: Had not the ingenious Mr. *Banister*[82] (the greatest *Virtuoso* we ever had on the Continent) been unfortunately taken out of this World, he would have given the best Account of the Plants of *America,* of any that ever yet made such an Attempt in these Parts. Not but we are satisfy'd, the Species of Vegetables in *Carolina,* are so numerous, that it requires more than one Man's Age to bring the chiefest Part of them into regular Classes; the Country being so different in its Situation and Soil, that what one place plentifully affords, another is absolutely a stranger to; yet we generally observe, that the greatest Variety is found in the Low Grounds, and Savanna's.

The Flower-Garden in *Carolina* is as yet arriv'd but to a very poor and jejune Perfection. We have only two sorts of Roses; the Clove-July [clove-gilly]-Flowers, Violets, Princes Feather, and *Tres Colores.* There has been nothing more cultivated in the

82. The Reverend John Banister (1650—May, 1692) was sent to Virginia by Bishop Henry Compton, the "Maecenas of botany." Banister collected many botanical specimens, not only for Compton's garden at Fulham Palace, but for several people in London interested in botany. Lawson must have been familiar with Banister's *Catalogus Plantarum in Virginia Observatarum* (1686) and other writings of Banister published in John Ray, *Historia Plantarum* (1704).

Flower-Garden, which, at present, occurs to my Memory; but as for the wild spontaneous Flowers of this Country, Nature has been so liberal, that I cannot name one tenth part of the valuable ones; And since, to give Specimens, would only swell the Volume, and give little Satisfaction to the Reader, I shall therefore proceed to the *Present State of Carolina,* and refer the Shrubs and other Vegetables of larger Growth, till hereafter, and then shall deliver them and the other Species in their Order.

THE

PRESENT STATE

OF

Carolina

WHEN we consider the Latitude and convenient Situation
of *Carolina,* had we no farther Confirmation thereof,
our Reason would inform us, that such a Place lay fairly to be
a delicious Country, being placed in that Girdle of the World
which affords Wine, Oil, Fruit, Grain, and Silk, with other rich
Commodities, besides a sweet Air, moderate Climate, and
fertile Soil; these are the Blessings (under Heaven's Protection)
that spin out the Thread of Life to its utmost Extent, and
crown our Days with the Sweets of Health and Plenty, which,
when join'd with Content, renders the Possessors the happiest
Race of Men upon Earth.

The Inhabitants of *Carolina,* thro' the Richness of the Soil,
live an easy and pleasant Life. The Land being of several sorts of
Compost, some stiff, others light, some marl, others rich black
Mould; here barren of Pine, but affording Pitch, Tar, and
Masts; there vastly rich, especially on the Freshes of the Rivers,
one part bearing great Timbers, others being Savanna's or
natural Meads, where no Trees grow for several Miles, adorn'd
by Nature with a pleasant Verdure, and beautiful Flowers,
frequent in no other Places, yielding abundance of Herbage for
Cattle, Sheep, and Horse. The Country in general affords
pleasant Seats, the Land (except in some few Places) being dry
and high Banks, parcell'd out into most convenient Necks, (by
the Creeks) easy to be fenced in for securing their Stocks to more
strict Boundaries, whereby, with a small trouble of fencing,

almost every Man may enjoy, to himself, an entire Plantation, or rather Park. These, with the other Benefits of Plenty of Fish, Wild-Fowl, Venison, and the other Conveniencies which this Summer-Country naturally furnishes, has induc'd a great many Families to leave the more Northerly Platations, and sit down under one of the mildest Governments in the World; in a Country that, with moderate Industry, will afford all the Necessaries of Life. We have yearly abundance of Strangers come among us, who chiefly strive to go Southerly to settle, because there is a vast Tract of rich Land betwixt the Place we are seated in, and *Cape-Fair,* and upon that River, and more Southerly, which is inhabited by none but a few *Indians,* who are at this time well affected to the *English,* and very desirous of their coming to live among them. The more Southerly, the milder Winters, with the Advantages of purchasing the Lords Land at the most easy and moderate Rate of any Lands in *America,* nay (allowing all Advantages thereto annex'd) I may say, the Universe does not afford such another; Besides, Men have a great Advantage of choosing good and commodious Tracts of Land at the first Seating of a Country or River, whereas the later Settlers are forced to purchase smaller Dividends of the old Standers [residents], and sometimes at very considerable Rates; as now in *Virginia* and *Maryland,* where a thousand Acres of good Land cannot be bought under twenty Shillings an Acre, besides two Shillings yearly Acknowledgment for every hundred Acres; which Sum, be it more or less, will serve to put the Merchant or Planter here into a good posture of Buildings, Slaves, and other Necessaries, when the Purchase of his Land comes to him on such easy Terms. And as our Grain and Pulse thrives with us to admiration, no less do our Stocks of Cattle, Horses, Sheep, and Swine multiply.

The Beef of *Carolina* equalizes the best that our neighbouring Colonies afford; the Oxen are of a great size when they are suffer'd to live to a fit Age. I have seen fat and good Beef at all times of the Year, but *October* and the cool Months are the Seasons we kill our Beeves in, when we intend them for Salting or Exportation; for then they are in their prime of Flesh, all coming from Grass, we never using any other Food for our Cattle. The Heifers bring Calves at eighteen or twenty Months old, which makes such a wonderful Increase, that many of our Planters, from very mean Beginnings, have rais'd themselves, and are now Masters of hundreds of fat Beeves, and other Cattle.

The Veal is very good and white, so is the Milk very pleasant and rich, there being, at present, considerable Quantities of Butter and Cheese made, that is very good, not only serving our own Necessities, but we send out a great deal among our Neighbours.

The Sheep thrive very well at present, having most commonly two Lambs at one yeaning: As the Country comes to be open'd, they prove still better, Change of Pasture being agreeable to that useful Creature. Mutton is (generally) exceeding Fat, and of a good Relish; their Wool is very fine, and proves a good Staple.

The Horses are well-shap'd and swift; the best of them would sell for ten or twelve Pounds in *England*. They prove excellent Drudges, and will travel incredible Journeys. They are troubled with very few Distempers, neither do the cloudy-fac'd grey Horses go blind here, as in *Europe*. As for *Spavins, Splints,* and *Ring-Bones,* they are here never met withal, as I can learn. Were we to have our Stallions and choice of Mares from *England,* or any other of a good Sort, and careful to keep them on the Highlands, we could not fail of a good Breed; but having been supply'd with our first Horses from the neighbouring Plantations, which were but mean, they do not as yet come up to the Excellency of the *English* Horses; tho' we generally find, that the Colt exceeds, in Beauty and Strength, its Sire and Dam.

The Pork exceeds any in *Europe;* the great Diversity and Goodness of the Acorns and Nuts which the Woods afford, making that Flesh of an excellent Taste, and produces great Quantities; so that *Carolina* (if not the chief) is not inferior, in this one Commodity, to any Colony in the hands of the *English*.

As for Goats, they have been found to thrive and increase well, but being mischievous to Orchards and other Trees, makes People decline keeping them.

Our Produce for Exportation to *Europe* and the Islands in *America,* are Beef, Pork, Tallow, Hides, Deer-Skins, Furs, Pitch, Tar, Wheat, *Indian*-Corn, Pease, Masts, Staves, Heading, Boards, and all sorts of Timber and Lumber for *Madera* and the *West-Indies;* Rozin, Turpentine, and several sorts of Gums and Tears, with some medicinal Drugs, are here produc'd; Besides Rice, and several other foreign Grains, which thrive very well. Good Bricks and Tiles are made, and several sorts of useful Earths, as Bole, Fullers-Earth, Oaker, and Tobacco-pipe-Clay, in great plenty;

Earths for the Potters Trade, and fine Sand for the Glass-makers. In building with Bricks, we make our Lime of Oyster-Shells, tho' we have great Store of Lime-stone, towards the Heads of our Rivers, where are Stones of all sorts that are useful, besides vast Quantities of excellent Marble. Iron-Stone we have plenty of, both in the Low-Grounds and on the Hills; Lead and Copper has been found, so has Antimony heretofore; But no Endeavours have been us'd to discover those Subteraneous Species; otherwise we might, in all probability, find out the best of Minerals, which are not wanting in *Carolina*. Hot Baths we have an account of from the *Indians* that frequent the Hill-Country, where a great likelihood appears of making Salt-peter, because the Earth, in many places, is strongly mix'd with a nitrous Salt, which is much coveted by the Beasts, who come at some Seasons in great Droves and Herds, and by their much licking of this Earth, make great Holes in those Banks, which sometimes lie at the heads of great Precipices, where their Eagerness after this Salt hastens their End, by falling down the high Banks, so that they are dash'd in Pieces. It must be confess'd, that the most noble and sweetest Part of this Country, is not inhabited by any but the Savages; and a great deal of the richest Part thereof, has no Inhabitants but the Beasts of the Wilderness: For, the *Indians* are not inclinable to settle in the richest Land, because the Timbers are too large for them to cut down, and too much burthen'd with Wood for their Labourers to make Plantations of; besides, the Healthfulness of those Hills is apparent, by the Gigantick Stature, and Gray-Heads, so common amongst the Savages that dwell near the Mountains. The great Creator of all things, having most wisely diffus'd his Blessings, by parcelling out the Vintages of the World, into such Lots, as his wonderful Foresight saw most proper, requisite, and convenient for the Habitations of his Creatures. Towards the Sea, we have the Conveniency of Trade, Transportation, and other Helps the Water affords; but oftentimes, those Advantages are attended with indifferent Land, a thick Air, and other Inconveniences; when backwards, near the Mountains, you meet with the richest Soil, a sweet, thin Air, dry Roads, pleasant small murmuring Streams, and several beneficial Productions and Species, which are unknown in the *European* World. One Part of this Country affords what the other is wholly a Stranger to.

We have *Chalybeate* Waters of several Tastes and different

Qualities; some purge, others work by the other Emunctories. We have, amongst the Inhabitants, a Water, that is, inwardly, a great Apersive, and, outwardly, cures Ulcers, Tettars, and Sores, by washing therewith.

There has been a Coal-Mine lately found near the *Mannakin* Town, above the Falls of *James*-River in *Virginia*, which proves very good, and is us'd by the *Smiths*, for their Forges; and we need not doubt of the same amongst us, towards the Heads of our Rivers; but the Plenty of Wood (which is much the better Fuel) makes us not inquisitive after Coal-Mines. Most of the *French*, who lived at that Town on *James*-River, are remov'd to *Trent*-River, in *North-Carolina*, where the rest were expected daily to come to them, when I came away, which was in *August, 1708.* They are much taken with the Pleasantness of that Country, and, indeed, are a very industrious People. At present, they make very good Linnen-Cloath and Thread, and are very well vers'd in cultivating Hemp and Flax, of both which they raise very considerable Quantities; and design to try an Essay of the Grape, for making of Wine.

As for those of our own Country in *Carolina*, some of the Men are very laborious, and make great Improvements in their Way; but I dare hardly give 'em that Character in general. The easy Way of living in that plentiful Country, makes a great many Planters very negligent, which, were they otherwise, that Colony might now have been in a far better Condition than it is, (as to Trade, and other Advantages) which an universal Industry would have led them into.

The Women are the most industrious Sex in that Place, and, by their good Houswifry, make a great deal of Cloath of their own Cotton, Wool and Flax; some of them keeping their Families (though large) very decently apparel'd, both with Linnens and Woollens, so that they have no occasion to run into the Merchant's Debt, or lay their Money out on Stores for Cloathing.

The *Christian* Natives of *Carolina* are a straight, clean-limb'd People; the Children being seldom or never troubled with Rickets, or those other Distempers, that the *Europeans* are visted withal. 'Tis next to a Miracle, to see one of them deform'd in Body. The Vicinity of the Sun makes Impression on the Men, who labour out of doors, or use the Water. As for those Women, that do not expose themselves to the Weather, they are often very fair, and generally as well featur'd, as you shall see any where, and have very brisk charming Eyes, which sets them off to Advantage. They marry very young; some at Thirteen or Fourteen; and She that stays till Twenty, is reckon'd a stale Maid; which is a very indifferent Character in that warm Country. The Women are very fruitful; most Houses being full of Little Ones. It has been observ'd, that Women long marry'd, and without Children, in other Places, have remov'd to *Carolina,* and become joyful Mothers. They have very easy Travail in their Child-bearing, in which they are so happy, as seldom to miscarry. Both Sexes are generally spare of Body, and not Cholerick, nor easily cast down at Disappointments and Losses, seldom immoderately grieving at Misfortunes, unless for the Loss of their nearest Relations and Friends, which seems to make a more than ordinary Impression upon them. Many of the Women are very handy in Canoes, and will manage them with great Dexterity and Skill, which they become accustomed to in this watry Country. They are ready to help their Husbands in any servile Work, as Planting, when the Season of the Weather requires Expedition; Pride seldom banishing good Houswifry. The Girls are not bred up to the Wheel, and Sewing only; but the Dairy and Affairs of the House they are very well acquainted withal; so that you shall see them, whilst very young, manage their Business with a great deal of Conduct and Alacrity. The Children of both Sexes are very docile, and learn any thing with a great deal of Ease and Method; and those that have the Advantages of Education, write good Hands, and prove good Accountants, which is most coveted, and indeed most necessary in these Parts. The young Men are commonly of a bashful, sober Behaviour; few proving Prodigals, to consume what the Industry of their Parents has left them, but commonly improve it. The marrying so young, carries a double Advantage with it, and that is, that the Parents see their Children provided for in Marriage, and the young married People are taught by their Parents, how to get their Living; for their Admonitions make great Impressions on their Children. I had heard (before I knew this new World) that the Natives of *America* were a short-liv'd People, which, by all the Observations I could ever make, proves quite contrary; for those who are born here, and in other colonies, live to as great Ages as any of the *Europeans,* the Climate being free from Consumptions, which Distemper, fatal to *England,* they are Strangers to. And as the Country becomes more clear'd of Wood, it still becomes more healthful to the Inhabitants, and less addicted to the Ague; which is incident to most new Comers into *America* from *Europe,* yet not mortal. A gentle Emetick seldom misses of driving it away, but if it is not too troublesome, 'tis better to let the Seasoning have its own Course, in which case, the Party is commonly free from it ever after, and very healthful.

And now, as to the other Advantages the Country affords, we cannot guess at them at present, because, as I said before, the best Part of this Country is not inhabited by the *English,* from whence probably will hereafter spring Productions that this Age does not dream of, and of much more Advantage to the Inhabitants than any things we are yet acquainted withal: And as for several Productions of other Countries, much in the same Latitude, we may expect, with good Management, they will become familiar to us, as Wine, Oil, Fruit, Silk, and other profitable Commodities, such as Drugs, Dyes, &c. And at present the Curious may have a large Field to satisfy and divert themselves in, as Collections of strange Beasts, Birds, Insects, Reptiles, Shells, Fishes, Minerals, Herbs, Flowers, Plants, Shrubs, intricate Roots, Gums, Tears [tars], Rozins, Dyes, and Stones, with several other that yield Satisfaction and Profit to those, whose Inclinations tend that Way. And as for what may be hop'd for, towards a happy Life and Being, by such as design to remove thither, I shall add this; That with prudent Management, I can affirm, by Experience, not by Hear-say, That any Person, with a small Beginning, may live very comfortably, and not only provide for the Necessaries of Life, but likewise for those that are to succeed him; Provisions being very plentiful, and of good Variety, to accommodate genteel House-keeping; and the neighbouring *Indians* are friendly, and in many Cases serviceable to us, in making us Wares to catch Fish in, for a small matter, which proves of great Advantage to large Families, because those Engines take great Quantities of many Sorts of Fish, that are very good and nourishing: Some of them hunt and fowl for us at reasonable Rates, the Country being as plentifully provided with all Sorts of Game, as any Part of *America;* the poorer Sort of Planters often get them to plant for them, by hiring them for that Season, or for so much Work, which commonly comes very reasonable. Moreover, it is remarkable, That no Place on the Continent of *America,* has seated an *English* Colony so free from Blood-shed, as *Carolina;* but all the others have been more damag'd and disturb'd by the *Indians,* than they have; which is worthy Notice, when we consider how oddly it was first planted with Inhabitants.

The Fishing-Trade in *Carolina* might be carried on to great Advantage, considering how many Sorts of excellent Fish our Sound and Rivers afford, which cure very well with Salt, as has been experienced by some small Quantities, which have been sent abroad, and yielded a good Price. As for the Whale-fishing, it is no otherwise regarded than by a few People who live on the Sand-Banks; and those only work on dead Fish cast on shoar, none being struck on our Coast, as they are to the Northward; altho' we have Plenty of Whales there. Great Plenty is generally the Ruin of Industry. Thus our Merchants are not many, nor have those few there be, apply'd themselves to the *European* Trade. The Planter sits contented at home, whilst his Oxen thrive and grow fat, and his Stocks daily increase; The fatted Porkets and Poultry are easily rais'd to his Table, and his Orchard affords him Liquor, so that he eats, and drinks away the Cares of the World, and desires no greater Happiness, than that which he daily enjoys. Whereas, not only the *European,* but also the *Indian*-Trade, might be carried on to a great Profit, because we lie as fairly for the Body of *Indians,* as any Settlement in *English-America;* And for the small Trade that has been carried on in that Way, the Dealers therein have throve as fast as any Men, and the soonest rais'd themselves of any People I have known in *Carolina.*

Lastly, As to the Climate, it is very healthful; our Summer is not so hot as in other places to the Eastward in the same Latitude; neither are we ever visited by Earthquakes, as many places in *Italy* and other Summer-Countries are. Our Northerly Winds, in Summer, cool the Air, and free us from pestilential Fevers, which *Spain, Barbary,* and the neighbouring Countries in *Europe, &c.* are visited withal. Our Sky is generally serene and clear, and the Air very thin, in comparison of many Parts of *Europe,* where Consumptions and Catarrhs reign amongst the Inhabitants. The Winter has several Fitts of sharp Weather, especially when the Wind is at N. W. which always clears the Sky, though never so thick before. However, such Weather is very agreeable to *European* Bodies, and makes them healthy. The N. E. Winds blowing in Winter, bring with them thick Weather, and, in the Spring, sometimes, blight the Fruits; but they very seldom endure long, being blown away by Westerly Winds, and then all becomes fair and clear again. Our Spring, in *Carolina,* is very beautiful, and the most pleasant Weather a Country can enjoy. The Fall is accompanied with cool Mornings, which come in towards the latter end of *August,* and so continue (most commonly) very moderate Weather till about *Christmas;* then Winter comes on apace. Tho' these Seasons are very piercing, yet the Cold is of no continuance. Perhaps, you will have cold Weather for three or four days at a time; then pleasant warm Weather follows, such as you have in *England,* about the latter end of *April* or beginning of *May.* In the Year 1707. we had the severest Winter in *Carolina,* that ever was known since the *English* came to settle there; for our Rivers, that were not above half a Mile wide, and fresh Water, were frozen over; and some of them, in the North-part of this Country, were passable for People to walk over.

One great Advantage of *North-Carolina* is, That we are not a Frontier, and near the Enemy; which proves very chargeable and troublesome, in time of War, to those Colonies that are so seated. Another great Advantage comes from its being near *Virginia,* where we come often to a good Market, at the Return of the *Guinea*-Ships for Negro's, and the Remnant of their Stores, which is very commodious for the *Indian*-Trade; besides, in War-time, we lie near at hand to go under their Convoy, and to sell our Provisions to the Tobacco-fleets; for the Planting of Tobacco generally in those Colonies, prevents their being supplyed with Stores, sufficient for victualling their Ships.

As for the Commodities, which are necessary to carry over to this Plantation, for Use and Merchandize, and are, therefore, requisite for those to have along with them, that intend to transport themselves thither; they are Guns, Powder and Shot, Flints, Linnens of all sorts, but chiefly ordinary Blues, *Osnabrugs* [coarse linen, originally made in Osnaburg, Germany], *Scotch* and *Irish* Linnen, and some fine: Mens and Womens Cloaths ready made up, some few Broad-Cloaths, Kerseys and Druggets; to which you must add *Haberdashers*-Wares, Hats about Five or Six Shillings apiece, and a few finer; a few Wiggs, not long, and pretty thin of Hair; thin Stuffs for Women; Iron-Work, as Nails, Spades, Axes, broad and narrow Hoes, Frows, Wedges, and Saws of all sorts, with other Tools for Carpenters, Joiners, Coopers, Shoemakers, Shave-locks, &c. all which, and others which are necessary for the Plantations, you may be inform'd of, and buy at very reasonable Rates, of Mr. *James Gilbert,* Ironmonger, in *Mitre-Tavern-Yard,* near *Aldgate.* You may also be used very kindly, for your Cuttlery-Ware, and other advantageous Merchandizes, and your Cargo's well sorted, by Capt. *Sharp,* at the *Blue gate* in *Cannon-street;* and for Earthen-Ware, Window-Glass, Grind-Stones, Mill-Stones, Paper, Ink-Powder, Saddles, Bridles, and what other things you are minded to take with you, for Pleasure or Ornament.

And now, I shall proceed to the rest of the Vegetables, that are common in *Carolina,* in reference to the Place where I left off, which is the *Natural History* of that Country.

THE

NATURAL HISTORY

OF

Carolina

Of the Vegetables of Carolina

THE spontaneous Shrubs of this Country, are, the Lark-heel-Tree; three sorts of Hony-Suckle-Tree, the first of which grows in Branches, as our Piemento-Tree does, that is, always in low, moist Ground; the other grows in clear, dry Land, the Flower more cut and lacerated; the third, which is the most beautiful, and, I think, the most charming Flower of its Colour, I ever saw, grows betwixt two and three Foot high, and for the most part, by the side of a swampy Wood, or on the Banks of our Rivers, but never near the Salt-Water. All the Sorts are white; the last grows in a great Bunch of these small Hony-Suckles set upon one chief Stem, and is commonly the Bigness of a large Turnep. Nothing can appear more beautiful than these Bushes, when in their Splendour, which is in *April* and *May*. The next is the Honey-Suckle of the Forest; it grows about a Foot high, bearing its Flowers on small Pedestals, several of them standing on the main Stock, which is the Thickness of a Wheat-Straw. We have also the Wood-bind, much the same as in *England;* Princes-feather, very large and beautiful in the Garden; *Tres-Colores*, branch'd Sun-flower, Double Poppies, Lupines, of several pretty sorts, spontaneous; and the *Sensible* Plant is said to be near the Mountains, which I have not yet seen. Saf-Flower; (and I believe, the Saffron of *England* would thrive here, if planted) the yellow Jessamin is wild in our Woods, of a pleasant Smell. Ever-Greens are here plentifully found, of a very quick

Growth, and pleasant Shade; Cypress, or white Cedar, the Pitch Pine, the yellow Pine, the white Pine with long Leaves; and the smaller Almond-Pine, which last bears Kernels in the Apple, tasting much like an Almond; and in some years there falls such plenty, as to make the Hogs fat. Horn-Beam; Cedar, two sorts; Holly, two sorts; Bay-Tree, two sorts; one the Dwarf-Bay, about twelve Foot high; the other the Bigness of a middling Pine-Tree, about two Foot and half Diameter; Laurel-Trees, in Height equalizing the lofty Oaks; the Berries and Leaves of this Tree dyes a Yellow; the Bay-Berries yield a Wax, which besides its Use in Chirurgery, makes Candles that, in burning, give a fragrant Smell. The Cedar-Berries are infused, and made Beer of, by the *Bermudians,* they are Carminative, and much of the Quality of Juniper-Berries; Yew and Box I never saw or heard of in this Country: There are two sorts of Myrtles, different in Leaf and Berry; the Berry yields Wax that makes Candles, the most lasting, and of the sweetest Smell imaginable. Some mix half Tallow with this Wax, others use it without Mixture; and these are fit for a Lady's Chamber, and incomparable to pass the Line withal, and other hot Countries, because they will stand, when others will melt, by the excessive Heat, down in the Binacles [pinnacles]. Ever-green Oak, two sorts; Gall-Berry-Tree, bearing a black Berry, with which the Women dye their Cloaths and Yarn black; 'tis a pretty Ever-green, and very plentiful, growing always in low swampy Grounds, and amongst Ponds. We have a Prim or Privet, which grows on the dry, barren, sandy Hills, by the Sound side; it bears a smaller sort than that in *England,* and grows into a round Bush, very beautiful. Last of Bushes, (except Savine, which grows every where wild) is the famous *Yaupon,* of which I find two sorts, if not three. I shall speak first of the Nature of this Plant, and afterwards account for the different Sorts. This *Yaupon,* call'd by the South-*Carolina* Indians, *Cassena,* is a Bush, that grows chiefly on the Sand-Banks and Islands, bordering on the Sea of *Carolina;* on this Coast it is plentifully found, and in no other Place that I know of. It grows the most like Box, of any Vegetable that I know, being very like it in Leaf, only dented exactly like Tea, but the Leaf somewhat fatter. I cannot say, whether it bears any Flower, but a Berry it does, about the Bigness of a Grain of Pepper, being first red, then brown when ripe, which is in *December;* Some of these Bushes grow to be twelve Foot high, others are three or four. The Wood thereof is brittle as Myrtle, and affords a light ash-colour'd Bark. There is sometimes found of it in Swamps and rich low Grounds, which has the same figured Leaf, only it is. larger, and of a deeper Green; This may be occasion'd by the Richness that attends the low Grounds thus situated. The third Sort has the same kind of Leaf, but never grows a Foot high, and is found both in rich, low Land, and on the Sand-Hills. I don't know that ever I found any Seed, or Berries on the dwarfish Sort, yet I find no Difference in Taste, when Infusion is made: Cattle and Sheep delight in this Plant very much, and so do the Deer, all which crop it very short, and browze thereon, wheresoever they meet with it. I have transplanted the Sand-Bank and dwarfish *Yaupon,* and find that the first Year, the Shrubs stood at a stand; but the second Year they throve as well as in their native Soil. This Plant is the *Indian* Tea, us'd and approv'd by all the Savages on the Coast of *Carolina,* and from them sent to the Westward *Indians,* and sold at a considerable Price. All which they cure after the same way, as they do for themselves; which is thus: They take this Plant (not only the Leaves, but the smaller Twigs along with them) and bruise it in a Mortar, till it becomes blackish, the Leaf being wholly defaced: Then they take it out, put it into one of their earthen Pots which is over the Fire, till it smoaks; stirring it all the time, till it is cur'd. Others take it, after it is bruis'd, and put it into a Bowl, to which they put live Coals, and cover them with the *Yaupon,* till they have done smoaking, often turning them over. After all, they spread it upon their Mats, and dry it in the Sun. to keep for Use. The *Spaniards* in *New-Spain* have this Plant very plentifully on the Coast of *Florida,* and hold it in great Esteem. Sometimes they cure it as the *Indians* do; or else beat it to a Powder, so mix it, as Coffee; yet before they drink it, they filter the same. They prefer it above all Liquids, to drink with Physick, to carry the same safely and speedily thro' the Passages, for which it is admirable, as I myself have experimented.

In the next Place, I shall speak of the *Timber* that *Carolina* affords, which is as follows.

Chesnut-Oak, is a very lofty Tree, clear of Boughs and Limbs, for fifty or 60 Foot. They bear sometimes four or five Foot through all clear Timber; and are the largest Oaks we have, yielding the fairest Plank. They grow chiefly in low Land, that is stiff and rich. I have seen of them so high, that a good Gun could not reach a Turkey, tho' loaded with Swan-Shot. They are call'd Chesnut, because of the Largeness and Sweetness of the Acorns.

White, Scaly-bark Oak; This is used, as the former, in building Sloops and Ships. Tho' it bears a large Acorn, yet it never grows to the Bulk and Height of the Chesnut Oak. It is so call'd, because of a scaly, broken, white Bark, that covers this Tree, growing on dry Land.

We have Red Oak, sometimes, in good Land, very large, and lofty. 'Tis a porous Wood, and used to rive into Rails for Fences. 'Tis not very durable; yet some use this, as well as the two former, for Pipe and Barrel-Staves. It makes good Clap boards.

Spanish Oak is free to rive, bears a whitish, smooth Bark; and rives very well into Clap-boards. It is accounted durable, therefore some use to build Vessels with it for the Sea; it proving well and durable. These all bear good Mast for the Swine.

Bastard-*Spanish* is an Oak betwixt the *Spanish* and Red Oak; the chief Use is for Fencing and Clap-boards. It bears good Acorns.

The next is Black Oak, which is esteem'd a durable Wood, under Water; but sometimes it is used in House-work. It bears a good Mast for Hogs.

White Iron, or Ring-Oak, is so call'd, from the Durability and lasting Quality of this Wood. It chiefly grows on dry, lean Land, and seldom fails of bearing a plentiful crop of Acorns. This Wood is found to be very durable, and is esteem'd the best Oak for Ship-work that we have in *Carolina;* for tho' Live Oak be more lasting, yet it seldom allows Planks of any considerable Length.

Turkey-Oak is so call'd from a small Acorn it bears, which the wild Turkeys feed on.

Live-Oak chiefly grows on dry, sandy Knolls. This is an Evergreen, and the most durable Oak all *America* affords. The Shortness of this Wood's Bowl, or Trunk, makes it unfit for Plank to build Ships withal. There are some few Trees, that would allow a Stock of twelve Foot, but the Firmness and great Weight thereof, frightens our Sawyers from the Fatigue that attends the cutting of this Timber. A Nail once driven therein, 'tis next to an Impossibility to draw it out. The Limbs thereof are so cur'd, that they serve for excellent Timbers, Knees, &c. for Vessels of any sort. The Acorns thereof are as sweet as Chesnuts, and the *Indians* draw an Oil from them, as sweet as that from the Olive, tho' of an Amber-Colour. With these Nuts, or Acorns, some have counterfeited the Cocoa, whereof they have made Chocolate, not to be distinguish'd by a good Palate. Window-Frames, Mallets, and Pins for Blocks, are made thereof, to an excellent Purpose. I knew two Trees of this Wood among the *Indians,* which were planted from the Acorn, and grew in the Freshes, and never saw any thing more beautiful of that kind. They are of an indifferent quick Growth; of which there are two sorts. The Acorns make very fine Pork.

Willow-Oak is a sort of Water-Oak. It grows in Ponds and Branches, and is useful for many things. It is so call'd, from the Leaf, which very much resembles a Willow.

The Live Oak grows in the fresh Water Ponds and Swamps, by the River sides, and in low Ground overflown with Water; and is a perennial Green.

Of Ash we have two sorts, agreeing nearly with the *English* in the Grain. One of our sorts is tough, like the *English,* but differs something in the Leaf, and much more in the Bark. Neither of them bears Keys. The Water-Ash is brittle. The Bark is Food for the Bevers.

There are two sorts of Elm; the first grows on our High-Land, and approaches our *English.* The *Indians* take the Bark of its Root, and beat it, whilst green, to a Pulp; and then dry it in the Chimney, where it becomes of a reddish Colour. This they use as a Sovereign Remedy to heal a Cut or green Wound, or any thing that is not corrupted. It is of a very glutinous Quality. The other Elm grows in low Ground, of whose Bark the *English* and *Indians* make Ropes; for as soon as the Sap rises, it strips off, with the greatest ease imaginable. It runs in *March,* or thereabouts.

The Tulip-Trees, which are, by the Planters, call'd Poplars, as nearest approaching that Wood in Grain, grow to a prodigious Bigness, some of them having been found One and twenty Foot in Circumference. I have been inform'd of a Tulip-Tree, that was ten Foot Diameter; and another, wherein a lusty Man had his Bed and Houshold Furniture, and liv'd in it, till his Labour got him a more fashionable Mansion. He afterwards became a noted Man, in his Country, for Wealth and Conduct. One of these sorts bears a white Tulip; the other a party-colour'd, mottled one. The Wood makes very pretty Wainscot, Shingles for Houses, and Planks for several Uses. It is reckon'd very lasting; especially, under Ground, for Mill-Work. The Buds, made into an Ointment, cure Scalds, Inflammations, and Burns. I saw several Bushels thereon. The Cattle are apt to eat of these Buds, which give a very odd Taste to the Milk.

Beech is here frequent, and very large. The Grain seems exactly the same as that in *Europe*. We make little Use thereof, save for Fire-Wood. 'Tis not a durable Timber. It affords a very sweet Nut, yet the Pork fed thereon (tho' sweet) is very oily, and ought to be harden'd with *Indian* Corn, before it is kill'd. Another sort call'd Buck-Beech is here found.

Horn-Beam grows, in some Places, very plentifully; yet the Plenty of other Wood makes it unregarded.

The Vertues of Sassafras are well known in *Europe*. This Wood sometimes grows to be above two Foot over, and is very durable and lasting, used for Bowls, Timbers, Posts for Houses, and other Things that require standing in the Ground. 'Tis very light. It bears a white Flower, which is very cleansing to the Blood, being eaten in the Spring, with other Sallating. The Berry, when ripe, is black; 'tis very oily, Carminative, and extremely prevalent in Clysters for the Colick. The Bark of the Root is a Specifick to those afflicted with the Gripes. The same in Powder, and a Lotion made thereof, is much used by the Savages, to mundify old Ulcers, and for several other Uses; being highly esteem'd among them.

Dog-Wood is plentiful on our light Land, inclining to a rich Soil. It flowers the first in the Woods; its white Blossom making the Forest very beautiful. It has a fine Grain, and serves for several Uses within doors; but is not durable. The Bark of this Root infused, is held an infallible Remedy against the Worms.

Laurel, before-mention'd; as to its Bigness and Use, I have seen Planks sawn of this Wood; but 'tis not found durable in the Weather; yet pretty enough for many other Uses.

Bay and Laurel generally delight in a low, swampy Ground. I know no Use they make of them, but for Fire-Wood, excepting what I spoke of before, amongst the Ever-Greens.

A famous Ever-Green I must now mention, which was forgotten amongst the rest. It is in Leaf like a Jessamine, but larger, and of a harder Nature. This grows up to a large Vine, and twists itself round the Trees it grows near, making a very fine Shade. I never saw any thing of that Nature outdo it, and if it be cut away close to the Ground, it will presently spring up again, it being impossible to destroy it, when once it has got

Root. 'Tis an ornamental Plant, and worth the Transplanting. Its Seed is a black Berry.

The Scarlet Trumpet-Vine bears a glorious red Flower, like a Bell, or Trumpet, and makes a Shade inferiour to none that I ever saw; yet it leaves us, when the Winter comes, and remains naked till the next Spring. It bears a large Cod, that holds its Seed.

The Maycock bears a glorious Flower, and Apple of an agreeable Sweet, mixt with an acid Taste. This is also a Summer-Vine.

The Indico grows plentifully in our Quarters.

The Bay-Tulip-Tree is a fine Ever-green which grows frequently here.

The sweet Gum-Tree, so call'd, because of the fragrant Gum it yields in the Spring-time, upon Incision of the Bark, or Wood. It cures the Herpes and Inflammations; being apply'd to the Morphew and Tettars. 'Tis an extraordinary Balsam, and of great Value to those who know how to use it. No Wood has scarce a better Grain; whereof fine Tables, Drawers, and other Furniture might be made. Some of it is curiously curl'd. It bears a round Bur, with a sort of Prickle, which is the Seed.

Of the Black Gum there grows, with us, two sorts; both fit for Cart-Naves. The one bears a black, well-tasted Berry, which the *Indians* mix with their Pulse and Soups, it giving 'em a pretty Flavour, and scarlet Colour. The Bears crop these Trees for the Berries, which they mightily covet, yet kill'd in that Season, they eat very unsavory; which must be occasion'd by this Fruit, because, at other times, when they feed on Mast, Bears-Flesh is a very well-tasted Food. The other Gum bears a Berry in shape like the other, tho' bitter and ill-tasted. This Tree (the *Indians* report) is never wounded by Lightning. It has no certain Grain; and it is almost impossible to split or rive it.

The white Gum, bearing a sort of long bunch'd Flowers, is the most curled and knotted Wood I ever saw, which would make curious Furniture, in case it was handled by a good Workman.

The red sort of Cedar is an Ever-green, of which *Carolina* affords Plenty. That on the Salts, grows generally on the Sandbanks; and that in the Freshes is found in the Swamps. Of this Wood, Tables, Wainscot, and other Necessaries, are made, and esteemed for its sweet Smell. It is as durable a Wood as any we have, therefore much used in Posts for Houses and Sills; likewise to build Sloops, Boats, &c. by reason the Worm will not touch it, for several Years. The Vessels built thereof are very durable, and good Swimmers. Of this Cedar, Ship-loads may be exported. It has been heretofore so plentiful in this Settlement, that they have fenced in Plantations with it, and the Coffins of the Dead are generally made thereof.

White Cedar, so call'd, because it nearly approaches the other Cedar, in Smell, Bark, and Leaf; only this grows taller, being as strait as an Arrow. It is extraordinary light, and free to rive. 'Tis good for Yard, Top-Masts, Booms and Boltsprits, being very tough. The best Shingles for Houses are made of this Wood, it being no Strain to the Roof, and never rots. Good Pails and other Vessels, free from Leakage, are likewise made thereof. The Bark of this and the red Cedar, the *Indians* use to make their Cabins of, which prove firm, and resist all Weathers.

Cypress is not an Ever-green with us, and is therefore call'd the bald Cypress, because the Leaves, during the Winter-Season, turn red, not recovering their Verdure till the Spring. These Trees are the largest for Height and Thickness, that we have in this Part of the World; some of them holding thirty-six Foot in Circumference. Upon Incision, they yield a sweet-smelling Grain, tho' not in great Quantities; and the Nuts which these Trees bear plentifully, yield a most odoriferous Balsam, that infallibly cures all new and green Wounds, which the Inhabitants are well acquainted withal. Of these great Trees the Pereaugers and Canoes are scoop'd and made; which sort of Vessels are chiefly to pass over the Rivers, Creeks, and Bays; and to transport Goods and Lumber from one River to another. Some are so large, as to carry thirty Barrels, tho' of one entire Piece of Timber. Others, that are split down the Bottom, and a piece added thereto, will carry eighty, or an hundred. Several have gone out of our Inlets on the Ocean to *Virginia*, laden with Pork, and other Produce of the Country. Of these Trees curious Boats for Pleasure may be made, and other necessary Craft. Some Years ago, a foolish Man in *Albemarl* and his Son, had got one of these Canoes deck'd. She held, as I take it, sixteen Barrels. He brought her to the Collectors, to be clear'd for *Barbados;* but the Officer took him for a Man that had lost his Senses, and argu'd the Danger and Impossibility of performing such a Voyage, in a hollow Tree; but the Fellow would hearken to no Advice of that kind, till the Gentleman told him, if he did not value his own Life, he valu'd his Reputation and Honesty, and so flatly refus'd clearing him; Upon which, the Canoe was sold, and, I think, remains in being still. This Wood is very lasting, and free from the Rot. A Canoe of it will outlast four Boats, and seldom wants Repair. They say, that a Chest made of this Wood, will suffer no Moth, or Vermine, to abide therein.

The Locust, for its enduring the Weather, is chosen for all sorts of Works that are exposed thereto. It bears a Leaf nearest the Liquorice-Plant. 'Tis a pretty tall Tree. Of this the *Indians* make their choicest Bows, it being very tough and flexible. We have little or none of this Wood in *Pampticough*.

The Honey-Tree bears as great a Resemblance to the Locust, as a Shallot does to an Onion. It is of that Species, but more prickly. They bear a Cod, one side whereof contains the Seed, the other the Honey; They will bear in five Years, from the Kernel. They were first brought (by the *Indian* Traders) and propagated, by their Seed, at the *Apamaticks* in *Virginia*. Last Year, I planted the Seed, and had them sprung up before I came from thence, which was in *August*. Of the Honey, very good Metheglin is made, there being Orchards planted in *Virginia* for that intent.

The Sorrel, or Sowr-Wood-Tree, is so call'd, because the Leaves taste like Sorrel. Some are about a Foot or ten Inches Diameter. I am unacquainted with its Vertues at present.

Of Pines, there are, in *Carolina*, at least, four sorts. The Pitch-Pine, growing to a great Bigness, most commonly has but a short Leaf. Its Wood (being replete with abundance of *Bitumen*) is so durable, that it seems to suffer no Decay, tho' exposed to all Weathers, for many Ages; and is used in several Domestick and Plantation Uses. This Tree affords the four great Necessaries, Pitch, Tar, Rozin, and Turpentine; which two last are extracted by tapping, and the Heat of the Sun, the other two by the Heat of the Fire.

The white and yellow Pines are saw'd into Planks for several Uses. They make Masts, Yards, and a great many other Necessaries therewith, the Pine being the most useful Tree in the Woods.

The Almond-Pine serves for Masts very well. As for the Dwarf-Pine, it is for Shew alone, being an Ever-green, as they all are.

The Hiccory is of the Walnut-kind, and bears a Nut as they do, of which there are found three sorts. The first is that which we call the common white Hiccory. It is not a durable Wood; for if cut down, and exposed to the Weather, it will be quite rotten, and spoil'd in three Years; as will likewise the Beech of this Country. Hiccory Nuts have very hard Shells, but excellent sweet Kernels, with which, in a plentiful Year, the old Hogs, that can crack them, fatten themselves, and make excellent Pork. These Nuts are gotten, in great Quantities, by the Savages, and laid up for Stores, of which they make several Dishes and Banquets. One of these I cannot forbear mentioning; it is this: They take these Nuts, and break them very small betwixt two Stones, till the Shells and Kernels are indifferent small; And this Powder you are presented withal in their Cabins, in little wooden Dishes; the Kernel dissolves in your Mouth, and the Shell is spit out. This tastes as well as any Almond. Another Dish is the Soup which they make of these Nuts, beaten, and put into Venison-Broth, which dissolves the Nut, and thickens, whilst the Shell precipitates, and remains at the bottom. This Broth tastes very rich. There is another sort, which we call red Hiccory, the Heart thereof being very red, firm and durable; of which Walking-Sticks, Mortars, Pestils, and several other fine Turnery-wares are made. The third is call'd the Flying-bark'd Hiccory, from its brittle and scaly Bark. It bears a Nut with a bitter Kernel and a soft Shell, like a *French* Walnut. Of this Wood, Coggs for Mills are made, *&c*. The Leaves smell very fragrant.

The Walnut-Tree of *America* is call'd Black Walnut. I suppose, that Name was, at first, to distinguish it from the Hiccories, it having a blacker Bark. This Tree grows, in good Land, to a prodigious Bigness. The Wood is very firm and durable, of which Tables and Chests of Drawers are made, and prove very well. Some of this is very knotty, which would make the best Returns for *England,* tho' the Masters of Vessels refuse it, not understanding its Goodness. 'Tis a very good and durable Wood, to bottom Vessels for the Sea withal; and they say, that it is never eaten by the Worm. The Nuts have a large Kernel, which is very oily, except lain by, a long time, to mellow. The Shell is very thick, as all the native Nuts of *America* are. When it has its yellow outward Coat on, it looks and smells much like a Lemon.

The Maple, of which we have two sorts, is used to make Trenchers, Spinning-wheels, *&c*. withal.

Chinkapin is a sort of Chesnut, whose Nuts are most commonly very plentiful; insomuch that the Hogs get fat with them. They are rounder and smaller than a Chesnut, but much sweeter. The Wood is much of the Nature of Chesnut, having a Leaf and Grain almost like it. It is used to timber Boats, Shallops, &c. and makes any thing that is to endure the Weather. This and the Hiccory are very tough Rods used to whip Horses withal; yet their Wood, in Substance, is very brittle. This Tree the Vine much delights to twist about. It's good Fire-Wood, but very sparkling, as well as Sassafras.

The Birch grows all on the Banks of our Rivers, very high up. I never saw a Tree on the Salts. It differs something, in Bark, from the *European* Birch. Its Buds in *April* are eaten by the Parrakeetos, which resort, from all Parts, at that Season, to feed thereon. Where this Wood grows, we are not yet seated; and as to the Wine, or other Profits it would yield, we are, at present, Strangers to.

The Willow, here, likewise differs both in Bark and Leaf. It is frequently found on the Banks of fresh Water, as the Birch is.

The Sycamore, in these Parts, grows in a low, swampy Land, by River-sides. Its Bark is quite different from the *English,* and the most beautiful I ever saw, being mottled and clowded with several Colours, as white, blue, &c. It bears no Keys but a Bur like the sweet Gum. Its Uses I am ignorant of.

I never saw any Aspin, but in *Rapahannock*-River, from whence I brought one, (that was presented me there as a great Present) but it died by the way.

Of Holly we have two sorts; one having a large Leaf, the other a smaller. They grow very thick in our low Woods. Many of them are very strait, and two Foot Diameter. They make good Trenchers, and other Turnery-Ware.

The Red-Bud-Tree bears a purple Lark-Heel, and is the best Sallad, of any Flower I ever saw. It is ripe in *April* and *May.* They grow in Trees, generally small, but some are a Foot Diameter.

Pelletory grows on the Sand-Banks and Islands. It is used to cure the Tooth-ach, by putting a Piece of the Bark in the Mouth, which being very hot, draws a Rhume from the Mouth, and causes much Spittle. The *Indians* use it to make their Composition, which they give to their young Men and Boys, when they are husquenaw'd, of which you shall hear farther, when I come to treat of the Customs, &c. of that People.

Arrow-Wood, growing on the Banks, is used, by the *Indians*, for Arrows and Gun-Sticks. It grows as strait, as if plain'd, and is of all Sizes. 'Tis as tough and pliable, as the smallest Canes.

The Chesnut-Tree of *Carolina*, grows up towards the hilly Part thereof, is a very large and durable Wood, and fit for House-Frames, Palisado's, Sills, and many other Uses. The Nut is smaller than those from *Portugal*, but sweeter.

This is no Tree, but call'd the Oak-Vine, by reason it bears a sort of Bur as the Oak does, and generally runs up those Trees. It's so porous, that you suck Liquors thro' a Length of two Foot.

Prickly-Ash grows up like a Pole; of which the *Indians* and *English* make Poles to set their Canoes along in Shoal-Water. It's very light, and full of Thorns or Prickles, bearing Berries in large Clusters, of a purple Colour, not much unlike the Alder. The Root of this Tree is Cathartick and Emetick, used in Cachexies.

The Poison Vine is so called, because it colours the Hands of those who handle it. What the Effects of it may be, I cannot relate; neither do I believe, that any has made an Experiment thereof. The Juice of this will stain Linnen, never to wash out. It marks a blackish blue Colour, which is done only by breaking a bit of the Vine off, and writing what you please therewith. I have thought, that the *East-India* Natives set their Colours, by some such Means, into their finest Callicoes. It runs up any Tree it meets withal, and clasps round about it. The Leaves are like Hemlock, and fall off in Winter.

Of Canes and Reeds we have many sorts. The hollow Reed, or Cane, such as Angling-Rods are made of, and *Weavers* use, we have great Plenty of, though none to the Northward of *James-River* in *Virginia*. They always grow in Branches and low Ground. Their Leaves endure the Winter, in which Season our Cattle eat them greedily. We have them (towards the Heads of our Rivers) so large, that one Joint will hold above a pint of Liquor.

The small *Bamboo* is next, which is a certain Vine, like the rest of these Species, growing in low Land. They seldom, with us, grow thicker than a Man's little Finger, and are very tough. Their Root is a round Ball, which the *Indians* boil as we do Garden-Roots, and eat them. When these Roots have been some time out of the Ground, they become hard, and make good Heads to the Canes, on which several pretty Figures may be cut.

There are several others of this kind, not thoroughly discover'd.

That *Palmeto* grows with us, which we call the dwarfish sort; but the *Palmeto*-Tree I have not yet met withal in *North-Carolina,* of which you have a Description elsewhere. We shall next treat of the Spontaneous Fruits of this Country; and then proceed to those that have been transplanted from *Europe,* and other Parts.

Among the natural Fruits, the Vine first takes place, of which I find six sorts, very well known. The first is the black *Bunch-Grapes,* which yield a Crimson Juice. These grow common, and bear plentifully. They are of a good Relish, though not large, yet well knit in the Clusters. They have a thickish Skin, and large Stone, which makes them not yield much Juice. There is another sort of Black-Grapes like the former, in all respects, save that their Juice is of a light Flesh-Colour, inclining to a White. I once saw a Spontaneous white Bunch-Grape in *Carolina;* but the Cattle browzing on the Sprouts thereof in the Spring, it died. Of those which we call *Fox-Grapes,* we have four sorts; two whereof are called Summer-Grapes, because ripe in *July;* the other two Winter-Fruit, because not ripe till *September* or *October.* The Summer Fox-Grapes grow not in Clusters, or great Bunches, but are about five or six in a Bunch, about the Bigness of a Damson, or larger. The black sort are frequent, the white not so commonly found. They always grow in Swamps, and low moist Lands, running sometimes very high, and being shady, and therefore proper for Arbours. They afford the largest Leaf I ever saw, to my remembrance, the Back of which is of a white Horse-flesh Colour. This Fruit always ripens in the Shade. I have transplanted them into my Orchard, and find they thrive well, if manured: A Neighbour of mine has done the same; mine were by Slips, his from the Roots, which thrive to Admiration, and bear Fruit, tho' not so juicy as the *European* Grape, but of a glutinous Nature. However, it is pleasant enough to eat.

The other Winter Fox-Grapes, are much of the same Bigness. These refuse no Ground, swampy or dry, but grow plentifully on the Sand-Hills along the Sea-Coast, and elsewhere, and are great Bearers. I have seen near twelve Bushels upon one Vine of the black sort. Some of these, when thoroughly ripe, have a very pretty vinous Taste, and eat very well, yet are glutinous. The white sort are clear and transparent, and indifferent small Stones. Being removed by the Slip of Root, they thrive well in our Gardens, and make pleasant Shades.

Persimmon is a Tree, that agrees with all Lands and Soils. Their Fruit, when ripe, is nearest our Medlar; if eaten before, draws your Mouth up like a Purse, being the greatest Astringent I ever met withal, therefore very useful in some Cases. The Fruit, if ripe, will presently cleanse a foul Wound, but causes Pain. The Fruit is rotten, when ripe, and commonly contains four flat Kernels, call'd Stones, which is the Seed. 'Tis said, the *Cortex Peruvianus* comes from a *Persimmon*-Tree, that grows in *New-Spain*. I have try'd the Drying of this Bark, to imitate it, which it does tolerably well, and agrees therewith. It is binding enough to work the same Effect. The Tree, in extraordinary Land, comes sometimes to two Foot Diameter, though not often. There are two sorts of this Fruit; one ripe in Summer, the other when the Frost visits us.

We have three sorts of Mulberries, besides the different Bigness of some Trees Fruit. The first is the common red Mulberry, whose Fruit is the earliest we have, (except the Strawberries) and very sweet. These Trees make a very fine Shade, to sit under in Summer-time. They are found wild in great Quantities, wherever the Land is light and rich; yet their Fruit is much better when they stand open. They are used instead of Raisins and Currants, and make several pretty Kickshaws. They yield a transparent Crimson Liquor, which would make good Wine; but few Peoples Inclinations in this Country tend that way. The others are a smooth-leav'd Mulberry, fit for the Silk-Worm. One bears a white Fruit, which is common; the other bears a small black Berry, very sweet. They would persuade me there, that the black Mulberry with the Silk-Worm smooth Leaf, was a white Mulberry, and changed its Fruit. The Wood hereof is very durable, and where the *Indians* cannot get Locust, they make use of this to make their Bows. This Tree grows extraordinary round and pleasant to the Eye.

The Hiccory, Walnut, Chinkapin and Chesnut, with their Fruits, we have mention'd before.

The Hazle-Nut grows plentifully in some places of this Country; especially, towards the Mountains; but ours are not so good as the *English* Nuts, having a much thicker Shell (like all the Fruits of *America*, that I ever met withal) which in Hardness exceeds those of *Europe*.

The Cherries of the Woods grow to be very large Trees. One sort, which is rarely found, is red, and not much unlike the Cornel-Berry. But the common Cherry grows high, and in Bunches, like *English* Currants, but much larger. They are of a bitterish sweet Relish, and are equally valuable with our small Black-Cherries, for an Infusion in Spirits. They yield a crimson Liquor, and are great Bearers.

Our Rasberries are of a purple Colour, and agreeable Relish, almost like the *English;* but I reckon them not quite so rich. When once planted, 'tis hard to root them out. They run wild all over the Country, and will bear the same Year you transplant them, as I have found by Experience.

The Hurts, Huckle-Berries, or Blues of this Country, are four sorts, which we are well acquainted withal; but more Species of this sort, and all others, Time and Enquiry must discover. The first sort is the same Blue or Bilberry, that grows plentifully in the *North* of *England,* and in other Places, commonly on your Heaths, Commons, and Woods, where Brakes or Fern grows.

The second sort grows on a small Bush in our *Savannas* and Meads, and in the Woods. They are larger than the common Fruit, and have larger Seed.

The third grows on the single Stem of a Stick that grows in low good Land, and on the Banks of Rivers. They grow three or four Foot high, and are very pleasant like the first sort, but larger.

The fourth sort grows upon Trees, some ten and twelve Foot high, and the Thickness of a Man's Arm; these are found in the Runs and low Grounds, and are very pleasant, and bear wonderfully. The *English* sometimes dry them in the Sun, and keep them to use in the Winter, instead of Currants. The *Indians* get many Bushels, and dry them on Mats, whereof they make Plum-Bread, and many other Eatables. They are good in Tarts, or infused in Liquors.

In the same Ground, commonly grows the *Piemento,* or All-Spice-Tree, whose Berries differ in shape from those in the *West-Indies,* being Taper or Conick, yet not inferiour to any of that sort. This Tree grows much like the Hurts, and is of the same Bigness. I have known it transplanted to high Land, where it thrives.

Our Dew-Berries are very good. But the Black-Berries are bitterish, and not so palatable, as in *England.*

The Sugar-Tree ought to have taken place before. It is found in no other parts of *Carolina* or *America,* that I ever learnt, but in Places that are near the Mountains. It's most like one sort of

Maple, of any Tree, and may be rank'd amongst that kind. This Tree, which, I am told, is of a very tedious Growth, is found very plentifully towards the Heads of some of our Rivers. The *Indians* tap it, and make Gourds to receive the Liquor, which Operation is done at distinct and proper times, when it best yields its Juice, of which, when the *Indians* have gotten enough, they carry it home, and boil it to a just Consistence of Sugar, which grains of itself, and serves for the same Uses, as other Sugar does.

The *Papau* is not a large Tree. I think, I never saw one a Foot through; but has the broadest Leaf of any Tree in the Woods, and bears an Apple about the Bigness of a Hen's Egg, yellow, soft, and as sweet, as any thing can well be. They make rare Puddings of this Fruit. The Apple contains a large Stone.

The wild Fig grows in *Virginia,* up in the Mountains, as I am inform'd by a Gentleman of my acquaintance, who is a Person of Credit, and a great Traveller in *America.* I shall be glad to have an Opportunity to make Tryal what Improvement might be made of this wild Fruit.

The wild Plums of *America* are of several sorts. Those which I can give an account of from my own Knowledge, I will, and leave the others till a farther Discovery. The most frequent is that which we call the common *Indian* Plum, of which there are two sorts, if not more. One of these is ripe much sooner than the other, and differs in the Bark; one of the Barks being very scaly, like our *American* Birch. These Trees, when in Blossom, smell as sweet as any Jessamine, and look as white as a Sheet, being something prickly. You may make it grow to what Shape you please; they are very ornamental about a House, and make a wonderful fine Shew at a Distance, in the Spring, because of their white Livery. Their Fruit is red, and very palatable to the sick. They are of a quick Growth, and will bear from the Stone in five Years, on their Stock. The *English* large black Plum thrives well, as does the Cherry, being grafted thereon.

The *American* Damsons are both black and white, and about the Bigness of an *European* Damson. They grow any where, if planted from the Stone or Slip; bear a white Blossom, and are a good Fruit. They are found on the Sand-Banks all along the Coast of *America.* I have planted several in my Orchard, that came from the Stone, which thrive well amongst the rest of my Trees. But they never grow to the Bigness of the other Trees now spoken of. These are plentiful Bearers.

There is a third sort of Plum about the Bigness of the Damson. The Tree is taller, seldom exceeding ten Inches in Thickness. The Plum seems to taste physically, yet I never found any
Operation it had, except to make their Lips sore, that eat them.
The Wood is something porous, but exceeds any Box, for a
beautiful Yellow.

There is a very pretty, bushy Tree, about seven or eight Foot
high, very spreading, which bears a Winter-Fruit, that is ripe in
October. They call 'em Currants, but they are nearer a Hurt. I
have eaten very pretty Tarts made thereof. They dry them instead of Currants. This Bush is very beautiful.

The *Bermudas* Currants grow in the Woods on a Bush, much
like the *European* Currant. Some People eat them very much;
but for my part, I can see nothing inviting in them, and reckon
them a very indifferent Fruit.

We have another Currant, which grows on the Banks of Rivers,
or where only Clay hath been thrown up. This Fruit is red, and
gone almost as soon as come. They are a pretty Fruit whilst they
last, and the Tree (for 'tis not a Bush) they grow upon, is a very
pleasant Vegetable.

The Haw-thorn grows plentifully in some parts of this Country. The Haws are quite different from those in *England,* being
four times as big, and of a very pleasant agreeable Taste. We
make no use of this Plant, nor any other, for Hedges, because
Timber is so plentiful at present. In my Judgment, the Honey-
Locust would be the fittest for Hedges; because it is very apt to
shoot forth many Sprouts and Succours from the Roots; besides,
it is of a quick Growth, and very prickly.

The Black Haw grows on a slender Tree, about the Height
of a Quince-Tree, or something higher, and bears the black
Haw, which People eat, and the Birds covet also. What Vertues
the Fruit or Wood is of, I cannot resolve you, at present.

Thus have I given an Account of all the Spontaneous Fruits of
Carolina, that have come to my Knowledge, excepting *Services,*
which I have seen in the *Indians* Hands, and eat of them, but
never saw, how nor where they grew. There may very well be
expected a great many more Fruits, which are the natural Product of this Country, when we consider the Fruitfulness of the
Soil and Climate, and account for the vast Tract of Land, (great
part of which is not yet found out) according to the Product of
that which is already discover'd, which (as I once hinted be-

fore) is not as yet arriv'd to our Knowledge, we having very little or no Correspondence amongst the mountainous Parts of this Province, and towards the Country of *Messiasippi,* all which we have strange Accounts of, and some very large ones, with respect to the different and noble Fruits, and several other Ornaments and Blessings of Nature which *Messiasippi* possesses; more to be coveted, than any of those we enjoy, to the Eastward of the Mountains: Yet when I came to discourse some of the Idolizers of that Country, I found it to be rather Novelty, than Truth and Reality, that induced those Persons to allow it such Excellencies above others. It may be a brave and fertile Country, as I believe it is; but I cannot be persuaded, that it can be near so advantageous as ours, which is much better situated for Trade, being faced all along with the Ocean, as the *English America* is; when the other is only a direct River, in the midst of a wild unknown Land, greatest part of whose Product must be fetch'd, or brought a great way, before it can come to a Market. Moreover, such great Rivers commonly allow of more Princes Territories than one; and thus nothing but War and Contention accompanies the Inhabitants thereof.

But not to trouble our Readers with any more of this, we will proceed, in the next place, to shew, what *Exotick* Fruits we have, that thrive well in *Carolina;* and what others, it may reasonably be suppos'd, would do there, were they brought thither and planted. In pursuance of which, I will set down a Catalogue of what Fruits we have; I mean Species: For should I pretend to give a regular Name to every one; it's neither possible for me to do it, nor for any one to understand it, when done; if we consider, that the chiefest part of our Fruit came from the Kernel, and some others from the Succours, or Sprouts of the Tree. First, we will begin with Apples; which are the

Golden Russet

Pearmain $\begin{cases} \text{Winter} \\ \text{Summer} \end{cases}$

Harvey-Apple, I cannot tell, whether the same as in *England.*

Winter Queening

Leather Coat

Juniting

Codlin

Redstreak
Long-stalk
Lady-Finger

The Golden Russet thrives well.

The Pearmains, of both sorts, are apt to speck, and rot on the Trees; and the Trees are damaged and cut off by the Worm, which breeds in the Forks, and other parts thereof; and often makes a Circumposition, by destroying the Bark round the Branches, till it dies.

Harvey-Apple; that which we call so, is esteem'd very good to make Cider of.

Winter Queening is a durable Apple, and makes good Cider.

Leather-Coat; both Apple and Tree stand well.

The Juniting is early ripe, and soon gone, in these warm Countries.

Codlin; no better, and fairer Fruit in the World; yet the Tree suffers the same Distemper, as the Pearmains, or rather worse; the Trees always dying before they come to their Growth.

The Redstreak thrives very well.

Long-stalk is a large Apple, with a long Stalk, and makes good Summer Cider.

We beat the first of our Codlin Cider, against reaping our Wheat, which is from the tenth of *June,* to the five and twentieth.

Lady-Finger, the long Apple, the same as in *England,* and full as good. We have innumerable sorts; some call'd Rope-Apples which are small Apples, hanging like Ropes of Onions; Flattings, Grigsons, Cheese-Apples, and a great number of Names, given according to every ones Discretion.

The *Warden-Pear* here proves a good eating Pear; and is not so long ripening as in *England.*

Katharine excellent.

Sugar-pear.

And several others without Name; The Bergamot we have not, nor either of the Bonne Chrestiennes, though I hear, they are all three in *Virginia.* Those sorts of Pears which we have, are as well relisht, as ever I eat any where; but that Fruit is of very short Continuance with us, for they are gone almost as soon as ripe.

I am not a Judge of the different sorts of Quinces, which they

call *Brunswick, Portugal,* and *Barbary;* But as to the Fruit, in
general, I believe no Place has fairer and better relisht. They
are very pleasant eaten raw. Of this Fruit, they make a Wine, or
Liquor, which they call Quince-Drink, and which I approve of
beyond any Drink which that Country affords, though a great
deal of Cider and some Perry is there made. The Quince-Drink
most commonly purges those that first drink it, and cleanses the
Body very well. The Argument of the Physicians, that they bind
People, is hereby contradicted, unless we allow the Quinces to
differ in the two Countries. The least Slip of this Tree stuck in
the Ground, comes to bear in three years.

All Peaches, with us, are standing; neither have we any Wall-
Fruit in *Carolina;* for we have Heat enough, and therefore do
not require it. We have a great many sorts of this Fruit, which
all thrive to Admiration, Peach-Trees coming to Perfection
(with us) as easily as the Weeds. A Peach falling on the Ground,
brings a Peach-Tree that shall bear in three years, or sometimes
sooner. Eating Peaches in our Orchards makes them come up so
thick from the Kernel, that we are forced to take a great deal of
Care to weed them out; otherwise they make our Land a Wilderness of Peach-Trees. They generally bear so full, that they break
great part of their Limbs down. We have likewise very fair Nec-
tarines, especially the red, that clings to the Stone, the other
yellow Fruit, that leaves the Stone; of the last, I have a Tree,
that, most Years, brings me fifteen or twenty Bushels. I see no
Foreign Fruit like this, for thriving in all sorts of Land, and bearing its Fruit to Admiration. I want to be satisfy'd about one sort
of this Fruit, which the *Indians* claim as their own, and affirm,
they had it growing amongst them, before any *Europeans* came
to *America.* The Fruit I will describe, as exactly as I can. The
Tree grows very large, most commonly as big as a handsome
Apple-tree; the Flowers are of a reddish, murrey Colour; the
Fruit is rather more downy, than the yellow Peach, and commonly very large and soft, being very full of Juice. They part
freely from the Stone, and the Stone is much thicker than all the
other Peach Stones we have, which seems to me, that it is a Spontaneous Fruit of *America;* yet in those Parts of *America* that we
inhabit, I never could hear that any Peach-Trees were ever found
growing in the Woods; neither have the foreign *Indians,* that
live remote from the *English,* any other sort. And those living
amongst us have a hundred of this sort for one other; they are a

hardy Fruit, and are seldom damaged by the North-East Blasts, as others are. Of this sort we make Vinegar; wherefore we call them Vinegar-Peaches, and sometimes *Indian*-Peaches.

This Tree grows to a vast Bigness, exceeding most Apple-Trees. They bear well, tho' sometimes an early Spring comes on in *February*, and perhaps, when the Tree is fully blown the Cloudy North-East-Winds which attend the end of, that Month, or the beginning of *March*, destroy most of the Fruit. The biggest Apricock-Tree I ever saw, as they told me, was grafted on a Peach-Stock, in the Ground. I know of no other sort with us, than the Common. We generally raise this Fruit from the Stone, which never fails to bring the same Fruit. Likewise our Peach-Stones effect the same, without so much as once missing, to produce the same sort that the Stone came from.

Damson, Damazeen, and a large round black Plum are all I have met withal in *Carolina*. They thrive well enough; the last to Admiration, and becomes a very large Tree, if in stiff Ground; otherwise they will not do well.

Of Figs we have two sorts; One is the low Bush-Fig, which bears a large Fruit. If the Winter happens to have much Frost, the tops thereof die, and in the Spring sprout again, and bear two or three good Crops.

The Tree-Fig is a lesser Fig, though very sweet. The Tree grows to a large Body and Shade, and generally brings a good Burden; especially, if in light Land. This Tree thrives no where better, than on the Sand-Banks by the Sea.

We have the common red and black Cherry, which bear well. I never saw any grafted in this Country, the common excepted, which was grafted on an *Indian* Plum-stock, and bore well. This is a good way, because our common Cherry-Trees are very apt to put Scions all round the Tree, for a great Distance, which must needs be prejudicial to the Tree and Fruit. Not only our Cherries are apt to do so, but our Apples and most other Fruit-Trees, which may chiefly be imputed to the Negligence and Unskilfulness of the Gardener. Our Cherries are ripe a Month sooner than in *Virginia*.

Goosberries I have seen of the smaller sort, but find they do not do so well as in *England*, and to the Northward. Want of Dressing may be some Reason for this.

Currants, White, Red, and Black, thrive here, as well as any where.

Rasberries, the red and white, I never saw any Trial made of. But there is no doubt of their thriving to Admiration, since those of the Country do so well.

The Mulberries are spontaneous. We have no others, than what I have already mentioned in the Class of Natural Fruits of *Carolina.*

Barberry red, with Stones, and without Stones, grow here.

Strawberries, not Foreign, but those of the Country, grow here in great Plenty. Last *April* I planted a Bed of two hundred Foot in Length, which bore the same Year.

Medlars we have none.

All sorts of Walnuts from *England, France,* and *Maderas,* thrive well from the Nut.

No Filberts, but Hazle-Nuts; the Filbert-Nut planted, becomes a good Hazle-Nut, and no better.

As for that noble Vegetable the Vine, without doubt, it may (in this Country) be improved, and brought to the same Perfection, as it is, at this Day, in the same Latitude in *Europe,* since the chiefest part of this Country is a deep, rich, black Mould, which is up towards the Freshes and Heads of our Rivers, being very rich and mix'd with Flint, Pebbles, and other Stones. And this sort of Soil is approv'd of (by all knowing Gardeners and Vigneroons) as a proper Earth, in which the Grape chiefly delights; and what seems to give a farther Confirmation hereof, is, that the largest Vines, that were ever discover'd to grow wild, are found in those Parts, oftentimes in such Plenty, and are so interwoven with one another, that 'tis impossible to pass through them. Moreover, in these Freshes, towards the Hills, the Vines are above five times bigger than those generally with us, who are seated in the Front-parts of this Country, adjoining to the Salts. Of the wild Vines, which are most of them great Bearers, some Wine has been made, which I drank of. It was very strong and well relisht; but what detains them all from offering at great quantities, they add, that this Grape has a large Stone, and a thick Skin, and consequently yields but a small Quantity of Wine. Some Essays of this Nature have been made by that Honourable Knight, Sir *Nathanael Johnson,*[83] in *South Carolina,* who, as I am inform'd, has rejected all Exotick Vines, and makes his Wine from the natural black Grape of *Carolina,* by

83. Governor of South Carolina, 1703–9.

grafting it upon its own Stock. What Improvement this may arrive to, I cannot tell; but in other Species, I own Grafting and Imbudding yields speedy Fruit, tho' I never found that it made them better.

New planted Colonies are generally attended with a Force and Necessity of Planting the known and approved Staple and Product of the Country, as well as all the Provisions their Families spend. Therefore we can entertain but small hopes of the Improvement of the Vine, till some skilful in dressing Vines shall appear amongst us, and go about it, with a Resolution, that Ordering the Vineyard shall be one half of their Employment. If this be begun and carried on, with that Assiduity and Resolution which it requires, then we may reasonably hope to see this a Wine-Country; for then, when it becomes a general Undertaking, every one will be capable to add something to the common Stock, of that which he has gain'd by his own Experience. This way would soon make the Burden light, and a great many shorter and exacter Curiosities, and real Truths would be found out in a short time. The trimming of Vines, as they do in *France,* that is, to a Stump, must either here be not follow'd, or we are not sensible of the exact time, when they ought to be thus pruned; for Experience has taught us, that the *European* Grape, suffer'd to run and expand itself at large, has been found to bear as well in *America,* as it does in *Europe;* when, at the same time, the same sort of Vine trimm'd to a Stump, as before spoken of, has born a poor Crop for one Year or two; and by its spilling, after cutting, emaciated, and in three or four Years, died. This Experiment, I believe, has never fail'd; for I have trimm'd the natural Vine the *French* way, which has been attended, at last, with the same Fate. Wherefore, it seems most expedient, to leave the Vines more Branches here, than in *Europe,* or let them run up Trees, as some do, in *Lombardy,* upon Elms. The Mulberries and *Chinkapin* are tough, and trimm'd to what you please, therefore fit Supporters of the Vines. Gelding and plucking away the Leaves, to hasten the ripening of this Fruit, may not be unnecessary, yet we see the natural wild Grape generally ripens in the Shade. Nature in this, and many others, may prove a sure Guide. The Twisting of the Stems to make the Grapes ripe together, loses no Juice, and may be beneficial, if done in Season. A very ingenious *French* Gentleman, and another from *Switzerland,* with whom I frequently converse, exclaim against that strict cutting of Vines, the generally approved Method of *France* and *Germany,* and say, that they were both out in their Judgment, till of late, Experience has taught them otherwise. Moreover, the *French* in *North Carolina* assure me, that if we should trim our Apple and other Fruit-Trees, as they do in *Europe,* we should spoil them. As for Apples and Plums, I have found by Experience, what they affirm to be true. The *French,* from the *Mannakin* Town on the Freshes of *James* River in *Virginia,* had, for the most part, removed themselves to *Carolina,* to live there, before I came away; and the rest were following, as their Minister, (Monsieur *Philip de Rixbourg* [Richbourg]) told me, who was at *Bath*-Town, when I was taking my leave of my Friends. He assur'd me, that their Intent was to propagate Vines, as far as their present Circumstances would permit; provided they could get any Slips of Vines, that would do. At the same time, I had gotten some Grape-Seed, which was of the *Jesuits* white Grape from *Madera*. The Seed came up very plentifully, and, I hope, will not degenerate, which if it happens not to do, the Seed may prove the best way to raise a Vineyard, as certainly it is most easy for Transportation. Yet I reckon we should have our Seed from a Country, where the Grape arrives to the utmost Perfection of Ripeness. These *French* Refugees have had small Encouragement in *Virginia,* because, at their first coming over, they took their Measures of Living, from *Europe;* which was all wrong; for the small Quantities of ten, fifteen, and twenty Acres to a Family did not hold out according to their way of Reckoning, by Reason they made very little or no Fodder; and the Winter there being much harder than with us, their Cattle fail'd; chiefly, because the *English* took up and survey'd all the Land round about them; so that they were hemm'd in on all Hands from providing more Land for themselves or their Children, all which is highly prejudicial in *America,* where the generality are bred up to Planting. One of these *French* Men being a Fowling, shot a Fowl in the River, upon which his Dog went down the Bank to bring it to his Master; but the Bank was so high and steep, that he could not get up again. Thereupon, the *French* Man went down, to help his Dog up, and breaking the Mould away, accidentally, with his Feet, he discover'd a very rich Coal-Mine. This Adventure he gave an Account of amongst the Neighbourhood, and presently one of the Gentlemen of that Part survey'd the Land, and the poor *French* Man got nothing by his Discovery. The *French* are good Neighbours amongst us, and give Examples of Industry, which is much wanted in this Country. They make good Flax, Hemp, Linnen-Cloth and Thread; which they exchange amongst the Neighbourhood for other Commodities, for which they have occasion.

We have hitherto made no Tryal of foreign Herbage; but, doubtless, it would thrive well; especially, *Sanfoin,* and those Grasses, that endure Heat, and dry Grounds. As for our Low Lands, such as Marshes, Savannas and Percoarson-Ground, which lies low, all of them naturally afford good Land for Pasturage.

We will next treat of the Beasts, which you shall have an Account of, as they have been discover'd.

The Beasts [84] *of* Carolina *are the*

Buffelo, or wild Beef.	*Water-Rat.*
Bear.	*Rabbet, two sorts.*
Panther.	*Elks.*
Cat-a-mount.	*Stags.*
Wild Cat.	*Fallow-Deer.*
Wolf.	*Squirrel, four sorts.*
Tyger.	*Fox.*
Polcat.	*Lion, and Jackall on the Lake.*
Otter.	*Rats, two sorts.*
Bever.	*Mice, two sorts.*
Musk-Rat.	*Moles.*
Possum.	*Weasel, Dormouse.*
Raccoon.	*Bearmouse.*
Minx.	

The *Buffelo* is a wild Beast of *America,* which has a Bunch on his Back, as the Cattle of St. *Laurence* are said to have. He seldom appears amongst the *English* Inhabitants, his chief Haunt being in the Land of *Messiasippi,* which is, for the most part, a plain Country; yet I have known some kill'd on the

84. The plate on "The Beasts of Carolina" appeared opposite page 180 of the 1709 edition, and the various pages on which these individual "beasts" were described were indicated in the plate—pages 115, 116, 118, 120, 121, 132, and 133.

Hilly Part of *Cape-Fair*-River, they passing the Ledges of vast Mountains from the said *Messiasippi,* before they can come near us. I have eaten of their Meat, but do not think it so good as our Beef; yet the younger Calves are cry'd up for excellent Food, as very likely they may be. It is conjectured, that these Buffelos, mixt in Breed with our tame Cattle, would much better the Breed for Largeness and Milk, which seems very probable. Of the wild Bull's Skin, Buff is made. The *Indians* cut the Skins into Quarters for the Ease of their Transportation, and make Beds to lie on. They spin the Hair into Garters, Girdles, Sashes, and the like, it being long and curled, and often of a chesnut or red Colour. These Monsters are found to weigh (as I am informed by a Traveller of Credit) from 1600 to 2400 Weight.

The Bears here are very common, though not so large as in *Groenland,* and the more Northern Countries of *Russia.* The Flesh of this Beast is very good, and nourishing, and not inferiour to the best Pork in Taste. It stands betwixt Beef and Pork, and the young Cubs are a Dish for the greatest *Epicure* living. I prefer their Flesh before any Beef, Veal, Pork, or Mutton; and they look as well as they eat, their fat being as white as Snow, and the sweetest of any Creature's in the World. If a Man drink a Quart thereof melted, it never will rise in his Stomach. We prefer it above all things, to fry Fish and other things in. Those that are Strangers to it, may judge otherwise; But I who have eaten a great deal of Bears Flesh in my Life-time (since my being an Inhabitant in *America*) do think it equalizes, if not excels, any Meat I ever eat in *Europe.* The Bacon made thereof is extraordinary Meat; but it must be well saved, otherwise it will rust. This Creature feeds upon all sorts of wild Fruits. When Herrings run, which is in *March,* the Flesh of such of those Bears as eat thereof, is nought, all that Season, and eats filthily. Neither is it good, when he feeds on Gum-berries, as I intimated before. They are great Devourers of Acorns, and oftentimes meet the Swine in the Woods, which they kill and eat, especially when they are hungry, and can find no other Food. Now and then they get into the Fields of *Indian* Corn, or *Maiz,* where they make a sad Havock, spoiling ten times as much as they eat.

The Potatos of this Country are so agreeable to them, that they never fail to sweep 'em all clean, if they chance to come in their way. They are seemingly a very clumsy Creature, yet are very nimble in running up Trees, and traversing every Limb thereof. When they come down, they run Tail foremost. At catching of Herrings, they are most expert Fishers. They sit by the Creek-sides, (which are very narrow) where the Fish run in; and there they take them up, as fast as it's possible they can dip their Paws into the Water. There is one thing more to be consider'd of this Creature, which is, that no Man, either Christian or *Indian*, has ever kill'd a She-bear with Young.

It is supposed, that the She-Bears, after Conception, hide themselves in some secret and undiscoverable Place, till they bring forth their Young, which, in all Probability, cannot be long; otherwise, the *Indians*, who hunt the Woods like Dogs, would, at some time or other, have found them out. Bear-Hunting is a great Sport in *America*, both with the *English* and *Indians*. Some Years ago, there were kill'd five hundred Bears, in two Counties of *Virginia*, in one Winter; and but two She-Bears amongst them all, which were not with Young, as I told you of the rest. The *English* have a breed of Dogs fit for this sport, about the size of Farmers Curs, and, by Practice, come to know the Scent of a Bear, which as soon as they have found, they run him, by the Nose, till they come up with him, and then bark and snap at him, till he trees, when the Huntsman shoots him out of the Trees, there being, for the most part, two or three with Guns, lest the first should miss, or not quite kill him. Though they are not naturally voracious, yet they are very fierce when wounded. The Dogs often bring him to a Bay, when wounded, and then the Huntsmen make other Shots, perhaps with the Pistols that are stuck in their Girdles. If a Dog is apt to fasten, and run into a Bear, he is not good, for the best Dog in *Europe* is nothing in their Paws; but if ever they get him in their Clutches, they blow his Skin from his Flesh, like a Bladder, and often kill him; or if he recovers it, he is never good for any thing after. As the Paws of this Creature, are held for the best bit about him, so is the Head esteem'd the worst, and always thrown away, for what reason I know not. I believe, none ever made Trial thereof, to know how it eats. The Oil of the Bear is very Sovereign for Strains, Aches, and old Pains. The fine Fur at the bottom of the Belly, is used for making Hats, in some places. The Fur itself is fit for several Uses; as for making Muffs, facing Caps, &c. but the black Cub-skin is preferable to all sorts of that kind, for Muffs. Its Grain is like Hog-Skin.

The *Panther* is of the Cat's kind; about the height of a very large Greyhound of a reddish Colour, the same as a Lion. He climbs Trees with the greatest Agility imaginable, is very strong-limb'd, catching a piece of Meat from any Creature he strikes at. His Tail is exceeding long; his Eyes look very fierce and lively, are large, and of a grayish Colour; his Prey is, Swines-flesh, Deer, or any thing he can take; no Creature is so nice and clean, as this, in his Food. When he has got his Prey, he fills his Belly with the Slaughter, and carefully lays up the Remainder, covering it very neatly with Leaves, which if any thing touches, he never eats any more of it. He purrs as Cats do; if taken when Young, is never to be reclaim'd from his wild Nature. He hollows like a Man in the Woods, when kill'd, which is by making him take a Tree, as the least Cur will presently do; then the Huntsmen shoot him; if they do not kill him outright, he is a dangerous Enemy, when wounded, especially to the Dogs that approach him. This Beast is the greatest Enemy to the Planter, of any Vermine in *Carolina*. His Flesh looks as well as any Shambles-Meat whatsoever; a great many People eat him, as choice Food; but I never tasted of a Panther, so cannot commend the Meat, by my own Experience. His Skin is a warm Covering for the *Indians* in Winter, though not esteem'd amongst the choice Furs. This Skin dress'd, makes fine Womens Shooes, or Mens Gloves.

The Mountain-Cat, so call'd, because he lives in the Mountainous Parts of *America*. He is a Beast of Prey, as the Panther is, and nearest to him in Bigness and Nature.

This Cat is quite different from those in *Europe;* being more nimble and fierce, and larger; his Tail does not exceed four Inches. He makes a very odd sort of Cry in the Woods, in the Night. He is spotted as the Leopard is, tho' some of them are not, (which may happen, when their Furs are out of Season) he climbs a Tree very dexterously, and preys as the Panther does. He is a great Destroyer of young Swine. I knew an Island, which was possess'd by these Vermine, unknown to the Planter, who put thereon a considerable Stock of Swine; but never took one back; for the wild Cats destroy'd them all. He takes most of his Prey by Surprize, getting up the Trees, which they pass by or under, and thence leaping directly upon them. Thus he takes Deer (which he cannot catch by running) and fastens his Teeth into their Shoulders and sucks them. They run with him, till they fall down for want of strength, and become a Prey to the Enemy. Hares, Birds, and all he meets, that he can conquer, he destroys. The Fur is approv'd to wear as a Stomacher, for weak and cold Stomachs. They are likewise used to line Muffs, and Coats withal, in cold Climates.

The Wolf of *Carolina,* is the Dog of the Woods. The *Indians* had no other Curs, before the Christians came amongst them. They are made domestick. When wild, they are neither so large, nor fierce, as the *European* Wolf. They are not Man-slayers; neither is any Creature in *Carolina,* unless wounded. They go in great Droves in the Night, to hunt Deer, which they do as well as the best Pack of Hounds. Nay, one of these will hunt down a Deer. They are often so poor, that they can hardly run. When they catch no Prey, they go to a Swamp, and fill their Belly full of Mud; if afterwards they chance to get any thing of Flesh, they will disgorge the Mud, and eat the other. When they hunt in the Night, that there is a great many together, they make the most hideous and frightful Noise, that ever was heard. The Fur makes good Muffs. The Skin dress'd to a Parchment makes the best Drum-Heads, and if tann'd makes the best sort of Shooes for the Summer-Countries.

Tygers are never met withal in the Settlement; but are more to the Westward, and are not numerous on this Side the Chain of Mountains. I once saw one, that was larger than a Panther, and seem'd to be a very bold Creature. The *Indians* that hunt in those Quarters, say, they are seldom met withal. It seems to differ from the Tyger of *Asia* and *Africa.*

Polcats or Skunks in *America,* are different from those in *Europe.* They are thicker, and of a great many Colours; not all alike, but each differing from another in the particular Colour. They smell like a Fox, but ten times stronger. When a Dog encounters them, they piss upon him, and he will not be sweet again in a Fortnight or more. The *Indians* love to eat their Flesh, which has no manner of ill Smell, when the Bladder is out. I know no use their Furs are put to. They are easily brought up tame.

There have been seen some Otters from the Westward of *Carolina,* which were of a white Colour, a little inclining to a yellow. They live on the same Prey here, as in *Europe,* and are the same in all other Respects; so I shall insist no farther on that Creature. Their Furs, if black, are valuable.

Bevers are very numerous in *Carolina,* their being abundance of their Dams in all Parts of the Country, where I have travel'd. They are the most industrious and greatest Artificers (in building their Dams and Houses) of any four-footed Creatures in the World. Their Food is chiefly the Barks of Trees and Shrubs, *viz.* Sassafras, Ash, Sweet-Gum, and several others. If you take them young, they become very tame and domestick, but are very mischievous in spoiling Orchards, by breaking the Trees, and blocking up your Doors in the Night, with the Sticks and Wood they bring thither. If they eat any thing that is salt, it kills them. Their Flesh is a sweet Food; especially, their Tail, which is held very dainty. There Fore-Feet are open, like a Dog's; their Hind-Feet webb'd like a Water-Fowl's. The Skins are good Furs for several Uses, which every one knows. The Leather is very thick; I have known Shooes made thereof in *Carolina,* which lasted well. It makes the best Hedgers Mittens that can be used.

Musk Rats frequent fresh Streams and no other; as the Bever does. He has a Cod of Musk, which is valuable, as is likewise his Fur.

The *Possum* is found no where but in *America.* He is the Wonder of all the Land-Animals, being the size of a Badger, and near that Colour. The Male's Pizzle is placed retrograde; and in time of Coition, they differ from all other Animals, turning Tail to Tail, as Dog and Bitch when ty'd. The Female, doubtless, breeds her Young at her Teats; for I have seen them stick fast thereto, when they have been no bigger than a small Rasberry, and seemingly inanimate. She has a Paunch, or false Belly, wherein she carries her Young, after they are from those Teats, till they can shift for themselves. Their Food is Roots, Poultry, or wild Fruits. They have no Hair on their Tails, but a sort of a Scale, or hard Crust, as the Bevers have. If a Cat has nine Lives, this Creature surely has nineteen; for if you break every Bone in their Skin, and mash their Skull, leaving them for Dead, you may come an hour after, and they will be gone quite away, or perhaps you meet them creeping away. They are a very stupid Creature, utterly neglecting their Safety. They are most like Rats of any thing. I have, for Necessity in the Wilderness, eaten of them. Their Flesh is very white, and well tasted; but their ugly Tails put me out of Conceit with that Fare. They climb Trees, as the Raccoons do. Their Fur is not esteem'd nor used, save that the *Indians* spin it into Girdles and Garters.

The *Raccoon* is of a dark-gray Colour; if taken young, is easily made tame, but is the drunkenest Creature living, if he can get any Liquor that is sweet and strong. They are rather more unlucky than a Monkey. When wild, they are very subtle in catching their Prey. Those that live in the Salt-Water, feed much on Oysters which they love. They watch the Oyster when it opens, and nimbly put in their Paw, and pluck out the Fish. Sometimes the Oyster shuts, and holds fast their Paw till the Tide comes in, that they are drown'd, tho' they swim very well. The way that this Animal catches Crabs, which he greatly admires, and which are plenty in *Carolina,* is worthy of Re-mark. When he intends to make a Prey of these Fish, he goes to a Marsh, where standing on the Land, he lets his Tail hang in the Water. This the Crab takes for a Bait, and fastens his Claws therein, which as soon as the *Raccoon* perceives, he, of a sudden, springs forward, a considerable way, on the Land, and brings the Crab along with him. As soon as the Fish finds himself out of his Element, he presently lets go his hold; and then the *Raccoon* encounters him, by getting him cross-wise in his Mouth, and devours him. There is a sort of small Land-Crab, which we call a *Fiddler,* that runs into a Hole when any thing pursues him. This Crab the *Raccoon* takes by putting his Fore-Foot in the Hole, and pulling him out. With a tame *Raccoon,* this Sport is very diverting. The Chief of his other Food is all sorts of wild Fruits, green Corn, and such as the Bear delights in. This and the *Possum* are much of a Bigness. The Fur makes good Hats and Linings. The Skin dress'd makes fine Womens Shooes.

The *Minx* is an Animal much like the *English* Filli-mart or Polcat. He is long, slender, and every way shap'd like him. His Haunts are chiefly in the Marshes, by the Seaside and Salt-Waters, where he lives on Fish, Fowl, Mice, and Insects. They are bold Thieves, and will steal any thing from you in

the Night, when asleep, as I can tell by Experience; for one Win-ter, by Misfortune, I ran my Ves-sel a-ground, and went often to the Banks, to kill wild Fowl, which we did a great many. One

Night, we had a mind to sleep on the Banks (the Weather being fair) and wrapt up the Geese which we had kill'd, and not eaten, very carefully, in the Sail of a Canoe, and folded it several Doubles, and for their better Security, laid 'em all Night under my Head. In the Morning when I wak'd, a Minx had eaten thro' every Fold of the Canoe's Sail, and thro' one of the Geese, most part of which was gone. These are likewise found high up in the Rivers, in whose sides they live; which is known by the abundance of Fresh-Water Muscle-Shells (such as you have in *England*) that lie at the Mouth of their Holes. This is an Enemy to the Tortois, whose Holes in the Sand, where they hide their Eggs, the *Minx* finds out, and scratches up and eats. The *Raccoons* and Crows do the same. The *Minx* may be made domestick, and were it not for his paying a Visit now and then to the Poultry, they are the greatest Destroyers of Rats and Mice, that are in the World. Their Skins, if good of that kind, are valuable, provided they are kill'd in Season.

The Water-Rat is found here the same as in *England*. The Water-Snakes are often found to have of these Rats in their Bellies.

That which the People of *Carolina* call a Hare, is nothing but a Hedge-Coney. They never borough in the Ground, but much frequent Marshes and Meadow-Land. They hide their Young in some Place secure from the Discovery of the Buck, as the *European* Rabbits do, and are of the same Colour; but if you start one of them, and pursue her, she takes into a hollow Tree, and there runs up as far as she can, in which Case the Hunter makes a Fire, and smoaks the Tree, which brings her down, and smothers her. At one time of the Year, great Bots or Maggots breed betwixt the Skin and the Flesh of these Creatures. They eat just as the *English* ones do; but I never saw one of them fat. We fire the Marshes, and then kill abundance.

The *English,* or *European* Coneys are here found, tho' but in one place that I ever knew of, which was in *Trent*-River, where they borough'd among the Rocks. I cannot believe, these are Natives of the Country, any otherwise than that they might come from aboard some Wreck; the Sea not being far off. I was told of several that were upon *Bodies* Island by *Ronoak,* which came from that Ship of *Bodies;* but I never saw any. However the Banks are no proper Abode of Safety, because of the many *Minxes* in those Quarters. I carried over some of

the tame sort from *England* to South *Carolina,* which bred
three times going over, we having a long Passage. I turn'd them
loose in a Plantation, and the young ones, and some of the old
ones bred great Maggots in their Testicles. At last, the great
Gust in *September,* 1700. brought a great deal of Rain, and
drown'd them all in their Holes. I intend to make a second tryal
of them in North *Carolina,* and doubt not but to secure them.

The Elk is a Monster of the Venison sort. His Skin is used al-
most in the same Nature as the *Buffelo*'s. Some take him for the red
Deer of *America;* but he is not: For, if brought and kept in
Company with one of that sort, of the contrary Sex, he will
never couple. His Flesh is not so sweet as the lesser Deers. His
Horns exceed (in Weight) all Creatures which the new World

affords. They will often resort and feed with the *Buffelo,* delighting in the same Range as they do.

The Stags of *Carolina* are lodg'd in the Mountains. They are not so large as in *Europe,* but much larger than any Fallow-Deer. They are always fat, I believe, with some delicate Herbage that grows on the Hills; for we find all Creatures that graze much fatter and better Meat on the Hills, than those in the Valleys: I mean towards and near the Sea. Some Deer on these Mountains afford the occidental *Bezoar,* not coming from a Goat, as some report. What sort of Beast affords the oriental *Bezoar,* I know not. The Tallow of the Harts make incomparable Candles. Their Horns and Hides are of the same Value, as others of their kind.

Fallow-Deer in *Carolina,* are taller and longer-legg'd, than in *Europe;* but neither run so fast, nor are so well haunch'd. Their Singles are much longer, and their Horns stand forward, as the others incline backward; neither do they beam, or bear their Antlers, as the *English* Deer do. Towards the Salts, they are not generally so fat and good Meat, as on the Hills. I have known some kill'd on the Salts in *January,* that have had abundance of Bots in their Throat, which keep them very poor. As the Summer approaches, these Bots come out, and turn into the finest Butterfly imaginable, being very large, and having black, white, and yellow Stripes. Deer-Skins are one of the best Commodities *Carolina* affords, to ship off for *England,* provided they be large.

Of Squirrels we have four Sorts. The first is the Fox-Squirrel, so call'd, because of his large Size, which is the Bigness of a Rabbet of two or three Months old. His Colour is commonly gray; yet I have seen several pied ones, and some reddish, and black; his chiefest Haunts are in the Piny Land, where the Almond Pine grows. There he provides his Winter-Store; they being a Nut that never fails of bearing. He may be made tame, and is very good Meat, when killed.

The next sort of Squirrel is much of the Nature of the *English,* only differing in Colour. Their Food is Nuts (of all sorts the Country affords) and Acorns. They eat well; and, like the Bear, are never found with young.

This Squirrel is gray, as well as the others. He is the least of the Three. His Food is much the same with the small gray Squirrels.

He has not Wings, as Birds or Bats have, there being a fine thin Skin cover'd with Hair, as the rest of the parts are. This is from the Fore-Feet to the Hinder-Feet, which is extended and holds so much Air, as buoys him up, from one Tree to another, that are greater distances asunder, than other Squirrels can reach by jumping or springing. He is made very tame, is an Enemy to a Cornfield, (as all Squirrels are) and eats only the germinating Eye of that Grain, which is very sweet.

Ground Squirrels are so call'd, because they never delight in running up Trees, and leaping from Tree to Tree. They are the smallest of all Squirrels. Their Tail is neither so long not bushy; but flattish. They are of a reddish Colour, and striped down each Side with black Rows, which make them very beautiful. They may be kept tame, in a little Box with Cotton. They and the Flying-Squirrels seldom stir out in Cold Weather, being tender Animals.

The Fox of *Carolina* is gray, but smells not as the Foxes in *Great-Britain,* and elsewhere. They have reddish Hair about their Ears, and are generally very fat; yet I never saw any one eat them. When hunted, they make a sorry Chace, because they run up Trees, when pursued. They are never to be made familiar and tame, as the Raccoon is. Their Furs, if in Season, are used for Muffs and other Ornaments. They live chiefly on Birds and Fowls, and such small Prey.

I have been inform'd by the *Indians,* that on a Lake of Water towards the Head of *Neus* River, there haunts a Creature, which frightens them all from Hunting thereabouts. They say, he is the Colour of a Panther, but cannot run up Trees; and that there abides with him a Creature like an *Englishman's* Dog, which runs faster than he can, and gets his Prey for him. They add, that there is no other of that Kind that ever they met withal; and that they have no other way to avoid him, but by running up a Tree. The Certainty of this I cannot affirm by my own Knowledge, yet they all agree in this Story. As for Lions, I never saw any in *America;* neither can I imagine, how they should come there.

Of Rats we have two sorts; the House-Rat, as in *Europe;* and the Marsh-Rat, which differs very much from the other, being more hairy, and has several other Distinctions, too long here to name.

Mice are the same here, as those in *England,* that belong to the House. There is one sort that poisons a Cat, as soon as she eats of them, which has sometimes happen'd. These Mice resort not to Houses.

The Dormouse is the same as in *England;* and so is the Weasel, which is very scarce.

The Bat or Rearmouse, the same as in *England.* The *Indian* Children are much addicted to eat Dirt, and so are some of the Christians. But roast a Bat on a Skewer, then pull the Skin off, and make the Child that eats Dirt, eat the roasted Rearmouse; and he will never eat Dirt again. This is held as an infallible Remedy. I have put this amongst the Beasts, as partaking of both Natures; of the Bird, and Mouse-Kind.

Having mention'd all the sorts of terrestrial or Land-Animals, which *Carolina* affords and are yet known to us, except the Tame and Domestick Creatures (of which I shall give an Account hereafter, when I come to treat of the Ways and Manners of Agriculture in that Province) I shall now proceed to the known *Insects* of that Place. Not that I pretend to give an ample Account of the whole Tribe, which is too numerous, and contains too great a Diversity of Species, many not yet discovered, and others that have slipt my Memory at present; But those which I can remember, I here present my Readers withal.

Insects [85] *of* Carolina

Allegators	*Long black Snake*
Rattle-Snakes	*King-Snake*
Ground Rattle-Snakes	*Green Snake*
Horn-Snakes	*Corn Snake*
Water-Snakes, four sorts	*Vipers black and gray*
Swamp Snakes, three sorts	*Tortois*
Red-bellied Land-Snakes	*Terebin Land and Water*
Red-back'd Snake	*Brimstone-Snake*
Black Truncheon Snake	*Egg, or Chicken-Snake*
Scorpion-Lizard	*Eel-Snake, or great Loach*
Green Lizard	*Brown Lizard*
Frogs, many sorts	*Rotten-wood Worm,* & c.

85. Webster's *Dictionary* defines an insect as "any of a class (Insecta) of small invertebrate animals, with three clearly defined body regions, *head, thorax,* and *abdomen,* with only three pairs of legs, and usually with wings, as beetles, bugs, bees, flies, etc." Obviously, Lawson's classification is different, and he does not explain the reasons for his classification.

The Allegator is the same, as the Crocodile, and differs only in Name. They frequent the sides of Rivers, in the Banks of which they make their Dwellings a great way under Ground; the Hole or Mouth of their Dens lying commonly two Foot under Water, after which it rises till it be considerably above the Surface thereof. Here it is, that this amphibious Monster dwells all the Winter, sleeping away his time till the Spring appears, when he comes from his Cave, and daily swims up and down the Streams. He always breeds in some fresh Stream, or clear Fountain of Water, yet seeks his Prey in the broad Salt Waters, that are brackish, not on the Sea-side, where I never met with any. He never devours Men in *Carolina*, but uses all ways to avoid them, yet he kills Swine and Dogs, the former as they come to feed in the Marshes, the others as they swim over the Creeks and Waters. They are very mischievous to the Wares made for taking Fish, into which they come to prey on the Fish that are caught in the Ware, from whence they cannot readily extricate themselves, and so break the Ware in Pieces, being a very strong Creature. This Animal, in these Parts, sometimes exceeds seventeen Foot long. It is impossible to kill them with a Gun, unless you chance to hit them about the Eyes, which is a much softer Place, than the rest of their impenetrable Armour. They roar, and make a hideous Noise against bad Weather, and before they come out of their Dens in the Spring. I was pretty much frightened with one of these once; which happened thus: I had built a House about half a Mile from an *Indian* Town, on the Fork of *Neus*-River, where I dwelt by my self, excepting a young *Indian* Fellow, and a Bull-Dog, that I had along with me. I had not then been so long a Sojourner in *America,* as to be throughly acquainted with this Creature. One of them had got his Nest directly under my House, which stood on pretty high Land, and by a Creek-side, in whose Banks his Entring-place was, his Den reaching the Ground directly on which my House stood. I was sitting alone by the Fire-side (about nine a Clock at Night, some time in *March*) the *Indian* Fellow being gone to the Town, to see his Relations; so that there was no body in the House but my self and my Dog; when, all of a sudden, this ill-favour'd Neighbour of mine, set up such a Roaring, that he made the House shake about my Ears, and so continued, like a Bittern, (but a hundred times louder, if possible) for four or five times. The Dog stared, as if

he was frightned out of his Senses; nor indeed, could I imagine
what it was, having never heard one of them before. Immediately
again I had another Lesson; and so a third. Being at that time
amongst none but Savages, I began to suspect, they were working some Piece of Conjuration under my House, to get away
my Goods; not but that, at another time, I have as little Faith
in their, or any others working Miracles, by diabolical Means, as
any Person living. At last, my Man came in, to whom when I had
told the Story, he laugh'd at me, and presently undeceiv'd me,
by telling me what it was that made that Noise. These Allegators lay Eggs, as the Ducks do; only they are longer shap'd,
larger, and a thicker Shell, than they have. How long they are in
hatching, I cannot tell; but, as the *Indians* say, it is most part
of the Summer, they always lay by a Spring-Side, the young living in and about the same, as soon as hatch'd. Their Eggs are
laid in Nests made in the Marshes, and contain twenty
or thirty Eggs. Some of these Creatures afford a great deal of Musk.
Their Tail, when cut of, looks very fair and white, seemingly
like the best of Veal. Some People have eaten thereof, and say,
it is delicate Meat, when they happen not to be musky. Their
Flesh is accounted proper for such as are troubled with the lame
Distemper, (a sort of Rhumatism) so is the Fat very prevailing
to remove Aches and Pains, by Unction. The Teeth of this Creature, when dead, are taken out, to make Chargers for Guns, being
of several Sizes, fit for all Loads. They are white, and would
make pretty Snuff Boxes, if wrought by an Artist. After the
Tail of the Allegator is separated from the Body, it will move
very freely for four days.

The Rattle-Snakes are found on all the Main of *America*, that
I ever had any Account of; being so call'd from the Rattle at
the end of their Tails, which is a Connexion of jointed Cover-
ings, of an excrementitious Matter, betwixt the Substance of
a Nail, and a Horn, though each *Tegmen* is very thin. Nature
seems to have design'd these, on purpose to give Warning of
such an approaching Danger, as the venomous Bite of these
Snakes is. Some of them grow to a very great Bigness, as six
Foot in Length, their Middle being the Thickness of the Small of a lusty Man's Leg. We have
an Account of much larger Serpents of this Kind;
but I never met them yet, although I have seen
and kill'd abundance in my time. They are of an

Orange, tawny, and blackish Colour, on the Back; differing (as all
Snakes do) in Colour, on the Belly; being of an Ash-Colour, inclining to Lead. The Male is easily distinguish'd from the Female, by a
black Velvet-Spot on his Head; and besides, his Head is smaller
shaped, and long. Their Bite is venomous, if not speedily remedied; especially, if the Wound be in a Vein, Nerve, Tendon,
or Sinew; when it is very difficult to cure. The *Indians* are the
best Physicians for the Bite of these and all other venomous
Creatures of this Country. There are four sorts of Snake-Roots
already discover'd, which Knowledge came from the *Indians,*
who have perform'd several great Cures. The Rattle-Snakes are
accounted the peaceablest in the World; for they never attack
any one, or injure them, unless they are trod upon, or molested.
The most Danger of being bit by these Snakes, is for those that
survey Land in *Carolina;* yet I never heard of any Surveyor that
was kill'd, or hurt by them. I have myself gone over several of
this Sort, and others; yet it pleased God, I never came to any
harm. They have the Power, or Art (I know not which to call
it) to charm Squirrels, Hares, Partridges, or any such thing, in
such a manner, that they run directly into their Mouths. This
I have seen by a Squirrel and one of these Rattle-Snakes; and
other Snakes have, in some measure, the same Power. The
Rattle-Snakes have many small Teeth, of which I cannot see
they make any use; for they swallow every thing whole; but the
Teeth which poison, are only four; two on each side of their
Upper-Jaws. These are bent like a Sickle, and hang loose as if by a
Joint. Towards the setting on of these, there is, in each Tooth, a
little Hole, wherein you may just get in the Point of a small
Needle. And here it is, that the Poison comes out, (which is as
green as Grass) and follows the Wound, made by the Point of
their Teeth. They are much more venomous in the Months
of *June* and *July,* than they are in *March, April* or *September.*
The hotter the Weather, the more poisonous. Neither may we
suppose, that they can renew their Poison as oft as they will;
for we have had a Person bit by one of these, who never rightly
recover'd it, and very hardly escaped with Life; a second Person
bit in the same Place by the same Snake, and receiv'd no more
Harm, that if bitten with a Rat. They cast their Skins every
Year, and commonly abide near the Place where the old Skin
lies. These cast Skins are used in Physick, and the Rattles are
reckon'd good to expedite the Birth. The Gall is made up into

Pills, with Clay, and kept for Use; being given in Pestilential Fevers and the Small-Pox. It is accounted a noble Remedy, known to few, and held as a great *Arcanum*. This Snake has two Nostrils on each side of his Nose. Their Venom, I have Reason to believe, effects no Harm, any otherwise than when darted into the Wound by the Serpents Teeth.

The Ground Rattle-Snake, wrong nam'd, because it has nothing like Rattles. It resembles the Rattle-Snake a little in Colour, but is darker, and never grows to any considerable Bigness, not exceeding a Foot, or sixteen Inches. He is reckon'd amongst the worst of Snakes; and stays out the longest of any Snake I know, before he returns (in the Fall of the Leaf) to his Hole.

Of the Horn-Snakes I never saw but two, that I remember. They are like the Rattle-Snake in Colour, but rather lighter. They hiss exactly like a Goose, when any thing approaches them. They strike at their Enemy with their Tail, and kill whatsoever they wound with it, which is arm'd at the End with a horny Substance, like a Cock's Spur. This is their Weapon. I have heard it credibly reported, by those who said they were Eye-Witnesses, that a small Locust-Tree, about the Thickness of a Man's Arm, being struck by one of these Snakes, at Ten a Clock in the Morning, then verdant and flourishing, at four in the Afternoon was dead, and the Leaves red and wither'd. Doubtless, be it how it will, they are very venomous. I think, the *Indians* do not pretend to cure their Wound.

Of Water-Snakes there are four sorts. The first is of the Horn-Snakes Colour, though less. The next is a very long Snake, differing in Colour, and will make nothing to swim over a River a League wide. They hang upon Birches and other Trees by the Water-Side. I had the Fortune once to have one of them leap into my Boat, as I was going up a narrow River; the Boat was full of Mats, which I was glad to take out, to get rid of him. They are reckon'd poisonous. A third is much of an *English* Adder's Colour, but always frequents the Salts, and lies under the Drift Seaweed, where they are in abundance, and are accounted mischievous, when they bite. The last is of a sooty black Colour, and frequents Ponds and Ditches. What his Qualities are, I cannot tell.

Of the Swamp-Snakes there are three sorts, which are very near akin to the Water-Snakes, and may be rank'd amongst them.

The Belly of the first is of a Carnation or Pink Colour; his Back a dirty brown; they are large, but have not much Venom in them, as ever I learnt. The next is a large Snake, of a brown Dirt Colour, and always abides in the Marshes.

The last is mottled, and very poisonous. They dwell in Swamps Sides, and Ponds, and have prodigious wide Mouths, and (though not long) arrive to the thickness of the Calf of a Man's Leg.

These frequent the Land altogether, and are so call'd because of their red Bellies, which incline to an Orange-Colour. Some have been bitten with these sort of Snakes, and not hurt; when others have suffer'd very much by them. Whether there be two sorts of these Snakes, which we make no Difference of, I cannot at present determine.

I never saw but one of these, which I stept over, and did not see him; till he that brought the Chain after me, spy'd him. He has a red Back, as the last has a red Belly. They are a long, slender Snake, and very rare to be met withal. I enquired of the *Indian* that was along with me, whether they were very venomous, who made Answer, that if he had bitten me, even the *Indian* could not have cured it.

This sort of Snake might very well have been rank'd with the Water-Snakes. They lie under Roots of Trees, and on the Banks of Rivers. When any thing disturbs them, they dart into the Water (which is Salt) like an Arrow out of a Bow. They are thick and the Shortest Snake I ever saw. What Good, or Harm, there is in them, I know not. Some of these Water-Snakes will swallow a black Land-Snake, half as long again as themselves.

The Scorpion Lizard, is no more like a Scorpion than a Hedge-Hog; but they very commonly call him a Scorpion. He is of the Lizard Kind, but much bigger; his Back is of a dark Copper-Colour; his Belly an Orange; he is very nimble in running up Trees, or on the Land, and is accounted very poisonous. He has the most Sets of Teeth in his Mouth and Throat, that ever I saw.

Green Lizards are very harmless and beautiful, having a little Bladder under their Throat, which they fill with Wind, and evacuate the same at Pleasure. They are of a most glorious Green, and very tame. They resort to the Walls of Houses in the Summer Season, and Stand gazing on a Man, without any Concern or Fear. There are several other Colours of these Lizards; but none so beautiful as the green ones are.

Of Frogs we have several sorts; the most famous is the Bull-Frog, so call'd, because he lows exactly like that Beast, which makes Strangers wonder (when by the side of a Marsh) what's the matter, for they hear the Frogs low, and can see no Cattle; he is very large. I believe, I have seen one with as much Meat on him, as a Pullet, if he had been dress'd. The small green Frogs get upon Trees, and make a Noise. There are several other colour'd small Frogs; but the Common Land-Frog is likest a Toad, only he leaps, and is not poisonous. He is a great Devourer of Ants, and the Snakes devour him. These Frogs baked and beat to Powder, and taken with Orrice-Root cures a Tympany.

The long, black Snake frequents the Land altogether, and is the nimblest Creature living. His Bite has no more Venom, than a Prick with a Pin. He is the best Mouser that can be; for he leaves not one of that Vermine alive, where he comes. He also kills the Rattle-Snake, wheresoever he meets him, by twisting his Head about the Neck of the Rattle-Snake, and whipping him to Death with his Tail. This Whipster haunts the Dairies of careless Housewives, and never misses to skim the Milk clear of the Cream. He is an excellent Egg-Merchant, for he does not suck the Eggs, but swallows them whole (as all Snakes do.) He will often swallow all the Eggs from under a Hen that sits, and coil himself under the Hen, in the Nest, where sometimes the Housewife finds him. This Snake, for all his Agility, is so brittle, that when he is pursued, and gets his Head into the Hole of a Tree, if any body gets hold of the other end, he will twist, and break himself off in the middle. One of these Snakes, whose Neck is no thicker that a Woman's little Finger, will swallow a Squirrel; so much does that part stretch, in all these Creatures.

The King-Snake is the longest of all others, and not common; no Snake (they say) will meddle with them. I think they are not accounted very venomous. The *Indians* make Girdles and Sashes of their Skins.

Green-Snakes are very small, tho' pretty (if any Beauty be allow'd to Snakes.) Every one makes himself very familiar with them, and puts them in their Bosom, because there is no manner of Harm in them.

The Corn-Snakes are but small ones; they are of a brown Colour, mixed with tawny. There is no more hurt in this, than in the green Snake.

Of those we call Vipers, there are two sorts. People call these Vipers, because they spread a very flat Head at any time when they are vex'd. One of these is a grayish like the *Italian* Viper, the other black and short; and is reckon'd amongst the worst of Snakes, for Venom.

Tortois, vulgarly call'd Turtle; I have rank'd these among the Insects, because they lay Eggs, and I did not know well where to put them. Among us there are three sorts. The first is the green Turtle, which is not common, but is sometimes found on our Coast. The next is the Hawks-bill, which is common. These two sorts are extraordinary Meat. The third is Logger-Head, which Kind scarce any one covets, except it be for the Eggs, which of this and all other Turtles, are very good Food. None of these sorts of Creatures Eggs will ever admit the White to be harder than a Jelly; yet the Yolk, with boiling, becomes as hard as any other Egg.

Of Terebins there are divers sorts, all which, to be brief, we will comprehend under the Distinction of Land and Water-Terebins.

The Land-Terebin is of several Sizes, but generally Round-Mouth'd, and not Hawks-Bill'd, as some are. The *Indians* eat them. Most of them are good Meat, except the very large ones; and they are good Food too, provided they are not Musky. They are an utter Enemy to the Rattle-Snake, for when the Terebin meets him, he catches hold of him a little below his Neck, and draws his Head into his Shell, which makes the Snake beat his Tail, and twist about with all the Strength and Violence imaginable, to get away; but the Terebin soon dispatches him, and there leaves him. These they call in *Europe* the Land Tortois; their Food is Snails, Tad-pools, or young Frogs, Mushrooms, and the Dew and Slime of the Earth and Ponds.

Water Terebins are small; containing about as much Meat as a Pullet, and are extraordinary Food; especially, in *May* and *June*. When they lay, their Eggs are very good; but they have so many Enemies that find them out, that the hundredth part never comes to Perfection. The Sun and Sand hatch them, which come out the Bigness of a small Chesnut, and seek their own Living.

We now come again to the Snakes. The Brimstone is so call'd, I believe, because it is almost of a Brimstone Colour. They might as well have call'd it a Glass-Snake, for it is as brittle as a Tobacco-Pipe, so that if you give it the least Touch of a small Twigg, it immediately breaks into several Pieces. Some affirm, that if you let it remain where you broke it, it will come together again. What Harm there is in this brittle Ware, I cannot tell; but I never knew any body hurt by them.

The Egg or Chicken-Snake is so call'd, because it is frequent about the Hen-Yard, and eats Eggs and Chickens, they are of a dusky Soot Colour, and will roll themselves round, and stick eighteen, or twenty Foot high, by the side of a smooth-bark'd Pine, where there is no manner of Hold, and there sun themselves, and sleep all the Sunny Part of the Day. There is no great matter of Poison in them.

The Wood-Worms are of a Copper, shining Colour, scarce so thick as your little Finger; are often found in Rotten-Trees. They are accounted venomous, in case they bite, though I never knew any thing hurt by them. They never exceed four or five Inches in length.

The Reptiles, or smaller *Insects*, are too numerous to relate here, this Country affording innumerable Quantities thereof; as the Flying-Stags with Horns, Beetles, Butterflies, Grashoppers, Locust, and several hundreds of uncouth Shapes, which in the Summer-Season are discovered here in *Carolina*, the Description of which requires a large Volume, which is not my Intent at present. Besides, what the Mountainous Part of this Land may hereafter lay open to our View, Time and Industry will discover, for we that have settled but a small Share of this large Province, cannot imagine, but there will be a great number of Discoveries made by those that shall come hereafter into the Back-part of this Land, and make Enquiries therein, when, at least, we consider that the Westward of *Carolina* is quite different in Soil, Air, Weather, Growth of Vegetables, and several Animals too, which we at present are wholly Strangers to, and to seek for. As to a right Knowledge thereof, I say, when another Age is come, the Ingenious then in being may stand upon the Shoulders of those that went before them, adding their own Experiments to what was delivered down to them by their Predecessors, and then there will be something towards a complete Natural History, which (in these days) would be no easie Undertaking to any Author that writes truly and compendiously, as he ought to do. It is sufficient at present, to write an honest and fair Account of any of the Settlements, in this new World, without wandring out of the Path of Truth, or bespattering any Man's Reputation any wise concern'd in the Government of the Colony; he that mixes Invectives with Relations of this Nature rendering himself suspected of Partiality in whatever he writes. For my part, I wish all well, and he that has received any severe Dealings from the Magistrate or his Superiours, had best examine himself well, if he was not first in the Fault; if so, then he can justly blame none but himself for what has happen'd to him.

Having thus gone thro' the *Insects*, as in the Table, except the Eel-Snake, (so call'd, though very improperly, because he is nothing but a Loach, that sucks, and cannot bite, as the Snakes do.) He is very large, commonly sixteen Inches, or a Foot and half long; having all the Properties that other Loaches have, and dwells in Pools and Waters, as they do. Notwithstanding, we have the same Loach as you have, in Bigness.

This is all that at present I shall mention, touching the *Insects*, and so go on to give an Account of the Fowls and Birds, that are properly found in *Carolina*, which are these.

Birds of Carolina [86]

Eagle bald	*Ring-tail*
Eagle gray	*Raven*
Fishing Hawk	*Crow*
Turkey Buzzard, or Vulture	*Black Birds, two sorts*
Herring-tail'd Hawk	*Buntings, two sorts*
Goshawk	*Pheasant*
Falcon	*Woodcock*
Merlin	*Snipe*
Sparrow-hawk	*Partridge*
Hobby	*Moorhen*
Jay	*Red Bird*
Green Plover	*East-India Bat*
Plover gray or whistling	*Martins, two sorts*
Pigeon	*Diveling, or Swift*
Turtle Dove	*Swallow*
Parrakeeto	*Humming Bird*

86. For an interesting article on this subject, see Waldo Lee McAtee, *The Birds in Lawson's* New Voyage to Carolina, 1709 (Raleigh: North Carolina Bird Club, 1955–56).

Thrush

Wood-Peckers, *five sorts*

Mocking-birds, *two sorts*

Cat-Bird

Cuckoo

Blue-Bird

Bulfinch

Nightingale

Hedge-Sparrow

Wren

Sparrows, *two sorts*

Lark

The Tom-Tit, *or* Ox-Eye

Owls, *two sorts*

Scritch Owl

Baltimore bird

Throstle, *no Singer*

Whippoo Will

Reed Sparrow

Weet bird

Rice bird

Cranes *and* Storks

Snow-birds

Yellow-wings

Water Fowl are,

Water Fowl.

Swans, *called* Trompeters

Swans, *called* Hoopers

Geese, *three sorts*

Brant gray

Brant white

Sea-pies *or pied* Curlues

Will Willets

Great Gray Gulls

Old Wives

Sea Cock

Curlues, *three sorts*

Coots

Kings-fisher

Loons, *two sorts*

Bitterns, *three sorts*

Hern gray

Hern white

Water Pheasant

Little gray Gull

Little Fisher, *or Dipper*

Gannet

Shear-water

Great black pied Gull

Marsh-hens

Blue Peter's

Sand-birds

Runners

Ducks, *as in* England

Ducks black, *all Summer*

Ducks pied, *build on Trees*

Ducks whistling, *at* Sapona

Ducks scarlet-eye *at* Esaw

Blue-wings

Widgeon

Teal, *two sorts*

Shovelers

Whisslers

Black Flusterers, *or bald* Coot

Turkeys *wild*

Fishermen

Divers

Raft Fowl

Bull-necks

Redheads

Tropick-birds

Pellican

Cormorant

Tutcocks

Swaddle-bills

Men [mew]

Sheldrakes

Bald Faces

Water Witch, *or Ware* Coot

As the Eagle is reckon'd the King of Birds I have begun with him. The first I shall speak of, is the bald Eagle; so call'd, because his Head, to the middle of his Neck, and his Tail, is as white as Snow. These Birds continually breed the Year round; for when the young Eagles are just down'd, with a sort of white woolly Feathers, the Hen-Eagle lays again, which Eggs are hatch'd by the Warmth of the young ones in the Nest, so that the Flight of one Brood makes Room for the next, that are but just hatch'd. They prey on any living thing they can catch. They are heavy of Flight, and cannot get their Food by Swiftness, to help which there is a Fishawk that catches Fishes, and suffers the Eagle to take them from her, although she is long-wing'd and a swift Flyer, and can make far better way in her Flight than the Eagle can. The bald Eagle attends the Gunners in Winter, with all the Obsequiousness imaginable, and when he shoots and kills any Fowl, the Eagle surely comes in for his Bird; and besides, those that are wounded, and escape the Fowler, fall to the Eagle's share. He is an excellent Artist at stealing young Pigs, which Prey he carries alive to his Nest, at which time the poor Pig makes such a Noise over Head, that Strangers that have heard them cry, and not seen the Bird and his Prey, have thought there were Flying Sows and Pigs in that Country. The Eagle's Nest is made of Twigs, Sticks and Rubbish. It is big enough to fill a handsome Carts Body, and commonly so full of nasty Bones and Carcasses that it stinks most offensively. This Eagle is not bald, till he is one or two years old.

The gray Eagle is altogether the same sort of Bird, as the Eagle in *Europe;* therefore, we shall treat no farther of him.

The Fishing-Hawk is the Eagle's Jackal, which most commonly (though not always) takes his Prey for him. He is a large Bird, being above two thirds as big as the Eagle. He builds his Nest as the Eagles do; that is, in a dead Cypress-Tree, either standing in, or hard by, the Water. The Eagle and this Bird seldom sit on a living Tree. He is of a gray pied Colour, and the most dexterous Fowl in Nature at Catching of Fish, which he wholly lives on, never eating any Flesh.

The Turkey-Buzzard of *Carolina* is a small Vulture, which lives on any dead Carcasses. They are about the Bigness of the Fishing-Hawk, and have a nasty Smell with them. They are of the Kites Colour, and are reported to be an Enemy to Snakes, by killing all they meet withal of that Kind.

The Herring, or Swallow-tail'd Hawk, is about the Bigness of a Falcon, but a much longer Bird. He is of a delicate Aurora-Colour; the Pinions of his Wings, and End of his Tail are black. He is a very beautiful Fowl, and never appears abroad but in the Summer. His Prey is chiefly on Snakes, and will kill the biggest we have, with a great deal of Dexterity and Ease.

Goshawks are very plentiful in *Carolina.* They are not seemingly so large as those from *Muscovy* [Russia]; but appear to be a very brisk Bird.

The Falcon is much the same as in *Europe,* and promises to be a brave Bird, tho' I never had any of them in my Hand; neither did I ever see any of them in any other Posture than on the Wing, which always happen'd to be in an Evening, and flying to the Westward; therefore, I believe, they have their Abode and Nest among the Mountains, where we may expect to find them, and several other Species that we are at present Strangers to.

The Merlin is a small Bird in *Europe,* but much smaller here; yet he very nimbly kills the smaller sorts of Birds, and sometimes the Partridge; if caught alive, he would be a great Rarity, because of his Beauty and Smalness.

The Sparrow-Hawk in *Carolina* is no bigger than a Field-fare in *England.* He flies at the Bush and sometimes kills a small Bird, but his chiefest Food is Reptiles, as Beetles, Grashoppers, and such small things. He is exactly of the same Colour, as the Sparrow-Hawk in *England,* only has a blackish Hood by his Eyes.

Hobbies are the same here as in *England,* and are not often met withal.

The Ring-tail is a short-wing'd Hawk, preying on Mice, and such Vermine in the Marshes, as in *England.*

Ravens, the same as in *England,* though very few. I have not seen above six in eight Years time.

Crows are here less than in *England.* They are as good Meat as a Pigeon; and never feed on any Carrion. They are great Enemies to the Corn-Fields; and cry and build almost like Rooks.

Of these we have two sorts, which are the worst Vermine in *America.* They fly sometimes in such Flocks, that they destroy every thing before them. They (both sorts) build in hollow Trees, as Starlings do. The first sort is near as big as a Dove, and is very white and delicate Food. The other sort is very beautiful, and about the Bigness of the Owsel. Part of their Head, next to the Bill, and the Pinions of their Wings, are of an Orange, and glorious Crimson Colour. They are as good Meat as the former, tho' very few here (where large Fowl are so plenty) ever trouble themselves to kill or dress them.

Of the Bunting-Larks we have two sorts, though the Heel of this Bird is not so long as in *Europe*. The first of these often accompany the Black-birds, and sing as the Bunting-Larks in *England* do, differing very little. The first sort has an Orange-Colour on the Tops of their Wings, and are as good Meat as those in *Europe*. The other sort is something less, of a lighter Colour; nothing differing therein from those in *England*, as to Feathers, Bigness, and Meat.

The Pheasant of *Carolina* differs some small matter from the *English* Pheasant, being not so big, and having some difference in Feather; yet he is not any wise inferiour in Delicacy, but is as good Meat, or rather finer. He haunts the back Woods, and is seldom found near the Inhabitants.

The Woodcocks live and breed here, though they are not in great plenty, as I have seen them in some Parts of *England*, and other Places. They want one third of the *English* Woodcock in Bigness; but differ not in Shape, or Feather, save that their Breast is of a Carnation Colour; and they make a Noise (when they are on the Wing) like the Bells about a Hawk's Legs. They are certainly as dainty Meat, as any in the World. Their Abode is in all Parts of this Country, in low, boggy Ground, Springs, Swamps, and Percoarsons.

The Snipes here frequent the same Places, as they do in *England*, and differ nothing from them. They are the only wild Bird that is nothing different from the Species of *Europe*, and keeps with us all the Year. In some Places, there are a great many of these Snipes.

Our Partridges in *Carolina*, very often take upon Trees, and have a sort of Whistle and Call, quite different from those in *England*. They are a very beautiful Bird, and great Destroyers of the Pease in Plantations; wherefore, they set Traps, and catch many of them. They have the same Feather, as in *Europe*; only the Cock wants the Horse-Shooe, in lieu of which he has a fair Half-Circle over each Eye. These (as well as the Woodcock) are less than the *European* Bird, but far finer Meat. They might be easily transported to any Place, because they take to eating, after caught.

The Moorhens are of the black-Game. I am inform'd, that the gray Game haunts the Hills. They never come into the Settlement, but keep in the hilly Parts.

Jays are here common, and very mischievous, in devouring our Fruit, and spoiling more than they eat. They are abundantly more beautiful, and finer feather'd than those in *Europe,* and not above half so big.

The Lap-wing or Green-Plover are here very common. They cry pretty much, as the *English* Plovers do; and differ not much in Feather, but want a third of their Bigness.

The gray or whistling Plover, are very scarce amongst us. I never saw any but three times, that fell and settled on the Ground. They differ very little from those in *Europe,* as far as I could discern. I have seen several great Flocks of them fly over head; therefore, believe, they inhabit the Valleys near the Mountains.

Our wild Pigeons, are like the Wood-Queese or Stock-Doves, only have a longer Tail. They leave us in the Summer. This sort of Pigeon (as I said before) is the most like our Stock-Doves, or Wood-Pigeons that we have in *England;* only these differ in their Tails, which are very long, much like a Parrakeeto's? You must understand, that these Birds do not breed amongst us, (who are settled at, and near the Mouths of the Rivers, as I have intimated to you before) but come down (especially in hard Winters) amongst the Inhabitants, in great Flocks, as they were seen to do in the Year 1707, which was the hardest Winter that ever was known, since *Carolina* has been seated by the Christians. And if that Country had such hard Weather, what must be expected of the severe Winters in *Pensylvania, New-York,* and *New-England,* where Winters are ten times (if possible) colder than with us. Although the Flocks are, in such Extremities, very numerous; yet they are not to be mention'd in Comparison with the great and infinite Numbers of these Fowl, that are met withal about a hundred, or a hundred and fifty, Miles to the Westward of the Places where we at present live; and where these Pigeons come down, in quest of a small sort of Acorns, which in those Parts are plentifully found. They are the same we call Turky-Acorns, because the wild Turkies feed very much thereon; And for the same Reason, those Trees that bear them, are call'd Turky-Oaks. I saw such prodigious Flocks of these Pigeons, in *January* or *February,*

1701-2, (which were in the hilly Country, between the great Nation of the *Esaw Indians,* and the pleasant Stream of *Sapona,* which is the West-Branch of *Clarendon,* or *Cape-Fair* River) that they had broke down the Limbs of a great many large Trees all over those Woods, whereon they chanced to sit and roost; especially the great Pines, which are a more brittle Wood, than our sorts of Oak are. These Pigeons, about Sun-Rise, when we were preparing to march on our Journey, would fly by us in such vast Flocks, that they would be near a Quarter of an Hour, before they were all pass'd by; and as soon as that Flock was gone, another would come; and so successively one after another, for great part of the Morning. It is observable, that wherever these Fowl come in such Numbers, as I saw them then, they clear all before them, scarce leaving one Acorn upon the Ground, which would, doubtless, be a great Prejudice to the Planters that should seat there, because their Swine would be thereby depriv'd of their Mast. When I saw such Flocks of the Pigeons I now speak of, none of our Company had any other sort of Shot, than that which is cast in Moulds, and was so very large, that we could not put above ten or a dozen of them into our largest Pieces; Wherefore, we made but an indifferent Hand of shooting them; although we commonly kill'd a Pigeon for every Shot. They were very fat, and as good Pigeons, as ever I eat. I enquired of the *Indians* that dwell'd in those Parts, where it was that those Pigeons bred, and they pointed towards the vast Ridge of Mountains, and said, they bred there. Now, whether they make their Nests in the Holes in the Rocks of those Mountains, or build in Trees, I could not learn; but they seem to me to be a Wood-Pigeon, that build in Trees, because of their frequent sitting thereon, and their Roosting on Trees always at Night, under which their Dung commonly lies half a Foot thick, and kills every thing that grows where it falls.

Turtle Doves are here very plentiful; they devour the Pease; for which Reason, People make Traps and catch them.

The Parrakeetos are of a green Colour, and Orange-Colour'd half way their Head. Of these and the Allegators, there is none found to the Northward of this Province. They visit us first, when Mulberries are ripe, which Fruit they love extremely. They peck the Apples, to eat the Kernels, so that the Fruit rots and perishes. They are mischievous to Orchards. They are often taken alive, and will become familiar and tame in two days. They have their Nests in hollow Trees, in low, swampy Ground. They devour the Birch-Buds in *April,* and lie hidden when the Weather is frosty and hard.

The Thrushes in *America,* are the same as in *England,* and red under the Wings. They never appear amongst us but in hard Weather, and presently leave us again.

Of Wood-peckers, we have four sorts. The first is as big as a Pigeon, being of a dark brown Colour, with a white Cross on his Back, his Eyes circled with white, and on his Head stands a Tuft of beautiful Scarlet Feathers. His Cry is heard a long way; and he flies from one rotten Tree to another, to get Grubs, which is the Food he lives on.

The second sort are of an Olive-Colour, striped with yellow. They eat Worms as well as Grubs, and are about the Bigness of those in *Europe.*

The third is the same Bigness as the last; he is pied with black and white, has a Crimson Head, without a Topping, and is a Plague to the Corn and Fruit; especially the Apples. He opens the Covering of the young Corn, so that the Rain gets in, and rots it.

The fourth sort of these Wood-peckers, is a black and white speckled, or mottled; the finest I ever saw. The Cock has a red Crown; he is not near so big as the others; his Food is Grubs, Corn, and other creeping Insects. He is not very wild, but will let one come up to him, then shifts on the other side the Tree, from your sight; and so dodges you for a long time together. He is about the size of an *English* Lark.

The Mocking-Bird is about as big as a Throstle in *England,* but longer; they are of a white, and gray Colour, and are held to be the Choristers of *America,* as indeed they are. They sing with the greatest Diversity of Notes, that is possible for a Bird to change to. They may be bred up, and will sing with us tame in Cages; yet I never take any of their Nests, altho' they build yearly in my Fruit-Trees, because I have their Company, as much as if tame, as to the singing Part. They often sit upon our Chimneys in Summer, there being then no Fire in them, and sing the whole Evening and most part of the Night. They are always attending our Dwellings; and feed upon Mulberries and other Berries and Fruits; especially the *Mechoacan*-berry [species of bindweed], which grows here very plentifully.

There is another sort call'd the Ground-Mocking-Bird. She is the same bigness, and of a Cinnamon Colour. This Bird sings excellently well, but is not so common amongst us as the former.

The Cat-Bird, so nam'd, because it makes a Noise exactly like young Cats. They have a blackish Head, and an Ash-coloured Body, and have no other Note that I know of. They are no bigger than a Lark, yet will fight a Crow or any other great Bird.

The Cuckoo of *Carolina* may not properly be so call'd, because she never uses that Cry; yet she is of the same Bigness and Feather, and sucks the Small-Birds Eggs, as the *English* Cuckoo does.

A Blue-Bird is the exact Bigness of a Robin-red-breast. The Cock has the same colour'd Breast as the Robin has, and his Back, and all the other Parts of him, are of as fine a Blue, as can possibly be seen in any thing in the World. He has a Cry, and a Whistle. They hide themselves all the Winter.

Bulfinches, in *America,* differ something from those in *Europe,* in their Feathers, tho' not in their Bigness. I never knew any one tame, therefore know not, what they might be brought to.

The Nightingales are different in Plumes from those in *Europe.* They always frequent the low Groves, where they sing very prettily all Night.

Hedge-Sparrows are here, though few Hedges. They differ scarce any thing in Plume or Bigness, only I never heard this Whistle, as the *English* one does; especially after Rain.

The Wren is the same as in *Europe,* yet I never heard any Note she has in *Carolina.*

Sparrows here differ in Feather from the *English.* We have several Species of Birds call'd Sparrows, one of them much resembling the Bird call'd a *Corinthian* Sparrow.

The Lark with us resorts to the Savannas, or natural Meads, and green Marshes. He is colour'd and heel'd as the Lark is; but his Breast is of a glittering fair Lemon-Colour, and he is as big as a Fieldfare, and very fine Food.

The Red-Birds (whose Cock is all over of a rich Scarlet Feather, with a tufted Crown on his Head, of the same Colour) are the Bigness of a Bunting-Lark, and very hardy, having a strong thick Bill. They will sing very prettily, when taken old, and put in a Cage. They are good Birds to turn a Cage with Bells; or if taught, as the Bulfinch is, I believe, would prove very docible.

East-India Bats or Musqueto Hawks, are the Bigness of a

Cuckoo, and much of the same Colour. They are so call'd, because the same sort is found in the *East-Indies*. They appear only in the Summer, and live on Flies, which they catch in the Air, as Gnats, Musquetos, &c.

Martins are here of two sorts. The first is the same as in *England;* the other as big as a Black-Bird. They have white Throats and Breasts, with black Backs. The Planters put Gourds on standing Poles, on purpose for these Fowl to build in, because they are a very Warlike Bird, and beat the Crows from the Plantations.

The Swift, or Diveling, the same as in *England.*

Swallows, the same as in *England.*

The Humming-Bird is the Miracle of all our wing'd Animals; He is feather'd as a Bird, and gets his Living as the Bees, by sucking the Honey from each Flower. In some of the larger sort of Flowers, he will bury himself, by diving to suck the bottom of it, so that he is quite cover'd, and oftentimes Children catch them in those Flowers, and keep them alive for five or six days. They are of different Colours, the Cock differing from the Hen. The Cock is of a green, red, *Aurora,* and other Colours mixt. He is much less than a Wren, and very nimble. His Nest is one of the greatest Pieces of Workmanship the whole Tribe of wing'd Animals can shew, it commonly hanging on a single Bryar, most artificially woven, a small Hole being left to go in and out at. The Eggs are the Bigness of Pease.

The Tom-Tit, or Ox-Eyes, as in *England.*

Of Owls we have two sorts; the smaller sort is like ours in *England;* the other sort is as big as a middling Goose, and has a prodigious Head. They make a fearful Hollowing in the Night-time, like a Man, whereby they often make Strangers lose their way in the Woods.

Scritch Owls, much the same as in *Europe.*

The *Baltimore-Bird,* so call'd from the Lord *Baltimore,* Proprietor of all *Maryland,* in which Province many of them are found. They are the Bigness of a Linnet, with yellow Wings, and beautiful in other Colours.

Throstle, the same Size and Feather as in *Europe,* but I never could hear any of them sing.

The Weet, so call'd because he cries always before Rain; he resembles nearest the Fire-tail.

Cranes use the Savannas, low Ground, and Frogs; they are above five Foot-high, when extended; are of a Cream Colour, and have a Crimson Spot on the Crown of their Heads. Their Quills are excellent for Pens; their Flesh makes the best Broth, yet is very hard to digest. Among them often frequent Storks, which are here seen, and no where besides in *America,* that I have yet heard of. The Cranes are easily bred up tame, and are excellent in a Garden to destroy Frogs, Worms, and other Vermine.

The Snow-Birds are most numerous in the North Parts of *America,* where there are great Snows. They visit us sometimes in *Carolina,* when the Weather is harder than ordinary. They are like the Stones Smach, or Wheat-Ears, and are delicate Meat.

These Yellow-Wings are a very small Bird, of a Linnet's Colour, but Wings as yellow as Gold. They frequent high up in our Rivers, and Creeks, and keep themselves in the thick Bushes, very difficult to be seen in the Spring. They sing very prettily.

Whippo-Will, so nam'd, because it makes those Words exactly. They are the Bigness of a Thrush, and call their Note under a Bush, on the Ground, hard to be seen, though you hear them never so plain. They are more plentiful in *Virginia,* than with us in *Carolina;* for I never heard but one that was near the Settlement, and that was hard-by an *Indian* Town.

This nearest resembles a Sparrow, and is the most common Small-Bird we have, therefore we call them so. They are brown, and red, cinnamon Colour, striped.

Of the Swans we have two sorts; the one we call Trompeters; because of a sort of trompeting Noise they make.

These are the largest sort we have, which come in great Flocks in the Winter, and stay, commonly, in the fresh Rivers till *February,* that the Spring comes on, when they go to the Lakes to breed. A Cygnet, that is, a last Year's Swan, is accounted a delicate Dish, as indeed it is. They are known by their Head and Feathers, which are not so white as Old ones.

The sort of Swans call'd Hoopers, are the least. They abide more in the Salt-Water, and are equally valuable, for Food, with the former. It is observable, that neither of these have a black Piece of horny Flesh down the Head, and Bill, as they have in *England.*

Of Geese we have three sorts, differing from each other only in size. Ours are not the common Geese that are in the Fens in *England,* but the other sorts, with black Heads and Necks.

The gray Brant, or Barnicle, is here very plentiful, as all other Water-Fowl are, in the Winter-Season. They are the same which they call Barnicles in *Great-Britain,* and are a very good Fowl, and eat well.

There is also a white Brant, very plentiful in *America.* This Bird is all over as white as Snow, except the Tips of his Wings, and those are black. They eat the Roots of Sedge and Grass in the Marshes and Savannas, which they tear up like Hogs. The best way to kill these Fowl is, to burn a Piece of Marsh, or Savanna, and as soon as it is burnt, they will come in great Flocks to get the Roots, where you kill what you please of them. They are as good Meat as the other, only their Feathers are stubbed, and good for little.

The Sea-Pie, or gray Curlue, is about the Bigness of a very large Pigeon, but longer. He has a long Bill as other Curlues have, which is the Colour of an *English* Owsel's, that is, yellow; as are his Legs. He frequents the Sand-beaches on the Sea-side, and when kill'd, is inferiour to no Fowl I ever eat of.

Will Willet is so called from his Cry, which he very exactly calls *Will Willet,* as he flies. His Bill is like a Curlue's, or Woodcock's, and has much such a Body as the other, yet not so tall. He is good Meat.

The great gray Gulls are good Meat, and as large as a Pullet. They lay large Eggs, which are found in very great Quantities, on the Islands in our Sound, in the Months of *June,* and *July.* The young Squabs are very good Victuals, and often prove a Relief to Travellers by Water, that have spent their Provisions.

Old Wives are a black and white pied Gull with extraordinary long Wings, and a golden colour'd Bill and Feet. He makes a dismal Noise, as he flies, and ever and anon dips his Bill in the Salt-Water. I never knew him eaten.

The Sea-Cock is a Gull that crows at Break of Day, and in the Morning, exactly like a Dunghil Cock, which Cry seems very pleasant in those uninhabited Places. He is never eaten.

Of Curlues there are three sorts, and vast Numbers of each. They have all long Bills, and differ neither in Colour, nor Shape, only in Size. The largest is as big as a good Hen, the smaller the Bigness of a Snipe, or something bigger.

We have three sorts of Bitterns in *Carolina.* The first is the same as in *England;* the second of a deep brown, with a great Topping, and yellowish white Throat and Breast, and is lesser than the former; the last is no bigger than a Woodcock, and near the Colour of the second.

We have the same Herns, as in *England.*

White Herns are here very plentiful. I have seen above thirty sit on one Tree, at a time. They are as white as Milk, and fly very slowly.

The Water-Pheasant (very improperly call'd so) are a Water-Fowl of the Duck-Kind, having a Topping, of pretty Feathers, which sets them out. They are very good Meat.

The little Gray-Gull is of a curious gray Colour, and abides near the Sea. He is about the Bigness of a Whistling-Plover, and delicate Food.

We have the little Dipper or Fisher, that catches Fish so dexterously, the same as you have in the Islands of *Scilly.*

We have of the same Ducks, and Mallards with green Heads, in great Flocks. They are accounted the coarsest sort of our Water-Fowl.

The black Duck is full as large as the other, and good Meat. She stays with us all the Summer, and breeds. These are made tame by some, and prove good Domesticks.

We have another Duck that stays with us all the Summer. She has a great Topping, is pied, and very beautiful. She builds her Nest in a Wood-pecker's Hole, very often sixty or seventy Foot high.

Towards the Mountains in the hilly Country, on the West-Branch of *Caip-Fair* Inlet, we saw great Flocks of pretty pied Ducks, that whistled as they flew, or as they fed. I did not kill any of them.

We kill'd a curious sort of Ducks, in the Country of the *Esaw-Indians,* which were of many beautiful Colours. Their Eyes were red, having a red Circle of Flesh for their Eyelids; and were very good to eat.

The Blue-Wings are less than a Duck, but fine Meat. These are the first Fowls that appear to us in the Fall of the Leaf, coming then in great Flocks, as we suppose, from *Canada,* and the Lakes that lie behind us.

Widgeons, the same as in *Europe,* are here in great Plenty.

We have the same Teal, as in *England,* and another sort that frequents the Fresh-Water, and are always nodding their Heads. They are smaller than the common Teal, and dainty Meat.

Shovellers (a sort of Duck) are gray, with a black Head. They are a very good Fowl.

These are called Whistlers, from the whistling Noise they make, as they fly.

Black Flusterers; some call these Old Wives. They are as black as Ink. The Cocks have white Faces. They always remain in the midst of Rivers, and feed upon drift Grass, Carnels or Sea-Nettles. They are the fattest Fowl I ever saw, and sometimes so heavy with Flesh, that they cannot rise out of the Water. They make an odd sort of Noise when they fly. What Meat they are, I could never learn. Some call these the great bald Coot.

The wild Turkeys I should have spoken of, when I treated of the Land-Fowl. There are great Flocks of these in *Carolina*. I have seen about five hundred in a Flock; some of them are very large. I never weigh'd any myself, but have been inform'd of one that weigh'd near sixty Pound Weight. I have seen half a Turkey feed eight hungry Men two Meals. Sometimes the wild breed with the tame ones, which, they reckon, makes them very hardy, as I believe it must. I see no manner of Difference betwixt the wild Turkeys and the tame ones; only the wild are ever of one Colour, (*viz.*) a dark gray, or brown, and are excellent Food. They feed on Acorns, Huckle-Berries, and many other sorts of Berries that *Carolina* affords. The Eggs taken from the Nest, and hatch'd under a Hen, will yet retain a wild Nature, and commonly leave you, and run wild at last, and will never be got into a House to roost, but always pearch on some high Tree, hard-by the House, and separate themselves from the tame sort, although (at the same time) they tread and breed together. I have been inform'd, that if you take these wild Eggs, when just on the point of being hatch'd, and dip them (for some small time) in a Bowl of Milk-warm Water, it will take off their wild Nature, and make them as tame and domestick as the others. Some *Indians* have brought these wild Breed hatch'd at home, to be a Decoy to bring others to roost near their Cabins, which they have shot. But to return to the Water-Fowl.

Fishermen are like a Duck, but have a narrow Bill, with Setts of Teeth. They live on very small Fish, which they catch as they swim along. They taste Fishy. The best way to order them, is, upon occasion, to pull out the Oil-Box from the Rump, and then bury them five or six Hours under Ground. Then they become tolerable.

Of Divers there are two sorts; the one pied, the other gray; both good Meat.

Raft-Fowl includes all the sorts of small Ducks and Teal, that go in Rafts along the Shoar, and are of several sorts, that we know no Name for.

These are a whitish Fowl, about the Bigness of a Brant; they come to us after *Christmas,* in very great Flocks, in all our Rivers. They are a very good Meat, but hard to kill, because hard to come near. They will dive and endure a great deal of Shot.

Red-Heads, a lesser Fowl than Bull-Necks, are very sweet Food, and plentiful in our Rivers and Creeks.

Tropick-Birds are a white Mew, with a forked Tail. They are so call'd, because they are plentifully met withal under the Tropicks, and thereabouts.

The Pellican of the Wilderness cannot be the same as ours; this being a Water-Fowl, with a great natural Wen or Pouch under his Throat, in which he keeps his Prey of Fish, which is what he lives on. He is Web-footed, like a Goose, and shap'd like a Duck, but is a very large Fowl, bigger than a Goose. He is never eaten as Food; They make Tobacco-pouches of his Maw.

Cormorants are very well known in some Parts of *England;* we have great Flocks of them with us, especially against the Herrings run, which is in *March* and *April;* then they sit upon Logs of dry Wood in the Water, and catch the Fish.

The Gannet is a large white Fowl, having one Part of his Wings black; he lives on Fish, as the Pellican. His Fat or Grease, is as yellow as Saffron, and the best thing known, to preserve Fire-Arms, from Rust.

Shear-Waters are a longer Fowl than a Duck; some of them lie on the Coast, whilst others range the Seas all over. Sometimes they are met five hundred Leagues from Land. They live without drinking any fresh Water.

We have a great pied Gull, black and white, which seems to have a black Hood on his Head; these lay very fair Eggs which are good; as are the young ones in the Season.

Marsh-Hen, much the same as in *Europe,* only she makes another sort of Noise, and much shriller.

The same as you call Water-Hens in *England,* are here very numerous, and not regarded for eating.

The Sand-Birds are about the Bigness of a Lark, and frequent our Sand-Beaches; they are a dainty Food, if you will bestow Time and Ammunition to kill them.

These are called Runners; because if you run after them, they will run along the Sands and not offer to get up; so that you may often drive them together to shoot as you please. They are a pleasant small Bird.

A sort of Snipe, but sucks not his Food; they are almost the same as in *England.*

Swaddle-Bills are a sort of an ash-colour'd Duck, which have an extraordinary broad Bill, and are good Meat; they are not common as the others are.

The same Mew as in *England,* being a white, slender Bird, with red Feet.

The same as in *England.*

The bald, or white Faces are a good Fowl. They cannot dive, and are easily shotten.

Water-Witch, or Ware-Coots, are a Fowl with Down and no Feathers; they dive incomparably, so that no Fowler can hit them. They can neither fly, nor go; but get into the Fish-wares, and cannot fly over the Rods, and so are taken.

Thus have we given an Account of what Fowl has come to our Knowledge, since our Abode in *Carolina;* except some that, perhaps, have slipt our Memory, and so are left out of our Catalogue. Proceed we now to treat of the Inhabitants of the Watry Element, which tho' we can as yet do but very imperfectly; yet we are willing to oblige the Curious with the best Account that is in our Power to present them withal.

Fish of Carolina

The Fish in the salt, and fresh Waters of *Carolina,*[87] are,

Whales, several sorts	*Mullets*
Thrashers	*Shad*
Divel-Fish	*Fat-Backs*
Sword-Fish	*Guard, white*
Crampois [grampus]	*Guard, green*
Bottle-Noses [dolphins]	*Scate or Stingray*
Porpoises	*Thornback*
Sharks, two sorts	*Congar-Eels*
Dog-Fish	*Lamprey-Eels*
Spanish-*Mackarel*	*Eels*

87. For a scientific article on this subject, see Henry W. Fowler, *A Study of the Fishes of the Southern Piedmont and Coastal Plain* (Philadelphia, 1945), pp. 91-92.

Cavallies

Boneto's

Blue-Fish

Drum, red

Drum-Fish, black

Angel-Fish

Bass, or Rock-Fish

Sheeps-Heads

Plaice

Flounder

Soles

Sun-Fish

Toad-Fish

Sea-Tench

Trouts of the Salt Water

Crocus [croaker]

Herring

Smelts

Shads

Breams

Taylors

Fresh-Water Fish are,

Sturgeon

Pike

Trouts

Gudgeon

Pearch English

Pearch, white

Pearch, brown, or Welch-men

Pearch, flat, and mottled, or
    Irishmen

Pearch small and flat, with red
    Spots, call'd round Robins

Carp

Roach

Dace

Loaches

Sucking-Fish

Cat-Fish

Grindals

Old-Wives

Fountain-Fish

White-Fish

The Shell-Fish are,

Large Crabs, call'd Stone-Crabs

Smaller flat Crabs

Oysters great and small

Cockles

Clams

Muscles

Conks

Skellop [scallop]

Man of Noses

Periwinkles, or Wilks

Sea-Snail-Horns

Fidlars

Runners

Spanish or Pearl-Oysters

Flattings

Tortois and Terebin, accounted
    for among the Insects

Finger-Fish [star fish]

Shrimps

Fresh Water

Craw-Fish

Muscles

Whales are very numerous, on the Coast of North *Carolina*, from which they make Oil, Bone, &c. to the great Advantage of those inhabiting the Sand-Banks, along the Ocean, where these Whales come ashore, none being struck or kill'd with a Harpoon in this Place, as they are to the Northward, and elsewhere; all those Fish being found dead on the Shoar, most commonly by those that inhabit the Banks, and Sea-side, where they dwell, for that Intent, and for the Benefit of Wrecks, which sometimes fall in upon that Shoar.

Of these Monsters there are four sorts; the first, which is most choice and rich, is the *Sperma Cati* Whale, from which the *Sperma Cati* is taken. These are rich Prizes; but I never heard but of one found on this Coast, which was near *Currituck*-Inlet.

The other sorts are of a prodigious Bigness. Of these the Bone and Oil is made; the Oil being the Blubber, or oily Flesh, or Fat of that Fish boil'd. These differ not only in Colour, some being pied, others not, but very much in shape, one being call'd a Bottle-Nosed Whale, the other a Shovel-Nose, which is as different as a Salmon from a Sturgeon. These Fish seldom come ashoar with their Tongues in their Heads, the Thrasher (which is the Whale's mortal Enemy, wheresoever he meets him) eating that out of his Head, as soon as he and the Sword-Fish have kill'd him. For when the Whale-catchers (in other Parts) kill any of these Fish, they eat the Tongue, and esteem it an excellent Dish.

There is another sort of these Whales, or great Fish, though not common. I never knew of above one of that sort, found on the Coast of North *Carolina,* and he was contrary, in Shape, to all others ever found before him; being sixty Foot in Length, and not above three or four Foot Diameter. Some *Indians* in *America* will go out to Sea, and get upon a Whales Back, and peg or plug up his Spouts, and so kill him.

The Thrashers are large Fish, and mortal Enemies to the Whale, as I said before. They make good Oil; but are seldom found.

The Divel-Fish lies at some of our Inlets, and, as near as I can describe him, is shap'd like a Scate, or Stingray; only he has on his Head a Pair of very thick strong Horns, and is of a monstrous Size, and Strength; for this Fish has been known to weigh a Sloop's Anchor, and run with the Vessel a League or two, and bring her back, against Tide, to almost the same Place. Doubtless, they may afford good Oil; but I have no Experience of any Profits which arise from them.

The Sword-Fish is the other of the Whale's Enemies, and joins with the Thrasher to destroy that Monster. After they have overcome him, they eat his Tongue, as I said before, and the Whale drives ashoar.

Crampois is a large Fish, and by some accounted a young Whale; but it is not so; neither is it more than twenty five or thirty Foot long. They spout as the Whale does, and when, taken yield good Oil.

Bottle-Noses are between the Crampois and Porpois, and lie near the Soundings. They are never seen to swim leisurely, as sometimes all other Fish do, but are continually running after their Prey in Great Shoals, like wild Horses, leaping now and then above the Water. The *French* esteem them good Food, and eat them both fresh and salt.

Porpoises are frequent, all over the Ocean and Rivers that are salt; nay, we have a Fresh-Water Lake in the great Sound of North *Carolina* that has Porpoises in it. And several sorts of other unknown Fish, as the *Indians* say, that we are wholly Strangers to. As to the Porpoises, they make good Oil; they prey upon other Fish as Drums, yet never are known to take a Bait, so as to be catch'd with a Hook.

Of these there are two sorts; one call'd *Paracooda* [Barracuda]-Noses; the other Shovel-Noses; they cannot take their Prey before they turn themselves on their Backs; wherefore some Negro's, and others, that can swim and dive well, go naked into the Water, with a Knife in their Hand, and fight the Shark, and very commonly kill him, or wound him so, that he turns Tail, and runs away. Their Livors make good Oil to dress Leather withal; the Bones found in their Head are said to hasten the Birth, and ease the Stone, by bringing it away. Their Meat is eaten in scarce times; but I never could away with it, though a great Lover of Fish. Their Back-Bone is of one entire Thickness. Of the Bones, or Joints, I have known Buttons made, which serve well enough in scarce Times, and remote Places.

The Dog-Fish are a small sort of the Shark Kind; and are caught with Hook and Line, fishing for Drums. They say, they are good Meat; but we have so many other sorts of delicate Fish, that I shall hardly ever make Tryal what they are.

Spanish Mackarel are, in Colour and Shape, like the common Mackarel, only much thicker. They are caught with Hook and Line at the Inlets, and sometimes out a little way at Sea.

They are a very fine hard Fish, and of good Taste. They are about two Foot long, or better.

Cavallies are taken in the same Places. They are of a brownish Colour, have exceeding small Scales, and a very thick Skin; they are as firm a Fish as ever I saw; therefore will keep sweet (in the hot Weather) two days, when others will stink in half a day, unless salted. They ought to be scaled as soon as taken; otherwise you must pull off the Skin and Scales, when boiled; the Skin being the choicest of the Fish. The Meat, which is white and large, is dress'd with this Fish.

Boneto's are a very palatable Fish, and near a Yard long. They haunt the Inlets and Water near the Ocean; and are killed with the Harpoon, and Fishgig.

The Blue Fish is one of our best Fishes, and always very fat. They are as long as a Salmon, and indeed, I think, full as good Meat. These Fish come (in the Fall of the Year) generally after there has been one black Frost, when there appear great Shoals of them. The *Hatteras Indians,* and others, run into the Sands of the Sea, and strike them, though some of these Fish have caused Sickness and violent Burnings after eating of them, which is found to proceed from the Gall that is broken in some of them, and is hurtful. Sometimes, many Cart-loads of these are thrown and left dry on the Sea side, which comes by their eager Pursuit of the small Fish, in which they run themselves ashoar, and the Tide leaving them, they cannot recover the Water again. They are called Blue-Fish, because they are of that Colour, and have a forked Tail, and are shaped like a Dolphin.

The Red Drum is a large Fish much bigger than the Blue-Fish. The Body of this is good firm Meat, but the Head is beyond all the Fish I ever met withal for an excellent Dish. We have greater Numbers of these Fish, than of any other sort. People go down and catch as many Barrels full as they please, with Hook and Line, especially every young Flood, when they bite. These are salted up, and transported to other Colonies, that are bare of Provisions.

Black Drums are a thicker-made Fish than the Red Drum, being shap'd like a fat Pig; they are a very good Fish, but not so common with us as to the Northward.

The Angel-Fish is shaped like an *English* Bream. He is so call'd, from his golden Colour, which shines all about his Head and Belly. This is accounted a very good Fish, as are most in these Parts. The *Bermudians* have the same sort of Fish, and esteem them very much.

Bass or Rock is both in Salt and Fresh-Water; when young, he much resembles a Grayling, but grows to the size of the large Cod-Fish. They are a very good firm Fish. Their Heads are souced, and make a noble Dish, if large.

Sheeps-Head has the general Vogue of being the choicest Fish in this Place. Indeed, it is a very delicate Fish, and well relish'd; yet I think, there are several others full as good as the Sheeps-Head. He is much of the Bigness of the Angel-Fish, and flat as he is; they sometimes weigh two or three Pound Weight. This Fish hath Teeth like a Sheep, and is therefore so call'd.

Plaice are here very large, and plentiful, being the same as in *England.*

Flounders should have gone amongst the Fresh-Water Fish, because they are caught there, in great Plenty.

Soles are a Fish we have but lately discover'd; they are as good, as in any other Part.

Mullets, the same as in *England,* and great Plenty in all Places where the Water is salt or brackish.

Shads are a sweet Fish, but very bony; they are very plentiful at some Seasons.

Fat-Backs are a small Fish, like Mullets, but the fattest ever known. They put nothing into the Pan, to fry these. They are excellent sweet Food.

The white Guard-Fish is shaped almost like a Pike, but slenderer; his Mouth has a long small Bill set with Teeth, in which he catches small Fish; his Scales are knit together like Armour. When they dress him, they strip him, taking off Scales and Skin together. His Meat is very white, and rather looks like Flesh than Fish. The *English* account them no good Fish; but the *Indians* do. The Gall of this Fish is green, and a violent Cathartick, if taken inwardly.

The green Guard is shaped, in all respects, like the other save that his Scales are very small and fine. He is indifferent good Meat; his Bones, when boil'd or fry'd, remain as green as Grass. The same sort of Fish come before the Mackarel in *England.*

Scate, or Stingray, the same as in *England,* and very common; but the great Plenty of other Fish makes these not regarded; for few or none eat them in *Carolina,* though they are almost at every ones Door.

Thornbacks are the same as in *England*. They are not so common as the Scate and Whip-Rays.

Congar-Eels always remain in the Salt-Water; they are much more known in the Northward Parts of *America*, than with us.

Lampreys are not common; I never saw but one, which was large, and caught by the *Indians*, in a Ware. They would not eat him, but gave him to me.

Eels are no where in the World better, or more plentiful, than in *Carolina*.

Sun-Fish are flat and rounder than a Bream, and are reckon'd a fine-tasted Fish, and not without Reason. They are much the size of Angel-Fish.

Toad-Fish are nothing but a Skin full of Prickles, and a few Bones; they are as ugly as a Toad, and preserv'd to look upon, and good for nothing else.

They are taken by a Bait, near the Inlet, or out at Sea a little way. They are blackish, and exactly like a Tench, except in the Back-fins, which have Prickles like a Pearch. They are as good, if not better than any Tench.

Trouts of the Salt-Water are exactly shaped like the Trouts in *Europe,* having blackish, not red Spots. They are in the Salts, and are not red within, but white, yet a very good Fish. They are so tender, that if they are in or near fresh Water, and a sudden Frost come, they are benumm'd, and float on the Surface of the Water, as if dead; and then they take up Canoe-Loads of them. If you put them into warm Water, they presently recover.

The Crocus is a Fish, in Shape like a Pearch, and in Taste like a Whiting. They croke and make a Noise in your Hand, when taken with Hook or Net. They are very good.

The Herrings in *Carolina* are not so large as in *Europe*. They spawn there in *March* and *April,* running up the fresh Rivers and small fresh Runs of Water in great Shoals, where they are taken. They become red if salted; and, drest with Vinegar and Oil, resemble an Anchovy very much; for they are far beyond an *English* Herring, when pickled.

The same as in *England;* they lie down a great way in the Sound, towards the Ocean, where (at some certain Seasons) are a great many very fine ones.

The fresh Water affords no such Bream as in *England,* that I have as yet discover'd; yet there is a Sea-Bream, which is a flat and thin Fish, as the *European* Breams are.

The Taylor is a Fish about the Bigness of a Trout, but of a bluish and green Colour, with a forked Tail, as a Mackarel has. They are a delicate Fish, and plentiful in our Salt-Waters. Infinite numbers of other Species will be hereafter discover'd as yet unknown to us; although I have seen and eaten of several other sorts of Fish, which are not here mention'd, because, as yet; they have no certain Names assign'd them. Therefore, I shall treat no farther of our Salt-Water Fish, but proceed to the Fresh.

The first of these is the Sturgeon, of which we have Plenty, all the fresh Parts of our Rivers being well stor'd therewith. The *Indians* upon and towards the Heads and Falls of our Rivers, strike a great many of these, and eat them; yet the *Indians* near the Salt-Waters will not eat them. I have seen an *Indian* strike one of these Fish, seven Foot long, and leave him on the Sands to be eaten by the Gulls. In *May*, they run up towards the Heads of the Rivers, where you see several hundreds of them in one day. The *Indians* have another way to take them, which is by Nets at the end of a Pole. The Bones of these Fish make good Nutmeg-Graters.

The Jack, Pike, or Pickerel, is exactly the same, in *Carolina*, as they are in *England*. Indeed, I never saw this Fish so big and large in *America*, as I have in *Europe*, these with us being seldom above two Foot long, as far as I have yet seen. They are very plentiful with us in *Carolina*, all our Creeks and Ponds being full of them. I once took out of a Ware, above three hundred of these Fish, at a time.

The same in *England* as in *Carolina;* but ours are a great way up the Rivers and Brooks, that are fresh, having swift Currents, and stony, and gravelly Bottoms.

The same Gudgeons as in *Europe* are found in *America*.

The same sort of Pearch as are in *England*, we have likewise in *Carolina*, though, I think, ours never rise to be so large as in *England*.

We have a white Pearch, so call'd, because he is of a Silver Colour, otherwise like the *English* Pearch. These we have in great Plenty, and they are preferable to the red ones.

The brown Pearch, which some call *Welch-men*, are the largest sort of Pearches that we have, and very firm, white and sweet Fish. These grow to be larger than any Carp, and are very frequent in every Creek and Pond.

The flat or mottled Pearch are shaped almost like a Bream. They are called *Irish-men,* being freckled or mottled with black, and blue Spots. They are never taken any where, but in the fresh Water. They are good Fish; but I do not approve of them, no more than of the other sorts of Pearch.

We have another sort of Pearch, which is the least sort of all, but as good Meat as any. These are distinguish'd from the other sorts, by the Name of *Round-Robins;* being flat, and very round-shap'd; they are spotted with red Spots very beautiful, and are easily caught with an Angle, as all the other sort of Pearches are.

We have the same Carp as you have in *England.*

And the same Roach; only scarce so large.

Dace are the same as yours too; but neither are these so large nor plentiful, as with you.

The same as in *England.*

Sucking-Fish are the nearest in Taste and Shape to a Barbel, only they have no Barbs.

Cat-Fish are a round blackish Fish, with a great flat Head, a wide Mouth, and no Scales; they something resemble Eels in Taste. Both this sort, and another that frequents the Salt Water, are very plentiful.

Grindals are a long scaled Fish with small Eyes; and frequent Ponds, Lakes, and slow-running Creeks and Swamps. They are a soft sorry Fish, and good for nothing; though some eat them for good Fish.

These are a bright scaly Fish, which frequent the Swamps, and fresh Runs; they seem to be between an *English* Roach and a Bream, and eat much like the latter. The *Indians* kill abundance of these, and barbakue them, till they are crisp, then transport them, in wooden Hurdles, to their Towns and Quarters.

The Fountain-Fish are a white sort which breed in the clear Running Springs and Fountains of Water, where the Clearness thereof makes them very difficult to be taken. I cannot say how good they are; because I have not as yet tasted of them.

The white Fish are very large; some being two Foot and a half long and more. They are found a great way up in the Freshes of the Rivers; and are firm Meat, and an extraordinary well-relish'd Fish.

Barbouts and Millers-Thumbs, are the very same here, in all respects, as they are in *England.* What more are in the fresh Waters we have not discover'd, but are satisfied, that we are not acquainted with one third part thereof; for we are told by the *Indians,* of a great many strange and uncouth shapes and sorts of Fish, which they have found in the Lakes laid down in my Chart. However as we can give no farther Account of these than by Hear-say; I proceed to treat of the Shell-Fish that are found in the Salt-Water, so far as they have already come to our Knowledge.

The large Crabs, which we call Stone-Crabs, are the same sort as in *England,* having black Tips at the end of their Claws. These are plentifully met withal, down in *Core* Sound, and the South Parts of North-*Carolina.*

The smaller flat Crabs I look upon to be the sweetest of all the Species. They are the Breadth of a lusty Man's Hand, or rather larger. These are innumerable, lying in most prodigious quantities, all over the Salts of *Carolina.* They are taken not only to eat, but are the best Bait for all sorts of Fish, that live in the Salt-Water. These Fish are mischievous to Night-Hooks, because they get away all the Bait from the Hooks.

Oysters, great and small, are found almost in every Creek and Gut of Salt-Water, and are very good and well-relish'd. The large Oysters are excellent, pickled.

One Cockle in *Carolina* is as big as five or six in *England.* They are often thrown upon the Sands on the Sound-Side, where the Gulls are always ready to open and eat them.

Clams are a sort of Cockles, only differing in Shell, which is thicker and not streak'd, or ribb'd. These are found throughout all the Sound and Salt-Water-Ponds. The Meat is the same for Look and Taste as the Cockle. These make an excellent strong Broth, and eat well, either roasted or pickled.

The Muscles in *Carolina* have a very large Shell, striped with Dents. They grow by the side of Ponds and Creeks, in Salt-Water, wherein you may get as many of them as you please. I do not like them so well as the *English* Muscle, which is no good Shell-Fish.

Some of the Shells of these are as large as a Man's Hand, but the lesser sort are the best Meat, and those not extraordinary. They are shap'd like the end of a Horses Yard. Of their Shells, the Peak or *Wampum* is made, which is the richest Commodity amongst the *Indians.* They breed like a long Thing shap'd like a Snake, but containing a sort of Joints, in the Hollowness whereof are thousands of small Coaks, no bigger then small Grains of Pepper.

The Skellops, if well dress'd, are a pretty Shell-Fish; but to eat them only roasted, without any other Addition, in my Judgment, are too luscious.

Man of Noses are a Shell-Fish commonly found amongst us. They are valued for increasing Vigour in Men, and making barren Women fruitful; but I think they have no need of that Fish; for the Women in *Carolina* are fruitful enough without their Helps.

Wilks, or Periwinkles, are not so large here, as in the Islands of *Scilly,* and in other Parts of *Europe,* though very sweet.

The Sea-Snail-Horn is large, and very good Meat; they are exactly shaped as other Snail-Horns are.

Fidlars are a sort of small Crabs, that lie in Holes in the Marshes. The Raccoons eat them very much. I never knew any one try, whether they were good Meat or no.

Runners live chiefly on the Sands, but sometimes run into the Sea. They have Holes in the Sand-Beaches and are a whitish sort of a Crab. Tho' small, they run as fast as a Man, and are good for nothing but to look at.

Spanish Oysters have a very thin Shell, and rough on the outside. They are very good Shell-Fish, and so large, that half a dozen are enow to satisfy an hungry Stomach.

The Flattings are inclosed in a broad, thin Shell, the whole Fish being flat. They are inferiour to no Shell-Fish this Country affords.

Finger-Fish are very plentiful in this Country; they are of the Length of a Man's Finger, and lie in the Bottom of the Water about one or two Foot deep. They are very good.

Shrimps are here very plentiful and good, and are to be taken with a Small-Bow-Net, in great Quantities.

The small Cockles are about the Bigness of the largest *English* Cockles, and differ nothing from them, unless in the Shells, which are striped cross-wise as well as long-wise.

The Fresh-Water Shell-Fish are,

Muscles, which are eaten by the *Indians,* after five or six hours Boiling, to make them tender, and then are good for nothing.

Craw-Fish, in the Brooks, and small Rivers of Water, amongst the *Tuskeruro Indians,* and up higher, are found very plentifully, and as good as any in the World.

And thus I have gone through the several Species of Fish, so far as they have come to my Knowledge, in the eight Years that I have lived in *Carolina.* I should have made a larger Discovery,

when travelling so far towards the Mountains, and amongst the
Hills, had it not been in the Winter-Season, which was improper
to make any Enquiry into any of the Species before recited.
Therefore, as my Intent was, I proceed to what remains of the
Present State of *Carolina*, having already accounted for the Animals, and Vegetables, as far as this Volume would allow of;
whereby the Remainder, though not exactly known, may yet be
guess'd at, if we consider what Latitude *Carolina* lies in, which
reaches from 29 to 36 deg. 30 min. Northern Latitude, as I have
before observ'd. Which Latitude is as fertile and pleasant, as
any in the World, as well for the Produce of Minerals, Fruit,
Grain, and Wine, as other rich Commodities. And indeed, all the
Experiments that have been made in *Carolina*, of the Fertility
and natural Advantages of the Country, have exceeded all Expectation, as affording some Commodities, which other Places,
in the same Latitude, do not. As for Minerals, as they are subterraneous Products, so, in all new Countries, they are the Species that are last discover'd; and especially, in *Carolina*, where
the *Indians* never look for any thing lower than the Superficies
of the Earth, being a Race of Men the least addicted to delving
of any People that inhabit so fine a Country as *Carolina* is. As
good if not better Mines than those the *Spaniards* possess in
America, lie full West from us; and I am certain, we have as
Mountainous Land, and as great Probability of having rich Minerals in *Carolina*, as any of those Parts that are already found to
be so rich therein. But, waving this Subject, till some other
Opportunity, I shall now give you some Observations in general,
concerning *Carolina;* which are, first, that it lies as convenient
for Trade as any of the Plantations in *America;* that we have
Plenty of Pitch, Tar, Skins of Deer, and Beeves, Furs, Rice,
Wheat, Rie, *Indian Grain,* sundry sorts of Pulse, Turpentine,
Rozin, Masts, Yards, Planks and Boards, Staves and Lumber,
Timber of many common sorts, fit for any Uses; Hemp, Flax,
Barley, Oats, Buck-Wheat, Beef, Pork, Tallow, Hides, Whale-
Bone and Oil, Wax, Cheese, Butter, &c. besides Drugs, Dyes,
Fruit, Silk, Cotton, Indico, Oil, and Wine that we need not
doubt of, as soon as we make a regular Essay, the Country being
adorn'd with pleasant Meadows, Rivers, Mountains, Valleys,
Hills, and rich Pastures, and blessed with wholesome pure Air;
especially a little backwards from the Sea, where the wild Beasts
inhabit, none of which are voracious. The Men are active, the

Women fruitful to Admiration, every House being full of Children, and several Women that have come hither barren, having presently prov'd fruitful. There cannot be a richer Soil, no Place abounding more in Flesh and Fowl, both wild and tame, besides Fish, Fruit, Grain, Cider, and many other pleasant Liquors; together with several other Necessaries for Life and Trade, that are daily found out, as new Discoveries are made. The Stone and Gout seldom trouble us; the Consumption we are wholly Strangers to, no Place affording a better Remedy for that Distemper, than *Carolina*. For Trade, we lie so near to *Virginia*, that we have the Advantage of their Convoys; as also Letters from thence, in two or three Days at most, in some Places in as few Hours. Add to this, that the great Number of Ships which come within those Capes, for *Virginia* and *Maryland*, take off our Provisions, and give us Bills of Exchange for *England*, which is Sterling Money. The Planters in *Virginia* and *Maryland* are forc'd to do the same, the great Quantities of Tobacco that are planted there, making Provisions scarce; and Tobacco is a Commodity oftentimes so low, as to bring nothing, whereas Provisions and Naval Stores never fail of a Market. Besides, where these are raised, in such Plenty as in *Carolina*, there always appears good Housekeeping, and Plenty of all manner of delicate Eatables. For Instance, the Pork of *Carolina* is very good, the younger Hogs fed on Peaches, Maiz, and such other natural Produce; being some of the sweetest Meat that the World affords, as is acknowledged by all Strangers that have been there. And as for the Beef, in *Pampticough,* and the Southward Parts, it proves extraordinary. We have not only Provisions plentiful, but Cloaths of our own Manufactures, which are made, and daily increase; Cotton, Wool, Hemp, and Flax, being of our own Growth; and the Women to be highly commended for their Industry in Spinning, and ordering their Houswifry to so great Advantage as they generally do; which is much more easy, by reason this happy Climate, visited with so mild Winters, is much warmer than the Northern Plantations, which saves abundance of Cloaths; fewer serving our Necessities, and those of our Servants. But this is not all; for we can go out with our Commodities, to any other Part of the *West-Indies,* or elsewhere, in the Depth of Winter; whereas, those in *New-England, New-York, Pensylvania,* and the Colonies to the Northward of us, cannot stir for Ice, but are fast lock'd into their Harbours. Besides, we can trade with South-*Carolina,* and pay no Duties or Customs, no more than their own Vessels, both North and South being under the same *Lords-Proprietors.* We have, as I observ'd before, another great Advantage, in not being a Frontier, and so continually alarm'd by the Enemy; and what has been accounted a Detriment to us, proves one of the greatest Advantages any People could wish; which is, our Country's being faced with a Sound near ten Leagues over in some Places, through which, although their be Water enough for as large Ships to come in at, as in any part hitherto seated in both *Carolinas;* yet the Difficulty of that Sound to Strangers, hinders them from attempting any Hostilities against us; and, at the same time, if we consider the Advantages thereof, nothing can appear to be a better Situation, than to be fronted with such a Bulwark, which secures us from our Enemies. Furthermore, our Distance from the Sea rids us of two Curses, which attend most other Parts of *America, viz.* Muskeetos, and the Worm-biting, which eats Ships Bottoms out; whereas at *Bath-Town,* there is no such thing known; and as for Muskeetos, they hinder us of as little Rest, as they do you in *England.* Add to this, the unaccountable Quantities of Fish this great Water, or Sound, supplies us withal, whenever we take the Pains to fish for them; Advantages I have no where met withal in *America,* except here. As for the Climate, we enjoy a very wholsome and serene Sky, and a pure and thin Air, the Sun seldom missing to give us his daily Blessing, unless now and then on a Winters Day, which is not often; and when cloudy, the first Appearance of a North-West Wind clears the Horizon, and restores the Light of the Sun. The Weather, in Summer, is very pleasant; the hotter Months being refresh'd with continual Breezes of cool reviving Air; and the Spring being as pleasant, and beautiful, as in any Place I ever was in. The Winter, most commonly, is so mild, that it looks like an Autumn, being now and then attended with clear and thin North-West Winds, that are sharp enough to regulate *English* Constitutions, and free them from a great many dangerous Distempers, that a continual Summer afflicts them withal, nothing being wanting, as to the natural Ornaments and Blessings of a Country, that conduce to make reasonable Men happy. And, for those that are otherwise, they are so much their own Enemies, where they are, that they will scarce ever be any ones Friends, or their own, when they are transplanted; so, it's much better for all sides, that they remain as they are. Not but that there are several good People, that, upon just Grounds, may be uneasy under their present Burdens; and such I would advise to remove to the Place I have been treating of, where they may enjoy their Liberty and Religion, and peaceably eat the Fruits of their Labour, and drink the Wine of their own Vineyards, without the Alarms of a troublesome worldly Life. If a Man be a *Botanist,* here is a plentiful Field of *Plants* to divert him in; If he be a *Gardner,* and delight in that pleasant and happy Life, he will meet with a Climate and Soil, that will further and promote his Designs, in as great a Measure, as any Man can wish for; and as for the Constitution of this Government, it is so mild and easy, in respect to the Properties and Liberties of a Subject, that without rehearsing the Particulars, I say once for all, it is the mildest and best establish'd Government in the World, and the Place where any Man may peaceably enjoy his own, without being invaded by another; Rank and Superiority ever giving Place to Justice and Equity, which is the Golden Rule that every Government ought to be built upon, and regulated by. Besides, it is worthy our Notice, that this Province has been settled, and continued the most free from the Insults and Barbarities of the *Indians,* of any Colony that was ever yet seated in *America;* which must be esteem'd as a particular Providence of God handed down from Heaven, to these People; especially, when we consider, how irregularly they settled North-*Carolina,* and yet how undisturb'd they have ever remain'd, free from any foreign Danger or Loss, even to this very Day. And what may well be look'd upon for as great a Miracle, this is a Place, where no Malefactors are found, deserving Death, or even a Prison for Debtors; there being no more than two Persons, that, as far as I have been able to learn, ever suffer'd as Criminals, although it has been a Settlement near sixty Years; One of whom was a *Turk* that committed *Murder;* the other, an old Woman, for *Witchcraft.* These, 'tis true, were on the Stage, and acted many Years, before I knew the Place; but as for the last, I wish it had been undone to this day; although they give a great many Arguments, to justifie the Deed, which I had rather they should have a Hand in, than myself; seeing I could never approve of taking Life away upon such Accusations, the Justice whereof I could never yet understand.

But, to return to the Subject in Hand; we there make extraordinary good Bricks throughout the Settlement. All sorts of Handicrafts, as *Carpenters, Joiners, Masons, Plaisterers, Shooe-makers, Tanners, Taylors, Weavers,* and most others, may, with small Beginnings, and God's Blessing, thrive very well in this Place, and provide Estates for their Children, Land being sold at a much cheaper Rate there, than in any other Place in *America,* and may, as I suppose, be purchased of the *Lords-Proprietors* here in *England,* or of the Governour there for the time being, by any that shall have a mind to transport them-selves to that Country. The Farmers that go thither (for which sort of Men it is a very thriving Place) should take with them some particular Seeds of Grass, as Trefoil, Clover-grass all sorts, Sanfoin, and Common Grass, or that which is a Rarity in *Europe;* especially, what has sprung and rose first from a warm Climate, and will endure the Sun without flinching. Likewise, if there be any extraordinary sort of Grain for Increase or Hardiness, and some Fruit-Trees of choice Kinds, they will be both profitable and pleasant to have with you, where you may see the Fruits of your Labour in Perfection, in a few Years. The necessary Instruments of Husbandry I need not acquaint the Husbandman withal; Hoes of all sorts, and Axes must be had, with Saws, Wedges, Augurs, Nails, Hammers, and what other Things may be necessary for building with Brick, or Stone, which sort your Inclination and Conveniency lead you to. For, after having look'd over this Treatise, you must needs be acquainted with the Nature of the Country, and therefore cannot but be Judges, what it is that you will chiefly want. As for Land, none need want it for taking up, even in the Places there seated on the Navigable Creeks, Rivers, and Harbours, without being driven into remoter Holes and Corners of the Country, for Set-tlements, which all are forced to do, who, at this day, settle in most or all of the other *English* Plantations in *America;* which are already become so populous, that a New-Comer cannot get a beneficial and commodious Seat, unless he purchases, when, in most Places in *Virginia* and *Maryland,* a thousand Acres of good Land, seated on a Navigable Water, will cost a thousand Pounds; whereas, with us, it is at present obtain'd for the fiftieth Part of the Money. Besides, our Land pays to the *Lords,* but an easy Quit-Rent, or yearly Acknowledgement; and the other Set-tlements pay two Shillings *per* hundred. All these things duly weighed, any rational Man that has a mind to purchase Land in the Plantations for a Settlement of himself and Family, will soon discover the Advantages that attend the Settlers and Purchasers of Land in *Carolina,* above all other Colonies in the *English* Dominions in *America.* And as there is a free Exercise of all Persuasions amongst Christians, the *Lords-Proprietors,* to encourage Ministers of the Church of *England,* have given free Land towards the Maintenance of a Church, and especially, for the Parish of *S. Thomas* in *Pampticough,* over-against the Town, is already laid out for a Glebe of two hundred and twenty three Acres of rich well-situated Land, that a Parsonage-House may be built upon. And now I shall proceed to give an Account of the *Indians,* their Customs and Ways of Living, with a short Dictionary of their Speech.

AN

ACCOUNT

OF THE

INDIANS

OF

North Carolina

THE *Indians,* which were the Inhabitants of *America,* when the *Spaniards* and other *Europeans* discover'd the several Parts of that Country, are the People which we reckon the Natives thereof; as indeed they were, when we first found out those Parts, and appear'd therein. Yet this has not wrought in me a full Satisfaction, to allow these People to have been the Ancient Dwellers of the New-World, or Tract of Land we call *America.* The Reasons that I have to think otherwise, are too many to set down here; but I shall give the Reader a few, before I proceed; and some others he will find scatter'd in my Writings elsewhere.

In *Carolina* (The Part I now treat of) are the fairest Marks of a Deluge, (that at some time has probably made strange Alterations, as to the Station that Country was then in) that ever I saw, or, I think, read of, in any History. Amongst the other Subterraneous Matters, that have been discover'd, we found, in digging of a Well that was twenty six foot deep, at the Bottom thereof, many large Pieces of the Tulip-Tree, and several other sorts of Wood, some of which were cut and notch'd, and some squared, as the Joices of a House are, which appear'd (in the Judgment of all that saw them) to be wrought with Iron

Instruments; it seeming impossible for any thing made of Stone, or what they were found to make use of, to cut Wood in that manner. It cannot be argu'd, that the Wood so cut, might float from some other Continent; because Hiccory and the Tulip-Tree are spontaneous in *America,* and in no other Places, that I could ever learn. It is to be acknowledg'd, that the *Spaniards* give us Relations of magnificent Buildings, which were raised by the *Indians* of *Mexico* and other Parts, which they discover'd, and conquer'd; amongst whom no Iron Instruments were found: But 'tis a great Misfortune, that no Person in that Expedition was so curious, as to take an exact Draught of the Fabricks of those People, which would have been a Discovery of great Value, and very acceptable to the Ingenious; for, as to the Politeness [Polishing] of Stones, it may be effected by Collision, and Grinding, which is of a contrary Nature, on several Accounts, and disproves not my Arguments, in the least.

The next is, the Earthen Pots that are often found under Ground, and at the Foot of the Banks where the Water has wash'd them away. They are for the most part broken in pieces; but we find them of a different sort, in Comparison of those the *Indians* use at this day, who have had no other, ever since the *English* discover'd *America.* The Bowels of the Earth cannot have alter'd them, since they are thicker, of another Shape, and Composition, and nearly approach to the Urns of the Ancient *Romans.*

Again, the Peaches, which are the only tame Fruit, or what is Foreign, that these People enjoy, which is an Eastern Product, and will keep and retain its vegetative and growing Faculty, the longest of any thing of that Nature, that I know of. The Stone, as I elsewhere have remark'd, is thicker than any other sort of the Peaches in *Europe,* or of the *European* sort, now growing in *America,* and is observed to grow if planted, after it has been for several Years laid by; and it seems very probable, that these People might come from some Eastern Country; for when you ask them whence their Fore-Fathers came, that first inhabited the Country, they will point to the Westward and say, *Where the Sun sleeps, our Forefathers came thence,* which, at that distance, may be reckon'd amongst the Eastern Parts of the World. And to this day, they are a shifting, wandring People; for I know some *Indian* Nations, that have chang'd their Settlements, many hundred Miles; sometimes no less than a thousand, as is prov'd by the *Savanna Indians,* who formerly lived on the Banks of the *Messiasippi,* and remov'd thence to the Head of one of the Rivers of South-*Carolina;* since which, (for some Dislike) most of them are remov'd to live in the Quarters of the *Iroquois* or *Sinnagars* [Senecas], which are on the Heads of the Rivers that disgorge themselves into the Bay of *Chesapeak.* I once met with a young *Indian* Woman, that had been brought from beyond the Mountains, and was sold a Slave into *Virginia.* She spoke the same Language, as the *Coranine* [Coree] *Indians,* that dwell near Cape-*Look-out,* allowing for some few Words, which were different, yet no otherwise, than that they might understand one another very well.

The *Indians* of North-*Carolina* are a well-shap'd clean-made People, of different Staturies, as the *Europeans* are, yet chiefly inclin'd to be tall. They are a very streight People, and never bend forwards, or stoop in the Shoulders, unless much overpower'd by old Age. Their Limbs are exceeding well-shap'd. As for their Legs and Feet, they are generally the handsomest in the World. Their Bodies are a little flat, which is occasion'd, by being laced hard down to a Board, in their Infancy. This is all the Cradle they have, which I shall describe at large elsewhere. Their Eyes are black, or of a dark Hazle; The White is marbled with red Streaks, which is ever common to these People, unless when sprung from a white Father or Mother. Their Colour is of a tawny, which would not be so dark, did they not dawb themselves with Bears Oil, and a Colour like burnt Cork. This is begun in their Infancy, and continued for a long time, which fills the Pores, and enables them better to endure the Extremity of the Weather. They are never bald on their Heads, although never so old, which, I believe, proceeds from their Heads being always uncover'd, and the greasing their Hair (so often as they do) with Bears Fat, which is a great Nourisher of the Hair, and causes it to grow very fast. Amongst the Bears Oil (when they intend to be fine) they mix a certain red Powder, that comes from a Scarlet Root which they get in the hilly Country, near the Foot of the great Ridge of Mountains, and it is no where else to be found. They have this Scarlet Root in great Esteem, and sell it for a very great Price, one to another. The Reason of its Value is, because they not only go a long way for it, but are in great Danger of the *Sinnagars* or *Iroquois,* who are mortal Enemies to all our *Indians,* and very often take them Captives, or kill them, before they return from this Voyage. The *Tus-keruros* and other *Indians* have often brought this Seed with them from the Mountains; but it would never grow in our Land. With this and Bears Grease they anoint their Heads and Temples, which is esteem'd as ornamental, as sweet Powder to our Hair. Besides, this Root has the Virtue of killing Lice, and suffers none to abide or breed in their Heads. For want of this Root, they sometimes use *Pecoon* [probably Pecan]-Root, which is of a Crimson Colour, but it is apt to die the Hair of an ugly Hue.

Their Eyes are commonly full and manly, and their Gate sedate and majestick. They never walk backward and forward as we do, nor contemplate on the Affairs of Loss and Gain; the things which daily perplex us. They are dexterous and steady both as to their Hands and Feet, to Admiration. They will walk over deep Brooks, and Creeks, on the smallest Poles, and that without any Fear or Concern. Nay, an *Indian* will walk on the Ridge of a Barn or House and look down the Gable-end, and spit upon the Ground, as unconcern'd, as if he was walking on *Terra firma*. In Running, Leaping, or any such other Exercise, their Legs seldom miscarry, and give them a Fall; and as for letting any thing fall out of their Hands, I never yet knew one Example. They are no Inventers of any Arts or Trades worthy mention; the Reason of which I take to be, that they are not possess'd with that Care and Thoughtfulness, how to provide for the Necessaries of Life, as the *Europeans* are; yet they will learn any thing very soon. I have known an *Indian* stock Guns better than most of our *Joiners*, although he never saw one stock'd before; and besides, his Working-Tool was only a sorry Knife. I have also known several of them that were Slaves to the *English*, learn Handicraft-Trades very well and speedily. I never saw a Dwarf amongst them, nor but one that was Hump-back'd. Their Teeth are yellow with Smoaking Tobacco, which both Men and Women are much addicted to. They tell us, that they had Tobacco amongst them, before the *Europeans* made any Discovery of that Continent. It differs in the Leaf from the sweet-scented, and *Oroonoko*, which are the Plants we raise and cultivate in *America*. Theirs differs likewise much in the Smell, when green, from our Tobacco, before cured. They do not use the same way to cure it as we do; and therefore, the Difference must be very considerable in Taste; for all Men (that know

Tobacco) must allow, that it is the Ordering thereof which gives a Hogoo [relish] to that Weed, rather than any Natural Relish it possesses, when green. Although they are great Smokers, yet they never are seen to take it in Snuff, or chew it.

They have no Hairs on their Faces (except some few) and those but little, nor is there often found any Hair under their Arm-Pits. They are continually plucking it away from their Faces, by the Roots. As for their Privities, since they wore Tail-Clouts, to cover their Nakedness, several of the Men have a deal of Hair thereon. It is to be observ'd, that the Head of the *Penis* is cover'd (throughout all the Nations of the *Indians* I ever saw) both in Old and Young. Although we reckon these a very smooth People, and free from Hair; yet I once saw a middle-aged Man, that was hairy all down his Back; the Hairs being above an Inch long.

As there are found very few, or scarce any, Deformed, or Cripples, amongst them, so neither did I ever see but one blind Man; and then they would give me no Account how his Blindness came. They had a Use for him, which was to lead him with a Girl, Woman, or Boy, by a String; so they put what Burdens they pleased upon his Back, and made him very serviceable upon all such Occasions. No People have better Eyes, or see better in the Night or Day, than the *Indians*. Some alledge, that the Smoke of the Pitch-Pine, which they chiefly burn, does both preserve and strengthen the Eyes; as, perhaps, it may do, because that Smoak never offends the Eyes, though you hold your Face over a great Fire thereof. This is occasion'd by the volatile Part of the Turpentine, which rises with the Smoke, and is of a friendly, balsamick Nature; for the Ashes of the Pine-Tree afford no fix'd Salt in them.

They let their Nails grow very long, which, they reckon, is the Use Nails are design'd for, and laugh at the *Europeans* for pairing theirs, which, they say, disarms them of that which Nature design'd them for.

They are not of so robust and strong Bodies, as to lift great Burdens, and endure Labour and slavish Work, as the *Europeans* are; yet some that are Slaves, prove very good and laborious: But, of themselves, they never work as the *English* do, taking care for no farther than what is absolutely necessary to support Life. In Travelling and Hunting, they are very indefatigable; because that carries a Pleasure along with the Profit. I have

known some of them very strong; and as for Running and Leap-
ing, they are extraordinary Fellows, and will dance for several
Nights together, with the greatest Briskness imaginable, their
Wind never failing them.

Their Dances are of different Natures; and for every sort of
Dance, they have a Tune, which is allotted for that Dance; as, if
it be a War-Dance, they have a warlike Song, wherein they express, with all the Passion and Vehemence imaginable, what
they intend to do with their Enemies; how they will kill, roast,
sculp, beat, and make Captive, such and such Numbers of them;
and how many they have destroy'd before. All these Songs are
made new for every Feast; nor is one and the same Song sung at
two several Festivals. Some one of the Nation (which has the
best Gift of expressing their Designs) is appointed by their
King, and War-Captains, to make these Songs.

Others are made for Feasts of another Nature; as, when several Towns, or sometimes, different Nations have made Peace
with one another; then the Song suits both Nations, and relates,
how the bad Spirit made them go to War, and destroy one another; but it shall never be so again; but that their Sons and
Daughters shall marry together, and the two Nations love one
another, and become as one People.

They have a third sort of Feasts and Dances, which are always
when the Harvest of Corn is ended, and in the Spring. The one,
to return Thanks to the good Spirit, for the Fruits of the Earth;
the other, to beg the same Blessings for the succeeding Year.
And, to encourage the young Men to labour stoutly, in planting
their Maiz and Pulse, they set a sort of an Idol in the Field,
which is dress'd up exactly like an *Indian,* having all the *Indians*
Habit, besides abundance of *Wampum,* and their Money, made
of Shells, that hangs about his Neck. The Image none of the
young Men dare approach; for the old ones will not suffer them
to come near him, but tell them, that he is some famous *Indian*
Warriour, that died a great while ago, and now is come amongst
them, to see if they work well, which if they do, he will go to
the good Spirit, and speak to him to send them Plenty of Corn,
and to make the young Men all expert Hunters and mighty
Warriours. All this while, the King and old Men sit round the
Image, and seemingly pay a profound Respect to the same. One
great Help to these *Indians,* in carrying on these Cheats, and
inducing Youth to do what they please, is, the uninterrupted

Silence, which is ever kept and observ'd, with all the Respect and Veneration imaginable.

At these Feasts, which are set out with all the Magnificence their Fare allows of, the Masquerades begin at Night, and not before. There is commonly a Fire made in the middle of the House, which is the largest in the Town, and is very often the Dwelling of their King, or War-Captain; where sit two Men on the Ground, upon a Mat; one with a Rattle, made of a Gourd, with some Beans in it; the other with a Drum, made of an earthen Pot, cover'd with a dress'd-Deer-Skin, and one Stick in his Hand to beat thereon; and so they both begin the Song appointed. At the same time, one drums, and the other rattles, which is all the artificial Musick of their own making I ever saw amongst them. To these two Instruments they sing, which carries no Air with it, but is a sort of unsavoury Jargon; yet their Cadences and Raising of their Voices are form'd with that Equality and Exactness, that (to us *Europeans*) it seems admirable, how they should continue these Songs, without once missing to agree, each with the others Note and Tune.

As for their Dancing, were there Masters of that Profession amongst them, as there are with us, they would dearly earn their Money; for these Creatures take the most Pains at it, that Men are able to endure. I have seen thirty odd together a dancing, and every one dropp'd down with Sweat, as if Water had been poured down their Backs. They use those hard Labours, to make them able to endure Fatigue, and improve their Wind, which indeed is very long and durable, it being a hard matter, in any Exercise, to dispossess them of it.

At these Feasts, they meet from all the Towns within fifty or sixty Miles round, where they buy and sell several Commodities, as we do at Fairs and Markets. Besides, they game very much, and often strip one another of all they have in the World; and what is more, I have known several of them play themselves away, so that they have remain'd the Winners Servants, till their Relations or themselves could pay the Money to redeem them; and when this happens, the Loser is never dejected or melancholy at the Loss, but laughs, and seems no less contented than if he had won. They never differ at Gaming, neither did I ever see a Dispute, about the Legality thereof, so much as rise amongst them.

Their chiefest Game is a sort of Arithmetick, which is man-

Indians around a fire

aged by a Parcel of small split Reeds, the Thickness of a small Bent; these are made very nicely, so that they part, and are tractable in their Hands. They are fifty one in Number, their Length about seven Inches; when they play, they throw part of them to their Antagonist; the Art is, to discover, upon sight, how many you have, and what you throw to him that plays with you. Some are so expert at their Numbers, that they will tell ten times together, what they throw out of their Hands. Although the whole Play is carried on with the quickest Motion it's possible to use, yet some are so expert at this Game, as to win great *Indian* Estates by this Play. A good Sett of these Reeds, fit to play withal, are valued and sold for a dress'd Doe-Skin.

They have several other Plays and Games; as, with the Kernels or Stones of Persimmons, which are in effect the same as our Dice, because Winning or Losing depend on which side appear uppermost, and how they happen to fall together.

Another Game is managed with a Batoon and a Ball, and resembles our Trap-ball; besides, several Nations have several Games and Pastimes, which are not used by others.

These Savages live in *Wigwams,* or Cabins built of Bark, which are made round like an Oven, to prevent any Damage by hard Gales of Wind. They make the Fire in the middle of the House, and have a Hole at the Top of the Roof right above the Fire, to let out the Smoke. These Dwellings are as hot as Stoves, where the *Indians* sleep and sweat all Night. The Floors thereof are never paved nor swept, so that they have always a loose Earth on them. They are often troubled with a multitude of Fleas, especially near the Places where they dress their Deer-Skins, because that Hair harbours them; yet I never felt any ill, unsavory Smell in their Cabins, whereas, should we live in our Houses, as they do, we should be poison'd with our own Nastiness; which confirms these *Indians* to be, as they really are, some of the sweetest People in the World.

The Bark they make their Cabins withal, is generally Cypress, or red or white Cedar; and sometimes, when they are a great way from any of these Woods, they make use of Pine-Bark, which is the worser sort. In building these Fabricks, they get very long Poles, of Pine, Cedar, Hiccory, or any Wood that will bend; these are the Thickness of the Small of a Man's Leg, at the thickest end, which they generally strip of the Bark, and warm them well in the Fire, which makes them tough and fit to

John White drawing

Indians dancing

bend; afterwards, they stick the thickest ends of them in the
Ground, about two Yards asunder, in a Circular Form, the distance they design the Cabin to be, (which is not always round,
but sometimes oval) then they bend the Tops and bring them
together, and bind their ends with Bark of Trees, that is proper
for that use, as Elm is, or sometimes the Moss that grows on the
Trees, and is a Yard or two long, and never rots; then they brace
them with other Poles, to make them strong; afterwards, cover
them all over with Bark, so that they are very warm and tight,
and will keep firm against all the Weathers that blow. They
have other sorts of Cabins without Windows, which are for
their Granaries, Skins, and Merchandizes; and others that are
cover'd over head; the rest left open for the Air. These have
Reed-Hurdles, like Tables, to lie and sit on, in Summer, and
serve for pleasant Banqueting-Houses in the hot Season of the
Year. The Cabins they dwell in have Benches all round, except
where the Door stands; on these they lay Beasts-Skins, and Mats
made of Rushes, whereon they sleep and loll. In one of these,
several Families commonly live, though all related to one another.

As to the *Indians* Food, it is of several sorts, which are as
follows.

Venison, and Fawns in the Bags, cut out of the Doe's Belly;
Fish of all sorts, the Lamprey-Eel excepted, and the Sturgeon
our Salt-Water *Indians* will not touch; Bear and Bever; Panther; Pole-cat; Wild-cat; Possum; Raccoon; Hares, and Squirrels, roasted with their Guts in; Snakes, all *Indians* will not eat
them, tho' some do; All wild Fruits that are palatable, some of
which they dry and keep against Winter, as all sort of Fruits, and
Peaches, which they dry, and make Quiddonies, and Cakes, that
are very pleasant, and a little tartish; young Wasps, when they
are white in the Combs, before they can fly, this is esteemed a
Dainty; All sorts of Tortois and Terebins; Shell-Fish, and Stingray, or Scate, dry'd; Gourds; Melons; Cucumbers; Squashes;
Pulse of all sorts; *Rockahomine* Meal, which is their Maiz,
parch'd and pounded into Powder; Fowl of all sorts, that are
eatable; Ground-Nuts, or wild Potato's; Acorns and Acorn Oil;
Wild-Bulls, Beef, Mutton, Pork, &c. from the *English; Indian*
Corn, or Maiz, made into several sorts of Bread; Ears of Corn
roasted in the Summer, or preserv'd against Winter.

The Victuals is common, throughout the whole Kindred Rela-

John White drawing

Indian man and woman eating

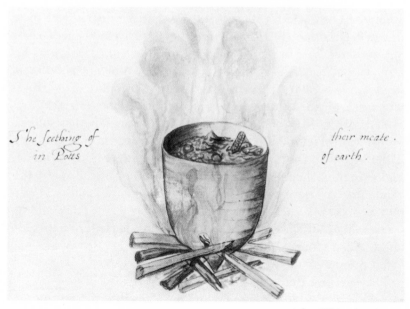

John White drawing

Cooking in an earthen pot

tions, and often to the whole Town; especially, when they are in Hunting-Quarters, then they all fare alike, whichsoever of them kills the Game. They are very kind, and charitable to one another, but more especially to those of their own Nation; for if any one of them has suffer'd any Loss, by Fire or otherwise, they order the griev'd Person to make a Feast, and invite them all thereto, which, on the day appointed, they come to, and after every Man's Mess of Victuals is dealt to him, one of their Speakers, or grave old Men, makes an Harangue, and acquaints the Company, That that Man's House has been burnt, wherein all his Goods were destroy'd; That he, and his Family, very narrowly escaped; That he is every Man's Friend in that Company; and, That it is all their Duties to help him, as he would do to any of them, had the like Misfortune befallen them. After this Oration is over, every Man, according to his Quality, throws him down upon the Ground some Present, which is commonly Beads, *Ronoak, Peak,* Skins or Furs, and which very often amounts to treble the Loss he has suffer'd. The same Assistance they give to any Man that wants to build a Cabin, or make a Canoe. They say, it is our Duty thus to do; for there are several Works that one Man cannot effect, therefore we must give him our Help, otherwise our Society will fall, and we shall be depriv'd of those urgent Necessities which Life requires. They have no Fence to part one anothers Lots in their Corn-Fields; but every Man knows his own, and it scarce ever happens, that they rob one another of so much as an Ear of Corn, which if any is found to do, he is sentenced by the Elders to work and plant for him that was robb'd, till he is recompensed for all the Damage he has suffer'd in his Corn-Field; and this is punctually perform'd, and the Thief held in Disgrace, that steals from any of his Country-Folks. It often happens, that a Woman is destitute of her Husband, and has a great many Children to maintain; such a Person they always help, and make their young men plant, reap, and do every thing that she is not capable of doing herself; yet they do not allow any one to be idle, but to employ themselves in some Work or other.

They never fight with one another, unless drunk, nor do you ever hear any Scolding amongst them. They say, the *Europeans* are always rangling and uneasy, and wonder they do not go out of this World, since they are so uneasy and discontented in it. All their Misfortunes and Losses end in Laughter; for if their

Cabins take Fire, and all their Goods are burnt therein, (indeed, all will strive to prevent farther Damage, whilst there is any Possibility) yet such a Misfortune ends in a hearty Fitt of Laughter, unless some of their Kinsfolks and Friends have lost their Lives; but then the Case is alter'd, and they become very pensive, and go into deep Mourning, which is continued for a considerable Time; sometimes longer, or shorter, according to the Dignity of the Person, and the Number of Relations he had near him.

The Burial of their Dead is perform'd with a great deal of Ceremony, in which one Nation differs, in some few Circumstances, from another, yet not so much but we may, by a general Relation, pretty nearly account for them all.

When an *Indian* is dead, the greater Person he was, the more expensive is his Funeral. The first thing which is done, is, to place the nearest Relations near the Corps, who mourn and weep very much, having their Hair hanging down their Shoulders, in a very forlorn manner. After the dead Person has lain a Day and a Night, in one of their Hurdles of Canes, commonly in some Out-House made for that purpose, those that officiate about the Funeral, go into the Town, and the first young Men they meet withal, that have Blankets or Match Coats on, whom they think fit for their Turn, they strip them from their Backs, who suffer them so to do, without any Resistance. In these they wrap the dead Bodies, and cover them with two or three Mats, which the *Indians* make of Rushes or Cane; and last of all, they have a long Web of woven Reeds, or hollow Canes, which is the Coffin of the *Indians,* and is brought round several times, and tied fast at both ends, which indeed, looks very decent and well. Then the Corps is brought out of the House, into the Orchard of Peach-Trees, where another Hurdle is made to receive it, about which comes all the Relations and Nation that the dead Person belong'd to, besides several from other Nations in Alliance with them; all which sit down on the Ground, upon Mats spread there, for that purpose; where the Doctor or Conjurer appears; and, after some time, makes a Sort of *O-yes,* at which all are very silent; then he begins to give an Account, who the dead Person was, and how stout a Man he approv'd himself; how many Enemies and Captives he had kill'd and taken; how strong, tall, and nimble he was; that he was a great Hunter, a Lover of his Country, and possess'd of a great many beautiful

John White drawing

Indian charnel house

Wives and Children, esteem'd the greatest of Blessings among these Savages, in which they have a true Notion. Thus this Orator runs on, highly extolling the dead Man, for his Valour, Conduct, Strength, Riches, and Good-Humour; and enumerating his Guns, Slaves and almost every thing he was possess'd of, when living. After which, he addresses himself to the People of that Town or Nation, and bids them supply the dead Man's Place, by following his steps, who, he assures them, is gone into the Country of Souls, (which they think lies a great way off, in this World, which the Sun visits, in his ordinary Course) and that he will have the Enjoyment of handsome young Women, great Store of Deer to hunt, never meet with Hunger, Cold or Fatigue, but every thing to answer his Expectation and Desire. This is the Heaven they propose to themselves; but, on the contrary, for those *Indians* that are lazy, thievish amongst themselves, bad Hunters, and no Warriours, nor of much Use to the Nation, to such they allot, in the next World, Hunger, Cold, Troubles, old ugly Women for their Companions, with Snakes, and all sorts of nasty Victuals to feed on. Thus is mark'd out their Heaven and Hell. After all this Harangue, he diverts the People with some of their Traditions, as when there was a violent hot Summer, or very hard Winter; when any notable Distempers rag'd amongst them; when they were at War with such and such Nations; how victorious they were; and what were the Names of their War-Captains. To prove the times more exactly, he produces the Records of the Country, which are a Parcel of Reeds, of different Lengths, with several distinct Marks, known to none but themselves; by which they seem to guess, very exactly, at Accidents that happen'd many Years ago; nay two or three Ages or more. The Reason I have to believe what they tell me, on this Account, is, because I have been at the Meetings of several *Indian* Nations; and they agreed, in relating the same Circumstances, as to Time, very exactly; as, for Example, they say, there was so hard a Winter in *Carolina*, 105 years ago, that the great Sound was frozen over, and the Wild Geese came into the Woods to eat Acorns, and that they were so tame, (I suppose, through Want) that they kill'd abundance in the Woods, by knocking them on the Head with Sticks.

But, to return to the dead Man. When this long Tale is ended, by him that spoke first; perhaps, a second begins another long

Story; so a third, and fourth, if there be so many Doctors present; which all tell one and the same thing. At last, the Corps
is brought away from that Hurdle to the Grave, by four young
Men, attended by the Relations, the King, old Men, and all the
Nation. When they come to the Sepulcre, which is about six Foot
deep, and eight Foot long, having at each end (that is, at the
Head and Foot) a Light-Wood, or Pitch-Pine Fork driven close
down the sides of the Grave, firmly into the Ground; (these
two Forks are to contain a Ridge-Pole, as you shall understand
presently) before they lay the Corps into the Grave, they cover
the bottom two or three times over with Bark of Trees, then
they let down the Corps (with two Belts, that the *Indians*
carry their Burdens withal) very leisurely, upon the said
Barks; then they lay over a Pole of the same Wood, in the two
Forks, and having a great many Pieces of Pitch-Pine Logs, about
two Foot and a half long, they stick them in the sides of the
Grave down each End, and near the Top thereof, where the
other Ends lie on the Ridge-Pole, so that they are declining
like the Roof of a House. These being very thick plac'd, they
cover them (many times double) with Bark; then they throw
the Earth thereon, that came out of the Grave, and beat it down
very firm; by this Means, the dead Body lies in a Vault, nothing touching him; so that when I saw this way of Burial, I
was mightily pleas'd with it, esteeming it very decent and
pretty, as having seen a great many Christians buried without
the tenth Part of that Ceremony and Decency. Now, when the
Flesh is rotted and moulder'd from the Bone, they take up the
Carcass, and clean the Bones, and joint them together; afterwards, they dress them up in pure white dress'd Deer-Skins,
and lay them amongst their Grandees and Kings in the *Quiogozon,* which is their Royal Tomb or Burial-Place of their
Kings and War-Captains. This is a very large magnificent
Cabin, (according to their Building) which is rais'd at the
Publick Charge of the Nation, and maintain'd in a great deal of
Form and Neatness. About seven foot high, is a Floor or Loft made,
on which lie all their Princes, and Great Men, that have died
for several hundred Years, all attir'd in the Dress I before told
you of. No Person is to have his Bones lie here, and to be thus
dress'd, unless he gives a round Sum of their Money to the Rulers,
for Admittance. If they remove never so far, to live in a Foreign
Country, they never fail to take all these dead Bones along

with them, though the Tediousness of their short daily Marches keeps them never so long on their Journey. They reverence and adore this *Quiogozon,* with all the Veneration and Respect that is possible for such a People to discharge, and had rather lose all, than have any Violence or Injury offer'd thereto. These Savages differ some small matter in their Burials; some burying right upwards, and otherwise, as you are acquainted withal in my Journal from South to North *Carolina;* Yet they all agree in their Mourning, which is, to appear every Night, at the Sepulcre, and howl and weep in a very dismal manner, having their Faces dawb'd over with Light-wood Soot, (which is the same as Lamp-black) and Bears Oil. This renders them as black as it is possible to make themselves, so that theirs very much resemble the Faces of Executed Men boil'd in Tar. If the dead Person was a Grandee, to carry on the Funeral Ceremonies, they hire People to cry and lament over the dead Man. Of this sort there are several, that practise it for a Livelihood, and are very expert at Shedding abundance of Tears, and howling like Wolves, and so discharging their Office with abundance of Hypocrisy and Art. The Women are never accompanied with these Ceremonies after Death; and to what World they allot that Sex, I never understood, unless, to wait on their dead Husbands; but they have more Wit, than some of the Eastern Nations, who sacrifice themselves to accompany their Husbands into the next World. It is the dead Man's Relations, by Blood, as his Uncles, Brothers, Sisters, Cousins, Sons, and Daughters, that mourn in good earnest, the Wives thinking their Duty is discharg'd, and that they are become free, when their Husband is dead; so, as fast as they can, look out for another, to supply his Place.

As for the *Indian* Women, which now happen in my Way; when young, and at Maturity, they are as fine-shap'd Creatures (take them generally) as any in the Universe. They are of a tawny Complexion; their Eyes very brisk and amorous; their Smiles afford the finest Composure a Face can possess; their Hands are of the finest Make, with small long Fingers, and as soft as their Cheeks; and their whole Bodies of a smooth Nature. They are not so uncouth or unlikely, as we suppose them; nor are they Strangers or not Proficients in the soft Passion. They are most of them mercenary, except the married Women, who sometimes bestow their Favours also to some or other, in their

Husbands Absence. For which they never ask any Reward. As for
the Report, that they are never found unconstant, like the *Europeans,* it is wholly false; for were the old World and the new
one put into a Pair of Scales (in point of Constancy) it would
be a hard Matter to discern which was the heavier. As for the
Trading Girls, which are those design'd to get Money by their
Natural Parts, these are discernable, by the Cut of their Hair;
their Tonsure differing from all others, of that Nation, who
are not of their Profession; which Method is intended to prevent Mistakes; for the Savages of *America* are desirous (if
possible) to keep their Wives to themselves, as well as those in
other Parts of the World. When any Addresses are made to one
of these Girls, she immediately acquaints her Parents therewith,
and they tell the King of it, (provided he that courts her be a
Stranger) his Majesty commonly being the principal Bawd of the
Nation he rules over, and there seldom being any of these
Winchester-Weddings agreed on, without his Royal Consent.
He likewise advises her what Bargain to make, and if it happens to be an *Indian* Trader that wants a Bed-fellow, and has
got Rum to sell, be sure, the King must have a large Dram for
a Fee, to confirm the Match. These *Indians,* that are of the elder
sort, when any such Question is put to them, will debate the
Matter amongst themselves with all the Sobriety and Seriousness
imaginable, every one of the Girl's Relations arguing the Advantage or Detriment that may ensue such a Night's Encounter;
all which is done with as much Steadiness and Reality, as if it
was the greatest Concern in the World, and not so much as
one Person shall be seen to smile, so long as the Debate holds,
making no Difference betwixt an Agreement of this Nature, and
a Bargain of any other. If they comply with the Men's Desire,
then a particular Bed is provided for them, either in a Cabin
by themselves, or else all the young people turn out, to another Lodging, that they may not spoil Sport; and if the old
People are in the same Cabin along with them all Night, they lie
as unconcern'd, as if they were so many Logs of Wood. If it be an
Indian of their own Town or Neighbourhood, that wants a Mistress, he comes to none but the Girl, who receives what she
thinks fit to ask him, and so lies all Night with him, without the
Consent of her Parents.

The *Indian* Traders are those which travel and abide amongst
the *Indians* for a long space of time; sometimes for a Year, two, or

John White drawing

Indian woman and young girl

three. These Men have commonly their *Indian* Wives, whereby they soon learn the *Indian* Tongue, keep a Friendship with the Savages; and, besides the Satisfaction of a She-Bed-Fellow, they find these *Indian* Girls very serviceable to them, on Account of dressing their Victuals, and instructing 'em in the Affairs and Customs of the Country. Moreover, such a Man gets a great Trade with the Savages; for when a Person that lives amongst them, is reserv'd from the Conversation of their Women, 'tis impossible for him ever to accomplish his Designs amongst that People.

But one great Misfortune which oftentimes attends those that converse with these Savage Women, is, that they get Children by them, which are seldom educated any otherwise than in a State of Infidelity; for it is a certain Rule and Custom, amongst all the savages of *America,* that I was ever acquainted withal, to let the Children always fall to the Woman's Lot; for it often happens, that two *Indians* that have liv'd together, as Man and Wife, in which Time they have had several Children; if they part, and another Man possesses her, all the Children go along with the Mother, and none with the Father. And therefore, on this Score, it ever seems impossible for the Christians to get their Children (which they have by these *Indian* Women) away from them; whereby they might bring them up in the Knowledge of the Christian Principles. Nevertheless, we often find, that *English* Men, and other *Europeans* that have been accustom'd to the Conversation of these savage Women, and their Way of Living, have been so allur'd with that careless sort of Life, as to be constant to their *Indian* Wife, and her Relations, so long as they liv'd, without ever desiring to return again amongst the *English,* although they had very fair Opportunities of Advantages amongst their Countrymen; of which sort I have known several.

As for the *Indian* Marriages, I have read and heard of a great deal of Form and Ceremony used, which I never saw, nor yet could learn in the Time I have been amongst them, any otherwise than I shall here give you an Account of; which is as follows.

When any young *Indian* has a Mind for such a Girl to his Wife, he, or some one for him, goes to the young Woman's Parents, if living; if not, to her nearest Relations; where they make Offers of the Match betwixt the Couple. The Relations reply, they will consider of it, which serves for a sufficient Answer, till there be a second Meeting about the Marriage, which is generally brought into Debate before all the Relations (that are old People) on both Sides; and sometimes the King, with all his great Men, give their Opinions therein. If it be agreed on, and the young Woman approve thereof, (for these Savages never give their Children in Marriage, without their own Consent) the Man pays so much for his Wife; and the handsomer she is, the greater Price she bears. Now, it often happens, that the Man has not so much of their Money ready, as he is to pay for his Wife; but if they know him to be a good Hunter, and that he can raise the Sum agreed for, in some few Moons, or any little time, they agree, she shall go along with him, as betroth'd, but he is not to have any Knowledge of her, till the utmost Payment is discharg'd; all which is punctually observ'd. Thus, they lie together under one Covering for several Months, and the Woman remains the same as she was when she first came to him. I doubt, our *Europeans* would be apt to break this Custom, but the *Indian* Men are not so vigorous and impatient in their Love as we are. Yet the Women are quite contrary, and those *Indian* Girls that have convers'd with the *English* and other *Europeans,* never care for the Conversation of their own Countrymen afterwards.

They never marry so near as a first Cousin; and although there is nothing more coveted amongst them, than to marry a Woman of their own Nation, yet when the Nation consists of a very few People (as now adays it often happens) so that they are all of them related to one another, then they look out for Husbands and Wives amongst Strangers. For if an *Indian* lies with his Sister, or any very near Relation, his Body is burnt, and his Ashes thrown into the River, as unworthy to remain on Earth; yet an *Indian* is allow'd to marry two Sisters, or his Brothers Wife. Although these People are call'd Savages, yet Sodomy is never heard of amongst them, and they are so far from the Practice of that beastly and loathsome Sin, that they have no Name for it in all their Language.

The Marriages of these *Indians* are no farther binding, than the Man and Woman agree together. Either of them has Liberty to leave the other, upon any frivolous Excuse they can make; yet whosoever takes the Woman that was another Man's before, and bought by him, as they all are, must certainly pay to her former Husband, whatsoever he gave for her. Nay, if she be a Widow, and her Husband died in Debt, whosoever takes her to Wife, pays all her Husband's Obligations, though never so many; yet the Woman is not required to pay any thing (unless she is willing) that was owing from her Husband, so long as she keeps Single. But if a Man courts her for a Nights Lodging, and obtains it, the Creditors will make him pay her Husband's Debts, and he may, if he will, take her for his Money, or sell her to another for his Wife. I have seen several of these Bargains driven in a day; for you may see Men selling their Wives as Men do Horses in a Fair, a Man being allow'd not only to change as often as he pleases, but likewise to have as many Wives as he is able to maintain. I have often seen, that very old *Indian* Men (that have been Grandees in their own Nation) have had three or four very likely young *Indian* Wives, which I have much wondered at, because to me they seem'd incapacitated to make good Use of one of them.

The young Men will go in the Night from one House to another, to visit the young Women, in which sort of Rambles they will spend the whole Night. In their Addresses they find no Delays, for if she is willing to entertain the Man, she gives him Encouragement and grants him Admittance; otherwise she withdraws her Face from him, and says, I cannot see you, either you or I must leave this Cabin, and sleep somewhere else this Night.

They are never to boast of their Intrigues with the Women. If they do, none of the Girls value them ever after, or admit of their Company in their Beds. This proceeds not on the score of Reputation, for there is no such thing (on that account) known amongst them; and although we may reckon them the greatest Libertines and most extravagant in their Embraces, yet they retain and possess a Modesty that requires those Passions never to be divulged.

The Trading Girls, after they have led that Course of Life, for several Years, in which time they scarce ever have a Child; (for they have an Art to destroy the Conception, and she that brings a Child in this Station, is accounted a Fool, and her Reputation is lessen'd thereby) at last they grow weary of so many, and betake themselves to a married State, or to the Company of one Man; neither does their having been common to so many any wise lessen their Fortunes, but rather augment them.

The Woman is not punish'd for Adultery, but 'tis the Man that makes the injur'd Person Satisfaction, which is the Law of

Nations practis'd amongst them all; and he that strives to evade such Satisfaction as the Husband demands, lives daily in Danger of his Life; yet when discharg'd, all Animosity is laid aside, and the Cuckold is very well pleased with his Bargain, whilst the Rival is laugh'd at by the whole Nation, for carrying on his Intrigue with no better Conduct, than to be discover'd and pay so dear for his Pleasure.

The *Indians* say, that the Woman is a weak Creature, and easily drawn away by the Man's Persuasion; for which Reason, they lay no Blame upon her, but the Man (that ought to be Master of his Passion) for persuading her to it.

They are of a very hale Constitution; their Breaths are as sweet as the Air they breathe in, and the Woman seems to be of that tender Composition, as if they were design'd rather for the Bed then Bondage. Yet their Love is never of that Force and Continuance, that any of them ever runs Mad, or makes away with themselves on that score. They never love beyond Retrieving their first Indifferency, and when slighted, are as ready to untie the Knot at one end, as you are at the other.

Yet I knew an *European* Man that had a Child or two by one of these *Indian* Women, and afterwards married a Christian, after which he came to pass away a Night with his *Indian* Mistress; but she made Answer that she then had forgot she ever knew him, and that she never lay with another Woman's Husband, so fell a crying, and took up the Child she had by him, and went out of the Cabin (away from him) in great Disorder.

The *Indian* Womens Work is to cook the Victuals for the whole Family, and to make Mats, Baskets, Girdles of Possum-Hair, and such-like. They never plant the Corn amongst us, as they do amongst the *Iroquois,* who are always at War and Hunting; therefore, the Plantation Work is left for the Women and Slaves to perform, and look after; whilst they are wandring all over the Continent betwixt the two Bays of *Mexico* and St. *Laurence.*

The Mats the *Indian* Women make, are of Rushes, and about five Foot high, and two Fathom long, and sew'd double, that is, two together; whereby they become very commodious to lay under our Beds, or to sleep on in the Summer Season in the Day-time, and for our Slaves in the Night.

There are other Mats made of Flags, which the *Tuskeruro In-dians* make, and sell to the Inhabitants.

The Baskets our Neighbouring *Indians* make, are all made of a very fine sort of Bulrushes, and sometimes of Silk-grass, which they work with Figures of Beasts, Birds, Fishes, &c.

A great way up in the Country, both Baskets and Mats are made of the split Reeds, which are only the outward shining Part of the Cane. Of these I have seen Mats, Baskets, and Dressing-Boxes, very artificially done.

The Savage Women of *America*, have very easy Travail with their Children; sometimes they bring Twins, and are brought to bed by themselves, when took at a Disadvantage; not but that they have Midwives amongst them, as well as Doctors, who make it their Profession (for Gain) to assist and deliver Women, and some of these Midwives are very knowing in several Medicines that *Carolina* affords, which certainly expedite, and make easy Births. Besides, they are unacquainted with those severe Pains which follow the Birth in our *European* Women. Their Remedies are a great Cause of this Easiness in that State; for the *Indian* Women will run up and down the Plantation, the same day, very briskly, and without any sign of Pain or Sickness; yet they look very meager and thin. Not but that we must allow a great deal owing to the Climate, and the natural Constitution of these Women, whose Course of Nature never visits them in such Quantities, as the *European* Women have. And tho' they never want Plenty of Milk, yet I never saw an *Indian* Woman with very large Breasts; neither does the youngest Wife ever fail of proving so good a Nurse, as to bring her Child up free from the Rickets and Disasters that proceed from the Teeth, with many other Distempers which attack our Infants in *England*, and other Parts of *Europe*. They let their Children suck till they are well grown, unless they prove big with Child sooner. They always nurse their own Children themselves, unless Sickness or Death prevents. I once saw a Nurse hired to give Suck to an *Indian* Woman's Child, which you have in my Journal. After Delivery, they absent the Company of a Man for forty days. As soon as the Child is born, they wash it in cold Water at the next Stream, and then bedawb it, as I have mention'd before. After which, the Husband takes care to provide a Cradle, which is soon made, consisting of a Piece of flat Wood, which they hew with their Hatchets to the Likeness of a Board; it is about two Foot long, and a Foot broad; to this they brace and tie the Child down very close, having, near the middle, a Stick fasten'd about two Inches from the Board, which is for the Child's Breech to rest on, under which they put a Wad of Moss, that receives the Child's Excrements, by which means they can shift the Moss, and keep all clean and sweet. Some Nations have very flat Heads, as you have heard in my Journal, which is made whilst tied on this Cradle, as that Relation informs you. These Cradles are apt to make the Body flat; yet they are the most portable things that can be invented; for there is a String which goes from one Corner of the Board to the other, whereby the Mother slings her Child on her Back; so the Infant's Back is towards hers, and its Face looks up towards the Sky. If it rains, she throws her Leather or Woollen Match-coat, over her Head, which covers the Child all over, and secures her and it from the Injuries of rainy Weather. The Savage Women quit all Company, and dress not their own Victuals, during their Purgations.

After they have had several children, they grow strangely out of Shape in their Bodies; As for Barrenness, I never knew any of their Women, that have not Children when marry'd.

The Womens Dress is, in severe Weather, a hairy Match-coat in the Nature of a Plad, which keeps out the Cold, and (as I said before) defends their Children from the Prejudices of the Weather. At other times, they have only a sort of Flap or Apron containing two Yards in Length, and better than half a Yard deep. Sometimes, it is a Deer-Skin dress'd white, and pointed or slit at the bottom, like Fringe. When this is clean, it becomes them very well. Others wear blue or red Flaps made of Bays and Plains, which they buy of the *English,* of both which they tuck in the Corners, to fasten the Garment, and sometimes make it fast with a Belt. All of them, when ripe, have a small String round the Waste, to which another is tied and comes between their Legs, where always is a Wad of Moss against the *Os pubis;* but never any Hair is there to be found: Sometimes, they wear *Indian* Shooes, or Moggizons, which are made after the same manner, as the Mens are.

The Hair of their Heads is made into a long Roll like a Horses Tail, and bound round with *Ronoak* or *Porcelan,* which is a sort of Beads they make of the Conk-Shells. Others that have not this, make a Leather-String serve.

The *Indian* Men have a Match-Coat of Hair, Furs, Feathers, or Cloth, as the Women have. Their Hair is roll'd up, on each Ear, as the Womens, only much shorter, and oftentimes a Roll on the

The aged man in his wynter garment.

John White drawing

Old Indian man

John White drawing

Indian elder or chief

Crown of the Head, or Temples, which is just as they fancy; there being no Strictness in their Dress. Betwixt their Legs comes a Piece of Cloth, that is tuck'd in by a Belt both before and behind. This is to hide their Nakedness, of which Decency they are very strict Observers, although never practised before the Christians came amongst them. They wear Shooes, of Bucks, and sometimes Bears Skin, which they tan in an Hour or two; with the Bark of Trees boil'd, wherein they put the Leather whilst hot, and let it remain a little while, whereby it becomes so qualify'd, as to endure Water and Dirt, without growing hard. These have no Heels, and are made as fit for the Feet, as a Glove is for the Hand, and are very easie to travel in, when one is a little us'd to them. When these Savages live near the Water, they frequent the Rivers in Summer-time very much, where both Men and Women very often in a day go in naked to wash themselves, though not both Sexes together.

Their Feather Match-Coats are very pretty, especially some of them, which are made extraordinary charming, containing several pretty Figures wrought in Feathers, making them seem like a fine Flower Silk-Shag; and when new and fresh, they become a Bed very well, instead of a Quilt. Some of another sort are made of Hare, Raccoon, Bever, or Squirrel-Skins, which are very warm. Others again are made of the green Part of the Skin of a Mallard's Head, which they sew perfectly well together, their Thread being either the Sinews of a Deer divided very small, or Silk-Grass. When these are finish'd, they look very finely, though they must needs be very troublesome to make. Some of their great Men, as Rulers and such, that have Plenty of Deer Skins by them, will often buy the *English*-made Coats, which they wear on Festivals and other Days of Visiting. Yet none ever buy any Breeches, saying, that they are too much confin'd in them, which prevents their Speed in running, &c.

We have some *Indians*, that are more civilized than the rest, which wear Hats, Shooes, Stockings, and Breeches, with very tolerable Linnen Shirts, which is not common amongst these Heathens. The *Paspitank Indians* did formerly keep Cattle, and make Butter.

These are them that wear the *English* Dress. Whether they have Cattle now or no, I am not certain; but I am of the Opinion, that such Inclinations in the Savages should meet with Encouragement, and every *Englishman* ought to do them Justice, and not defraud them of their Land, which has been allotted them formerly by the Government; for if we do not shew them Examples of Justice and Vertue, we can never bring them to believe us to be a worthier Race of Men than themselves.

The Dresses of these People are so different, according to the Nation that they belong to, that it is impossible to recount all the whimsical Figures that they sometimes make by their Antick Dresses. Besides, *Carolina* is a warm Country, and very mild in its Winters, to what *Virginia, Maryland, Pensylvania, New-York,* the *Jerseys,* and *New-England* are; wherefore, our *Indians* Habit very much differs from the Dresses that appear amongst the Savages who inhabit those cold Countries; in regard their chiefest Cloathing for the Winter-Season is made of the Furs of Bever, Raccoon, and other Northern Furs, that our Climate is not acquainted withal, they producing some Furs, as the *Monack,* Moor, Marten, Black Fox, and others to us unknown.

Their Dress in Peace and War, is quite different. Besides, when they go to War, their Hair is comb'd out by the Women, and done over very much with Bears Grease, and red Root; with Feathers, Wings, Rings, Copper, and *Peak,* or *Wampum* in their Ears. Moreover, they buy Vermillion of the *Indian* Traders, wherewith they paint their Faces all over red, and commonly make a Circle of Black about one Eye, and another Circle of White about the other, whilst others bedawb their Faces with Tobacco-Pipe Clay, Lampblack, black Lead, and divers other Colours, which they make with the several sorts of Minerals and Earths that they get in different Parts of the Country, where they hunt and travel. When these Creatures are thus painted, they make the most frightful Figures that can be imitated by Men, and seem more like Devils than Humane Creatures. You may be sure, that they are about some Mischief, when you see them thus painted; for in all the Hostilities which have ever been acted against the *English* at any time, in several of the Plantations of *America,* the Savages always appear'd in this Disguize, whereby they might never after be discover'd, or known by any of the Christians that should happen to see them after they had made their Escape; for it is impossible, ever to know an *Indian* under these Colours, although he has been at your House a thousand times, and you know him, at other times, as well as you do any Person living. As for their Women, they never use any Paint on their Faces; neither do they ever carry them along

The manner of their attire and
painting them selues when
they goe to their generall
huntinges or at theire
Solemne feasts.

John White drawing

Indian in body paint

with them into the Field, when they intend any Expedition, leaving them at home with the old Men and Children.

Some of the *Indians* wear great Bobs in their Ears, and sometimes in the Holes thereof they put Eagles and other Birds, Feathers, for a Trophy. When they kill any Fowl, they commonly pluck off the downy Feathers, and stick them all over their Heads. Some (both Men and Women) wear great Necklaces of their Money made of Shells. They often wear Bracelets made of Brass, and sometimes of Iron Wire.

Their Money is of different sorts, but all made of Shells, which are found on the Coast of *Carolina*, which are very large and hard, so that they are very difficult to cut. Some *English* Smiths have try'd to drill this sort of Shell-Money, and thereby thought to get an Advantage; but it prov'd so hard, that nothing could be gain'd. They often times make, of this Shell, a sort of Gorge, which they wear about their Neck in a string; so it hangs on their Collar, whereon sometimes is engraven a Cross, or some odd sort of Figure, which comes next in their Fancy. There are other sorts valued at a Doe-Skin, yet the Gorges will sometimes sell for three or four Buck-Skins ready drest. There be others, that eight of them go readily for a Doe Skin; but the general and current Species of all the *Indians* in *Carolina*, and, I believe, all over the Continent, as far as the Bay of *Mexico*, is that which we call *Peak*, and *Ronoak*; but *Peak* more especially. This is that which at *New-York*, they call *Wampum*, and have used it as current Money amongst the Inhabitants for a great many Years. This is what many Writers call *Porcelan*, and is made at *New-York* in great Quantities, and with us in some measure. Five Cubits of this purchase a dress'd Doe-Skin, and seven or eight purchase a dress'd Buck-Skin. An *English*-man could not afford to make so much of this *Wampum* for five or ten times the Value; for it is made out of a vast great Shell, of which that Country affords Plenty; where it is ground smaller than the small End of a Tobacco-Pipe, or a large Wheat-Straw. Four or five of these make an Inch, and every one is to be drill'd through, and made as smooth as Glass, and so strung, as Beds are, and a Cubit of the *Indian* Measure contains as much in Length, as will reach from the Elbow to the End of the little Finger. They never stand to question, whether it is a tall Man, or a short one, that measures it; but if this *Wampum Peak* be black or purple, as some Part of that Shell is, then it is twice the

Value. This the *Indians* grind on Stones and other things, till they make it current, but the Drilling is the most difficult to the *English*-men, which the *Indians* manage with a Nail stuck in a Cane or Reed. Thus they roll it continually on their Thighs, with their Right-hand, holding the Bit of Shell with their Left, so in time they drill a Hole quite through it, which is a very tedious Work; but especially in making their *Ronoak,* four of which will scarce make one Length of *Wampum.* The *Indians* are a People that never value their time, so that they can afford to make them, and never need to fear the *English* will take the Trade out of their Hands. This is the Money with which you may buy Skins, Furs, Slaves, or any thing the *Indians* have; it being the Mammon (as our Money is to us) that entices and persuades them to do any thing, and part with every thing they possess, except their Children for Slaves. As for their Wives, they are often sold, and their Daughters violated for it. With this they buy off Murders; and whatsoever a Man can do that is ill, this *Wampum* will quit him of, and make him, in their Opinion, good and vertuous, though never so black before.

All the *Indians* give a Name to their Children, which is not the same as the Father or Mother, but what they fancy. This Name they keep, (if Boys) till they arrive to the Age of a War-riour, which is sixteen or seventeen Years; then they take a Name to themselves, sometimes, *Eagle, Panther, Allegator,* or some such wild Creature; esteeming nothing on Earth worthy to give them a Name, but these Wild-Fowl, and Beasts. Some again take the Name of a Fish, which they keep as long as they live.

The King is the Ruler of the Nation, and has others under him, to assist him, as his War-Captains, and Counsellors, who are pick'd out and chosen from among the ancientest Men of the Nation he is King of. These meet him in all general Councils and Debates, concerning War, Peace, Trade, Hunting, and all the Adventures and Accidents of Humane Affairs, which ap-pear within their Verge; where all Affairs are discoursed of and argued *pro* and *con,* very deliberately (without making any manner of Parties or Divisions) for the Good of the Publick; for, as they meet there to treat, they discharge their Duty with all the Integrity imaginable, never looking towards their Own Inter-est, before the Publick Good. After every Man has given his Opinion, that which has most Voices, or, in Summing up, is found the most reasonable, that they make use of without any

Jars and Wrangling, and put it in Execution, the first Opportunity that offers.

The Succession falls not to the King's Son, but to his Sister's Son, which is a sure way to prevent Impostors in the Succession. Sometimes they poison the Heir to make way for another, which is not seldom done, when they do not approve of the Youth that is to succeed them. The King himself is commonly chief Doctor in that Cure.

They are so well versed in Poison, that they are often found to poison whole Families; nay, most of a Town; and which is most to be admired, they will poison a running Spring, or Fountain of Water, so that whosoever drinks thereof, shall infallible die. When the Offender is discover'd, his very relations urge for Death, whom nothing will appease, but the most cruel Torment imaginable, which is executed in the most publick Manner that it's possible to act such a Tragedy in. For all the whole Nation, and all the *Indians* within a hundred Mile (if it is possible to send for them) are summon'd to come and appear at such a Place and Time, to see and rejoyce at the Torments and Death of such a Person, who is the common and profess'd Enemy to all the friendly *Indians* thereabouts, who now lies under the Condemnation of the whole Nation, and accordingly is to be put to Death. Then all appear (young and old) from all the adjacent Parts, and meet, with all the Expressions of Joy, to consummate this horrid and barbarous Feast, which is carried on after this dismal Manner. First, they bring the Prisoner to the Place appointed for the Execution, where he is set down on his Breech on the Ground. Then they all get about him, and you shall not see one sorrowful or dejected Countenance amongst them, but all very merrily dispos'd, as if some Comedy was to be acted, instead of a Tragedy. He that is appointed to be the chief Executioner, takes a Knife, and bids him hold out his Hands, which he does, and then cuts round the Wrist through the Skin, which is drawn off like a Glove, and flead quite off at the Fingers Ends; then they break his Joints and Bones, and buffet and torment him after a very inhumane Manner, till some violent Blow perhaps ends his Days; then they burn him to Ashes, and throw them down the River. Afterwards they eat, drink and are merry, repeating all the Actions of the Tormentors and the Prisoner, with a great deal of Mirth and Satisfaction. This Accusation is laid against an

Indian Heroe sometimes wrongfully, or when they have a mind to get rid of a Man that has more Courage and Conduct than his neighbouring Kings or great Men; then they alledge the Practice of poisoning *Indians* against him, and make a Rehearsal of every *Indian* that died for a year or two, and say, that they were poison'd by such an *Indian;* which Reports stir up all the Relations of the deceased against the said Person, and by such means make him away presently. In some Affairs, these Savages are very reserv'd and politick, and will attend a long time with a great deal of Patience, to bring about their Designs; they being never impatient or hasty in executing any of their Designs of Revenge.

Now I am gone so far in giving an Account of the *Indians* Temper, I will proceed; and can give you no other Character of them, but that they are a very wary People, and are never hasty or impatient. They will endure a great many Misfortunes, Losses, and Disapointments without shewing themselves, in the least, vex'd or uneasy. When they go by Water, if there proves a Head-Wind, they never vex and fret as the *Europeans* do, and let what Misfortune come to them, as will or can happen, they never relent. Besides, there is one Vice very common every where, which I never found amongst them, which is Envying other Mens Happiness, because their Station is not equal to, or above, their Neighbours. Of this Sin I cannot say I ever saw an Example, though they are a People that set as great a Value upon themselves, as any sort of Men in the World; upon which Account they find something Valuable in themselves above Riches. Thus, he that is a good Warriour, is the proudest Creature living; and he that is an expert Hunter, is esteem'd by the People and himself; yet all these are natural Vertues and Gifts, and not Riches, which are as often in the Possession of a Fool as a Wise-man. Several of the *Indians* are possess'd of a great many Skins, *Wampum*, Ammunition, and what other things are esteem'd Riches amongst them; yet such an *Indian* is no more esteem'd amongst them, than any other ordinary Fellow, provided he has no personal Endowments, which are the Ornaments that must gain him an Esteem among them; for a great Dealer, amongst the *Indians,* is no otherwise respected and esteemed, than as a Man that strains his Wits, and fatigues himself, to furnish others with Necessaries of Life, that live much easier and enjoy more of the World, than he himself does with all his Pelf. If they are taken Captives, and expect a miserable Exit, they sing; if Death approach them in Sickness, they are not afraid of it; nor are ever heard to say, Grant me some time. They know by Instinct, and daily Example, that they must die; wherefore, they have that great and noble Gift to submit to every thing that happens, and value nothing that attacks them.

Their Cruelty to their Prisoners of War is what they are seemingly guilty of an Error in, (I mean as to a natural Failing) because they strive to invent the most inhumane Butcheries for them, that the Devils themselves could invent, or hammer out of Hell; they esteeming Death no Punishment, but rather an Advantage to him, that is exported out of this into another World.

Therefore, they inflict on them Torments, wherein they prolong Life in that miserable state as long as they can, and never miss Skulping of them, as they call it, which is, to cut off the Skin from the Temples, and taking the whole Head of Hair along with it, as if it was a Night-cap. Sometimes, they take the Top of the Skull along with it; all which they preserve, and carefully keep by them, for a Trophy of their Conquest over their Enemies. Others keep their Enemies Teeth, which are taken in War, whilst others split the Pitch-Pine into Splinters, and stick them into the Prisoners Body yet alive. Thus they light them, which burn like so many Torches; and in this manner, they make him dance round a great Fire, every one buffeting and deriding him, till he expires, when every one strives to get a Bone or some Relick of this unfortunate Captive. One of the young Fellows, that has been at the Wars, and has had the Fortune to take a Captive, returns the proudest Creature on Earth, and sets such a Value on himself, that he knows not how to contain himself in his Senses. The *Iroquois,* or *Sinnagars,* are the most Warlike *Indians* that we know of, being always at War, and not to be persuaded from that Way of Living, by any Argument that can be used. If you go to persuade them to live peaceably with the *Tuskeruros,* and let them be one People, and in case those *Indians* desire it, and will submit to them, they will answer you, that they cannot live without War, which they have ever been used to; and that if Peace be made with the *Indians* they now war withal, they must find out some others to wage War against; for, for them to live in Peace, is to live out of their Element, War, Conquest, and Murder, being what they delight in, and value themselves for. When they take a Slave, and intend to keep him to Work in their Fields, they flea the Skin from the Setting on of his Toes to the middle of his Foot, so cut off one half of his Feet, wrapping the Skin over the Wounds, and healing them. By this cruel Method, the *Indian* Captive is hinder'd from making his Escape, for he can neither run fast or go any where, but his Feet are more easily traced and discover'd. Yet I know one Man who made his Escape from them, tho' they had thus disabled him, as you may see in my Journal.

The *Indians* ground their Wars on Enmity, not on Interest, as the *Europeans* generally do; for the Loss of the meanest Person in the Nation, they will go to War and lay all at Stake, and prosecute their Design to the utmost; till the Nation they were injur'd by, be wholly destroy'd, or make them that Satisfaction which they demand. They are very politick, in waging, and carrying on their War, first by advising with all the ancient Men of Conduct and Reason, that belong to their Nation; such as superannuated War-Captains, and those that have been Counsellors for many Years, and whose Advice has commonly succeeded very well. They have likewise their Field Counsellors, who are accustomed to Ambuscades, and Surprizes, which Methods are commonly used by the Savages; for I scarce ever heard of a Field-Battle fought amongst them.

One of their Expeditions afforded an Instance, worthy mention, which was thus; Two Nations of *Indians* here in *Carolina* were at War together, and a Party of each were in the Forest ranging to see what Enemies they could take. The lesser Number found they were discover'd, and could not well get over a River (that lay betwixt them and their home) without engaging the other Party, whose Numbers were much the greater; so they call'd a Council, which met, and having weigh'd their present Circumstances with a great deal of Argument and Debate, for a considerable time, and found their Enemies Advantage, and that they could expect no Success in Engaging such an unequal Number; they, at last, concluded on this Stratagem, which, in my Opinion, carried a great deal of Policy along with it. It was, That the same Night, they should make a great Fire, which they were certain would be discover'd by the adverse Party, and there dress up Logs of Wood in their Cloaths, and make them exactly seem like *Indians,* that were asleep by the Fire-side; (which is their Way, when in the Woods) so, *said they,* our Enemies will fire upon these Images, supposing them to be us, who will lie in Ambuscade, and, after their Guns are unloaded, shall deal well enough with them. This Result was immediately put in Execution, and the Fire was made by the side of a Valley, where they lay perdu very advantageously. Thus, a little before Break of Day, (which commonly is the Hour they surprize their Enemies in) the *Indians* came down to their Fire, and at once fired in upon those Logs in the *Indians* Cloaths, and run up to them, expecting they had kill'd every Man dead; but they found themselves mistaken, for then the other *Indians,* who had lain all the Night stark-naked in the Bottom, attack'd them with their loaded Pieces, which so surprized them, that every Man was taken Prisoner, and brought in bound to their Town.

Another Instance was betwixt the *Machapunga Indians,* and the *Coranine's,* on the Sand-Banks; which was as follows. The *Machapungas* were invited to a Feast, by the *Coranines;* (which two Nations had been a long time at War together, and had lately concluded a Peace.) Thereupon, the *Machapunga Indians* took the Advantage of coming to the *Coranines* Feast, which was to avoid all Suspicion, and their King, who, of a Savage, is a great Politician and very stout, order'd all his Men to carry their *Tamahauks* along with them, hidden under their Match-Coats, which they did; and being acquainted when to fall on, by the Word given, they all (upon this Design) set forward for the Feast, and came to the *Coranine* Town, where they had gotten Victuals, Fruit, and such things as make an *Indian* Entertainment, all ready to make these new Friends welcome, which they did; and, after Dinner, towards the Evening, (as it is customary amongst them) they went to Dancing, all together; so when the *Machapunga* King saw the best Opportunity offer, he gave the Word, and his Men pull'd their *Tamahauks* or Hatchets from under their Match-Coats, and kill'd several, and took the rest Prisoners, except some few that were not present, and about four or five that escap'd. The Prisoners they sold Slaves to the *English.* At the time this was done, those *Indians* had nothing but Bows and Arrows, neither side having Guns.

The *Indians* are very revengeful, and never forget an Injury done, till they have receiv'd Satisfaction. Yet they are the freest People from Heats and Passions (which possess the *Europeans*) of any I ever heard of. They never call any Man to account for what he did, when he was drunk; but say, it was the Drink that caused his Misbehaviour, therefore he ought to be forgiven: They never frequent a Christian's House that is given to Passion, nor will they ever buy or sell with him, if they can get the same Commodities of any other Person; for they say, such Men are mad Wolves, and no more Men.

They know not what Jealousy is, because they never think their Wives are unconstant, unless they are Eye-witnesses thereof. They are generally very bashful, especially the young Maids, who when they come into a strange Cabin, where they are not acquainted, never ask for any thing, though never so hungry or thirsty, but sit down, without speaking a Word (be it never so long) till some of the House asks them a Question, or falls into Discourse, with the Stranger. I never saw a Scold amongst them, and to their Children they are extraordinary tender and indulgent; neither did I ever see a Parent correct a Child, excepting one Woman, that was the King's Wife, and she (indeed) did possess a Temper that is not commonly found amongst them. They are free from all manner of Compliments, except Shaking of Hands, and Scratching on the Shoulder, which two are the greatest Marks of Sincerity and Friendship, that can be shew'd one to another. They cannot express *fare you well;* but when they leave the House, will say, *I go straightway,* which is to intimate their Departure; and if the Man of the House has any Message to send by the going Man, he may acquaint him therewith. Their Tongue allows not to say, *Sir, I am your Servants;* because they have no different Titles for Man, only King, War-Captain, Old Man, or Young Man, which respect the Stations and Circumstances Men are employ'd in, and arriv'd to, and not Ceremony. As for Servant, they have no such thing, except Slave, and their Dogs, Cats, tame or domestick Beasts, and Birds, are call'd by the same Name: For the *Indian* Word for Slave includes them all. So when an *Indian* tells you he has got a Slave for you, it may (in general Terms, as they use) be a young Eagle, a Dog, Otter, or any other thing of that Nature, which is obsequiously to depend on the Master for its Sustenance.

They are never fearful in the Night, nor do the Thoughts of Spirits ever trouble them; such as the many Hobgoblins and Bugbears that we suck in with our Milk, and the Foolery of our Nurses and Servants suggest to us; who by their idle Tales of

Fairies, and Witches, make such Impressions on our tender Years, that at Maturity, we carry Pigmies Souls, in Giants Bodies and ever after, are thereby so much depriv'd of Reason, and unman'd, as never to be Masters of half the Bravery Nature design'd for us.

Not but that the *Indians* have as many Lying Stories of Spirits and Conjurers, as any People in the World; but they tell it with no Disadvantage to themselves; for the great Esteem which the Old Men bring themselves to, is by making the others believe their Familiarity with Devils and Spirits, and how great a Correspondence they have therewith, which if it once gains Credit, they ever after are held in the greatest Veneration imaginable, and whatever they after impose upon the People, is receiv'd as infallible. They are so little startled at the Thoughts of another World, that they not seldom murder themselves; as for Instance, a *Bear*-River *Indian*, a very likely young Fellow, about twenty Years of Age, whose Mother was angry at his drinking of too much Rum, and chid him for it, thereupon reply'd, he would have her satisfied, and he would do the like no more; upon which he made his Words good; for he went aside, and shot himself dead. This was a Son of the politick King of the *Machapunga*, I spoke of before, and has the most Cunning of any *Indian* I ever met withal.

Most of the Savages are much addicted to Drunkenness, a Vice they never were acquainted with, till the Christians came amongst them. Some of them refrain drinking strong Liquors, but very few of that sort are found amongst them. Their chief Liquor is Rum, without any Mixture. This the *English* bring amongst them, and buy Skins, Furs, Slaves and other of their Commodities therewith. They never are contented with a little, but when once begun, they must make themselves quite drunk; otherwise they will never rest, but sell all they have in the World, rather than not have their full Dose. In these drunken Frolicks, (which are always carried on in the Night) they sometimes murder one another, fall into the Fire, fall down Precipices, and break their Necks, with several other Misfortunes which this drinking of Rum brings upon them; and tho' they are sensible of it, yet they have no Power to refrain this Enemy. About five years ago, when *Landgrave Daniel* [Robert Daniel was not governor until 1716–17] was Governour, he summon'd in all the *Indian* Kings and Rulers to meet, and in a full Meeting of the Government and Council, with those *Indians*, they agreed upon a firm Peace, and the *Indian* Rulers desired no Rum might be sold to them, which was granted, and a Law made, that inflicted a Penalty on those that sold Rum to the Heathens; but it was never strictly observ'd, and besides, the young *Indians* were so disgusted at that Article, that they threatened to kill the *Indians* that made it, unless it was laid aside, and they might have Rum sold them, when they went to the *Englishmens* Houses to buy it.

Some of the Heathens are so very poor, that they have no Manner of Cloaths, save a Wad of Moss to hide their Nakedness. These are either lusty and will not work; otherwise, they are given to Gaming or Drunkenness; yet these get Victuals as well as the rest, because that is common amongst them, If they are caught in theft they are Slaves till they repay the Person, (as I mention'd before) but to steal from the *English* they reckon no Harm. Not but that I have known some few Savages that have been as free from Theft as any of the Christians. When they have a Design to lie with a Woman, which they cannot obtain any otherwise than by a larger Reward than they are able to give, they then strive to make her drunk, which a great many of them will be; then they take the Advantage, to do with them what they please, and sometimes in their Drunkenness, cut off their Hair and sell it to the *English*, which is the greatest Affront can be offer'd them. They never value Time; for if they be going out to hunt, fish, or any other indifferent Business, you may keep them in talk as long as you please, so you but keep them in Discourse, and seem pleased with their Company; yet none are more expeditious and safer Messengers than they, when any extraordinary Business that they are sent about requires it.

When they are upon travelling the Woods, they keep a constant Pace, neither will they stride over a Tree that lies cross the Path, but always go round it, which is quite contrary to the Custom of the *English,* and other *Europeans.* When they cut with a Knife, the Edge is towards them, whereas we always cut and whittle from us. Nor did I ever see one of them left-handed. Before the Christians came amongst them, not knowing the Use of Steel and Flints, they got their Fire with Sticks, which by vehement Collision, or Rubbing together, take Fire. This Method they will sometimes practise now, when it has happen'd thro' rainy Weather, or some other Accident, that they have wet their Spunk, which is a sort of soft corky Substance, generally of a Cinnamon Colour, and grows in the concave part of an Oak, Hiccory, and several other Woods, being dug out with an Ax, and always kept by the *Indians*, instead of Tinder or Touch-wood, both which it exceeds. You are to understand, that the two Sticks they use to strike Fire withal, are never of one sort of Wood, but always differ from each other.

They are expert Travellers, and though they have not the Use of our artificial Compass, yet they understand the North-point exactly, let them be in never so great a Wilderness. One Guide is a short Moss, that grows upon some Trees, exactly on the North-Side thereof.

Besides, they have Names for eight of the thirty two Points, and call the Winds by their several Names, as we do; but indeed more properly, for the North-West Wind is called the cold Wind; the North-East the wet Wind; the South the warm Wind; and so agreeably of the rest. Sometimes it happens, that they have a large River or Lake to pass over, and the Weather is very foggy, as it often happens in the Spring and Fall of the Leaf; so that they cannot see which Course to steer: In such a Case, they being on one side of the River, or Lake, they know well enough what Course such a Place (which they intend for) bears from them. Therefore, they get a great many Sticks and Chunks of Wood in their Canoe, and then set off directly for their Port, and now and then throw over a Piece of Wood, which directs them, by seeing how the Stick bears from the Canoes Stern, which they always observe to keep right aft; and this is the *Indian* Compass by which they will go over a broad Water of ten or twenty Leagues wide. They will find the Head of any River, though it is five six or seven hundred miles off, and they never were there, in their Lives before; as is often prov'd, by their appointing to meet on the Head of such a River, where perhaps, none of them ever was before, but where they shall rendezvous exactly at the prefixt time; and if they meet with any Obstruction, they leave certain Marks in the Way, where they that come after will understand how many have pass'd by already, and which way they are gone. Besides, in their War Expeditions, they have very certain Hieroglyphicks, whereby each Party informs the other of the Success or Losses they have met withal; all which is so exactly perform'd by their Sylvian

Marks and Characters, that they are never at a Loss to understand one another. Yet there was never found any Letters amongst the Savages of *Carolina;* nor, I believe, among any other Natives in *America,* that were possess'd with any manner of Writing or Learning throughout all the Discoveries of the New-World. They will draw Maps, very exactly, of all the Rivers, Towns, Mountains, and Roads, or what you shall enquire of them, which you may draw by their Directions, and come to a small matter of Latitude, reckoning by their Days Journeys. These Maps they will draw in the Ashes of the Fire, and sometimes upon a Mat or Piece of Bark. I have put a Pen and Ink into a Savage's Hand, and he has drawn me the Rivers, Bays, and other Parts of a Country, which afterwards I have found to agree with a great deal of Nicety: But you must be very much in their Favour, otherwise they will never make these Discoveries to you; especially, if it be in their own Quarters. And as for Mines of Silver and other Metals, we are satisfied we have enow, and those very rich, in *Carolina* and its adjacent Parts; some of which the *Indians* are acquainted withal, although no Enquirers thereafter, but what came, and were discover'd, by Chance; yet they say, it is this Metal that the *English* covet, as they do their *Peak* and *Ronoak;* and that we have gain'd Ground of them wherever we have come. Now, say they, if we should discover these Minerals to the *English,* they would settle at or near these Mountains, and bereave us of the best Hunting-Quarters we have, as they have already done wherever they have inhabited; so by that means, we shall be driven to some unknown Country, to live, hunt, and get our Bread in. These are the Reasons that the Savages give, for not making known what they are acquainted withal, of that Nature. And indeed, all Men that have ever gone upon those Discoveries, allow them to be good; more especially, my ingenious Friend Mr. *Francis-Louis Mitchell* [Head of a Swiss Land company], of *Bern* in *Switzerland,* who has been, for several Years, very indefatigable and strict in his Discoveries amongst those vast Ledges of Mountains, and spacious Tracts of Land, lying towards the Heads of the great Bays and Rivers of *Virginia, Maryland,* and *Pensylvania,* where he has discover'd a spacious Country inhabited by none but the Savages, and not many of them; who yet are of a very friendly Nature to the Christians. This Gentleman has been employ'd by the Canton of *Bern,* to find out a Tract of Land in the *English America,* where that Republick might settle some of their People; which Proposal, I believe, is now in a fair way towards a Conclusion, between her Majesty of *Great-Britain* and that Canton. Which must needs be of great Advantage to both; and as for ourselves, I believe, no Man that is in his Wits, and understands the Situation and Affairs of *America,* but will allow, nothing can be of more Security and Advantage to the Crown and Subjects of *Great-Britain,* than to have our Frontiers secured by a warlike People, and our Friends, as the *Switzers* are; especially when we have more *Indians* than we can civilize, and so many Christian Enemies lying on the back of us, that we do not know how long or short a time it may be, before they visit us. Add to these, the Effects and Product that may be expected from those Mountains; which may hereafter prove of great Advantage to the *British* Monarchy, and none more fit than an industrious People, bred in a mountainous Country, and inur'd to all the Fatigues of War and Travel, to improve a Country. Thus we have no room to doubt, but as soon as any of those Parts are seated by the *Switzers,* a great many *Britains* will strive to live amongst them, for the Benefit of the sweet Air and healthful Climate, which that Country affords, were it only for the Cultivating of Hemp, Flax, Wine, and other valuable Staples, which those People are fully acquainted withal: Not to mention the Advantages already discover'd by that worthy Gentleman I just now spoke of, who is highly deserving of the Conduct and Management of such an Affair, as that wise Canton has entrusted him withal.

When these Savages go a hunting, they commonly go out in great Numbers, and oftentimes a great many Days Journey from home, beginning at the coming in of the Winter; that is, when the Leaves are fallen from the Trees, and are become dry. 'Tis then they burn the Woods, by setting Fire to the Leaves, and wither'd Bent and Grass, which they do with a Match made of the black Moss that hangs on the Trees in *Carolina,* and is sometimes above six Foot long. This, when dead, becomes black, (tho' of an Ash-Colour before) and will then hold Fire as well as the best Match we have in *Europe.* In Places, where this Moss is not found, (as towards the Mountains) they make Lintels of the Bark of Cypress beaten, which serve as well. Thus they go and fire the Woods for many Miles, and drive the Deer and other Game into small Necks of Land and Isthmus's, where they kill and destroy what they please. In these Hunting-Quarters, they have their Wives and Ladies of the Camp, where they eat all the Fruits and Dainties of that Country, and live in all the Mirth and Jollity, which it is possible for such People to entertain themselves withal. Here it is, that they get their Complement of Deer-Skins and Furs to trade with the *English,* (the Deer-Skins being in Season in Winter, which is contrary to *England.*) All small Game, as Turkeys, Ducks, and small Vermine, they commonly kill with Bow and Arrow, thinking it not worth throwing Powder and Shot after them. Of Turkeys they have abundance; especially, in Oak-Land, as most of it is, that lies any distance backwards. I have been often in their Hunting-Quarters, where a roasted or barbakued Turkey, eaten with Bears Fat, is held a good Dish; and indeed, I approve of it very well; for the Bears Grease is the sweetest and least offensive to the Stomach (as I said before) of any Fat of Animals I ever tasted. The Savage Men never beat their Corn to make Bread; but that is the Womens Work, especially the Girls, of whom you shall see four beating with long great Pestils in a narrow wooden Mortar; and every one keeps her Stroke so exactly, that 'tis worthy of Admiration. Their Cookery continues from Morning till Night. The Hunting makes them hungry; and the *Indians* are a People that always eat very often, not seldom getting up at Midnight, to eat. They plant a great many sorts of Pulse, Part of which they eat green in the Summer, keeping great Quantities for their Winter-Store, which they carry along with them into the Hunting-Quarters, and eat them.

The small red Pease is very common with them, and they eat a great deal of that and other sorts boil'd with their Meat, or eaten with Bears Fat, which Food makes them break Wind backwards, which the Men frequently do, and laugh heartily at it, it being accounted no ill Manners amongst the *Indians:* Yet the Women are more modest, than to follow that ill Custom. At their setting out, they have *Indians* to attend their Hunting-Camp, that are not good and expert Hunters; therefore are employ'd to carry Burdens, to get Bark for the Cabins, and other Servile Work; also to go backward and forward, to their Towns, to carry News to the old People, whom they leave behind them. The Women are forced to carry their Loads of Grain and other Provisions, and get Fire-Wood; for a good Hunter, or Warriour in these Expeditions, is employ'd in no

other Business, than the Affairs of Game and Battle. The wild
Fruits which are dry'd in the Summer, over Fires, on Hurdles
and in the Sun, are now brought into the Field; as are likewise
the Cakes and Quiddonies of Peaches, and that Fruit and
Bilberries dry'd, of which they stew and make Fruit-Bread and
Cakes. In some parts, where Pigeons are plentiful, they get of
their Fat enough to supply their Winter Stores. Thus they abide
in these Quarters, all the Winter long, till the Time approach
for planting their Maiz and other Fruits. In these quarters, at
Spare-hours, the Women make Baskets and Mats to lie upon,
and those that are not extraordinary Hunters, make Bowls,
Dishes, and Spoons, of Gum-wood, and the Tulip-Tree; others
(where they find a Vein of white Clay, fit for their purpose,
make Tobacco-pipes, all which are often transported to other
Indians, that perhaps have greater Plenty of Deer and other
Game; so they buy (with these Manufactures) their raw Skins,
with the Hair on, which our neighbouring *Indians* bring to their
Towns, and, in the Summer-time, make the Slaves and sorry
Hunters dress them, the Winter-Sun being not strong enough
to dry them; and those that are dry'd in the Cabins are black
and nasty with the Lightwood Smoke, which they commonly
burn. Their Way of dressing their Skins is by soaking them in
Water, so they get the Hair off, with an Instrument made of the
Bone of a Deer's Foot; yet some use a sort of Iron Drawing-
Knife, which they purchase of the *English,* and after the Hair is
off, they dissolve Deers Brains, (which beforehand are made in a
Cake and baked in the Embers) in a Bowl of Water, so soak the
Skins therein, till the Brains have suck'd up the Water; then
they dry it gently, and keep working it with an Oyster-Shell, or
some such thing, to scrape withal, till it is dry; whereby it becomes soft and pliable. Yet these so dress'd will not endure wet,
but become hard thereby; which to prevent, they either cure
them in the Smoke, or tan them with Bark, as before observ'd; not
but that young *Indian* Corn, beaten to a Pulp, will effect the
same as the Brains. They are not only good Hunters of the wild
Beasts and Game of the Forest, but very expert in taking the
Fish of the Rivers and Waters near which they inhabit, and
are acquainted withal. Thus they that live a great way up the
Rivers practise Striking Sturgeon and Rock-fish, or Bass, when
they come up the Rivers to spawn; besides the vast Shoals of
Sturgeon which they kill and take with Snares, as we do Pike in

Europe. The Herrings in *March* and *April* run a great way up the Rivers and fresh Streams to spawn, where the Savages make great Wares, with Hedges that hinder their Passage only in the Middle, where an artificial Pound is made to take them in; so that they cannot return. This Method is in use all over the fresh Streams, to catch Trout and the other Species of Fish which those Parts afford. Their taking of Craw-fish is so pleasant, that I cannot pass it by without mention; When they have a mind to get these Shell-fish, they take a Piece of Venison, and half-barbakue or roast it; then they cut it into thin Slices, which Slices they stick through with Reeds about six Inches asunder, betwixt Piece and Piece; then the Reeds are made sharp at one end; and so they stick a great many of them down in the bottom of the Water (thus baited) in the small Brooks and Runs, which the Craw-fish frequent. Thus the *Indians* sit by, and tend those baited Sticks, every now and then taking them up, to see how many are at the Bait; where they generally find abundance; so take them off, and put them in a Basket for the purpose, and stick the Reeds down again. By this Method, they will, in a little time, catch several Bushels, which are as good, as any I ever eat. Those *Indians* that frequent the Salt-Waters, take abundance of Fish, some very large, and of several sorts, which to preserve, they first barbakue, then pull the Fish to Pieces, so dry it in the Sun, whereby it keeps for Transportation; as for Scate, Oysters, Cockles, and several sorts of Shell-fish, they open and dry them upon Hurdles, having a constant Fire under them. The Hurdles are made of Reeds or Canes in the shape of a Gridiron. Thus they dry several Bushels of these Fish, and keep them for their Necessities. At the time when they are on the Salts, and Sea Coasts, they have another Fishery, that is for a little Shell-fish, which those in *England* call Blackmoors Teeth. These they catch by tying Bits of Oysters to a long String, which they lay in such places, as, they know, those Shell-Fish haunt. These Fish get hold of the Oysters, and suck them in, so that they pull up those long Strings, and take great Quantities of them, which they carry a great way into the main Land, to trade with the remote *Indians,* where they are of great Value; but never near the Sea, by reason they are common, therefore not esteem'd. Besides, the Youth and *Indian* Boys go in the Night, and one holding a Lightwood Torch, the other has a Bow and Arrows, and the Fire directing him to see the Fish, he shoots them with the Arrows;

and thus they kill a great many of the smaller Fry, and some-times pretty large ones. It is an establish'd Custom amongst all these Natives, that the young Hunter never eats of that Buck, Bear, Fish, or any other Game, which happens to be the first they kill of that sort; because they believe, if he should eat thereof, he would never after be fortunate in Hunting. The like foolish Ceremony they hold, when they have made a Ware to take Fish withal; if a big-belly'd Woman eat of the first Dish that is caught in it, they say, that Ware will never take much Fish; and as for killing of Snakes, they avoid it, if they lie in their way, be-cause their Opinion is, that some of the Serpents Kindred would kill some of the Savages Relations, that should destroy him: They have thousands of these foolish Ceremonies and Beliefs, which they are strict Observers of. Moreover, several Customs are found in some Families, which others keep not; as for Example, two Families of the *Machapunga Indians,* use the *Jewish* Custom of Circumcision,[88] and the rest do not; neither did I ever know any others amongst the *Indians,* that practis'd any such thing; and perhaps, if you ask them, what is the Reason they do so, they will make you no Manner of Answer; which is as much as to say, I will not tell you. Many other Customs they have, for which they will render no Reason or Account; and to pretend to give a true Description of their Religion, it is im-possible; for there are a great many of their Absurdities, which, for some Reason, they reserve as a Secret amongst themselves; or otherwise, they are jealous of their Weakness in the practising them; so that they never acquaint any Christian with the Knowl-edge thereof, let Writers pretend what they will; for I have known them amongst their Idols and dead Kings in their *Quiogozon* for several Days, where I could never get Admit-tance, to see what they were doing, though I was at great Friendship with the King and great Men; but all my Persua-sions avail'd me nothing. Neither were any but the King, with the Conjurer, and some few old Men, in that House; as for the young Men, and chiefest Numbers of the *Indians,* they were kept as ignorant of what the Elders were doing, as myself.

They all believe, that this World is round, and that there are two Spirits; the one good, the other bad: The good one they reckon to be the Author and Maker of every thing, and say, that

88. See Frank G. Speck, "Remnants of the Machapunga Indians of North Carolina," *American Anthropologist,* Vol. 18 (April–June, 1916), 271–76.

it is he, that gives them the Fruits of the Earth, and has taught them to hunt, fish, and be wise enough to overpower the Beasts of the Wilderness, and all other Creatures, that they may be assistant, and beneficial to Man; to which they add, that the *Quera,* or good Spirit, has been very kind to the *English* Men, to teach them to make Guns, and Ammunition, besides a great many other Necessaries, that are helpful to Man, all which, they say, will be deliver'd to them, when that good Spirit sees fit. They do not believe, that God punishes any Man either in this Life, or that to come; but that he delights in doing good, and in giving the Fruits of the Earth, and instructing us in making several useful and ornamental things. They say, it is a bad Spirit (who lives separate from the good one) that torments us with Sicknesses, Disappointments, Losses, Hunger, Travel, and all the Misfortunes, that Humane Life is incident to. How they are treated in the next World, I have already mention'd, and, as I said before, they are very resolute in dying, when in the Hands of Savage Enemies; yet I saw one of their young Men, a very likely Person, condemn'd, on a *Sunday,* for Killing a Negro, and burning the House. I took good Notice of his Behaviour, when he was brought out of the House to die, which was the next Morning after Sentence, but he chang'd his Countenance with Trembling, and was in the greatest Fear and Agony. I never saw any Person under his Circumstances, which, perhaps, might be occasion'd by his being deliver'd up by his own Nation (which was the *Tuskeruro's*) and executed by us, that are not their common Enemies, though he met with more Favour than he would have receiv'd at the Hands of Savages; for he was only hang'd on a Tree, near the Place where the Murder was committed; and the three Kings, that but the day before shew'd such a Reluctancy to deliver him up, (but would have given another in his Room) when he was hang'd, pull'd him by the Hand, and said, *Thou wilt never play any more Rogues Tricks in this World; whither art thou gone to shew thy Tricks now?* Which shews these Savages to be what they really are, (*viz*) a People that will save their own Men if they can, but if the Safety of all the People lies at Stake, they will deliver up the most innocent Person living, and be so far from Concern, when they have made themselves easy thereby, that they will laugh at their Misfortunes, and never pity or think of them more.

Their Priests are the Conjurers and Doctors of the Nation.

I shall mention some of their Methods, and Practices; and so leave them to the Judgment of the Reader. As I told you before, the Priests make their Orations at every Feast, or other great Meeting of the *Indians.* I happen'd to be at one of these great Meetings, which was at the Funeral of a *Tuskeruro Indian,* that was slain with Lightning at a Feast, the day before, where I was amongst the rest; it was in *July,* and a very fair day, where, in the Afternoon, about six or seven a Clock, as they were dealing out their Victuals, there appear'd a little black Cloud to the North West, which spread and brought with it Rain, Wind and Lightning; so we went out from the Place where we were all at Victuals, and went down to the Cabins where I left the *Indians,* and went to lie in my Canoe, which was convenient enough to keep me dry. The Lightning came so terrible, and down in long Streams, that I was afraid it would have taken hold of a Barrel of Powder I had in my Vessel, and so blown me up; but it pleas'd God, that it did me no Harm; yet the Violence of the Wind had blown all the Water away, where I rid at Anchor, so that my Canoe lay dry, and some *Indian* Women came with Torches in their Hands to the side of the Canoe, and told me, an *Indian* was kill'd with Lightning. The next day, (I think) he was buried, and I stay'd to see the Ceremony, and was very tractable to help the *Indians* to trim their Reeds, and make the Coffin, which pleased them very much, because I had a mind to see the Interment. Before he was Interr'd according to their Custom, they dealt every one some hot Victuals, which he took and did what he would with: Then the Doctor began to talk, and told the People what Lightning was, and that it kill'd every thing that dwelt upon the Earth; nay, the very Fishes did not escape; for it often reach'd the Porpoises and other Fish, and destroy'd them; that every thing strove to shun it, except the Mice, who, he said, were the busiest in eating their Corn in the Fields, when it lightned the most. He added, that no Wood or Tree could withstand it, except the black Gum, and that it would run round that Tree a great many times, to enter therein, but could not effect it. Now you must understand, that sort of Gum will not split or rive; therefore, I suppose, the Story might arise from thence. At last, he began to tell the most ridiculous absurd Parcel of Lyes about Lightning, that could be; as that an *Indian* of that Nation had once got Lightning in the Likeness of a Partridge; That no other

Lightning could harm him, whilst he had that about him; and that after he had kept it for several Years, it got away from him; so that he then became as liable to be struck with Lightning, as any other Person. There was present at the same time, an *Indian* that had liv'd from his Youth, chiefly in an *English* House; so I call'd to him, and told him, what a Parcel of Lyes the Conjurer told, not doubting but he thought so, as well as I, but I found to the contrary; for he reply'd, that I was much mistaken, for that old Man (who, I believe was upwards of an hundred Years old) did never tell Lyes; and as for what he said, it was very true, for he knew it himself to be so. Thereupon, seeing the Fellow's Ignorance, I talk'd no more about it. Then the Doctor proceeded to tell a long Tale of a great Rattle-Snake, which, a great while ago, liv'd by a Creek in that River (which was *Neus*) and that it kill'd abundance of *Indians;* but at last, a bald Eagle kill'd it, and they were rid of a Serpent, that us'd to devour whole Canoes full of *Indians,* at a time. I have been something tedious upon this Subject, on purpose to shew what strange ridiculous Stories these Wretches are inclinable to believe. I suppose, these Doctors understand a little better themselves, than to give Credit to any such Fooleries; for I reckon them the cunningest Knaves in all the Pack. I will therefore begin with their Physick and Surgery, which is next: You must know, that the Doctors or Conjurers, to gain a greater Credit amongst these People, tell them, that all Distempers are the Effects of evil Spirits, or the bad Spirit, which has struck them with this or that Malady; therefore, none of these Physicians undertakes any Distemper, but that he comes to an Exorcism, to effect the Cure, and acquaints the sick Party's Friends, that he must converse with the good Spirit, to know whether the Patient will recover or not; if so, then he will drive out the bad Spirit, and the Patient will become well. Now, the general way of their Behaviour in curing the Sick, (a great deal of which I have seen, and shall give some Account thereof, in as brief a manner as possible) is, when an *Indian* is sick, if they think there is much Danger of Life, and that he is a great Man or hath good Friends, the Doctor is sent for. As soon as the Doctor comes into the Cabin, the sick Person is sat on a Mat or Skin, stark-naked, lying on his Back, and all uncover'd, except some small Trifle that covers their Nakedness when ripe, otherwise in very young Children, there is nothing about them. In this manner, the Patient lies, when the Conjurer appears; and the King of that Nation comes to attend him with a Rattle made of a Gourd with Pease in it. This the King delivers into the Doctor's Hand, whilst another brings a Bowl of Water, and sets it down: Then the Doctor begins, and utters some few Words very softly; afterwards he smells of the Patient's Navel and Belly, and sometimes scarifies him a little with a Flint, or an Instrument made of Rattle-Snakes Teeth for that purpose; then he sucks the Patient, and gets out a Mouthful of Blood and *Serum,* but *Serum* chiefly; which, perhaps, may be a better Method in many Cases, than to take away great Quantities of Blood, as is commonly practis'd; which he spits in the Bowl of Water. Then he begins to mutter, and talk apace, and, at last, to cut Capers, and clap his Hands on his Breech and Sides, till he gets into a Sweat, so that a Stranger would think he was running mad; now and then sucking the Patient, and so, at times, keeps sucking till he has got a great Quantity of very ill-coloured Matter out of the Belly, Arms, Breast, Forehead, Temples, Neck, and most Parts, still continuing his Grimaces, and antick Postures, which are not to be match'd in *Bedlam:* At last, you will see the Doctor all over of a dropping Sweat, and scarce able to utter one Word, having quite spent himself; then he will cease for a while, and so begin again, till he comes in the same Pitch of Raving and seeming Madness, as before, (all this time the sick Body never so much as moves, although, doubtless, the Lancing and Sucking must be a great Punishment to them; but they, certainly, are the patientest and most steady People under any Burden, that I ever saw in my Life.) At last, the Conjurer makes an end, and tells the Patient's Friends, whether the Person will live or die; and then one that waits at this Ceremony, takes the Blood away, (which remains in a Lump, in the middle of the Water) and buries it in the Ground, in a Place unknown to any one, but he that inters it. Now, I believe a great deal of Imposture in these Fellows; yet I never knew their Judgment fail, though I have seen them give their Opinion after this Manner, several times: Some affirm, that there is a smell of Brimstone in the Cabins, when they are Conjuring, which I cannot contradict. Which way it may come, I will not argue, but proceed to a Relation or two, which I have from a great many Persons, and some of them worthy of Credit.

The first is, of a certain *Indian,* that one rainy Night, under-

min'd a House made of Logs, (such as the *Swedes* in *America*
very often make, and are very strong) which belong'd to *Seth
Southwell* [Sothel, last governor of Albemarle County, 1682–
1689], Esq; Governor of *North-Carolina,* and one of the Proprietors. There was but one place the *Indian* could get in at,
which was very narrow; the rest was secur'd, by having Barrels of
Pork and other Provisions set against the side of the House, so
that if this *Indian* had not exactly hit the very Place he
undermin'd, it had been impossible for him to have got therein,
because of the full Barrels that stood round the House, and
barricadoed it within. The *Indian* stole sixty or eighty dress'd
Deer-Skins, besides Blankets, Powder, Shot and Rum, (this
being the *Indian* Store-House, where the Trading Goods were
kept.) Now, the *Indian* had made his Escape, but dropt some of
the Skins by the way, and they track'd his Foot-steps, and found
him to be an *Indian;* then they guess'd who it was, because none
but that *Indian* had lately been near the House. Thereupon,
the Governor sent to the *Indian* Town that he belong'd to,
which was the *Tuskeruro's,* and acquainted them that if they did
not deliver up the *Indian,* who had committed the Robbery, he
would take a Course with them, that would not be very agreeable. Upon this, the *Indians* of the Town he belong'd to, brought
him in bound, and deliver'd him up to the Governor, who laid
him in Irons. At the same time, it happen'd, that a Robbery was
committed amongst themselves, at the *Indian* Town, and this
Prisoner was one of their Conjurers; so the *Indians* came down
to the Governor's House, and acquainted him with what had
happen'd amongst them, and that a great Quantity of *Peak,*
was stoln away out of one of their Cabins, and no one could find
out the Thief, unless he would let the Prisoner conjure for it,
who was the only Man they had at making such Discoveries.
The Governor was content he should try his Skill for them, but
not to have the Prisoners Irons taken off, which was very well
approved of. The *Indian* was brought out in his Fetters, where
were the Governor's Family, and several others of the Neighbourhood, now living, to see this Experiment; which he perform'd thus:

The Conjurer order'd three Fires to be made in a triangular
Form, which was accordingly done; then he was hoodwink'd very
securely, with a dress'd Deer-Skin, two or three doubles, over
his Face. After he had made some Motions, as they always do, he

went directly out of one of the three Gaps, as exactly as if he had not been blindfolded, and kept muttering to himself, having a Stick in his Hand, with which, after some time, he struck two Strokes very hard upon the Ground, and made thereon a Cross, after which he told the *Indian's* Name that had stoln the Goods, and said, that he would have a Cross on his Back; which prov'd true; for when they took and search'd him, there appear'd two great Wheals on his Back, one cross the other; for the Thief was at Governor *Southwell's* House, and was under no Apprehension of being discover'd. The *Indians* proffer'd to sell him as a Slave to the Governor, but he refused to buy him; so they took him bound away.

Another Instance, of the like Nature, happen'd at the same House. One of the *Tuskeruro* Kings had brought in a Slave to the same Governor, to whom he had sold him; and before he return'd, fell sick at the Governor's House; upon which, the Doctor that belong'd to this King's Nation, was sent for, being a Man that was held to be the greatest Conjurer amongst them. It was three Days, before he could arrive, and he appear'd (when he came) to be a very little Man, and so old, that his Hair was as white as ever was seen. When he approach'd the sick King, he order'd a Bowl of Water to be brought him, and three Chunks of Wood, which was immediately done. Then he took the Water, and set it by him, and spurted a little on him, and with the three Pieces of Wood, he made a Place to stand on, whereby he was rais'd higher; (he being a very low statur'd Man) then he took a String of *Ronoak,* which is the same as a String of small Beads; this he held by one End, between his Fingers; the other End touch'd the King's Stomach, as he stood on the Logs. Then he began to talk, and at length, the By-standers thought really, that they heard somebody talk to him, but saw no more than what first came in. At last, this String of Beads, which hung thus perpendicular, turn'd up as an Eel would do, and without any Motion of his, they came all up (in a lump) under his Hand, and hung so for a considerable time, he never closing his Hand, and at length return'd to their pristine Length and Shape, at which the Spectators were much frightened. Then he told the Company, that he would recover, and that his Distemper would remove into his Leg, all which happen'd to be exactly as the *Indian* Doctor had told. These are Matters of Fact, and I can, at this day, prove the Truth thereof by several substantial

Evidences, that are Men of Reputation, there being more than a dozen People present, when this was perform'd; most of whom are now alive.

There are a great many other Stories, of this Nature, which are seemingly true, being told by Persons that affirm they were Eye-Witnesses thereof; as, that they have seen one *Roncommock* (a *Chuwou Indian*, and a great Conjurer) take a Reed about two Foot long in his Mouth, and stand by a Creek-side, where he call'd twice or thrice with the Reed in his Mouth; and, at last, has open'd his Arms, and fled over the Creek, which might be near a quarter of a Mile wide or more; but I shall urge no Man's Belief, but tell my own; which is, that I believe the two first Accounts, which were acted at Mr. *Southwell's* Planatation, as firmly as any Man can believe any thing of that which is told him by honest Men, and he has not seen; not at all doubting the Credit of my Authors.

The Cures I have seen perform'd by the *Indians,* are too many to repeat here; so I shall only mention some few, and their Method. They cure Scald-heads infallibly, and never miss. Their chief Remedy as I have seen them make use of, is, the Oil of Acorns, but from which sort of Oak I am not certain. They cure Burns beyond Credit. I have seen a Man burnt in such a manner, (when drunk) by falling into a Fire, that I did not think he could recover; yet they cur'd him in ten Days, so that he went about. I knew another blown up with Powder, that was cured to Admiration. I never saw an *Indian* have an Ulcer, or foul Wound in my Life; neither is there any such thing to be found amongst them. They cure the Pox, by a Berry that salivates, as *Mercury* does; yet they use Sweating and Decoctions very much with it; as they do, almost on every Occasion; and when they are thoroughly heated, they leap into the River. The Pox is frequent in some of these Nations; amongst which I knew one Woman die of it; and they could not, or would not, cure her. Before she died, she was worn away to a Skeleton, yet walk'd up and down to the last. We had a Planter in *Carolina*, who had got an Ulcer in his Leg, which had troubled him a great many Years; at last, he apply'd himself to one of these *Indian* Conjurers, who was a *Pampticough Indian,* and was not to give the Value of fifteen Shillings for the Cure. Now, I am not positive, whether he wash'd the Ulcer with any thing, before he used what I am now going to speak of, which was nothing but the rotten

doated Grains of *Indian* Corn, beaten to Powder, and the soft
Down growing on a Turkey's Rump. This dry'd the Ulcer up
immediately, and no other Fontanel was made to discharge the
Matter, he remaining a healthful Man, till the time he had the
Misfortune to be drown'd, which was many Years after. Another
Instance (not of my own Knowledge, but I had it confirm'd by
several Dwellers in *Maryland,* where it was done) was, of an
honest Planter that had been possess'd with a strange Lingring
Distemper, not usual amongst them, under which he emaciated,
and grew every Month worse than another, it having held him
several Years, in which time he had made Tryal of several
Doctors, as they call them, which, I suppose, were Ship-Surgeons.
In the beginning of this Distemper, the Patient was very well to
pass, and was possess'd of several Slaves, which the Doctors
purged all away, and the poor Man was so far from mending,
that he grew worse and worse every day. But it happen'd, that,
one day, as his Wife and he were commiserating his miserable
Condition, and that he could not expect to recover, but look'd
for Death very speedily, and condoling the Misery he should
leave his Wife and Family in, since all his Negro's were gone. At
that time, I say, it happen'd, that an *Indian* was in the same
Room, who had frequented the House for many Years, and so
was become as one of the Family, and would sometimes be at
this Planter's House, and at other times amongst the *Indians.*

This Savage, hearing what they talk'd of, and having a great
Love for the Sick Man, made this Reply to what he had heard.
*Brother, you have been a long time Sick; and, I know, you have
given away your Slaves to your* English *Doctors: What made
you do so, and now become poor? They do not know how to cure
you; for it is an* Indian *Distemper, which your People know not
the Nature of. If it had been an* English *Disease, probably they
could have cured you; and had you come to me at first, I would
have cured you for a small matter, without taking away your
Servants that made Corn for you and your Family to eat; and
yet, if you will give me a Blanket to keep me warm, and some
Powder and Shot to kill Deer withal, I will do my best to make
you well still.* The Man was low in Courage and Pocket too, and
made the *Indian* this Reply. *Jack, my Distemper is past Cure,
and if our* English *Doctors cannot cure it, I am sure, the* Indians
cannot. But his Wife accosted her Husband in very mild terms,
and told him, he did not know, but God might be pleased to

give a Blessing to that *Indian's* Undertaking more than he had done to the *English;* and farther added; *if you die, I cannot be much more miserable, by giving this small matter to the* Indian; *so I pray you, my Dear, take my Advice, and try him;* to which, by her Persuasions, he consented. After the Bargain was concluded, the *Indian* went into the Woods, and brought in both Herbs and Roots, of which he made a Decoction, and gave it the Man to drink, and bad him go to bed, saying, it should not be long, before he came again, which the Patient perform'd as he had ordered; and the Potion he had administred made him sweat after the most violent manner that could be, whereby he smell'd very offensively both to himself, and they that were about him; but in the Evening, towards Night, *Jack* came, with a great Rattle-Snake in his Hand alive, which frightned the People almost out of their Senses; and he told his Patient, that he must take that to Bed to him; at which the Man was in a great Consternation, and told the *Indian,* he was resolv'd, to let no Snake come into his Bed, for he might as well die of the Distemper he had, as be kill'd with the Bite of that Serpent. To which the *Indian* reply'd, he could not bite him now, nor do him any Harm; for he had taken out his Poison-teeth, and shew'd him, that they were gone. At last, with much Persuasion, he admitted the Snake's Company, which the *Indian* put about his Middle, and order'd nobody to take him away upon any account, which was strictly observ'd, although the Snake girded him as hard for a great while) as if he had been drawn in by a Belt, which one pull'd at, with all his strength. At last, the Snake's Twitches grew weaker and weaker, till, by degrees, he felt him not; and opening the Bed, he was found dead, and the Man thought himself better. The *Indian* came in the Morning, and seeing the Snake dead, told the Man, that his Distemper was dead along with that Snake, which prov'd so as he said; for the Man speedily recover'd his Health, and became perfectly well.

They cure the Spleen (which they are much addicted to) by burning with a Reed. They lay the Patient on his Back, so put a hollow Cane into the Fire, where they burn the End thereof, till it is very hot, and on Fire at the end. Then they lay a Piece of thin Leather on the Patient's Belly, between the Pit of the Stomach and the Navel, so press the hot Reed on the Leather, which burns the Patient so that you may ever after see the

Impression of the Reed where it was laid on, which Mark never
goes off so long as he lives. This is used for the Belly-Ach sometimes. They can colour their Hair black, though sometimes it is
reddish, which they do with the Seed of a Flower that grows
commonly in their Plantations. I believe this would change the
reddest Hair into perfect black. They make use of no Minerals
in their Physick, and not much of Animals; but chiefly rely on
Vegetables. They have several Remedies for the Tooth-ach,
which often drive away the Pain; but if they fail, they have
Recourse to punching out the Tooth, with a small Cane set
against the same, on a Bit of Leather. Then they strike the Reed,
and so drive out the Tooth; and howsoever it may seem to the
Europeans, I prefer it before the common way of drawing Teeth
by those Instruments than endanger the Jaw, and a Flux of
Blood often follows, which this Method of a Punch never is attended withal; neither is it half the Pain. The Spontaneous
Plants of *America* the Savages are well acquainted withal; and a
Flux of Blood never follows any of their Operations. They are
wholly Strangers to Amputation, and for what natural Issues
of Blood happen immoderately, they are not to seek for a certain
and speedy Cure. Tears, Rozins, and Gums, I have not dis-
cover'd that they make much use of; And as for Purging and
Emeticks, so much in fashion with us, they never apply themselves to, unless in drinking vast Quantities of their *Yaupon* or
Tea, and vomiting it up again, as clear as they drink it. This is a
Custom amongst all those that can procure that Plant, in which
manner they take it every other Morning, or oftner; by which
Method they keep their Stomachs clean, without pricking the
Coats, and straining Nature, as every Purge is an Enemy to.
Besides, the great Diuretick Quality of their Tea carries off a
great deal, that perhaps might prejudice their Health, by Agues,
and Fevers, which all watry Countries are addicted to; for
which reason, I believe, it is, that the *Indians* are not so much
addicted to that Distemper, as we are, they preventing its
seizing upon them, by this Plant alone. Moreover, I have remark'd, that it is only those Places bordering on the Ocean and
great Rivers, that this Distemper is frequent in, and only on
and near the same Places this Evergreen is to be found; and none
up towards the Mountains, where these Agues seldom or never
appear; Nature having provided suitable Remedies, in all Countries, proper for the Maladies that are common thereto. The

Savages of *Carolina* have this Tea in Veneration, above all the
Plants they are acquainted withal, and tell you, the Discovery
thereof was by an infirm *Indian*, that labour'd under the
Burden of many rugged Distempers, and could not be cured by
all their Doctors; so, one day, he fell asleep, and dreamt, that
if he took a Decoction of the Tree that grew at his Head, he
would certainly be cured; upon which he awoke, and saw the
Yaupon or Cassena-Tree, which was not there when he fell
asleep. He follow'd the Direction of his Dream, and became
perfectly well in a short time. Now, I suppose, no Man has so
little Sense as to believe this Fable; yet it lets us see what they
intend thereby, and that it has, doubtless, work'd Feats enough,
to gain it such an Esteem amongst these Savages, who are too
well versed in Vegetables, to be brought to a continual use of
any one of them, upon a meer Conceit or Fancy, without some
apparent Benefit they found thereby; especially, when we are
sensible, they drink the Juices of Plants, to free Nature of her
Burdens, and not out of Foppery and Fashion, as other Nations
are oftentimes found to do. Amongst all the Discoveries of
America, by the Missionaries of the *French* and *Spaniards*, I
wonder none of them was so kind to the World, as to have kept
a Catalogue of the Distempers they found the Savages capable
of curing, and their Method of Cure; which might have been of
some Advantage to our *Materia Medica* at home, when deliver'd by Men of Learning, and other Qualifications, as most
of them are. Authors generally tell us, that the Savages are well
enough acquainted with those Plants which their Climate affords,
and that some of them effect great Cures, but by what Means,
and in what Form, we are left in the dark. The Bark of the Root
of the Sassafras-Tree, I have observ'd, is much used by them.
They generally torrefy it in the Embers, so strip off the Bark
from the Root, beating it to a Consistence fit to spread, so lay
it on the griev'd Part; which both cleanses a fowl Ulcer; and
after Scarrification, being apply'd to a Contusion, or Swelling,
draws forth the Pain, and reduces the Part to its pristine State
of Health, as I have often seen effected. Fats and Unguents
never appear in their Chirurgery, when the Skin is once broke.
The Fats of Animals are used by them, to render their Limbs
pliable, and when wearied, to relieve the Joints, and this not
often, because they approve of the Sweating-House (in such
cases) above all things. The Salts they mix with their Bread and

Soupe, to give them a Relish, are *Alkalis,* (viz.) Ashes, and calcined Bones of Deer, and other Animals. Sallads, they never eat any; as for Pepper and Mustard, they reckon us little better than Madmen, to make use of it amongst our Victuals. They are never troubled with the Scurvy, Dropsy, nor Stone. The Phthisick, Asthma, and Diabetes, they are wholly Strangers to; neither do I remember I ever saw one Paralytick amongst them. The Gout, I cannot be certain whether they know what it is, or not. Indeed, I never saw any Nodes or Swellings, which attend the Gout in *Europe;* yet they have a sort of Rhumatism or Burning of the Limbs, which tortures them grievously, at which time their Legs are so hot, that they employ the young People continually to pour Water down them. I never saw but one or two thus afflicted. The Struma is not uncommon amongst these Savages, and another Distemper, which is, in some respects, like the Pox, but is attended with no *Gonorrhoea.* This not seldom bereaves them of their Nose. I have seen three or four of them render'd most miserable Spectacles by this Distemper. Yet, when they have been so negligent, as to let it run on so far without curbing of it; at last, they make shift to patch themselves up, and live for many years after; and such Men commonly turn Doctors. I have known two or three of these no-nose Doctors in great Esteem amongst these Savages. The Juice of the Tulip-Tree is used as a proper Remedy for this Distemper. What Knowledge they have in Anatomy, I cannot tell, neither did I ever see them employ themselves therein, unless, as I told you before, when they make the Skeletons of their Kings and great Mens Bones.

The *Indians* are very careless and negligent of their Health; as, by Drunkenness, Wading in the Water, irregular Diet and Lodging, and a thousand other Disorders, (that would kill an *European*) which they daily use. They boil and roast their Meat extraordinary much, and eat abundance of Broth, except the Savages whom we call the naked *Indians,* who never eat any Soupe. They travel from the Banks of the *Messiasippi,* to war against the *Sinnagars* or *Iroquois,* and are (if equal Numbers) commonly too hard for them. They will lie and sleep in the Woods without Fire, being inur'd thereto. They are the hardiest of all *Indians,* and run so fast, that they are never taken, neither do any *Indians* outrun them, if they are pursu'd. Their Savage Enemies say, their Nimbleness and Wind proceeds from their never eating any Broth. The Small-Pox has been fatal to them;

they do not often escape, when they are seiz'd with that Distemper, which is a contrary Fever to what they ever knew. Most
certain, it had never visited *America,* before the Discovery thereof
by the Christians. Their running into the Water, in the Extremity
of this Disease, strikes it in, and kills all that use it. Now they are
become a little wiser; but formerly it destroy'd whole Towns,
without leaving one *Indian* alive in the Village. The Plague was
never known amongst them, that I could learn by what Enquiry I
have made: These Savages use Scarrification almost in all Distempers. Their chief Instruments for that Operation is the Teeth of
Rattle-Snakes, which they poison withal. They take them out of
the Snake's Head, and suck out the Poison with their Mouths,
(and so keep them for use) and spit out the Venom, which is
green, and are never damag'd thereby. The Small-Pox and Rum
have made such a Destruction amongst them, that, on good
grounds, I do believe, there is not the sixth Savage living within
two hundred Miles of all our Settlements, as there were fifty Years
ago. These poor Creatures have so many Enemies to destroy them,
that it's a wonder one of them is left alive near us. The Small-pox
I have acquainted you withal above, and so I have of Rum, and
shall only add, that they have got a way to carry it back to the
Westward *Indians,* who never knew what it was, till within very
few Years. Now they have it brought them by the *Tuskeruro's,*
and other Neighbour-*Indians,* but the *Tuskeruro's* chiefly, who
carry it in Rundlets several hundred Miles, amongst other *Indians.* Sometimes they cannot forbear breaking their Cargo, but
sit down in the Woods, and drink it all up, and then hollow and
shout like so many *Bedlamites.* I accidentally once met with one
of these drunken Crews, and was amaz'd to see a Parcel of
drunken Savages so far from any *Englishman's* House; but the
Indians I had in Company inform'd me, that they were Merchants, and had drunk all their Stock, as is very common for them
to do. But when they happen to carry it safe, (which is seldom,
without drinking some part of it, and filling it up with Water)
and come to an *Indian* Town, those that buy Rum of them have
so many Mouthfuls for a Buck-Skin, they never using any other
Measure; and for this purpose, the Buyer always makes Choice of
his Man, which is one that has the greatest Mouth, whom he
brings to the Market with a Bowl to put it in. The Seller looks
narrowly to the Man's Mouth that measures it, and if he happens
to swallow any down, either through Wilfulness or otherwise, the

Merchant or some of his Party, does not scruple to knock the Fellow down, exclaiming against him for false Measure. Thereupon, the Buyer finds another Mouthpiece to measure the Rum by; so that this Trading is very agreeable to the Spectators, to see such a deal of Quarrelling and Controversy, as often happens, about it, and is very diverting.

Another Destroyer of them, is, the Art they have, and often practise, of poisoning one another; which is done by a large, white, spungy Root, that grows in the Fresh-Marshes, which is one of their Poisons; not but that they have many other Drugs, which they poison one another withal.

Lastly, the continual Wars these Savages maintain, one Nation against another, which sometimes hold for some Ages, killing and making Captives, till they become so weak thereby, that they are forced to make Peace for want of Recruits, to supply their Wars; and the Difference of Languages, that is found amongst these Heathens, seems altogether strange. For it often apears, that every dozen Miles, you meet with an *Indian* Town, that is quite different from the others you last parted withal; and what a little supplies this Defect is, that the most powerful Nation of these Savages scorns to treat or trade with any others (of fewer Numbers and less Power) in any other Tongue but their own, which serves for the *Lingua* of the Country, with which we travel and deal; as for Example, we see that the *Tuskeruro's* are most numerous in *North-Carolina,* therefore their Tongue is understood by some in every Town of all the *Indians* near us. And here I shall insert a small Dictionary of every Tongue, though not Alphabetically digested.

English.	Tuskeruro.	Pampticough.	Woccon.
One	*Unche*	*Weembot*	*Tonne*
Two	*Necte*	*Neshinnauh*	*Num-perre*
Three	*Ohs-sah*	*Nish-wonner*	*Nam-mee*
Four	*Untoc*	*Yau-Ooner*	*Punnum-punne*
Five	*Ouch-whe*	*Umperren*	*Webtau*
Six	*Houeyoc*	*Who-yeoc*	*Is-sto*
Seven	*Chauh-noc*	*Top-po-osh*	*Nommis-sau*
Eight	*Nec-kara*	*Nau-haush-shoo*	*Nupsau*
Nine	*Wearah*	*Pach-ic-conk*	*Weihere*
Ten	*Wartsauh*	*Cosh*	*Soone noponne*

English.	Tuskeruro.	Pampticough.	Woccon.
Eleven	Unche scauwhau		Tonne hauk pea
Twelve	Nectec scaukhau		Soone nomme
Twenty	Wartsau scauhau		Winnop
Thirty	Ossa te wartsau		
Hundred	Youch se		
Thousand	Ki you se		
Rum	Oonaquod	Weesaccon	Yup-se
Blankets	Oorewa	Mattosh	Roo-iune
White	Ware-occa	Wop-poshaumosh	Waurraupa
Red	Cotcoo-rea	Mish-cosk	Yauta
Black or blue, idem	Caw-hunshe	Mow-cottowosh	Yah-testea
Gunpowder	Ou-kn	Pungue	Rooeyam
Shot	Cauna	Ar-rounser	Week
Axe	Au-nuka	Tomma-hick	Tau-unta winnik
Knife	Oosocke nauh	Rig-cosq	Wee
Tobacco	Charho	Hooh-pau	Uu-coone
Shirt	Ough-tre's		Tacca-pitteneer
Shoes	Oo-ross-soo		Wee-kessoo
Hat	Trossa	Mottau-quahan	Intome-posswa
Fire	Utchar	Tinda	Yau
Water	Awoo	Umpe	Ejau
Coat	Ouswox Kawhitchra	Taus-won	Rummissau
Awl or Needle	Oose-waure	Moc-cose	Wonsh-shee
A Hoe	Wauche-wocnoc	Rosh-shocquon	Rooe-pau
Salt	Cheek-ha		
Paint	Quaunt	Chumon	Whooyeonne

English.	Tuskeruro.	Pampticough.	Woccon.
Ronoak	*Nauh-houreot*	*Mis-kis-su*	*Rummaer*
Peak	*Chu-teche*	*Ronoak*	*Erroco*
Gun	*Auk-noc*	*Gau hooptop*	*Wittape*
Gun-Lock	*Oo-teste*	*Gun tock Seike*	*Noonkosso*
Flints	*Ou-negh-ra*	*Hinds*	*Matt-teer*
A Flap	*Oukhaure*	*Rappatoc*	*Rhooeyau*
Belt	*Oona-teste*	*Maachone*	*Wee-kau*
Scissors and Tobacco-Tongues	*Cheh-ra*		*Toc-koop*
A Kettle	*Oowaiana*		*Tooseawau*
A Pot	*Ocnock*		
Acorns	*Kooawa*		*Roosomme*
A Pine-Tree	*Heigta*	*Oonossa*	*Hooheh*
Englishman	*Nickreruroh*	*Tosh shonte*	*Wintsohore*
Indians	*Unqua*	*Nuppin*	*Yauh-he*

English.	Tuskeruro.	Woccon.
A Horse	*A hots*	*Yenwetoa*
Swine	*Watsquerre*	*Nommewarraupau*
Moss	*Auoona hau*	*Itto*
Raw skin undrest	*Ootahawa*	*Teep*
Buckskin	*Ocques*	*Rookau*
Fawn-skin	*Ottea*	*Wisto*
Bear-skin	*Oochehara*	*Ourka*
Fox-skin	*Che-chou*	*Hannatockore*
Raccoon-skin	*Roo-sotto*	*Auher*
Squirrel-skin	*Sost*	*Yehau*
Wildcat-skin	*Cauhauweana*	
Panther-skin	*Caunerex*	*Wattau*
Wolf	*Squarrena*	*Tire kiro*
Min[k]	*Chac-kauene*	*Soccon*
Otter	*Chaunoc*	*Wetkes*
A Mat	*Ooyethne*	*Soppepepor*
Basket	*Ooyaura*	*Rookeppa*
Feathers	*Oosnooqua*	*Soppe*

English.	Tuskeruro.	Woccon.
Drest-skin	Cotcoo	Rauhau
A Turkey	Coona	Yauta
A Duck	Sooeau	Welka
A King	Teethha	Roamore
Fat	Ootsaure	Yendare
Soft	Uisauwanne	Roosomme
Hard or heavy	Waucots ne	Itte teraugh
A Rope	Utsera	Trauhe
A Possum	Che-ra	
Day	Ootauh-ne	
Pestel	Tic-caugh-ne	Miyau
A Mortar	Ootic caugh-ne	Yosso
Stockings	Way haushe	
A Creek	Wackena	
A River	Ahunt wackena	
A Man	Entequos	
Old Man	Occooahawa	
Young Man	Quottis	
Woman	Con-noowa	
Old Woman	Cusquerre	Yicau
Potato's	Untone	Wauk
A Stick	Chinqua	
Wood	Ouyunkgue	Yonne
House	Oinouse	Ouke
A Cow	Ous-sarunt	Noppinjure
A Snake	Us-quauh-ne	Yau-hauk
A Rat	Rusquiana	Wittan
A Goose	Au-hoohaha	Auhaun
A Swan	Oorhast	Atter
Allegator	Utsererauh	Monwittetan
A Crab	Royare cou	Wunneau
A Canoe	Ooshunnawa	Watt
A Box	Ooanoo	Yopoonitsa
A Bowl	Ortse	Cotsoo
A Spoon	Oughquere	Cotsau
A Path	Wauh-hauhne	Yaub
Sun or Moon	Heita	Wittapare
Wind	Hoonoch	Yuncor
A Star	Uttewiraratse	Wattapi untakeer

English.	Tuskeruro.	Woccon.
Rain	*Untuch*	*Yawowa*
	Auhuntwood	
Night	*Oosottoo*	*Yantoha*
A Rundlet	*Oohunawa*	*Ynpyupseunne*
An Eel	*Cuhn-na*	
A T—d	*Utquera*	*Pulawa*
A F—t	*Uttena*	*Pautyau*
A Cable	*Utquichra*	
Wife	*Kateocca*	*Yecauau*
A Child	*Woccanookne*	
A Boy	*Wariaugh*	
Infant	*Utserosta*	
Ears	*Ooethnat*	
Fishgig	*Ootosne*	*Weetipsa*
A Comb	*Oonaquitchra*	*Sacketoome posswa*
A Cake bak't	*Ooneck*	
A Head	*Ootaure*	*Poppe*
Hair	*Oowaara*	*Tumme*
Brother	*Caunotka*	*Yenrauhe*
I	*Ee*	
Thou	*Eets*	
There	*Ka*	
Homine	*Cotquerre*	*Roocauwa*
Bread	*Ootocnare*	*Ikettau*
Broath	*Ook-hoo*	
Corn	*Oonaha*	*Cese*
	Oonave	
	Oosare	
	Oosha	
Pease	*Saugh-he*	*Coosauk*
A Bag	*Uttaqua*	*Ekoocromon*
Fish	*Cunshe*	*Yacunne*
A Louse	*Cheeoq*	*Eppesyau*
A Flea	*Nauocq*	
Small Ropes	*Utsera utquichra*	
A Button	*Tic-hah*	*Rummissauwoune*
Breeches	*Wahunshe*	*Rooeyaukitte*
Stockings	*Oowissera*	*Rooesoo posson*
Day	*Wauwoc-hook*	*Waukhaway*

English.	Tuskeruro.	Woccon.
Mad	Cosseraunte	Rockcumne
Angry	Cotcheroore	Roocheha
Afraid	Werricauna	Reheshiwan
Smoak	Oo-teighne	Too-she
A Thief or Rogue	Katichlei	
A Dog	Cheeth	Tauh-he
A Reed	Cauna	Weekwonne
Lightwood	Kakoo	Sek
To morrow	Jureha	Kittape
Now	Kahunk	
To day	Kawa	
A little while ago	Kakoowa	Yauka
Yesterday	Oousotto	Yottoha
How many	Ut-tewots	Tontarinte
How far	Untateawa	
Will you go along with me	Unta hah	Quauke
Go you	Its warke	Yuppa me
Give it me	Cotshau	Mothei
That's all	Ut chat	Cuttaune
A Cubit length	Kihoosocca	Ishewounaup
Dead	Whaharia	Caure
A Gourd or Bottle	Utchaawa	Wattape
A lazy Fellow	Wattattoo watse	Tontaunete
Englishman is thirsty	Oukwockaninni- wock	
I will sell you Goods very cheap	Wausthanocha	Nau hou hoore-ene
All the Indians are drunk	Connaugh jost twane	Nonnupper
Have you got anything to eat	Utta-ana-wox	Noccoo Eraute
I am sick	Connauwox	Waurepa
A Fish-Hook	Oos-skinna	
Don't lose it	Oon est nonne it quost	
A Tobacco-pipe	Oosquaana	Intom
I remember it	Oonutsauka	Aucummate

English.	Tuskeruro.	Woccon.
Let it alone	*Tnotsaurauweek*	*Sauhau*
Peaches	*Roo-ooe*	*Yonne*
Walnuts	*Rootau-ooe*	
Hickery Nuts	*Rootau*	*Nimmia*
A *Jew's*-Harp	*Ooratsa*	*Wottiyau*
I forget it	*Merrauka*	
Northwest-Wind	*Hothooka*	
Snow	*Acaunque*	*Wawawa*

To repeat more of this *Indian* Jargon, would be to trouble the Reader; and as an Account how imperfect they are in their Moods and Tenses, has been given by several already, I shall only add, that their Languages or Tongues are so deficient, that you cannot suppose the *Indians* ever could express themselves in such a Flight of Stile, as Authors would have you believe. They are so far from it, that they are but just able to make one another understand readily what they talk about. As for the two Consonants *L* and *F*, I never knew them in any *Indian* Speech I have met withal; yet I must tell you, that they have such a Way of abbreviating their Speech, when in their great Councils and Debates, that the young Men do not understand what they treat about, when they hear them argue. It is wonderful, what has occasion'd so many different Speeches as the Savages have. The three Nations I now mention'd, do not live above ten Leagues distant, and two of them, *viz.* the *Tuskeruro's* and the *Woccon,* are not two Leagues asunder; yet their Speech differs in every Word thereof, except one, which is *Tsaure, Cockles,* which is in both Tongues the same, and nothing else. Now this Difference of Speech causes Jealousies and Fears amongst them, which bring Wars, wherein they destroy one another; otherwise the Christians had not (in all Probability) settled *America* so easily, as they have done, had these Tribes of Savages united themselves into one People or general Interest, or were they so but every hundred Miles. In short, they are an odd sort of People under the Circumstances they are at present, and have some such uncouth Ways in their Management and Course of Living, that it seems a Miracle to us, how they bring about their Designs, as they do, when their Ways are commonly quite contrary to ours. I believe, they are (as to this Life) a very happy People; and were it not for the Feuds amongst themselves, they would enjoy the happiest State (in this World) of all Mankind.

They met with Enemies when we came amongst them; for they are no nearer Christianity now, than they were at the first Discovery, to all Appearance. They have learnt several Vices of the *Europeans,* but not one Vertue, as I know of. Drunkenness was a Stranger, when we found them out, and Swearing their Speech cannot express; yet those that speak *English,* learn to swear the first thing they talk of. It's true, they have some Vertues and some Vices; but how the Christians can bring these People into the Bosom of the Church, is a Proposal that ought to be form'd and follow'd by the wisest Heads and best Christians. After I have given one Remark or two farther, of some of their strange Practices and Notions, I will give my Opinion, how I think, in probability, it may be (if possible) effected, and so shall conclude this Treatise of *Carolina.*

They are a very craving People, and if a Man give them any thing of a Present, they think it obliges him to give them another; and so on, till he has given them all he has; for they have no Bounds of Satisfaction in that way; and if they give you any thing, it is to receive twice the Value of it. They have no Consideration that you will want what you give them; for their way of Living is so contrary to ours, that neither we nor they can fathom one anothers Designs and Methods. They call Rum and Physick by one Name, which implies that Rum make People sick, as when they have taken any poisonous Plant; yet they cannot forbear Rum. They make Offerings of their First-Fruits, and the more serious sort of them throw into the Ashes, near the Fire, the first Bit or Spoonful of every Meal they sit down to, which, they say, is the same to them, as the pulling off our Hats, and talking, when we go to Victuals, is to us. They name the Months very agreeably, as one is the Herring-Month, another the Strawberry-Month, another the Mulberry-Month. Others name them by the Trees that blossom; especially, the Dogwood-Tree; or they say, we will return when Turkey-Cocks gobble, that is in *March* and *April.* The Age of the Moon they understand, but know no different Name for Sun and Moon. They can guess well at the time of the Day, by the Sun's Height. Their Age they number by Winters, and say, such a Man or Woman is so many Winters old. They have no Sabbath, or Day of Rest. Their Slaves are not over-burden'd with Work, and so not driven by Severity to seek for that Relief. Those that are acquainted with the *English,* and speak the Tongue, know when *Sunday* comes; besides, the *Indians* have a distinct Name for

Christmas which they call *Winnick Keshuse,* or the *Englishmans Gods Moon.* There is one most abominable Custom amongst them, which they call *Husquenawing* their young Men; which I have not made any Mention of as yet, so will give you an Account of it here. You must know, that most commonly, once a Year, or, at farthest, once in two Years, these People take up so many of their young Men, as they think are able to undergo it, and *husquenaugh* them, which is to make them obedient and respective to their Superiors, and (as they say) is the same to them, as it is to us to send our Children to School, to be taught good Breeding and Letters. This House of Correction is a large strong Cabin, made on purpose for the Reception of the young Men and Boys, that have not passed this Graduation already; and it is always at *Christmas* that they *husquenaugh* their Youth, which is by bringing them into this House, and keeping them dark all the time, where they more than half-starve them. Besides, they give them Pellitory-Bark, and several intoxicating Plants, that make them go raving mad as ever were any People in the World; and you may hear them make the most dismal and hellish Cries, and Howlings, that ever humane Creatures express'd; all which continues about five or six Weeks, and the little Meat they eat, is the nastiest, loathsome stuff, and mixt with all manner of Filth it's possible to get. After the Time is expired, they are brought out of the Cabin, which never is in the Town, but always a distance off, and guarded by a Jaylor or two, who watch by Turns. Now, when they first come out, they are as poor as ever any Creatures were; for you must know several die under this diabolical Purgation. Moreover, they either really are, or pretend to be dumb, and do not speak for several Days; I think, twenty or thirty; and look so gastly, and are so chang'd, that it's next to an Impossibility to know them again, although you was never so well acquainted with them before. I would fain have gone into the mad House, and have seen them in their time of Purgatory, but the King would not suffer it, because, he told me, they would do me, or any other white Man, an Injury, that ventured in amongst them; so I desisted. They play this Prank with Girls as well as Boys, and I believe it a miserable Life they endure, because I have known several of them run away, at that time, to avoid it. Now, the Savages say, if it was not for this, they could never keep their Youth in Subjection, besides that it hardens them ever after to the Fatigues of War, Hunting, and all manner of Hardship, which their way of living exposes them to.

Besides, they add, that it carries off those infirm weak Bodies, that would have been only a Burden and Disgrace to their Nation, and saves the Victuals and Cloathing for better People, that would have been expended on such useless Creatures. These Savages are described in their proper Colours, but by a very few; for those that generally write Histories of this new World, are such as Interest, Preferment, and Merchandize, drew thither, and know no more of that People than I do of the *Laplanders,* which is only by Hear-say. And if we will make just Remarks, how near such Relations generally approach Truth and Nicety, we shall find very few of them worthy of Entertainment; and as for the other part of the Volume, it is generally stufft with Invectives against the Government they lived under, on which Stage is commonly acted greater Barbarities, in Murdering worthy Mens Reputations, than all the Savages in the new World are capable of equalizing, or so much as imitating.

And since I hinted at a Regulation of the Savages, and to propose a way to convert them to Christianity, I will first particularize the several Nations of *Indians* that are our Neighbours, and then proceed to what I promis'd.

Tuskeruro Indians are fifteen Towns, *viz. Haruta, Waqui, Contah-nah, Anna Ooka, Conauh-Kare Harooka, Una Nauhan, Kentanuska, Chunaneets, Kenta, Eno, Naur-hegh-ne, Oonossoora, Tosneoc, Nonawharitse, Nursoorooka;* Fighting Men 1200. *Waccon.* Towns 2, *Yupwauremau, Tooptatmeer,* Fighting Men 120. *Machapunga,* Town 1, *Maramiskeet,* Fighting Men 30. *Bear* River, Town 1, *Raudauqua-quank,* Fighting Men 50. *Maherring Indians,* Town 1, *Maherring* River, Fighting Men 50. *Chuwon Indians,* Town 1, *Bennets* Creek, Fighting Men 15. *Paspatank Indians,* Town 1, *Paspatank* River, Fighting Men 10. *Poteskeit,* Town 1, *North* River, Fighting Men 30. *Nottaway Indians,* Town 1, *Winoack* Creek, Fighting Men 30. *Hatteras* Town 1, Sand Banks, Fighting Men 16. *Connamox Indians,* Towns 2, *Coranine, Raruta,* Fighting Men 25. *Neus Indians,* Towns 2, *Chattooka, Rouconk,* Fighting Men 15. *Pampticough Indians,* Town 1, *Island,* Fighting Men 15. *Jaupim Indians,* 6 People. These five Nations of the *Totero's, Sapona's, Keiauwee's, Aconechos,* and *Schoccories,* are lately come amongst us, and may contain, in all, about 750 Men, Women and Children. Total 4780.

Now, there appears to be one thousand six hundred and twelve Fighting Men, of our Neighbouring *Indians;* and probably, there are three Fifths of Women and Children, not including Old Men, which amounts to four thousand and thirty Savages, besides the five Nations lately come. Now, as I before hinted, we will see what grounds there are to make these People serviceable to us, and better themselves thereby.

On a fair Scheme, we must first allow these Savages what really belongs to them, that is, what good Qualities, and natural Endowments, they possess, whereby they being in their proper Colours, the Event may be better guess'd at, and fathom'd.

First, they are as apt to learn any Handicraft, as any People that the World affords; I will except none; as is seen by their Canoes and Stauking Heads, which they make of themselves; but to my purpose, the *Indian* Slaves in South *Carolina*, and elsewhere, make my Argument good.

Secondly, we have no disciplin'd Men in *Europe,* but what have, at one time or other, been branded with Mutining, and Murmuring against their Chiefs. These Savages are never found guilty of that great Crime in a Soldier; I challenge all Mankind to tell me of one Instance of it; besides, they never prove Traitors to their Native Country, but rather chuse Death than partake and side with the Enemy.

They naturally possess the Righteous Man's Gift; they are Patient under all Afflictions, and have a great many other Natural Vertues, which I have slightly touch'd throughout the Account of these Savages.

They are really better to us, than we are to them; they always give us Victuals at their Quarters, and take care we are arm'd against Hunger and Thirst: We do not so by them (generally speaking) but let them walk by our Doors Hungry, and do not often relieve them. We look upon them with Scorn and Disdain, and think them little better than Beasts in Humane Shape, though if well examined, we shall find that, for all our Religion and Education, we possess more Moral Deformities, and Evils than these Savages do, or are acquainted withal.

We reckon them Slaves in Comparison to us, and Intruders, as oft as they enter our Houses, or hunt near our Dwellings. But if we will admit Reason to be our Guide, she will inform us, that these *Indians* are the freest People in the World, and so far from being Intruders upon us, that we have abandon'd our own Native Soil, to drive them out, and possess theirs; neither have we any true Balance, in Judging of these poor Heathens, because we

neither give Allowance for their Natural Disposition, nor the
Sylvian Education, and strange Customs, (uncouth to us) they lie
under and have ever been train'd up to; these are false Measures
for Christians to take, and indeed no Man can be reckon'd a
Moralist only, who will not make choice and use, of better Rules
to walk and act by: We trade with them, it's true, but to what
End? Not to shew them the Steps of Vertue, and the Golden Rule,
to do as we would be done by. No, we have furnished them with
the Vice of Drunkenness, which is the open Road to all others,
and daily cheat them in every thing we sell, and esteem it a Gift of
Christianity, not to sell to them so cheap as we do to the Christians, as we call our selves. Pray let me know where is there to be
found one Sacred Command or Precept of our Master, that coun-
sels us to such Behaviour? Besides, I believe it will not appear, but
that all the Wars, which we have had with the Savages, were
occasion'd by the unjust Dealings of the Christians towards them.
I can name more than a few, which my own Enquiry has given me
a right Understanding of, and I am afraid the remainder (if they
come to the test) will prove themselves Birds of the same Feather.

As we are in Christian Duty bound, so we must act and behave
ourselves to these Savages, if we either intend to be serviceable in
converting them to the Knowledge of the Gospel, or discharge the
Duty which every Man, within the Pale of the Christian Church,
is bound to do. Upon this Score, we ought to shew a Tenderness
for these Heathens under the weight of Infidelity; let us cherish
their good Deeds, and, with Mildness and Clemency, make them
sensible and forwarn them of their ill ones; let our Dealings be
just to them in every Respect, and shew no ill Example, whereby
they may think we advise them to practise that which we will not
be conformable to ourselves: Let them have cheap Penniworths
(without Guile in our Trading with them) and learn them the
Mysteries of our Handicrafts, as well as our Religion, otherwise
we deal unjustly by them. But it is highly necessary to be brought
in Practice, which is, to give Encouragement to the ordinary
People, and those of a lower Rank, that they might marry with
these *Indians,* and come into Plantations, and Houses, where so
many Acres of Land and some Gratuity of Money, (out of a
publick Stock) are given to the new-married Couple; and that the
Indians might have Encouragement to send their Children Ap-
prentices to proper Masters, that would be kind to them, and
make them Masters of a Trade, whereby they would be drawn to

live amongst us, and become Members of the same Ecclesiastical and Civil Government we are under; then we should have great Advantages to make daily Conversions amongst them, when they saw that we were kind and just to them in all our Dealings. Moreover, by the *Indians* Marrying with the Christians, and coming into Plantations with their *English* Husbands, or Wives, they would become Christians, and their Idolatry would be quite forgotten, and, in all probability, a better Worship come in its Stead; for were the *Jews* engrafted thus, and alienated from the Worship and Conversation of *Jews*, their Abominations would vanish, and be no more.

Thus we should be let into a better Understanding of the *Indian* Tongue, by our new Converts; and the whole Body of these People would arrive to the Knowledge of our Religion and Customs, and become as one People with us. By this Method also, we should have a true Knowledge of all the *Indians* Skill in Medicine and Surgery; they would inform us of the Situation of our Rivers, Lakes, and Tracts of Land in the Lords Dominions, where by their Assistance, greater Discoveries may be made than has been hitherto found out, and by their Accompanying us in our Expeditions, we might civilize a great many other Nations of the Savages, and daily add to our Strength in Trade, and Interest; so that we might be sufficiently enabled to conquer, or maintain our Ground, against all the Enemies to the Crown of *England* in *America*, both Christian and Savage.

What Children we have of theirs, to learn Trades, &c. ought to be put into those Hands that are Men of the best Lives and Characters, and that are not only strict Observers of their Religion, but also of a mild, winning and sweet Disposition, that these *Indian* Parents may often go and see how well their Children are dealt with, which would much win them to our Ways of Living, Mildness being a Vertue the *Indians* are in love withal, for they do not practise beating and correcting their Children, as we do. A general Complaint is, that it seems impossible to convert these People to Christianity, as, at first sight, it does; and as for those in *New Spain*, they have the Prayer of that Church in Latin by Rote, and know the external Behaviour at Mass and Sermons; yet scarce any of them are steady and abide with constancy in good Works, and the Duties of the Christian Church. We find that the *Fuentes* and several other of the noted *Indian* Families about *Mexico*, and in other parts of *New Spain*, had given several large Gifts to the

Altar, and outwardly seem'd fond of their new Religion; yet those that were the greatest Zealots outwards, on a strict Enquiry, were found guilty of Idolatry and Witchcraft; and this seems to proceed from their Cohabiting, which, as I have noted before, gives Opportunities of Cabals to recal their ancient pristine Infidelity and Superstitions. They never argue against our Religion, but with all imaginable Indifference own, that it is most proper for us that have been brought up in it.

In my opinion, it's better for Christians of a mean Fortune to marry with the Civiliz'd *Indians*, than to suffer the Hardships of four or five years Servitude, in which they meet with Sickness and Seasonings amidst a Crowd of other Afflictions, which the Tyranny of a bad Master lays upon such poor Souls, all which those acquainted with our Tobacco Plantations are not Strangers to.

This seems to be a more reasonable Method of converting the *Indians*, than to set up our Christian Banner in a Field of Blood, as the *Spaniards* have done in *New Spain*, and baptize one hundred with the Sword for one at the Font. Whilst we make way for a Christian Colony through a Field of Blood, and defraud, and make away with those that one day may be wanted in this World, and in the next appear against us, we make way for a more potent Christian Enemy to invade us hereafter, of which we may repent, when too late.

APPENDIXES

THE SECOND

CHARTER

GRANTED BY

KING CHARLES II

TO THE

Proprietors of Carolina

C HARLES II. by the Grace of God, &c. Whereas by Our Letters Patents, bearing Date the Four and Twentieth Day of *March,* in the Fifteenth Year of Our Reign, We were Graciously Pleas'd to Grant unto Our right Trusty, and right Well-beloved Cousin and Counsellor *Edward* Earl of *Clarendon,* our High Chancellor of *England,* Our right Trusty, and right entirely Beloved Cousin and Counsellor, *George* Duke of *Albemarle,* Master of our Horse, Our right Trusty and Well Beloved *William,* now Earl of *Craven,* our right Trusty and well-beloved Counsellor, *John* Lord *Berkeley,* our right Trusty, and well-beloved Counsellor, *Anthony* Lord *Ashley,* Chancellor of our Exchequer, our right Trusty and Well-beloved Counsellor Sir *George Carterett* Knight and Baronet, Vice-Chamberlain of our Houshold, Our right Trusty and well-beloved, Sir *John Colleton* Knight and Baronet, and Sir *William Berkeley* Knight, all that Province, Territory, or Tract of Ground, called *Carolina,* situate, lying and being within our Dominions of *America,* Extending from the *North* End of the Island, called *Luke Island,* which lyeth in the *Southern Virginia* Seas, and within six and thirty Degrees of the *Northern* Latitude; and to the *West,* as far as the *South* Seas; and so respectively as far as the River of *Mathias,* which bordereth upon the Coast of

Florida, and within One and Thirty Degrees of the *Northern* Latitude, and so *West* in a direct Line, as far as the *South* Seas aforesaid.

Now, know Ye, that We, at the Humble Request of the said Grandees in the aforesaid Letters Patents named, and as a farther Mark of Our especial Favour towards them, We are Graciously Pleased to Enlarge Our said Grant unto them, according to the Bounds and Limits hereafter Specifyed, and in Favour to the Pious and Noble Purpose of the said *Edward* Earl of *Clarendon, George* Duke of *Albemarle, William* Earl of *Craven, John* Lord *Berkeley, Anthony* Lord *Ashley,* Sir *George Carterett,* Sir *John Colleton,* and Sir *William Berkeley,* their Heirs and Assigns, all that Province, Territory, or Tract of Ground, situate, lying, and being within Our Dominions of *America* aforesaid, extending *North* and *Westward,* as far as the *North* End of *Carahtuke* River, or *Gulet,* upon a streight *Westerly* Line, to *Wyonoake* Creek, which lies within, or about the Degrees of Thirty Six, and Thirty Minutes *Northern* Latitude, and so *West,* in a direct Line, as far as the *South* Seas; and *South* and *Westward,* as far as the Degrees of Twenty Nine Inclusive *Northern* Latitude, and so *West* in a direct Line, as far as the *South* Seas; together with all and singular Ports, Harbours, Bays, Rivers and Islets, belonging unto the Province or Territory, aforesaid. And also, all the Soil, Lands, Fields, Woods, Mountains, Ferms, Lakes, Rivers, Bays and Islets, situate, or being within the Bounds, or Limits, last before mentioned; with the Fishing of all sorts of Fish, *Whales, Sturgeons,* and all other Royal Fishes in the Sea, Bays, Islets and Rivers, within the Premises, and the Fish therein taken; together with the Royalty of the Sea, upon the Coast within the Limits aforesaid. And moreover, all Veins, Mines and Quarries, as well discovered as not discover'd, of Gold, Silver, Gems and Precious Stones, and all other whatsoever; be it of Stones, Metal, or any other thing found, or to be found within the Province, Territory, Islets and Limits aforesaid.

And furthermore, the Patronage and Advowsons of all the Churches and Chappels, which as the Christian Religion shall encrease within the Province, Territory, Isles and Limits aforesaid, shall happen hereafter to be erected; together with Licence and Power to build and found Churches, Chappels and Oratories in convenient and fit places, within the said Bounds and Limits; and to cause them to be Dedicated and Consecrated, according to the Ecclesiastical Laws of Our Kingdom of *England;* together with all and singular, the like, and as ample Rights, Jurisdictions, Privileges, Prerogatives, Royalties, Liberties, Immunities and Franchises, of what Kind soever, within the Territory, Isles, Islets and Limits aforesaid. To have, hold, use, exercise and enjoy the same, as amply, fully, and in as ample Manner, as any Bishop of *Durham* in Our Kingdom of *England,* ever heretofore had, held, used, or enjoyed, or of right ought, or could have, use, or enjoy; and them the said *Edward* Earl of *Clarendon, George* Duke of *Albemarle, William* Earl of *Craven, John* Lord *Berkeley, Anthony* Lord *Ashley,* Sir *George Carterett,* Sir *John Colleton,* and Sir *William Berkeley,* their Heirs and Assigns; We do by these Presents, for Us, Our Heirs and Successors, make, create and constitute the true and absolute Lords and Proprietors of the said Province, or Territory, and of all other the Premises, saving always the Faith, Allegiance and Sovereign Dominion due to Us, our Heirs and Successors, for the same; to have, hold, possess and enjoy the said Province, Territory, Islets, and all and singular, other the Premises, to them the said *Edward* Earl of *Clarendon, George* Duke of *Albemarle, William* Earl of *Craven, John* Lord *Berkeley, Anthony* Lord *Ashley,* Sir *George Carterett,* Sir *John Colleton* and Sir *William Berkeley,* their Heirs and Assigns, for Ever, to be holden of Us, Our Heirs and Successors, as of Our Mannor of *East Greenwich,* in *Kent,* in free and common Soccage, and not in *Capite,* or by *Knights Service,* yielding and paying yearly to Us, Our Heirs and Successors, for the same, the fourth Part of all Goods and Silver Oar, which within the Limits hereby Granted, shall from Time to Time, happen to be found, over and besides the Yearly Rent of Twenty Marks and the fourth part of the Gold and Silver Oar, in and by the said recited Letters Patents reserved and payable.

And that the Province, or Territory hereby granted and described, may be dignifyed with as large Titles and Privileges, as any other Parts of our Dominions and Territories in that Region; Know ye, That We, of our farther Grace, certain Knowledge and meer Motion, have thought fit to annex the same Tract of Ground and Territory, unto the same Province of *Carolina;* and out of the Fulness of our Royal Power and Prerogative, We do for Us, our Heirs and Successors, annex and unite the same to the said Province of *Carolina.* And forasmuch as We have made and ordained the aforesaid *Edward* Earl of *Clarendon, George* Duke of *Albe-*

marle, William Earl of *Craven, John* Lord *Berkeley, Anthony* Lord *Ashley,* Sir *George Carterett,* Sir *John Colleton,* and Sir *William Berkeley,* their Heirs and Assigns, the true Lords and Proprietors of all the Province or Territory aforesaid; Know ye therefore moreover, that We reposing especial Trust and Confidence in their Fidelity, Wisdom, Justice and provident Circumspection for Us, our Heirs and Successors, do grant full and absolute Power, by virtue of these Presents, to them the said *Edward* Earl of *Clarendon, George* Duke of *Albemarle, William* Earl of *Craven, John* Lord *Berkeley, Anthony* Lord *Ashley,* Sir *George Carterett,* Sir *John Colleton,* and Sir *William Berkeley,* and their Heirs and Assigns, for the good and happy Government of the said whole Province or Territory, full Power and Authority to erect, constitute, and make several Counties, Baronies, and Colonies, of and within the said Provinces, Territories, Lands and Hereditaments, in and by the said recited Letters Patents, and these Presents, granted, or mentioned to be granted, as aforesaid, with several and distinct Jurisdictions, Powers, Liberties and Privileges. And also, to ordain, make and enact, and under their Seals, to publish any Laws and Constitutions whatsoever, either appertaining to the publick State of the said whole Province or Territory, or of any distinct or particular County, Barony or Colony, of or within the same, or to the private Utility of particular Persons, according to their best Discretion, by and with the Advice, Assent and Approbation of the Freemen of the said Province or Territory, or of the Freemen of the County, Barony or Colony, for which such Law or Constitution shall be made, or the greatest Part of them, or of their Delegates or Deputies, whom for enacting of the said Laws, when, and as often as need shall require, We will that the said *Edward* Earl of *Clarendon, George* Duke of *Albemarle, William* Earl of *Craven, John* Lord *Berkeley, Anthony* Lord *Ashley,* Sir *George Carterett,* Sir *John Colleton* and Sir *William Berkeley,* and their Heirs or Assigns, shall from Time to Time, assemble in such Manner and Form as to them shall seem best: And the same Laws duly to execute upon all People within the said Province or Territory, County, Barony or Colony, and the Limits thereof, for the Time being, which shall be constituted under the Power and Government of them, or any of them, either sailing towards the said Province or Territory of *Carolina,* or returning from thence towards *England,* or any other of our, or foreign Dominions, by Imposition of Penalties, Imprisonment, or any other Punishment:

Yea, if it shall be needful, and the Quality of the Offence require it, by taking away Member and Life, either by them, the said *Edward* Earl of *Clarendon, George* Duke of *Albemarle, William* Earl of *Craven, John* Lord *Berkeley, Anthony* Lord *Ashley,* Sir *George Carterett,* Sir *John Colleton,* and Sir *William Berkeley,* and their Heirs, or by them or their Deputies, Lieutenants, Judges, Justices, Magistrates, or Officers whatsoever, as well within the said Province, as at Sea, in such Manner and Form, as unto the said *Edward* Earl of *Clarendon, George* Duke of *Albemarle, William* Earl of *Craven, John* Lord *Berkeley, Anthony* Lord *Ashley,* Sir *George Carterett,* Sir *John Colleton,* and Sir *William Berkeley,* and their Heirs, shall seem most convenient: Also, to remit, release, pardon and abolish, whether before Judgment or after, all Crimes and Offences whatsoever, against the said Laws; and to do all and every other Thing and Things, which unto the compleat Establishment of Justice, unto Courts, Sessions and Forms of Judicature, and Manners of proceedings therein, do belong, altho' in these Presents, express Mention is not made thereof; and by Judges, to him or them delegated to award, process, hold Please, and determine in all the said Courts and Places of Judicature, all Actions, Suits and Causes whatsoever, as well criminal as civil, real, mixt, personal, or of any other Kind or Nature whatsoever: Which Laws so as aforesaid, to be published, Our Pleasure is, and We do enjoyn, require and command, shall be absolutely firm and available in Law; and that all the Leige People of Us, our Heirs and Successors, within the said Province or Territory, do observe and keep the same inviolably in those Parts, so far as they concern them, under the Pains and Penalties therein expressed; or to be expressed; provided nevertheless, that the said Laws be consonant to Reason, and as near as may be conveniently, agreeable to the Laws and Customs of this our Realm of *England.*

And because such Assemblies of Free-holders cannot be so suddenly called, as there may be Occasion to require the same; We do therefore by these Presents, give and grant unto the said *Edward* Earl of *Clarendon, George* Duke of *Albemarle, William* Earl of *Craven, John* Lord *Berkeley, Anthony* Lord *Ashley,* Sir *George Carterett,* Sir *John Colleton,* and Sir *William Berkeley,* their Heirs and Assigns, by themselves or their Magistrates in that Behalf, lawfully authorized, full Power and Authority from Time to Time, to make and ordain fit and wholsome Orders and Ordinances, within the Province or Territory aforesaid, or any County, Barony or Province, of or within the same, to be kept and observed, as well for the keeping of the Peace, as for the better Government of the People there abiding, and to publish the same to all to whom it may concern: Which Ordinances we do, by these Presents, streightly charge and command to be inviolably observed within the same Province, Counties, Territories, Baronies, and Provinces, under the Penalties therein expressed; so as such Ordinances be reasonable and not repugnant or contrary, but as near as may be agreeable to the Laws and Statutes of this our Kingdom of *England;* and so as the same Ordinances do not extend to the binding, charging or taking away of the Right or Interest of any Person or Persons, in their freehold Goods, or Chattels, whatsoever.

And to the end the said Province or Territory, may be the more happily encreased by the Multitude of People resorting thither, and may likewise be the more strongly defended from the Incursions of Savages and other Enemies, Pirates, and Robbers.

Therefore, We for Us, Our Heirs and Successors, do give and grant by these Presents, Power, License and Liberty unto all the Leige People of Us, our Heirs and Successors in our Kingdom of *England,* or elsewhere, within any other our Dominions, Islands, Colonies or Plantations; (excepting those who shall be especially forbidden) to transport themselves and Families into the said Province or Territory, with convenient Shipping, and fitting Provisions; and there to settle themselves, dwell and inhabit, any Law, Act, Statute, Ordinance, or other Thing to the contrary in any wise, notwithstanding.

And we will also, and of Our especial Grace, for Us, our Heirs and Successors, do streightly enjoyn, ordain, constitute and demand, That the said Province or Territory, shall be of our Allegiance; and that all and singular, the Subjects and Leige People of Us, our Heirs and Successors, transported, or to be transported into the said Province, and the Children of them, and such as shall descend from them, there born, or hereafter to be born, be, and shall be Denizens and Lieges of Us, our Heirs and Successors of this our Kingdom of *England,* and be in all Things, held, treated and reputed as the Liege faithful People of Us, our Heirs and Successors, born within this our said Kingdom, or any other of our Dominions; and may inherit, or otherwise purchase and receive, take, hold, buy and possess any Lands, Tenements or

Hereditaments, within the said Places, and them may occupy, and enjoy, sell, alien and bequeath; as likewise, all Liberties, Franchises and Privileges of this our Kingdom, and of other our Dominions aforesaid, may freely and quietly have, possess and enjoy, as our Liege People born within the same, without the Molestation, Vexation, Trouble or Grievance of Us, Our Heirs and Successors, any Act, Statute, Ordinance, or Provision to the contrary, notwithstanding.

And furthermore, That Our Subjects of this Our said Kingdom of *England,* and other our Dominions, may be the rather encouraged to undertake this Expedition, with ready and chearful Minds; Know Ye, That We, of Our especial Grace, certain Knowledge and meer Motion, do give and grant, by virtue of these Presents, as well to the said *Edward* Earl of *Clarendon, George* Duke of *Albemarle, William* Earl of *Craven, John* Lord *Berkeley, Anthony* Lord *Ashley,* Sir *George Carterett,* Sir *John Colleton,* and Sir *William Berkeley,* and their Heirs, as unto all others as shall, from time to time, repair unto the said Province or Territory, with a Purpose to inhabit there, or to trade with the Natives thereof; Full Liberty and License to lade and freight in every Port whatsoever, of Us, our Heirs and Successors; and into the said Province of *Carolina,* by them, their Servants and Assigns, to transport all and singular, their Goods, Wares and Merchandizes: as likewise, all sort of Grain whatsoever, and any other Thing whatsoever, necessary for their Food and Cloathing, not prohibited by the Laws and Statutes of our Kingdom and Dominions, to be carried out of the same, without any Lett or Molestation of Us, our Heirs and Successors, or of any other our Officers or Ministers whatsoever; saving also to Us, our Heirs and Successors, the Customs, and other Duties and Payments due for the said Wares and Merchandizes, according to the several Rates of the Place from whence the same shall be transported.

We will also, and by these Presents, for Us, our Heirs and Successors, do give and grant License by this our Charter, unto the said *Edward* Earl of *Clarendon, George* Duke of *Albemarle, William* Earl of *Craven, John* Lord *Berkeley, Anthony* Lord *Ashley,* Sir *George Carterett,* Sir *John Colleton,* and Sir *William Berkeley,* their Heirs and Assigns, and to all the Inhabitants and Dwellers in the Province or Territory aforesaid, both present and to come, full Power and Authority to import or unlade by themselves, or their Servants, Factors or Assigns, all Merchandizes and

Goods whatsoever, that shall arise of the Fruits and Commodities of the said Province or Territory, either by Land or Sea, into any the Ports of Us, our Heirs and Successors, in our Kingdom of *Engl. Scotl.* or *Ireland,* or otherwise, to dispose of the said Goods, in the said Ports. And if need be, within one year next after the unlading, to lade the said Merchandizes and Goods again in the same, or other Ships; and to export the same into any other Countries, either of our Dominins or foreign, being in Amity with Us, our Heirs and Successors, so as they pay such Customs, Subsidies and other Duties for the same to Us, our Heirs and Successors, as the rest of our Subjects of this our Kingdom, for the Time being, shall be bound to pay. Beyond which We will not that the Inhabitants of the said Province or Territory, shall be any ways charged. Provided, nevertheless, and our Will and Pleasure is, and we have further, for the Considerations aforesaid, of our special Grace, certain Knowledge and meer Motion, given and granted, and by these Presents, for Us, our Heirs and Successors, do give and grant unto the said *Edward* Earl of *Clarendon, George* Duke of *Albemarle, William* Earl of *Craven, John* Lord *Berkeley, Anthony* Lord *Ashley,* Sir *George Carterett,* Sir *John Colleton,* and Sir *William Berkeley,* their Heirs and Assigns, full and free License, Liberty, Power and Authority, at any Time or Times, from and after the Feast of St. *Michael* the Arch-Angel, which shall be in the Year of our Lord Christ, One Thousand, Six Hundred, Sixty and Seven; as well to import and bring into any our Dominions from the said Province of *Carolina,* or any Part thereof, the several Goods and Commodities herein after mentioned; That is to say, Silks, Wines, Currants, Raisons, Capers, Wax, Almonds, Oil and Olives, without paying or answering to Us, our Heirs and Successors, any Custom, Impost, or other Duty, for, or in respect thereof, for and during the Time and Space of Seven Years to commence and be accompted from and after the first Importation of Four Tons of any the said Goods, in any one Bottom Ship or Vessel, from the said Province or Territory, into any of our Dominions; as also, to export and carry out of any of our Dominions into the said Province or Territory, Custom-free, all sorts of Tools, which shall be useful or necessary for the Planters there, in the Accommodation and Improvement of the Premises, any thing before in these Presents contained, or any Law, Act, Statute, Prohibition, or other Matter or Thing, heretofore had, made, enacted or provided, or hereafter to be had, made, enacted or provided, in any wise notwithstanding.

And furthermore, of our more ample and especial Grace, certain Knowledge and meer Motion, We do for Us, our Heirs and Successors, grant unto the said *Edward* Earl of *Clarendon, George* Duke of *Albemarle, William* Earl of *Craven, John* Lord *Berkeley, Anthony* Lord *Ashley,* Sir *George Carterett,* Sir *John Colleton,* and Sir *Will. Berkeley,* their Heirs and Assigns, full and absolute Power and Authority to make, erect and constitute within the said Province or Territory, and the Isles and Islets aforesaid, such and so many Sea-Ports, Harbours, Creeks and other Places for discharge and unlading of Goods and Merchandizes out of Ships, Boats, and other Vessels, and for lading of them in such and so many Places, as with such Jurisdictions, Privileges and Franchises, unto the said Ports belonging, as to them shall seem most expedient; And that all and singular, the Ships, Boats and other Vessels, which shall come for Merchandizes, and trade into the said Province or Territory, or shall depart out of the same, shall be laden and unladen at such Ports only, as shall be erected and constituted by the said *Edward* Earl of *Clarendon, George* Duke of *Albemarle, William* Earl of *Craven, John* Lord *Berkeley, Anthony* Lord *Ashley,* Sir *George Carterett,* Sir *John Colleton,* and Sir *William Berkeley,* their Heirs and Assigns, and not elsewhere, any Use, Custom, or any thing to the contrary in any wise notwithstanding.

And we do furthermore will, appoint and ordain, and by these Presents, for Us, our Heirs and Successors, do grant unto the said *Edward* Earl of *Clarendon, George* Duke of *Albemarle, William* Earl of *Craven, John* Lord *Berkeley, Anthony* Lord *Ashley,* Sir *George Carterett,* Sir *John Colleton* and Sir *William Berkeley,* their Heirs and Assigns, That they the said *Edward* Earl of *Clarendon, George* Duke of *Albemarle, William* Earl of *Craven, John* Lord *Berkeley, Anthony* Lord *Ashley,* Sir *George Carterett,* Sir *John Colleton,* and Sir *William Berkeley,* their Heirs and Assigns, may from Time to Time, for ever, have and enjoy the Customs and Subsidies in the Ports, Harbours, Creeks and other Places, within the Province aforesaid, payable for the Goods, Merchandizes and Wares there laded, or to be laded or unladed, the said Customs to be reasonably assessed upon any Occasion by themselves, and by and with the Consent of the free People, or the greater Part of them, as aforesaid; to whom We give Power by these Presents, for Us, our Heirs and Successors, upon just Cause and in a due Proportion to assess and impose the same.

And further, of our especial Grace, certain Knowledge and meer Motion, we have given, granted and confirmed, and by these Presents, for Us, our Heirs and Successors, do give, grant and confirm unto the said *Edward* Earl of *Clarendon, George* Duke of *Albemarle, William* Earl of *Craven, John* Lord *Berkeley, Anthony* Lord *Ashley,* Sir *George Carterett,* Sir *John Colleton,* and Sir *William Berkeley,* their Heirs and Assigns, full and absolute Power, License and Authority, that they the said *Edward* Earl of *Clarendon, George* Duke of *Albemarle, William* Earl of *Craven, John* Lord *Berkeley, Anthony* Lord *Ashley,* Sir *George Carterett,* Sir *John Colleton,* and Sir *William Berkeley,* their Heirs and Assigns, from Time to Time, hereafter for ever, at his and their Will and Pleasure, may assign, alien, grant, demise or enfeoff the Premises or any Part or Parcel thereof to him or them, that shall be willing to purchase the same; and to such Person and Persons, as they shall think fit, to have, and to hold to them the said Person or Persons, their Heirs and Assigns, in Fee simple or in Fee Tayle, or for the Term of Life or Lives, or Years to be held of them, the said *Edward* Earl of *Clarendon, George* Duke of *Albemarle, William* Earl of *Craven, John* Lord *Berkeley, Anthony* Lord *Ashley,* Sir *George Carterett,* Sir *John Colleton,* and Sir *William Berkeley,* their Heirs and Assigns, by such Rents, Services and Customs, as shall seem fit to them the said *Edward* Earl of *Clarendon, George* Duke of *Albemarle, William* Earl of *Craven, John* Lord *Berkeley, Anthony* Lord *Ashley,* Sir *George Carterett,* Sir *John Colleton,* and *William Berkeley,* their Heirs and Assigns, and not of Us, our Heirs and Successors: And to the same Person and Persons, and to all and every of them, We do give and grant by these Presents, for Us, our Heirs and Successors, License, Authority and Power, that such Person or Persons, may have and take the Premises, or any Parcel thereof, of the said *Edward* Earl of *Clarendon, George* Duke of *Albemarle, William* Earl of *Craven, John* Lord *Berkeley, Anthony* Lord *Ashley,* Sir *George Carterett,* Sir *John Colleton,* and Sir *William Berkeley,* their Heirs and Assigns, and the same to hold to themselves, their Heirs or Assigns, in what Estate of Inheritance soever, in Fee simple, or in Fee Tayle, or otherwise, as to them the said *Edward* Earl of *Clarendon, George* Duke of *Albemarle, William* Earl of *Craven, John* Lord *Berkeley,*

Anthony Lord *Ashley,* Sir *George Carterett,* Sir *John Colleton,* and Sir *William Berkeley,* their Heirs and Assigns, shall seem expedient; The Statute in the Parliament of *Edward,* Son of King *Henry,* heretofore King of *England,* our Predecessor, commonly called, The Statute of *Quia Emptores Terrar;* or any other Statute, Act, Ordinance, Use, Law, Custom, any other Matter, Cause or Thing heretofore published or provided to the contrary, in any wise notwithstanding.

And because many Persons born and inhabiting in the said Province for their Deserts and Services may expect, and be capable of Marks of Honour and Favour, which, in respect of the great Distance cannot conveniently be conferred by Us; our Will and Pleasure therefore is, and We do by these Presents, give and grant unto the said *Edward* Earl of *Clarendon, George* Duke of *Albemarle, William* Lord *Craven, John* Lord *Berkeley, Anthony* Lord *Ashley,* Sir *George Carterett,* Sir *John Colleton,* and Sir *William Berkeley,* their Heirs and Assigns, full Power and Authority to give and confer unto, and upon such of the Inhabitants of the said Province, or Territory, as they shall think, do, or shall merit the same, such Marks of Favour, and Titles of Honour, as they shall think fit, so as their Titles of Honours be not the same as are enjoyed by, or conferred upon any of the Subjects of this Our Kingdom of *England.*

And further also, We do by these Presents, for Us, Our Heirs and Successors, give and Grant, License to them the *Edward* Earl of *Clarendon, George* Duke of *Albemarle, William* Earl of *Craven, John* Lord *Berkeley, Anthony* Lord *Ashley,* Sir *George Carterett,* Sir *John Colleton* and Sir *William Berkeley,* their Heirs and Assigns, full Power, Liberty and License, to Erect, Raise and Build within the said Province and Places aforesaid, or any Part or Parts thereof, such and so many Forts, Fortresses, Castles, Cities, Boroughs, Towns, Villages and other Fortifications whatsoever; and the same or any of them to Fortify and Furnish with Ordnance, Powder, Shot, Armour and all other Weapons, Ammunition and Habiliments of War, both Defensive and Offensive, as shall be thought fit and convenient for the Safety and Welfare of the said Province, and Places, or any Part thereof; and the same, or any of them, from Time to Time, as Occasion shall require, to Dismantle, Disfurnish, Demolish and Pull down; And also to Place, Constitute and Appoint in, or over all, or any of the said Castles, Forts, Fortifications, Cities, Towns and Places afore-

said, Governours, Deputy Governours, Magistrates, Sheriffs and
other Officers, Civil and Military, as to them shall seem meet; and
to the said Cities, Boroughs, Towns, Villages, or any other Place
or Places, within the said Province or Territory, to Grant Letters
or Charters of Incorporation, with all Liberties, Franchises and
Privileges requisite, or usual, to, or within this our Kingdom of
England granted, or belonging; And in the same Cities, Boroughs,
Towns and other Places, to Constitute, Erect and Appoint such,
and so many Markets, Marts and Fairs as shall in that Behalf be
thought fit and necessary; And further also, to Erect and Make in
the Province or Territory aforesaid, or any Part thereof, so many
Mannors with such Signories as to them shall seem meet and
convenient, and in every of the same Mannors to have and to hold
a court-Baron, with all Things whatsoever, which to a Court-
Baron do belong, and to have and to hold Views of Frank Pledge,
and Court-Leet, for the Conservation of the Peace, and better
Government of those Parts, with such Limits, Jurisdiction and
Precincts, as by the said *Edward* Earl of *Clarendon, George* Duke
of *Albemarle, William* Earl of *Craven, John* Lord *Berkeley, Anthony* Lord *Ashley,* Sir *George Carterett,* Sir *John Colleton,* and
Sir *William Berkeley,* or their Heirs, shall be appointed for that
purpose, with all things whatsoever, which to a Court-Leet, or
view of Franck Pledge, do belong; the same Courts to be holden
by Stewards, to be Deputed and Authorized by said *Edward* Earl
of *Clarendon, George* Duke of *Albemarle, William* Earl of
Craven, John Lord *Berkeley, Anthony* Lord *Ashley,* Sir *George
Carterett,* Sir *John Colleton,* and Sir *William Berkeley,* or their
Heirs, by the Lords of the Manors and Leets, for the Time being,
when the same shall be Erected.

And because that in so remote a Country, and Situate among so
many Barbarous Nations, the Invasions as well of Savages as other
Enemies, Pirates, and Robbers may Probably be feared; Therefore We have Given, and for Us, Our Heirs and Successors do give
Power by these Presents, unto the Said *Edward* Earl of *Clarendon,
George* Duke of *Albemarle, William* Earl of *Craven, John* Lord
Berkeley, Anthony Lord *Ashley,* Sir *George Carterett,* Sir *John
Colleton,* and Sir *William Berkeley,* their Heirs or Assigns by
themselves, or their Captains, or their Officers to Levy, Muster
and Train up all sorts of Men, of what Condition soever, or
wheresoever Born, whether in the said Province, or elsewhere, for
the Time being; and to make War and pursue the Enemies afore-

said, as well by Sea, as by Land; yea, even without the Limits of the said Province, and by God's Assistance, to Vanquish and Take them, and being Taken, to put them to Death by the Law of War, and to save them at their Pleasure; And to do all and every other thing, which to the Charge and Office of a Captain General of an Army belongeth, or hath accustomed to belong, as fully and freely as any Captain General of an Army hath had the same.

Also, Our Will and Pleasure is, and by this Our Charter, We do give and grant unto the said *Edward* Earl of *Clarendon, George* Duke of *Albemarle, William* Lord *Craven, John* Lord *Berkeley, Anthony* Lord *Ashley,* Sir *George Carterett,* Sir *John Colleton,* and Sir *William Berkeley,* their Heirs and Assigns, full Power, Liberty and Authority, in Case of Rebellion, Tumult, or Sedition (if any should happen, which God forbid) either upon the Land within the Province aforesaid, or upon the main Sea, in making a Voyage thither, or returning from thence, by him and themselves, their Captains, Deputies or Officers, to be authorized under his or their Seals, for that purpose: To whom also for Us, our Heirs and Successors, We do give and grant by these Presents, full Power and Authority to exercise Martial Law against mutinous and seditious Persons of those Parts; such as shall refuse to submit themselves to their Government, or shall refuse to serve in the Wars, or shall fly to the Enemy, or forsake their Colours or Ensigns, or be Loiterers or Stragglers, or otherwise howsoever offending against Law, Custom, or Military Discipline, as freely, and in as ample Manner and Form as any Captain General of an Army, by virtue of his Office, might, or hath accustomed to use the same.

And Our further Pleasure is, and by these Presents, for Us, our Heirs and Successors, We do grant unto the said *Edward* Earl of *Clarendon, George* Duke of *Albemarle, William* Earl of *Craven, John* Lord *Berkeley, Anthony* Lord *Ashley,* Sir *George Carterett,* Sir *John Colleton,* and Sir *William Berkeley,* their Heirs and Assigns, and to the Tenants and Inhabitants of the said Province, or Territory, both present and to come, and to every of them, that the said Province, or Territory, and the Tenants and Inhabitants thereof, shall not from henceforth, be held or reputed any Member, or Part of any Colony whatsoever, in *America* or elsewhere, now transported or made, or hereafter to be transported or made; nor shall be depending on, or subject to their Government in any Thing, but be absolutely separated and divided from the same: And our Pleasure is, by these Presents, That they may be separated, and that they be subject immediately to our Crown of *England,* as depending thereof for ever. And that the Inhabitants of the said Province or Territory, or any of them, shall at any Time hereafter, be compelled or compellible, or be any ways subject, or liable to appear or answer to any Matter, Suit, Cause, or Plaint whatsoever, out of the Province or Territory aforesaid, in any other of our Islands, Colonies or Dominions in *America,* or elsewhere, other than in our Realm of *England* and Dominion of *Wales.*

And because it may happen, That some of the People and Inhabitants of the said Province, cannot in their private Opinions conform to the Publick Exercise of Religion according to the Liturgy, Forms and Ceremonies of the Church of *England,* or take or subscribe the Oaths and Articles made and established in that Behalf: And for that the same, by reason of the remote Distances of those Places, will, as we hope, be no Breach of the Unity, and Conformity, Established in this Nation; Our Will and Pleasure therefore is, and We do by these Presents for Us, Our Heirs, and Successors, Give and Grant unto the said *Edward* Earl of *Clarendon, George* Duke of *Albemarle, William* Earl of *Craven, John* Lord *Berkeley, Anthony* Lord *Ashley,* Sir *George Carterett,* Sir *John Colleton,* and Sir *William Berkeley,* their Heirs and Assigns, full and free Licence, Liberty and Authority, by such Ways and Means as they shall think fit, To Give and Grant unto such Person any Persons, Inhabiting, and being within the said Province or Territory, hereby or by the said recited Letters Patents, mentioned to be granted as aforesaid, or any Part thereof, such Indulgencies and Dispensations, in that Behalf, for, and during such Time and Times, and with such Limitations and Restrictions, as they the said *Edward* Earl of *Clarendon, George* Duke of *Albemarle, William* Earl of *Craven, John* Lord *Berkeley, Anthony* Lord *Ashley,* Sir *George Carterett,* Sir *John Colleton,* and Sir *William Berkeley,* their Heirs, or Assigns, shall in their Discretion think fit and reasonable. And that no Person or Persons, unto whom such Liberty shall be given, shall be any way molested, punished, disquieted, or called in question for any Differences in Opinion or Practice, in Matters of Religious Concernment, who do not actually disturb the civil Peace of the Province, County or Colony, that they shall make their abode in. But all and every such Person and Persons, may from Time to Time, and at all Times, freely and quietly have and enjoy his and their Judgment and Consciences, in Matters of Religion, throughout all the said Province, or Colony, they behaving themselves peaceably, and not using this Liberty to Licentiousness, nor to the Civil Injury or outward Disturbance of others. Any Law, Statute or Clause contained, or to be contained, Usage or Customs of our Realm of *England* to the contrary hereof in any wise, notwithstanding.

And in Case it shall happen, that any Doubts or Questions should arise concerning the True Sense and Understanding of any Word, Clause, or Sentence, contained in this Our present Charter, We Will, Ordain, and Command, that at all Times, and in all Things, such Interpretations be made thereof, and allow'd in all and every of Our Courts whatsoever, as Lawfully may be Adjudged most Advantageous and Favourable to the said *Edward* Earl of *Clarendon, George* Duke of *Albemarle, William* Earl of *Craven, John* Lord *Berkeley, Anthony* Lord *Ashley,* Sir *George Carterett,* Sir *John Colleton,* and Sir *William Berkeley,* their Heirs and Assigns, although Express Mention, *&c.*

Witness our Self at *Westminster,* the Thirtieth Day of *June,* in the Seventeenth Year of our Reign.

Per Ipsum Regem.

A N

ABSTRACT

OF THE

CONSTITUTION

OF

Carolina

A s to the Government of *Carolina,* the Laws of *England* are there in Force; yet the Lords-Proprietors, by their Deputies, have Power, with the Consent of the Inhabitants, to make By-Laws for the better Government of the said Province; so that no Law can be made, or Money rais'd, unless the Inhabitants, or their Representatives, consent thereto: One Law which they have in South-*Carolina* deserves particular Mention, which is, their Method of chusing Juries, it being done by making a considerable Number of Paper-Billets, on which are written the Names of as many of the most substantial Freeholders. These Billets are put into a Hat, out of which Twenty-four are chosen by the next Child that appears. Then, out of those Twenty-four, Twelve are chosen at the next Court, after the same manner; which is an infallible way to prevent all Manner of Fraud.

North and South-*Carolina* Settlements are distant from one another some hundreds of Miles; so that Necessity compels each Colony to keep to themselves, a Governour, Council and Assembly. The Governor represents the Lord-Palatine; the rest of the Counsellors are the Lord-Deputies; who, of themselves, make a Palatines Court, and a Court of Chancery; wherein they pass several Orders of Council, much of the Nature of the Prince's Proclamation; which continues no longer in Force, than the next Assembly. Likewise, they grant several sorts of Commissions, Warrants, &c. yet Military Commissions lie wholly in the Governor's Power; but Making of War or Peace, in all, or the Majority of the Lords-Deputies; by whom (the Governor being one) it is determin'd, and by whose Commissions all other Magistrates act. On these Heads they have settled, and maintain an admirable Constitution of Government, for the lasting Peace, Security, and Wellbeing of all the Inhabitants. The way of any ones taking up his Land in *Carolina,* due to him either by Purchasing it of the Lords Proprietors here in *England,* who keep their Board at *Craven-House* in *Drury-Lane, London,* the first *Thursday* in every Month; or if purchas'd in *Carolina,* is after this manner: He first looks out for a Place to his Mind, that is not already possess'd by any other; then applies himself to the Governor and Lords Proprietors Deputies, and shews what Right he hath to such a Tract of Land, either by Purchase of the Lords in *England,* or by an Entry in the Surveyor-General's Office, in order to purchase of the Governor and Lords Deputies there in *Carolina,* who thereupon issue out their Warrant-Land as is due to him. Who making Certificate, that he had measured out so much Land and the Bounds, a Deed is prepared of Course, by the Secretary, which is sign'd by the Governor and the Lords Proprietors Deputies, and the Proprietors Seal affix'd to it, and register'd in the Secretaries Office, which is a good Coveyance in Law of the Land therein mention'd, to the Party and his Heirs for ever.

Thus have I given you as large and exact an Account of *Carolina,* as the Discovery of so few Years (in this great and extensive Land) would permit. Which flourishing Country will, doubtless, in time, increase the Number of its Productions, and afford us plentifully those Necessaries and rich Commodities, which the *Streights, Turky* and other Countries supply us withal at present and not seldom in their own Shipping; whereas, were those Merchandizes the Produce of an *English* Plantation, and brought us home by our own Hands and Bottoms, of what Advantage such an Improvement would be to the Crown of *Great-Britain,* and the People in general, I leave to Men of Reason and Experience to judge. I do intend (if God permit) by future Voyages (after my Arrival in *Carolina*) to pierce into the Body of the Continent,

and what Discoveries and Observations I shall, at any time hereafter, make, will be communicated to my Correspondents in *England,* to be publish'd, having furnish'd myself with Instruments
and other Necessaries for such Voyages.

For the better Understanding of this Country, I have already
drawn a very large and exact Map thereof, as far as any Discoveries have been yet made, either by others or my self, and have
spared neither Cost nor Pains, to procure the most correct Maps
and Journals thereof, that are extant in Print, or in Manuscript.
This Map containing nine Sheets of Imperial Paper, and now sit
for engraving, begins at Cape *Henry* in *Virginia,* 37 deg. N. Lat.
and contains all the Coasts of *Carolina,* or *Florida,* with the
Bahama Islands, great Part of the Bay of *Mexico,* and the Island
of *Cuba,* to the Southward, and several Degrees to the Westward
of the *Messiasippi* River, with all the *Indian* Nations and Villages, and their Numbers, which of them are subject to *Carolina,*
and trade with their People, what Places are convenient Factories and Forts, to increase and secure our Trade on the *Messiasippi,* and what Forts and Factories the *French* and *Spaniards* have
gain'd in those Latitudes, especially on the great River and the
Neighbouring Streams; all which they illegally possess, since the
very Mouth of the River *Messiasippi* is in the King of *England's*
Grant to the Lords Proprietors of *Carolina,* it falling something to
the Northward of 29 Degr. *North* Lat. whose Claim and Right I
question not, but a Peace will adjust, and restore, which every
Englishman is bound in Duty and Interest, to wish for; if we
consider how advantageously they have seated themselves,
whereby to disturb the Peace and Interest of all the *English*
Plantations on the Continent of *America.*

FINIS.

LETTERS FROM

JOHN LAWSON

TO JAMES PETIVER OF LONDON,

in the Sloane Collection

of the British Museum

Bath County on Pampicough River
North Carolina, April 12th, 1701
Recd. Aug. 4 1701 [another hand]

Good Sr.

I have sent you a letter dated from Albemarl County in North Carolina by wch. I design yr. advertismts. in order to for yr. collections of Animals Vegitables etc. I shall be very industrious in that Imploy I hope to yr. satisfaction & my own, thinking it a more than sufficient Reward to have the Conversation of so great a Vertuosi. I shall shortly goe for the Sea Board which voyage I hope will furnish me wth. shells (according to yr. Request to Mr. Bohun & Mr. Ellis whose letters of yrs. to them I have as for Cortez Elutheria I have laid onto & will use every means I possibly can to procure it butterflies, & other Insects you may depend on w'tever our new Settlement affords fish likewise—I cam about Xmas last to that place by land, from Ashley River in the lat. 32:45 for Okakro Inlet wch. this River runs to Sr. my Service to Major Golstead

I am yr. most devoted
att Commands
John Lawson

pray send me yr.
Opinion concerning the
Distillation of Spirits from Malt, molasses, figs, apples, Cherries, peaches etc wch. fruit we have plenty. My journal of my Voage through Carolina I shall send you when you desire Sr.

Adieu

Direct for me att pamplicough River in North Carolina to be left for me at Collonl Quarme's in Philadelphia, Pensilvania I shall (God willing) send you some collections by Octobr. by way of Pensilvania or Virginia.

Portsmouth [England] Jany. 11th 1709

Worthy Sr.

Excuse me for my neglect in not returning you due acknoledment for yr. kind present of Mr. Ray's book of Phisick, which I hope to make a suitable return, for soon after arrivall in America. The root I believe to be excellent in the collick, & a great carminative, yt.   in balls wth. ye   must needs retain their virtues being made up into balls as for ye Citron laudanum I have given some few drops to a poor Patient wch. did him a great kindness in giving him rest in a Delirium. I think these to be choice remedies & fit for transportation to our parts, the wind is northerly & I doubt we shall stay here longer than we wish for. therefore if you please to send some parcels for sale & ye price I doubt not but they will do great deal of good amongst us & answer yr. expectation in ye returns, if you will have money send [word?] or returned in any commodity ye Carolina or virginia affords. If you have none made up I desire you would send ye root Coming by One of our ships when I showd it to [him] he desired me to get him some & he would pay for it, but I could not re—— him of ye price if yr. last months memoirs be out pray send me one & half a dozen [corks] for ye vials, being quarts are to small to stop them, you may send them by ye Portsmouth Coach Monday next who ——— from ye White Hart in Southward. Our palatine Children do grow apace, we have lost above 40 already, they are chiefly very youngest ones, the men & women are generally in health. we are to be conveyed by Mr. Jno. Norris with a Squadron of 4 or 5 men of war & goe wth. ye first settled easterly wind. I shall call for it att ye coachmans on Tuesday night, but let it be directed to be left for me at Mr. Binkes Collector of Portsmouth. This is wt. I can think on att present until my arrival in America you shall my monthly observations wth. yr. Collections, those wth. respects to yr. selfe & all that ——— after me

Sr. I subscibe yr.

most humble Servant

John Lawson

If Mr. London would
oblige me wth. something by
the next Virginia fleet I shall not

forget to make him a grateful return. Direct to be left for me at Collonl James Wilsons in Ebroboth [York] Rr. in Virginia & by a James Rr. Ship if possible. I hope you will not forget ye grape seeds & Cork acorns. I desire of Juniper berries & Buckthorn berries of this years growth pr. ye Coach if possible pray sr. excuse this boldness.

N. Carolina Neus Rr. Xber. 30th 1710

Sr.

Excuse me not writing sooner wch. was by reason of my too much business. At that time I have sent a small box of Collections to Mr. William Williamson's att Kicquolan in Virginia in order to be sent to Mr. Dawsons for you & Mr. Bellers. I hope they are come safe to you by this time being they went from me in July last to Virginia. They had a direction to be left at Mrs. Mary Masons att ye white horse in Cannon Street Since wch. I have writt to my Correspondent in Virginia if not gone to direct them for you too to be left at Mr. Dawsons. In ye box are for you 4 vials of Insects all plants that are in yr. own paper those in ye white are for Mr. Fettiplace Rolley & all ye bird skins and snake skins they are preserved wth. a liquor he gave me & some few fossells being I have more of a collection for you. Ye preserving liquor is quite gone so that I can do nothing this winter to ye Water fowl wch. is a great loss in our Collections & missing all this Season I could not keep an exact Dyary As you & I proposed until July last when I began & shall very strictly continue ye year 1711 from ye first of January wth. ye weather & wt. our happens worthy of Notice in this Collony. This Winter here has been the finest weather I ever saw being equall to yr May to June. We have very plentifull crops of all grains & pulses, ect. & ye greatest mass of all sorts of acorns for swine that ever yet was known. The Swiss gentlemen have arrived safe wth. their people & go on bravely & will (in all probability) live very nobly in a little time, which they will make of ye Palatines I cannot guess being they are the most Sloathful people I ever yet saw above one half of them are dead of ye spotted fever wch. took them in the Ship fluxes & the Dropsy. When they are taken sick they go to bed & there lye until they dye or recover & cannot be persuaded to ye Contrary, although many of them were dispatched thereby. Above one half of them are dead, one reason & ye Chiefest was being they were twice as ought to have been in a healthful ship. The great ship I went in got safe into Virginia in about 9 weeks & we buried our Capt Carpenter & his mate & one passenger, & a great many palatines, one in 24 hours. The other Ship was taken on ye Coast by a Martinigo

man, a Sloop, who treated them very well. She came not in untill a
month after us. I hope ye next news I hear from you will be of a peace
which will be very welcome to all America. I found Virginia a little
sickly at my arrivall (wch. was about ye 25th of March last) both
them & Negro's but ye latter chiefly. I have not time now to write you
those observations I have made this year wch. my business would
admitt of but shall send you them in the next. Of every plant I intended to have gotten two, one of them to have kept myself that I
might have yr. Judgment upon each plant & sending one ye No.
thereof I might have been thoroughly acquainted therewith but ye
paper would not hould out besides you sent only large brown paper &
no small to collect in, & I find that many of our plants & tender
flowers lost their colours & beauty in brown paper, wch. may be
much better preserved in white as my own experience Inform-
me the bottles are too small & too narrow mouths for some large
snakes, etc. I can no ways preserve snakes, Lizards & small birds but in
Spirits. I had a curious liquor of Mr. Fettiplace Bellers that preserved
bird-skins very well it is all gone I have made a liquor of my own
which does it reasonably well wch. is aloes, myrrh, allom & tobacco
steept in rum. I take his to be something of that nature but it gives
them a shining varnish wch. mine does not pray get his recipe & speak
to him to send a quantity If God prolongs my dayes my Intention is
this.

To make a strict collection of all of plants I can meet withall in
Carolina always keeping one of a sort by me giving an account of ye
time & day they were gotten, when they first appearing, wt soil of
ground, wn. the flower seed & disapear & wt. individuall uses the
Indians or English make thereof & to have it enough of the same & to
let me know how near they agree to the European plants of ye same
species & how in they differ besides I would send seeds of all ye
physicall plants & flowers to be planted in England. As for the trees
the time they bred flower bring their ripe fruit & soil I hope to
Comply wth. most of them this year 1711.

Beast the most easy to discover fully their kinds for being they are not
many as the other tribes are.

Birds to procure all of this place both land & water fowls from ye
Eagle to the wren, to know if possible the age they arrive to, how &
where they build their nests, of what material & form, the coulour of
their eggs and time of their Incubation & flight, their food, beauty &
colour, of wt. medicinall uses if any. if rarily designedd to the Life,
this would Illustrate such a history very much, their musical notes &
cryes must not be omitted, wch. of them abide with us all ye

year & those that go away, and wt. strange birds tempestuous weather winds unusual seasons & other evidence affords us.

Fishes their species names here how far they agree with those of Europe & wherein not, their food usuall haunts best virtues time of breed & running to Scowne, as they call it, wt. are all ye year when in season which of them delight in salt water & of others in fresh streams, Lakes, ponds, springs, etc. wt. species are found in ponds that are often destitute of water in drye seasons whether spawn may be transported for propogating strange species of fish & how far.

Insects the months they appear to us in the places of their resort, how they breed & wt. changes they undergo, their food, makes, & parts this may be very well done by hav[ing] a many small Phyals or boxes wth. descriptions of every Insect contained in each bottle & when you receive them You may rank them on wyer pins in little drawers as you think fitt having yr notes constantly by you.

Fossills as Earths, shells, stones, Mettalls, Minerals, stratas, paints, Phisicall Earths, where & when found & what subterranean matters are yet discovered & wt. methods has been heretofore taken to discover & work mines of all sorts.

Of ye nature of Soyles & Lan wt. agriculture they are most fitt for as to Orchards, Gardens, grain, pasturage, Exotick plants, how they thrive & what Species may be expected to agree both with their Climate, as fruits, timber, trees for pleasure, grain of all sorts garden seeds & seeds of all usefull sorts, of grapes, of the nature & disposition of our spontaneous vines if they are to be melorated & made profitable and how wch is ye best way to bring in foreign viands that they may thrive whether by ye seed or by slips or roots. how fruit came first from ye seed to be melorated to ye perfection they are at now in Europe. I think grafting not so absolutely necessary in hott climates as in Cold, since ye best peaches & apples I ever have eat in Carolina came from ye seed wch. will not do (I presume) in great Brittain as to ye Vine a great help might be had from ye Event the planters of Madeira Cape of Good Hope & other new Collonies had in planting them, were we acquainted therewith of ye making wine its vapour & fermentation, the making of fruit as raissins, figgs, prunes, etc. on account of this kind would be extremely pleasant & profitable.

The present estate of such a new Country as this wh. weather each day & month affords in season for fruits, fish, fowl, etc. Their way of living, cooking, dayry, seasons of planting, reaping, Advancemt of trade, Increase of Stocke of cattle sheep etc wt. designs are in hand to Inrich ye country & wt. experiments have been made and how far they have answered ye design. Their buildings, fencing, fortifications &

improvemn'ts of barren lands, dredging of marshes & other improvements, wt ——— mountains, valleys, nations of Indians, naturall waters, springs, cataracts & other naturall varieties are discovered, wt. other accidents are of moment as to such who dyed & who recovered & wt. means was used for ye same either by the Xhain ? or Indian practitioners. I hope transactions hereby faithfully communicated to you & such Ingenious Gentlemen of ye Royal Society wth. their remarks on ye same will be a foundation towards a Compleat History of these parts wch. I heartily wish I may live to tell you ——— I shall be ready & glad at all times when I can wth. my ——— be anyways servicable towards compleating so good an undertaking I shall be glad at all time wn. opportunity sends, to hear from you & Mr. Roller & to have yr. Instructions Sr. I Recd yr. parcells of Physik wth. yr. printed papers but neither ye price of the former nor any Lr. fro you. Mr. Michell gave them to me att his arrivall. I must take the freedom to remember you of the promise in getting for me from Barcelona & other places you correspond wth. grape seeds, Cork acorns & fruits. My humble Service to Mr. London whom I am Collecting for and shall send them by the next Shipps & return him thanks for his civilities when in England, and am sorry we had not room in the Ship, to have taken them along wth. me

---

[Insert]
I have some more plants collected but of books being not full I omitt sending them untill compleated. Sr. pardon this freedom I take wth. you. I only tell you my Intentions & beg yr. Advice & am & shall ever Remain to the utmost of my power

Sr.
Yr. most humble Servant
to command
John Lawson

Mr. Pettiver
I would have you send your Bottles & paper to Mr. Danson, for I think I shall goe by Wednesday so want'em now to putt on board. If you'd please according to yr. promise to send me ye receipt for pickling wallnutts I should think my Selfe obliged to you and should be proud to see you before I goe aboard

I am yr. humble Servt.
John Lawson

Monday Morning 7 o'clock
from ye rose tree in

Cannon Street & Corner
of Abchurch Lane
please to send ye rect
in a penny post Letter &
direction where you [torn and missing]

July 24, 1711

Mr Pettiver

Sr. I hope long since you have Received ye Collection of plants & Insects in 4 vials wch I sent for you along wth. Mr. Fettiplace Boller's things directed to be left att Mrs. Mary Masons at the white horse in Cannon Street London I have now sent you by our Govrs. Lady one book of plants very slovingly packt up wch. I hope when you hear ye distracted Circumstances our Country has laboured under you will Excuse I have more collected at my home at Neus but could not send them to you now being I have not been there since January last I hope you have received all my Lrs. heretofore directed to you wch. I Refer my sel to & shall be extremely glad att all times of yr. Correspondence pray Sr. Excuse my brevity at this time wch. I cannot hinder but assure you I am at all times

Sr. Yr. most sincere Friend
& most humble Servt.
John Lawson

Vir July ye 24th 1711
   Rec Oct 20 1711
        ——
         12
Now here on business off
—— homewards this week
Anger Walbroke ye White
   Hart near Stock Markett [Part of these notes at bottom left had been trimmed when mounted]

JOHN LAWSON'S WILL[1]

No. Carolina

Bath Towne

IN THE NAME OF GOD, AMEN, ye 12th day of August 1708. I, John Lawson, of Bath Towne, in the Province of North Carolina, Gent., being of perfect mind & memory, thanks be given unto God therefore, calling to mind the mortality of my body & knowing that it is appointed for men once to dye, Doe make and Ordayne this my last will and testament, that is to Say, principally & first of all, I give a[nd] recommend my body to ye Earth, & my Soul to Allmighty God that gave it.

Impris., I give & bequeath to my Dearly beloved Hannah Smith, the house & Lott I now live in, to enjoy the same during her Naturall life & also one third part of my Personale Estate in No. Carolina to her proper Use & behoofe & for her to dispose of ye Same as She Thinks fitt.

Item, I give ye remainder of my Estate, both Personall & reale, to my Daughter, Isabella, of Bath Town and to the brother & sister (which her mother is w'th Child off at this present) to them Equally to Enjoy (vizt.) that Each of them two shall Enjoy & inheritt alike an Equall part of all my Estate that I dye Possessed of, the Land to be parted & devided when they shall arrive att twenty one years of age or Marry. And if it shall please God that her Mother, Hannah Smith, shall have more than one Child at a Birth, which she is now with Child off, that then, every Child of hers by me shall Enjoy an equall part of my Estate.

1. J. Bryan Grimes, comp., *North Carolina Wills and Inventories: Copied from Original and Recorded Wills and Inventories in the Office of the Secretary of State* (Raleigh: Edwards & Broughton, 1912), 280–81. The original will is missing, but it is recorded in Will Book, 1712–22.

And [I] Doe hereby Constitute, make & Ordayne ye Commis' of ye Court of Bath County w'th Mrs. Hannah Smith, the Ex'rs. of this my last will and Testament all & Singular my lands tenem'ts & Messauges, & I doe hereby utterly disallow, revoke & disannull all & every other former Testaments, Wills, Legacy's & Bequests & Exrs. by me in any way before named, Willed & bequeathed, ratyfying & Confirming this & no other to be my last will & testament.

In Witness whereof, I have hereunto Sett my hand & Seal ye day & Year above Written.

JOHN LAWSON (Seal)

Signed, Sealed, published &
declared by ye sd. John Lawson,
as his last will & testament in the
presence of us ye Subscribers:
   WM. W. HAWKOCK
   RICH'D SMITH
   JAMES LEIGH
Recorded in Will Book No. 2, page 98, office of
the Secretary of State, Raleigh, N.C.

INDEX

INDEX

A

Abbott's Creek, xiii. *See also* Rocky River

Abstract of the Constitution of Carolina, 264–66

Account of the Founding of New Bern, by Von Graffenried, quoted, xxviii

"Account of the Indians of North Carolina," by John Lawson, 172–233

Achonechy, 62. *See also* Occaneechi

Acorns, 33, 51, 74, 75, 77, 88, 99–100, 129, 145, 153, 182, 226, 269

Adams, Percy G., *Travelers and Travel Liars,* lii

Adshusheer, Indian village, xiv, 61–63

Adultery, among Indians, 41–42

Advantages of Carolina, 94

Adventure, ship of William Hilton, 79

Age, of Indians numbered by winters, 240

Aged, Indian respect for, 43

Agriculture, xliii, 80, 131, 271. *See also* Crops, Farming

Ague, 92, 229

Albemarle, County of, xxxix, 69, 103, 224, 267

Albemarle, Duke of, xxiv, 3

Albemarle Sound, 80, 103

Alcoholic drinks, 18. *See also* Rum

Alder, 74, 107

Alderson, Simon of Bath, xxii

Aldgate, London, 95

Allen, Matt H., quoted on Lawson's death, xxxiv

Alligators (Allegators), 58, 131–33, 146, 204; eaten by Indians, 58; teeth used for chargers for guns, 133

Allspice tree described, 110

Almond pine, 104

Alum (Allum), 270

Alumni Cantabrigienses, cited, xvii

Alumni Oxonieses, cited, xvii

Amazons, 45

America, xi, xvii, xxxvii, xlii, 3, 5, 9–11, 18–19, 25, 28, 42, 51, 81–84, 91–92, 111, 118, 147–48, 150, 161–62, 166, 168–73, 175, 190, 201, 214, 224, 230, 232, 244, 268, 270

American Antiquarian Society *Proceedings,* cited, xvi

Americanischer Wegewiser . . . , Johann Rudolff Ochs, xl, lii

Ammunition, 22, 27, 61, 206, 220. *See also* Guns

Amputation practiced by Indians, 229

Angel fish, 156, 159–60

Angelica, 83

Angling rods for fishing, 107

Animals, xli–xlii, 166–67, 229, 231, 267,

Anise, 83

Anne, Queen of Great Britain, xxvi, 215

Antidotes for snake bites, 84

Antimony, 89

Appalachian Mountains, 52. *See also* Mountains

Apparel, 20, 70. *See also* Clothing, Dress

Appetites of Indians, 216

Apple, maycock, 102

Apples and apple trees, 113–16, 119, 146, 271, 267

Appleton's Cyclopedia of American Biography, quoted, xvi

Apothecaries, xli, xvi. *See also* Petiver, James

Apprenticeship of John Lawson in London, xvi

Apricots and apricot trees, 116

Archaeologists and archaeological research, xiii, 56

Arithmetick, Indian game of, described, 178–80

Arrows, 28, 38, 63, 75–76, 80, 107, 209, 216, 218,

Arrowwood tree, 107

Artichokes, ground, 83

Asarum, 84

Ashe, S. A., *Biographical History of North Carolina*, xv, xl

Asheboro, 56

Ashley, Maurice, Lord Proprietor of Carolina, 3

Ashley River, South Carolina, 8, 14, 20, 24, 48, 267

Ash tree, 74, 100

Aspen, (Aspin), 106

Asthma, 231

Atlantic Ocean, 6, 16, 17, 21, 68

Attitudes of whites toward Indians, 243

Augurs, 170

Aurea Virga (Golden Rod), 48, 84

Avendabaugh, Indian village of, 16

Axes, xx, 94, 170

B

Babies, Indian, 196–97

Babylon, 80

Backhook Indians, 30

Bacon, bear meat, 121

Bagnios, 55

Bald eagle, 222

Baldface, waterfowl, 141, 155

Balm, 83

Balsam from cypress used in treatment of wounds, 103

Baltimore, Lord, of Maryland, 149

Baltimore bird or oriole, 141, 149

Bamboo, described, 107

Banister, John, Virginia botanist and author, xli, 84

Banquet-house, Indian, 42–43, 86, 182

Barbadoes, West Indies, 8, 79; explorers from, describe Cape Fear region, 79

Barbarities, Indian, xxxvi, xxxvii, 242

Barbary coast, 93

Barbary quinces, 115

Barbecue (Barbacue), from venison, 25, 42, 118, 163

Barbecued (Barbacued) peaches, 24

Barberry, 117

Barbout, fish, 163–64

Bark, Indian uses, 17, 68, 70; as drugs, 17; tanning, 24; in burial, 28; cabins, 42, 180

Barley, 24, 81, 166; cakes from, 24

Barracuda, 158

Barrels, 16, 103, 221, 224; staves, 99

Barrow, William, of Bath, xxii

Barter, for furs, 18

Basil (Bazil), 83

Baskets, 34, 75, 77, 195–96, 217

Bass, 72, 156, 160, 217. *See also* Rockfish

Bassett, J. S., historian, quoted, xxi, xxxvii

Bastard Spanish oak, 99

Bastardy, xxxvii

Bath, town of, xxii; town commissioners of, xxii, xxiv, xxxvii, xl, 119, 168, 274

Bath County, xxii, xli, 67, 267, 275

Bathing, Indian, 17, 48, 55, 200, 226

Bats, 130, 131

Bawds, 41

Bayberry, 97

Bays, 16–17, 101, 103, 214

Bay tree, 32, 70, 74, 97, 102

Beads, xiii, 24, 27–28, 47, 76–77, 184, 225. *See also* Money

Beans, 24, 82, 178

Bear, 17, 28, 31, 44, 54, 59, 61–62, 120–23; meat, 44; oil used as medicine, 28, 31, 62, 122, 201, 216

Beards and mustaches, worn by Indians, 58

Bear hunting, 122, 219

Bearmouse, described, 120, 131

Bear River Indians, 211, 242

Bear skins, 200

Beasts, xliii, lii, 33, 39, 89, 92, 166, 182, 196, 204, 210, 217, 220; "Beasts of Carolina," 120–31

Beasts of prey, 33

Beatty, R. C., and Mulloy, W. J., translators of *William Byrd's Natural History of Virginia,* liii

Beaufort, Henry, Duke of, Lord Proprietor of Carolina, 3

Beaver, 100, 120, 125; traps, 54; tail for food, 66; dams of, 125; skins and furs, 200–1

Bed-fellow, desire of whites for Indian, 46

Beds and bedding, 22, 121

Beech, 74, 80, 101; nuts for pigs, 101

Beef and beef cattle, 70, 87–88, 166–67, 182

Beef, buffalo, 121

Beer, 8; from cedar berries, 97; from corn, 81

Bees, 149

Beets, 83

Beetles, 139, 143

Belgium, 26

Belief, Indian, that world is round, 219

Bells, 44, 148; used in war dances, 148

Bell's Island, South Carolina, xii, 14

Bellyache, and how treated by Indians, 27, 229

Bennett's Creek, Indian village, 242

Bergamot, 114

Berkeley, Edmund and Dorothy Smith, *John Clayton: Pioneer of American Botany,* quoted, xli, xliii

Berkeley, William, Lord Proprietor of Carolina, 3

Bermudas sails, 17

Bermudians, 70, 97, 160

Bern, Switzerland, xxvi, xl, liii, 214

Berries, 17, 37, 147, 153. See also names of varieties

Bezoar, stone, 54; for medicine, 129

Big Alamance River, xiv

Bilberries, 217. See also Blueberries

Bills of exchange, 167

Bindweed, 147

Birch, 106, 111

Birds, xli, xliii, lii, liii–liv, 48, 52, 70, 92, 112, 130, 166, 196, 203, 210, 270, 271; "Birds of Carolina," 140–55

Birth control practiced by Indians, 194

Birth rate of North Carolina settlers, 91

Biscuit (Bisket), 61

Bittern, 141, 151

Blackamoor's teeth, shell fish, 218

Blackberries, 34, 110,

Blackbird, 140

Black bread, 81

Black cherries, 116

Black flusterer, bird, 141, 152

Black fox, 201

Black grape, 108, 117

Black gum, 102, 221

Black House, Indian village, 29

Black oak, 99

Black truncheon snake, 131, 136

Black walnut, 105

Blankets, 185, 224, 227

Bleeding, how Indians stopped it, 229

Blocks, 100

Blood cleansing, by quince drink, 115

Bloodletting and purification, 101, 223

Bloodstone, 37

Blount, John Gray, papers, xxiv

Blueberries, 34

Bluebird, 141, 148

Bluefish, 156, 159

Blue peter, waterfowl, 141

Bluestone, 56

Bluewings, bird, 141, 152

Boards, 74, 88. See also Planks

Boats, 74, 75, 76, 103, 106, 135. See also Ships

Bobart, Jacob, English botanist, xliii

Bogs, 32. See also Swamps, Pocosins

Bole, 38, 88

Bonavis, peas, 82

Bonito (Boneto), 155, 159

"Bonny, Bonny," cry of Indians, 76, 77

Booms, 103

Borage, 83

Botanical Garden, Fulham Palace, London, xli

Botanists and botany, xvi, xli, xliii, 84, 169

Bottled nose delphin, 155, 158. *See also* Dolphin

Bottles, 272

Boundary dispute with Virginia, xx, xviii, xix, xxii,

Boundary line commissioners, xliv. *See also* Moseley, Edward; Lawson, John

Bowls, 14, 101, 217

Bows, 28, 38, 76, 80, 106, 109, 209, 216, 218. *See also* Arrows

Bowsprits, 103

Box trees, 34

Boxwood, 97

Boyd, Thomas, appraiser of Lawson's estate, xxxix

Boyd, W. K., historian, cited, xv, xxii

Brant, waterfowl, gray and white, 141, 151, 154

Bread, 8, 24, 30, 34, 42, 50, 62, 81

Bream, 156, 161

Breeches, 200

Brice, William, an incorporator of Bath, xxii

Bricks, 8, 21, 170; houses of, 8, 21; how made, 89

Brickell, Dr. John, *Natural History of North Carolina,* lii

Bridles, 95

Brigantines, 68. *See also* Boats, Ships

Brimstone, 223

Brimstone snake, 131, 139

British Museum, letter from quoted, xvi, xli, xliii

Broadcloths, 94

Brothel houses of Indians, 41. *See also* Adultery

Brough Hall, Yorkshire, England, xv–xvi

Brown lizard, 131, 139

Brunswick quinces, 115

Brussels sand, 37

Bry, Theodore de, illustrations, 179, 181, 183, 186, 191, 198, 199, 202

Bubbling springs, xii

Buckskins, 47, 204

Buckthorn berries, 269

Buckwheat, 82, 166

Buff, from buffalo skin, 121

Buffalo, 54, 120–21. *See also* Beef

Bugloss, 83

Building materials, 170

Buildings, 8, 24, 87, 271. *See also* Houses

Bullfinch, 141, 148

Bullfrog, 137

Bull neck, waterfowl, 141

Bull's Island, South Carolina, xii, 14, 16

Bulrushes, 42, 78, 182, 196

Bunch grapes, 108

Bunting lark, 140

Burial customs, Indian, xiii, 28, 66, 185, 221

Bush, fig, 116

Bushel beans, 82

Burdock and its use in medicine, 84

Burke's *Baronetage,* cited, xvi

Burmillions, 83

Burnet, 83

Burning, at stake, xxxvi; of prisoners alive, 207; in medicine, for certain diseases, 228

Burns, how treated by Indians, 84, 226

Burras, John, xxii

Burrington, George, Governor of North Carolina, xviii

Butter, 50, 88, 166, 200

Butterflies, xli, 129, 139, 267

Byrd, William, of Virginia, xxi–xxii, xxxvi, xxxvii; *Natural History of Virginia,* liii

C

Cabbage, 83

Cabins of Indians, description of, 25, 27, 29, 52, 103, 180, 182, 185, 217, 221–23, 241

Cakes, 182, 217

Calavancies peas, 82

Cambridge University, xvii

Camden, South Carolina, 38

Camomile (Camomil), 84

Canada, 5

Candles, how they were made, 97, 129

Cane and reeds, their uses, 17, 77, 107, 185, 196, 204, 218, 229

Canoes, construction of and uses, xii, 13–14, 16, 19–22, 66, 75–76, 78, 91, 103–4, 127, 213, 221–22, 243

Cape Fear (Cape Fair), 55, 62, 68, 72, 78, 87, 167

Cape Fear River, 53, 60, 72, 79, 121, 146

Cape Fear Inlet, 152
Cape Fear area, described by William Hilton, 79
Cape Hatteras, described, 71
Cape Lookout, described, 72, 174
Captives, of Indians scalped, 177
Caraway (Carawa), 83
Carduus benedictus, 83
Carlisle Bay, Barbados, 79
Carminiatives, 268. *See also* Drugs, Medicines
Carolina, xi, xxiv, xxvi, xxxix, xliii, 3, 6, 7, 9, 19, 32, 58, 61, 63, 68, 70, 81–82, 84–87, 92, 95, 99, 104, 115, 132, 139, 142, 144–45, 150–51, 153, 160, 162, 164–67, 171–72, 187, 196, 201, 203, 208, 214, 226, 230, 267, 268; 1665 charter of, 249–63; map of, xxxix
Carp, 156, 163
Carpenters, 94, 170
Carraway Creek, xiii
Carriage, of Indian women, 59
Carrot, 82
Cart-naves, 102
Carteret, George, Lord Proprietor of Carolina, 3
Cartwright, John, Surveyor for North Carolina, xviii
Cary (Carey), Thomas and Rebellion, xix, xxiv, xliv, 14
Cashaw, 83
Cassena tree, 230. *See also* Yaupon
Cassetta, Indian, cabin of, 34
Catamount, described, 120, 123
Catawba (Kadapahaw) Indians, xii–xiii, 46, 49–50
Catawba River, xiii, 49
Catbird, 141, 148
Catechna, Indian village, xxxii–xxxiii
Catfish, 156, 163
Cathartics, 160. *See also* Drugs, Medicine
Catnip (Nep), 83
Cats, 131
Cattle, 10, 11, 14, 23, 69, 78–80, 86–88, 98, 107–8, 119–21, 200, 271; ranges for, 34, 65
Cauliflower, 83
Cavallies, fish, 156, 159
Cavalry, South Carolina, 10
Caves, 57

Cedar, bark and berries, 10, 97, 102, 180; beer, 97
Ceremonies, Indian, 219. *See also* Feasts, Dances
Chalybeate (Chalybeat) water, 89
Chandler, John, John Lawson apprenticed to, xvi
Channel, Cape Fear River, 78
Character of settlers, 90
Charleston, South Carolina, xi–xii, 8, 13, 17, 21, 24, 31, harbor described, 8; Huguenot Church, 9
Charlotte, North Carolina, xiii
Chastity of Indian women, 193
Charter of Carolina, 1663 boundaries, xix; 1665 boundaries, xix; Second Charter, 249–63
Chatooka, town, xviii, 66
Chatooka (Chattookau) River, branch of Neuse, 66
Cheating of Indians by whites, 244
Cheese, 88, 116; apples, 114
Chenco, Indian game, 62
Cherokee Mountains, liii
Cherries, 109–10, 111, 116, 267
Chesapeake Bay, xxxix, 174
  pin) trees and nuts, 24, 34, 105,
Chestnut, 58, 99, 105–7, 109
Chestnut oak, 51, 98–99
Chickanee Indians, xii, 38. *See also* Wateree Indians
Chicken snake, 138
Chief Justice of North Carolina, xviii, xx, xxvi. *See also* Gale, Christopher
Chiefs, Indian. *See* Kings, Indian
Childbirth among Indians, 91, 196, 192
Children, Indian, docility of, 91
Chinquapin (Chinkapin, Thinkapin) trees and nuts, 24, 34, 105, 109, 118
Chirurgery, 26, 97. *See also* Medicine
Chives, 83
Chocolate, 100
Chowan River, v, xxvii, 80
Chowan (Chuwon) Indians, 226, 242; precinct, 69
Christians and Christianity, in Carolina, xxx, 6, 11, 19, 44, 45, 52, 80–81, 90, 145, 171, 188, 192, 200–1, 211, 214, 232, 240, 242, 244–45

Christmas, Indian name for, 241
Church of England, xvii, 171
Church of Geneva, 20
Cid, community in North Carolina, xiii
Cider, 114–15, 167
Circumcision practiced by Machapunga Indians, 219
Citron laudanum, xlii, 268
Clam, shellfish, 16, 156, 164
Clapboards, 99
Clarendon County, present, South Carolina, 24
Clarendon River, 53, 79, 146. See also Cape Fear River
Clary, 83
Clay, 56, 76, 88; 201, 217; for bricks and tile, 88
Clayton, John, Virginia botanist, xli, xliii–xliv
Climate, of Carolina, 8, 17, 25, 86, 93, 168, 170, 271
Clergy, 5
Clerk of court, Lawson, xxiv
Clothes (Cloaths), 167, 197
Clothing of Indians, 18, 20, 25, 31, 39, 94, 212
Clothmaking, 90
Clove-gilly (july) flower, 84
Clovergrass, 170
Coal mine in Virginia, 90, 119
Coast and coastal section, xiv–xv, xl, xxxix. See also Seacoast
Cockle, 10, 156, 164, 218
Cocks, how prepared for eating, 62
Cocoa, synthetic, from acorns, 99–100
Codlin apple, 113, 114
Coe, Joffre, 56
Coemtha, xxxii
Coffee, 98
Coffins, Indians, made of cedar, 103, 185, 221
Cogs (Coggs) for mills, 105
Cohabitation of whites with Indians, 46–47. See also Adultery
Coins, English, 69
Coleworts, 83
Colic (Cholick), xliii, 36, 101, 268; treatment for, 101
Colic (Cholick) root, xlii
Collins, Richard, xxii
Cologne, 56

Colonial Records of North Carolina, xix–xxlv, xxvi, xxxi
Colonies and their problems, xxvi, 118
Collections of Lawson, 269
Collectors, in Albemarle, 103
Colleton, John, Lord Proprietor of Carolina, 3
Columbines, 83
Columbus, 25
Comfrey, 83
Comments on Cape Fear region by New England settlers, 79
Commissioners of Bath, xxii
Commissioners of North Carolina-Virginia boundary line, xix–xxi
Commodities of Carolina, 8–9, 27, 86, 92, 94, 178
Compton, Henry, Bishop of London, xli, 84
Conch (Conk), 16, 164. See also Shells
Concord, North Carolina, xiii
Congar eels, 155, 161
Congaree Indians, xii, 23, 31, 33–35, 37–38, 46, 48, 57
Congaree River, xii, 21
Congaree Town, xii, 33
Conjurers and conjuration, 27, 30, 55, 211, 219, 221–25
Connamox Indians, 242
Constancy of Indian women, 190
Consumption, 91, 167. See also Disease
Contentnea Creek or River, xiv, xxxiii
Contusions, Indian treatment of, 230. See also Medicine
Convoy system, 94, 167
Cony, 73. See also Rabbit
Cookery, Indian, 24, 42, 58. See also various vegetables, fish, fruit
Cooper River, South Carolina, 8, 9, 13
Coopers, 94
Coots, 141, 152, 155. See also Fowl
Copper, 89, 201,
Coranine Indians, 209, 242. See also Core (Coree) Indians
Core (Coree) Indians, xxxiii, 174
Core Sound, 164
Coriander, 83
Cork acorns, 272
Cormorant, 141, 154

Corn, 23–24, 30, 35, 39, 45–46, 59, 65–66, 70, 77, 80–81, 88, 101, 121, 126, 166, 177, 216–17, 227, 269; fields, 56, 76, 82, 130, 143, 221; destroyed by crows, 143. *See also* Maize

Corn bread, 216

Corn harvest dance, 177

Corn mill, 79

Corn snake, 131, 138

Cornwall County, England, 7

Correction, Indian house of, 241

Cortex Peruvianus, 109. *See also* Medicine

Cortez, Elutheria, 267

Cor Tom, King of Coree Indians, xxxiii

Cotechny, Indian town, xxxiii

Cotton and cotton cloth, 90, 166, 167

Council, Carolina, xix, xviii, 211; of England, xxi; of Indians, 204; of Virginia, xx–xxi; of war (Indian) 204

Courtesans, 25, 26. *See also* Mistresses

Courtship, Indian, 45, 47

Country of souls, 187

Cow dung and its use, 83

Cowes, England, xi, 7

Crab, 126, 156, 164

Craft, sailing, 21, 51

Craftsmen, 94–95

Crampois (Grampois), fish, 155, 158

Crane, 23, 25, 73, 79, 141, 149–50. *See also* Storks

Crane Island, 78

Crawfish, 66, 156, 165, 218

Craven, William, Lord Proprietor of Carolina, 3

Craven House, London, xxxix

Craven Precinct, xxxvii

Creeks, xiii, xv, xviii, xl, 16–17, 21–22, 50–51, 54, 63, 67, 83, 86, 103, 150, 154, 170, 222, 226

Cribs, Indian, described, 23

Crimes, among Indians, 27, 169. *See also* Murder, Theft, Witchcraft

Criolos, 25

Cripples, rare among Indians, 176

Croaker, fish, 156, 161

Crocodile, 132. *See also* Alligator

Crops, in North Carolina, 269. *See also* Agriculture, Corn, and other individual crops

Crow, 127, 140, 143, 148

Crown, of England, xx, 9

Cruelty of Indians to captives, 207

Cuckholds, 195

Cuckoo, 141, 148

Cucumber, 83, 182

Cumin (Cummin), 83

Cumming, William P., *The Southeast in Early Maps,* xxxix; quoted, xl

Curaçao, Dutch West Indian island, 10

Cures, performed by Indians, 84, 90, 226, 228–29

Curlew, 16, 79, 141, 151

Currant, 110, 112, 116, 271

Currents of rivers, 19

Currituck, bar and harbour, 70; inlet, 68, 157; sound, 68, 70

Customs, Indian, 58, 219, 221, 241

Customs duties, 168

Cutlass, 59

Cutlery ware, 95

Cygnet, 150

Cypress trees, 16, 20, 24, 28, 74, 97, 103; bark for cabins, 180, 215

D

Dace, fish, 156, 163

Dairying, Indian. *See* cattle

Damson plum, 111, 116

Dances, of Indians, 44–45, 177–78

Daniel, Robert, Landgrave and Governor of South Carolina, xxii, 211

Danson, John, Lord Proprietor of Carolina, 3

Darien, Isthmus, ship from, 14

Daughters of Thunder, 43

Daw, Nicholas, of Bath, xxii

Death, Indian attitude toward, 185, 187, 219–21

Deck gun, 69

Decoctions, 226. *See also* Medicine

Deep River, xiv

Deer, 14–15, 17, 20, 33, 44, 54, 58, 66, 73–74, 98, 124, 182, 187, 200, 215, 217, 219, 227, 231

Deer skins, 29–30, 39, 66, 70, 76, 88, 166, 178, 180, 188, 203, 216, 224, 232; as money, 203. *See also* Money

Delirium, Indian treatment of, 268

Deluge, Indian idea of flood, 172

Depre, David, resident of Bath, xxii
Dereham, Richard, resident of Bath, xx
Derwent, Yorkshire, England, 48
Description of Carolina, Lawson's account, 68–95
Description of North Carolina natives, 90–91
Devil, Indian idea of, 55
Devilfish, 155, 157
Dewberry, 110
Diabetes, Indian treatment of, 231
Diary of Lawson, xliii, 269
Dice, 178, 180
Dictionary of American Biography, xv, xvi
Dictionary of National Biography, xvi
"Dictionary of Speech of some Indian tribes of North Carolina," by Lawson, 171, 233–39
Die provinz, xl, lii
Dill, Alonzo, Governor Tryon and His Palace, xviii, xxvi–xxvii, 83
Dipper, bird, 141, 152
Discovery of North Carolina, 68
Direction points observed by Indians, 213
Disease, xxvii, xxx, xlii, liii, 17, 18, 25, 26, 34, 36, 54, 90, 91, 167, 196, 227, 268, 269. See also Distemper, individual diseases
Dishes, 217. See also Food
Dissenters, South Carolina, xviii, 9
Distemper, 17, 25, 34, 90–91, 196, 222, 225, 227, 229–32; of horses, 88
Distillation of spirits, 267
Diveling or swift, bird, 140, 149
Diver, waterfowl, 141, 153
Divorce among Indians, 40
Dix Island, South Carolina, xii, 14
Dock, 83, 84
Doctors, Indian xii, 20, 25–26, 54, 66, 188, 221–23, 225, 227, 230–31, 272. See also Medicine, Remedies, Practitioners
Dog, xviii, 10, 37, 44, 122, 130, 132; kennels, 30
Dogfish, 155, 158
Dogwood, 240
Dogwood tree month, 240
Dolphin, 155, 158. See also Bottlenoses

Domestic affairs of Indians, 91
Domesticated animals of Indians. See Dog, Horses
Dories, 20
Dormouse, 120, 131. See also Weasel
Drawers, chests of, Indian, 102. See also Furniture
Dredge, flower, 83
Dress of Indians, 44, 197, 200–1
Dress of troops, South Carolina, 10
Driftwood, 76
Dropsy and its treatment, xxx, 231, 260
Drugs, xlii, 17, 54, 88, 92, 166, 229, 233, 270. See also Medicine
Druggets, 94
Drums, 44, 62
Drum, fish, 159, 178
Drunkenness, of Indians, xxx, 18, 33, 210–12, 231, 240, 244
Dry walls, making of by Indians, 51
Duck, 16, 50, 74, 79, 133, 141, 152, 216
Dukeville power station, xiii
Durham, North Carolina, xiv, xix, 61
Dutch, inhabitants of New York, x–xi, 8; architecture, 8
Dwarf bay tree, 97
Dwarf pine, 104
Dwellings, Indian, 42, 180. See also Cabins, Houses
Dyes, 92, 97, 166
Dying of hair by Indians, 229

E

Eagles, 203–4, 210, 222; bald, 140, 142; gray, 140, 142
Early plan of Bath, xxiv
Earthenpots and earthenware, 95, 173
Earth for potter's trade, 89
Earths, 271
Earthquakes, 93
East India bat, 140
East Indies, 149
Economic history, liii. See also Agriculture, Industry, Trade
Eden, Land of, liii
Edenton, xix, liii
Editions of Lawson's book, xliv, l–liii
Education, xvii, 5, 9, 91, 243–44; of Indians, 57
Eel, 131, 139, 155, 161, 182, 225

Eel snake, 131, 139. *See also* Loach
Egg or chicken snake, 131, 138–39
Elecampane, 83
Elizabeth I, Queen of England, 68
Elk, 54, 120, 128
Elm, 100, 182
Embalming, Indian method of, 28
Emetics, 92, 229. *See also* Medicine
Emunctories, 90. *See also* Medicine
England, xv, xvi–xvii, xix–xx, xxvi, xxxiv, liii, 7–8, 18–20, 32, 34, 38, 50, 83, 88, 91, 96–97, 116, 127–29, 143–44, 149–50, 152, 154–55, 160–63, 168, 170, 196, 215–16, 218, 244, 268
English, people, xi, xii, xiv, xxiv, xxx, 10, 17–18, 21, 24, 25, 34–35, 42–43, 51, 56, 59, 61, 63, 66–67, 69, 78–80, 87, 92, 100, 106, 110, 127, 144, 147–48, 160, 163, 168, 170–71, 173, 176, 182, 192–93, 197, 200–1, 203, 211–212, 214, 216, 220, 222, 228, 232, 240, 244, 270
English currants, 110
English diseases, 227
English editions of Lawson's book, xl, xliv–lii
English language, 46, 240
Eno Indians, 61–66
Eno River, xiv, 63
Eno (Enoe) Will, Lawson's guide, xiv, 61, 62, 64, 66
Epidemics, Indian, 25. *See also* Diseases, Medicine
Esaw Indians, 46, 49, 146, 152. *See also* Catawba Indians, Kadapahaw Indians
Eugee, Monsieur, French planter in South Carolina, 20
Europe, 6, 9, 19, 25, 48, 52, 65, 81, 88, 93, 101, 142–45, 148, 152, 154, 161–62, 170, 173, 196, 243
European bean, 82
European grape, 108
Europeans, 17, 41, 57, 83, 90, 91, 115, 118, 127, 172–76, 178, 192–93, 196, 205–6, 208–9, 212, 229, 240
Evergreen oak, 97
Evergreens, 70, 96, 101–4; used in medicines, 229
Exorcism, Indian method of, 30. *See also* Conjurers

Exports, 88. *See also* Trade and traders

F

Fabian, Peter, of Barbados, 79
Fairs, Indian, 178. *See also* Trade and traders
Falcon, 140, 143
Fall of year in North Carolina, 94
Fallow deer, 120, 129
Falls of Neuse Creek (River), xiv, 64
Families, large in North Carolina, 91, 167
Farmers, advice to, 170
Farm implements, 170
Fatback, fish, 155, 160
Fauna of North Carolina, xv, liv. *See also* Animals, Birds, Fish and fishing, Fish of Carolina
Fawn. *See* Deer
Feasts, Indian, 42, 53, 177–78; of corn harvest, 42; funeral, 221
Feathers, Indian use of, 28, 44, 155, 197, 200–1, 203
Fecundity of women in North Carolina, 91, 165, 167
Fees, Indian, for cures, 226. *See also* Medicine, Doctors
Fences, 51, 59, 86, 99, 184
Ferry, xii
Fertility of Soil, xiv. *See also* Agriculture, Crops in North Carolina
Festination, 43
Festivals, Indian, 45. *See also* Feasts, Ceremonies, Dances
Feverfew, 84
Fevers, and Indian treatment of, 17, 24, 134, 229, 232, 269
Fidlars, 126, 156, 165. *See also* Crab
Fieldfare, bird, 48
Field peas, 82
Fields, corn, 221. *See also* Agriculture, Crops
Fig, 111, 116, 267, 271
Filbert nuts, 117
Filth of Indians, 180, 241
Finger fish, 156, 165
Fingernails, worn long by Indians, 176
Fire arms, 154
Fire making, Indian method described, 212
Firewood, 101, 106, 216

Fish and fishing, xli, xliii, lii, 7–8, 33, 38, 49, 51, 72, 78, 87, 92, 126, 152, 154, 155–65, 167–68, 182, 217–19, 221, 271; trade, 93; fried in bear's fat, 121; methods, 158–59, 161, 164, 218; Indian shooting with bow and arrow, 218; industry, 218, 220
Fisher, bird, 141–42
Fisherman, bird, 141, 153
Fisherman, waterfowl, 141
Fish (Fishing) hawk, 140, 142
Fish hooks, 57
Fish of Carolina, Lawson's account, 155–65
Fits, Indian treatment of, 66
Flanders, 26,
Flat Heads, name for Waxhaw Indians, 39–40, 197
Flatting, shellfish, 156, 165
Flatting apples, 114
Flax, and flax cloth 90, 120, 166–67, 215
Fleet, 19
Flemish brick buildings in New York, 8
Flies, 14, 30
Flints, used to make fire, 212
Flocks of pigeons and wild turkies, 146, 153
Flood, 12; Indian description of, 45
Flora, xv, liv. See also Plants
Florida, 98
Flos virginis, virginity, 41
Flounder, 156, 160
Flower gardens, 84–85
Flowers, 70, 85–86, 92, 270; listed, 84–85
Fluxes and treatment of, xxx, 269
Flyingbark hickory, 105
Flying squirrels, 130
Flying stags, 139
Food, 7, 23, 25, 33–34, 36, 39, 51, 58, 143, 150, 157, 167, 209, 216, 221; Indian food listed, 182–84. See also Cookery, names of plants and animals
Fording streams, 60
Forests, cleared, xxx; burned by Indians, 215
Forges, 90
Fort Motte, South Carolina, xii
Fort Raleigh, "Virginia," 69

Forts and fortifications, xi, xiii, 8, 52, 56, 271
Fort San Marcos, St. Augustine, Florida, 10
Fossils, xliii, 269, 271
Fountain fish, 156, 163
Fowl, 16, 51, 79, 87, 126, 130, 167, 182, 204, 271
Fowler, Henry W., Study on Fishes, 155
Fox, 120, 130, 201
Fox grapes, 108
Fox squirrels, 129
France, 5, 20, 118
Freedom, 11, 19, 87, 169, 264–66
Free stones, 48, 49, 56, 59
French Huguenots, in South Carolina, 9; in Virginia, 119
Frenchmen, xii, 17
French settlers in North Carolina, xii, 5, 10, 16, 19–20, 22–23, 25, 36, 90, 119, 158, 230
Freshes, 17, 21, 23
Fresh water fish, 156–63
Frogs, 131, 137, 149
Frontier, Carolina not a, 94, 168
Fruit and fruit trees, 57, 83, 86, 92–93, 108–16, 121, 126, 166–67, 170, 173, 182, 209, 216–17, 267, 271–72
Fruit bread, 217
Frows, 94
Fuel, 212. See also Wood
Fulham Palace, London, xli, 84
Fullers earth, 37, 88
Funeral ceremonies, of Indians, 28, 189, 221. See also Mourners
Fur, 8, 18, 39, 70, 88, 166, 184, 197, 201, 204, 211, 216
Furniture making, 102
Fuzee, 59

G

Gale, Christopher, Chief Justice of North Carolina, xx–xxi, xxiv, xxvi; quoted on Lawson's death, xxxvi
Gallberry oak, 97
Gallian, French planter in South Carolina, xii, 21, 22
Gambling, by Indians, 178, 212
Game, 17, 19, 20, 40, 54, 92, 184, 216–17, 219. See also Hunters and

hunting, names of birds and animals

Games, Indian, 34, 178–79

Gannet, 16, 141, 154

Gardeners, 169

Garden roots, 82

Gardens, 271

Garlic (Garlick), 83

Garters, Indian, 28, 121; of racoon, 126

Geese, 16, 23, 54, 79, 127, 141, 150–51, 154

General Assembly, xxii

Georgia, 11

German editions of Lawson, xxvii

German migration to America, xxxvii

Gibson, Captain, of Glasgow, 14

Gilbert, James, English iron-monger, 95

Girdles, 28, 121, 126, 137, 195; of raccoon, 126; of snake's skins, 137; of possum hair, 195

Glasgow, Scotland, 14

Glebe land, 171

Glover, William, leader of anti-Cary forces, xix

Gnats, 149

Goats, 56, 88

God, Indian idea of, 18, 57, 220–21, 227. *See also* Religion

Golden rod, 48, 84

Golden russet apple, 113–14

Goldsboro, North Carolina, xiv

Gonorrhea among Indians, 25; treatment of, 231

Gooseberry, 116

Goose Creek, South Carolina, French Church, 9

Goshawk, 140, 143

Gourds, and uses of, 28, 37, 44–45, 83, 111, 149, 178, 182, 223

Gout and its treatment, 167, 231

Government of North Carolina, xix, 9, 87, 140, 169, 201, 211–12, 244; *See also* Governors, individual governors

Government of Indian tribes, 42–43, 57, 204

Governors, xviii, xix, 5, 49, 170, 224, 226

Graffenried, Christopher Von (De), xxiv, xxvi–xxvii, xxx–xxiv, xxxvi; account of Lawson's capture and execution, xxxvi; account of the founding of New Bern, xxvi–xxxiii

Grafting fruit trees by Indians, 118, 271

Grain, 34, 39, 44, 81, 86–87, 166–67, 170, 269, 271. *See also* Corn, Wheat

Granary, 23, 30, 182

Grain mill, xxiv, xxx

Grampus (Crampois), 155, 158

Granite, 37. *See also* Marble, Rocks

Granville, Lord, 3

Grapes and grape vines, xxxi, lii, liii, 57, 74, 90, 108, 117, 118, 269, 271

Grass, 38, 52, 56, 73–74, 78, 170

Grasshoppers, 139, 143

Gravel, 24. *See also* Granite, Marble

Gravesend, England, xxvi

Graves of Indians, 188. *See also* Tombs

Gray squirrels, 129

Great black pied gull, 141, 154

Great Britain, xi, 9, 151, 215, 271

Great Falls, South Carolina, xii

Great gray gulls, 141, 151

Green lizard, 131, 136–37

Green plover, 140, 145

Green River, 73, 75

Greensboro, North Carolina, xix

Green snake, 131, 138

Green turtle, 138

Greenville, North Carolina, xiv

Grifton, North Carolina, xiv

Grigson apples, 114

Grimes, J. B., *North Carolina Wills and Inventories . . .* , xxxvii, 274

Grindle (Grindal) fish, 156, 163

Grind stones, 95

Gripes, treatment of, 101

Ground ivy, 84

Ground nuts, 182

Ground rattlesnakes, 131, 135

Ground squirrels, 130

Gruel, 35

Guard fish, 155, 160

Gudgeon, fish, 156, 162

Guide, Indian, xi–xii, xiv–xv, 13, 21, 23, 29, 37, 39, 46, 50, 54, 62–63, 72, *See also* Will, Eno; Scipio

Guinea corn, 82

Guinea slave ships, 94

Gulf of Mexico, 11

Gull, 16, 141, 151–52, 154

Gum tree and gums, 88, 217, 221, 229
Guns, 20, 22, 27–28, 38, 51, 55, 69, 76–77, 80, 92, 94, 175, 187, 208, 220; Indian skill with, 33

H

Haberdashers wares, 94
Hair, of Indians, 176
Hamburg editions of Lawson's book, xliv, xlv, xlviii, l
Hammers, 170
Hampton, Virginia, xxvii
Hancock, King of Tuscarora Indians, xxxiii
Handicrafts, 170, 175, 343–44. *See also* Arrows, Baskets, Bowls, Canoes, Clothes, Dishes, Drums, Girdles, Ladles, Mats, Music, Pipes, Spoons
Hangings by Indians, 220
Happy hunting ground, Indian idea of, 187
Harbors, 11, 13, 70, 167, 170
Hare. *See* Rabbit
Harrison, Nathaniel, Virginia boundary line commissioner, xx–xxi
Harriss, Francis Latham, Lawson's *History of North Carolina*, xvii, l, lii
Hart's-tongue, 84
Harvest of corn, feast, 42
Harvey, John, Governor of North Carolina, xx
Harvey apples, 113–14
Hatchets, Indian, 77, 209
Hats, 94, 122–23, 126, 200. *See also* Raccoon, Bear
Hatteras, Cape, 68; Inlet, 71–72; described by Indians, 69, 159, 242
Havens of North Carolina, 70. *See also* Ports
Haw Old Fields, 61
Haw River, xiv, 60–61
Hawks, F. L., *History of North Carolina*, xl
Hawk's bells, 45
Hawksbill turtle, 138
Hawthorn, 112
Haw tree, 112
Hayes, James, Lawson's master in London, xvi
Hazlenut, 109, 117
Head deformation of Indians, 39–40

Headings, 88
Health of Indians, 91, 231. *See also* Disease, Distemper, Medicine
Health Springs, South Carolina, xii
Heaven, Indian idea of, 187
Hecklefield, John, xxii
Hedge-coney, 127. *See also* Rabbit
Hedge sparrow, 141, 148
Heighwarrie River. *See* Uwharrie River
Hell, Indian idea of, 187
Hemlock, 107
Hemp, 90, 120, 166–67, 215
Herbs, 48, 83–85, 92, 120, 228. *See also* Drugs, Medicine
Hern (Heron), 141, 152
Herpes and treatment of, 102
Herring, 121, 156, 160, 218; herring-month, 240
Herring-tailed hawk, 140, 143
Hickerau, Indian village, 29
Hickory trees and nuts, 34, 104, 105, 109, 180, 173, 213
Hides, and their uses, 70, 88, 166. *See also* Deerskins, Bear skins, Raccoon
Hieroglyphics, Indian, 213
High-Land-Point, named by Barbadians, 75
High Point, 56
High Rock Lake, xiii
Hill country, xxxix, 89
Hillsborough, North Carolina, xiv, 59
Hilton, William, of Barbados, account of Cape Fear area, 70–79
Hilton's River, 75, 78
Historia plantarium, xli, 84. *See also* Ray, John
History of North Carolina, by John Lawson, 1714 ed., xv
Hobby, bird, 140, 143
Hoes, 81, 94, 170
Hogoo (relish), v, 176
Hogs, 16, 26, 34, 44, 51, 64–65, 82, 97, 105–6, 151, 167; stolen by Indians, 64
Holloman, Charles R., quoted, xviii
Holly, 74, 97, 106
Hominy meal, 182
Honey, 55; locust, 55, 104
Honeysuckle, 70, 96
Hook and Backhook Indians, 30
Hooper, bird, 141, 150

Horn, plant, 83
Hornbeam tree, 97, 101
Horn snakes, 131, 135
Horse-bells, 44
Horseradish, 83
Horses, 8, 10, 44–45, 49, 52, 54–56, 60, 69, 86, 87–88; Indian attitude toward, 44; prices of, 88
Hortus Siccus of English plants, xlii
Hospitality of Indians, 22, 167, 243; of planters, 70
Hot baths, 89
Housekeeping, by colonists, 92, 167; by Indians, 23, 76
Houseleek, 84
House rats, 130
Houses, 8, 20–21, 24, 100, 107, 224; of Indians, 65
Huckleberry, 34, 110, 153
Huger, Monsieur, French planter in South Carolina, 19–20
Hugh Town, Scilly Islands, 7
Hummingbird, 140
Humpbacked Indian, 65
Hunters and hunting, 7, 14, 29, 54, 64, 142, 176, 214–16, 220
Hunting quarters and grounds of Indians, xiv, xxx, 31, 184
Hurricane, Sept., 1700, 15, 24, 128
Hurts, 112
Husbandry and husbandmen in North Carolina, 69, 81. *See also* Agriculture
Husquenaughing young Indian men, 241
Huts of Indians, 23, 76. *See also* Cabins of Indians, Houses
Hyde, Edward, Governor of North Carolina, xxi, xxxiii, xliv
Hyssop, 83

I

Idea of future life, Indian, 58, 187
Idols and idolatry, Indian, 219, 244–45
Immigrants to England from Europe, xxvi
Implements, xxvi. *See also* Agriculture, Tools
Indians, v, xii–xv, xvii–xviii, xx, xxiv, xxx–xxxiv, xxxvi, lii, 5–6, 10, 13–14, 16–22, 24–25, 27, 30–35,

37–39, 40, 42–44, 46, 49, 54, 59, 69, 72, 75–80, 82, 87, 89, 92–93, 97–98, 100, 107, 109–12, 115, 121–22, 126, 130, 132, 134, 136–37, 146, 150, 152–53, 157–60, 162–66, 169, 172–76, 270, 272; trade and traders, xi, 93; men and women, xii, 20, 77, 189–90; towns and villages, xiii–xiv, xvii, 132, 150; words, xv, 233–39; kings, xxxii; torture by, xxxvi, 59; language, 36, 233–39; plantations, 38
Indian Fort, xiii
Indian grain, 166
Indian peaches, 116
Indian peas, 82
Indian pilot, 22, 33
Indian plum, 111
Indian tea, 98. *See also* Yaupon
Indian words, xv; list prepared by Lawson, 233–39
Indies, xvii, 7
Indigo (Indico), plant, 102, 166
Industriousness of French settlers in North Carolina, 19, 120
Infants, care of by Indians, 196–97, 204
Inflammations, treatment by Indians, 102
Inhabitants of North Carolina, 86
Ink-powder, 95
Inlets, 11, 68, 70–72, 152, 267
Insects, xli–xliii, lii, liv, 14, 23, 92, 126, 267, 269, 271, 273; defined and listed, 131–40
Instruments, musical, of Indians, 178
Interment of dead Indians, 28, 221. *See also* Sepulchres, Tombs
Ireland, lii–liii, 94
Irish linen, 163
Irishmen, fish, 163
Iron ore and iron tools, 32, 46, 69, 94–95, 89, 172–73, 203, 217
Irons, prisoners of Indians placed in, 234
Iroquoian Indians, 35, 50, 174, 195, 207, 231
Islands, 8, 75
Isle of Wight, England, 7
Italy, 93
Ivy, 84

J

Jack, Indian physician, 227

Jade, horse, 44

James River, Virginia, xxvii, 49, 90, 119

Jamestown, South Carolina, xii

Jamestown weed, 84

Jaupim Indians, 242

Jay bird, 140, 145

Jellyfish, 16

Jenner, Samuel, Swiss land speculator, liii

Jennings, Edward, President of Virginia Council, xx

Jennito (Seneca) Indians, 49–50

Jessamine, 70, 96, 101, 111

Jesuits, 119

Jewish customs among Machapunga Indians, 219

Jews, 244

Johnson, Sir Nathaniel, Governor of South Carolina, 117

Joiners, 94, 170, 175

Jones, Fred, quoted, xix, 6

Journal of Lawson's voyage to Carolina, xv, 6, 189, 267

Juniper berries and their use, 97, 269

Juniting apple, 113–14

Justice, fairly administered in North Carolina, 169

K

Kadapahaw Indians, xiii. See Catawba Indians

Katharine pear, 114

Kerseys, 94

Ketch, described, 8, 68

Keyauwee Indians, xiii, 53, 56, 57, 242; Town, xiii, 56; Jack, King of tribe, 227

Kickshaw, 109. See Mulberry

Kicotan, Virginia, 269

Kidnapping of Indians by whites, xxx–xxxi

Kidney beans, 82

Kingfisher, 141

King of England, xxxiv

Kings, Indian, xii, 27–29, 39, 42–43, 34, 54, 77, 204, 219–20, 223, 225, 241

Kingsnake, 131, 137

Knight, Tobias, appraiser of Lawson's estate, xxxix

Knives, and how used by Indians, 39, 212, 217

Kocherthal, Joshua, Das verlangte, xxiv

L

Labor and laborers in North Carolina, 20, 89, 92

Ladles, Indian, 64

Lady-finger apple, 114

Lakes, 21, 164, 244, 271

Lambs, 88; quarters, 83

Lampblack, 201

Lamprey eel, 155, 161, 182

Lancaster County, South Carolina, 39

Land in North Carolina, and its fertility, xx, xxi, xxiv, xxvi, xxvii, xxx, 6, 31, 33–34, 75, 87, 89, 244; sales at Bath, xxii; purchased for site of New Bern, xxvii; prices, 87, 170–71; purchases, 200–1

Land frog, 137

Landgraves in Carolina, 211

Landholdings, of Indians, 17; of Edward Moseley, xviii

Land of Eden, land tract in Virginia, liii

Land terrapins (Terabins), 138

Languages, Indian, list by Lawson, 233–39

Lapwing, 145

Lark, 141, 148

Lark-heel tree, 96, 106. See also Redbud

Latitude of North Carolina, 166

Laudanum, xlii, 268. See also Medicine, Drugs

Laurel, and its uses, 70, 97, 101

Lavender, 83

Law enforcement, problem of, xx, 19

Lawson, Andrew, father of John, xvi

Lawson, Isaac, scientist, xvi

Lawson, John, 4, 11, 17–19, 21, 30, 38, 40, 42, 55, 267, 269, 274–75; map by, x, xix–xl, 66, 68; biographical sketch, xii–liv; plan for Bath, xxiv; book by, and various editions, xix, xxvi, xxx, xl; letters to James Petiver, xxx, 267–74; trial by Indians, xxxiii–xxxiv; journal by, 13–67; will of, 67, 274–75; dictionary of English, Tuscarora, Pamlico, and Wocoon words, 233–39

Lawson's Creek, xviii

Lawson-Vischer Map, xl
Laziness of Indians, 38
Lead, 56–57, 89, 201; used by Indians to paint faces, 56
Leager ladies, 26, 49, 158
Leather, materials and uses, 197, 200, 228–29
Leather coat apples, 114
Lederer, John, explorer and author, xl
Lee, Philip, map maker, xxxix
Leeds, England, 61
Leeks, 82
Lefler, Hugh T., and A. R. Newsome, *North Carolina*, xviii, xxxi
Legends of Indians, 69, 226. *See also* Flood, Rattlesnake
L'Grand, Monsieur, French planter in South Carolina, 20
Leigh, James, 275
L' Jandro, Monsieur, French planter in South Carolina, 20
Lemma, 38
Lemnos, Island, 38
Lemons, 11
Lettuce, 83
Lexington, North Carolina, xiii
Liberty of North Carolina people, 169
Lice and how Indians killed them, 175
Licorice (Liquorice) plant, 104
Life, easy for settlers, 86, 87, 93; longevity of Indians, 91
Lightwood, use of, 217
Lilleloo, method of making, v, 30
Lime of oyster shells, 89
Limes, 11
Limestone, 89
Linen, 90, 94, 120, 200
Lion, 120
Liquor, 18, 93, 115, 167, 211, 270. *See also* Alcoholic drinks, Rum
Little Alamance River, North Carolina, xiv
Little fisher, 141, 152
Little gray gull, 141, 152
Live oak, 99–100
Livestock, 14. *See also* Cattle, Horses
Lixivium, 30. *See* Medicine
Lizard, 270
Loach, fish, 156
Loblolly, food, 35, 44, 45

Locust, insect, 139
Locust tree, 55, 104, 109
Lodges of Indians, xii. *See also* Cabins of Indians
Loggerhead turtle, 138
London, xvi, xxiv, xxvi, xxxvii, xxxix, xli, xliii
London, George, xli–xliii, 268
London, William, xli
London Society of Apothecaries, xvi
Long, Anthony, of Barbados, account, 70–79
Long black snake, 131, 137
Longevity of Indians, 91
Longstalk apple, 114
Loons, 141
Lords Proprietors of Carolina, xi, xviii–xx, xxvi, xxxiv, xxxvi, xxxix, 3, 9, 80, 87, 168, 170–71, 249–63
Loretto, pilgrimage to, 47
Lost Colony, reasons for failure, 68–70
Love making among Indians, 41, 45, 192–93
Ludwell, Philip, Virginia boundary line commissioner, xx–xxi
Luellyn, Dr. Maurice, of Bath, xxiv
Lues venera, 25. *See also* Gonorrhea
Lumber, 8, 88, 103, 166
Lupines, 96
Lynch's River, South Carolina, xii

M

McAtee, W. L., *The Birds in Lawson's New Voyage to Carolina,* 140
Machapunga Indians, 209, 211, 219, 242
Mackerel, 155
Madeira, 88, 119
Madison, James, xlvi
Maggots, 128
Maidenheads, 40. *See also* Virginity
Maize, 30, 44, 81–82, 121, 167, 177, 182, 217. *See also* Corn, Grain
Marjoram, 83
Maladies, 229. *See also* Disease, Distemper
Mallard, 16, 79, 200
Mallets, 100
Malt, 267
Mammals, species described, 120–31
Mannakin Town, Virginia, 90, 119
Man of nose, shellfish, 156, 165

Mansion, 100. *See also* Houses

Manufactures, 167

Manuring land, 80. *See* Agriculture, Crops

Maple, tree and sugar 74, 105, 111

Map of Carolina by Lawson, x, xix, xxxviii–xl, xxxix, 66, 68, 164

Maps, drawn by Indians, 214

Maps of the Southeast, xxxix–xl

Marble, land and rocks, xii, xxxix, 37, 48, 50, 52, 56, 59, 65, 89. *See also* Granite, Rocks

Marigold, 83

Markets, Indian, 178. *See also* Trade and traders

Marl, 45, 51, 76

Marriage, Indian, 35, 40, 190, 192; forced, 190; white with Indian, 244; white marriages at early age, 91

Marshes, 21, 34, 73, 75, 83, 84, 120, 127, 148, 151, 272

Marsh hens, 141, 154

Marsh rats, 130

Marsh weeds, 84

Martin, bird, 140, 148–49

Martin, Joel, landholder in Bath, xxii, xxiv

Maryland, xi, xxvi, liii, 9, 81, 87, 149, 167, 170, 201, 214, 227

Marten, fur of, 201

Masons, 170

Masquerades, Indian, 178

Massacre, Indian, xxxiii–xxxvi

Massey, English trader, 61

Mast, for swine, 99. *See also* Acorns

Masts, for ships, 74, 86, 88, 166

Match coat, 18, 28, 185, 197, 200, 209. *See also* Clothing of Indians

Materia medica, 230

Matriarchal policy of Indians, 205

Mats, 77, 178, 182, 195, 196, 217, 222

Mattamuskeet Indians, 242

Maycock, 102

May River, xxxix

Meadows, 70, 75, 127, 148, 166

Meal, Indian, how prepared, 35, 51

Measurement, Indian methods of, linear, 205; liquid, 232

Meat, 36, 42, 45, 66, 82, 144, 151–53, 155, 158–59, 164, 165, 216; how prepared by Indians, 36, 231, 241

Mechoacan berry, 147

Mecklenburg County, North Carolina, 39

Medicine, and medical practices of Indians, xvi, xliii, lii–liii, 17, 24, 48, 54, 84, 88, 90, 92, 97, 98, 101, 115, 122, 160, 196, 222, 226, 228, 244, 270

Medlars, 117

Medleys, 44

Meeting houses, Indian, 9

Meherrin Indians, xxx, 242

Melons, 182

Men (Mew) 141, 155

Mercenary Indian women, 189–90

Merchants, 5, 11, 19, 87, 93, 95, 182, 233. *See also* Trade and Traders

Merlin, 140, 143

Metals, 271

Metheglin, 104

Mexico, 173, 293, 244

Mice, 120, 127, 130, 221

Michel, Luis, Swiss land promoter, xx, xxiv

Midwives, Indian, 196

Militia, South Carolina, 10

Milk, 88

Mill, grain, xxiv, xxx, 100; stones, 95–96

Miller's thumb, fish, 163–64

Milling, J. C., *Red Carolinians,* 18, 34

Minerals and mining, xxvi, 11, 38, 56–57, 89–90, 92, 166, 201, 214, 229, 271

Mineral waters, 89–90

Ministers, 9, 171

Mink (Minx), 120, 126–27

Mint, 84

Miraculous peas, 82

Missionaries, 5, 230

Mississippi River, and region, 5, 8, 113, 121, 174, 231

Mistresses, Indian, of whites, 25, 36, 190, 195. *See also* Adultery

Mitchell, Francis-Louis, 214

Moccasins (Moccosins), Indian, 47, 55, 197, 200

Mocking bird, 141, 147–48

Monacan, Virginia. *See* Mannakin Town

Molasses, 70, 267

Moles, 120

Monack, fur, 201

Money, English and Indian, 9–11, 167, 177, 188, 190, 193–94, 203–4, 214, 224–26, 268. *See also* Beads, Peak, Roanoak

Monks rhubarb, 83

Monroe, North Carolina, xii

Months, Indian names for, 240

Monuments, Indian, 50

Mooney, James, quoted, 17, 23–24, 38

Moor fur, 201

Moor hen, 140, 145

Moore, James, Governor of South Carolina, 48

Morphew, treatment for, 102

Mortar and pestle, 105, 216

Mortality, of Indians, 45, 232; of Palatines, 268–69

Moseley, Edward, xviii, xx–xxii, xxxix, xliv, li–liii

Mosquito (Musquito), 14, 149, 168

Moss, and its uses, 35, 182, 197

Moths, 104

Mountains, xxxi, lii, 6, 11, 17, 21, 32–33, 37, 51–53, 55–57, 89–90, 96, 111, 113, 129, 139, 143, 146, 152, 166, 174–75, 214–15, 229, 272

Mount Bonny, named by Barbadians, 77

Mount Skerry, names by Barbadians, 76

Mourners, Indian, *See* Funeral ceremonies

Mouse. *See* Mice

Moustaches (Mustaches), Indian, 58

Muffs, Indians, from bear fur, 123

Mulberry, trees and fruit, 74, 109, 117, 118, 146

Mulberry-month, 240

Mules, 56

Mullein, 84

Mullet, 72, 78, 155, 160

Mulloy, W. J., and R. C. Beatty, translators of *William Byrd's Natural History of Virginia*, liii

Murder, 169, 204, 220, 242

Muscovy (Russia), 143

Music, Indian, 33, 44–45, 178

Muskmelons, 83

Muskrat, 120, 125

Mussel (Muscle) shells, 127, 156, 164–65

Mustard, 231

Mutton, 11, 88, 121, 182

Myrrh, 270

Myrtle, 70, 97–98; wax used to make candles, 97–98

N

Nails, 94, 99, 170, 204

Names, of Indian children, how given, 204; Indian nations, 242; towns, 242

Nanticokes peas, 82

Narratives of Early Carolina, cited, 79

Natural history, xvi, xli–xliii, lii–liv, 6, 11, 95, 96–171

Naturalists, xl, liii

Naturalization law of 1709, English, xxvi

Naval stores, 11, 167; *See also* Tar, Pitch, Rosin, Turpentine

Navigation, Indian method of, 213. *See also* Canoes, Ships and shipbuilding

Necoes, Indian village, xx, 72

Nectarine, 115

Negroes, xxxi, xxxiv, xxxvi, 16, 20, 81, 94, 220, 227, 270. *See also* Slaves

Nelson's Ferry, South Carolina, 24

Nettle, 83

Neuse River, xiv, xvii, xxvi–xxvii, xxxi, xxxiii, 64, 66, 130, 222, 242, 269, 273

New Bern, v, xviii, xxii, xxiv, xxxiv, xxvii, xxxi, xlii, 66

New England, 8, 70, 79, 145, 167, 201. *See also* Trade and Traders

New Jersey, 201

New Map of Carolina, by Thornton, Modren, Lea, xxxix

New Orleans, 8

New Netherland, 8

New Spain, 98, 244–45

New World, xi, xvii. *See also* America

New York, city and colony, xi, 8, 35, 145, 167, 201, 203

Nightingale, 141, 148

Nightshade, 84

No-nosed Indian doctor, xii, 27

North Carolina, xii–xiii, xv, xvi–xix, xxxvii–xli, xliii–xliv, liii, 11, 13, 35, 59, 90, 156, 158, 164, 169, 172, 189, 219, 224, 267–70, 274

Noses, loss of due to syphilis, 26, 231

Northern colonies, 8, 81
Nottoway Indians, 242
Nottoway River, xxii
Nuts, 17, 23, 34, 88, 129

O

Oak, 33, 50, 64, 74, 80, 97, 107, 145, 213, 226
Oak-land, 216
Oak vine, 107
Oat, 81, 166
Occaneechi, town or village, xiv, 59–60
Occaneechi (Achonechy, Aconecho) Indians, xiv, 64, 242
Occaneechi Trail or Trading Path, 59
Ocean, 46, 51; hardship of voyage, xxvii. See also Atlantic Ocean
Ocher (Oaker), 88
Ochs, J. R., Americanischer Wegewiser . . . , xl, lii
Ocracoke (Ocacock) Inlet, and harbor, 68, 71, 267
Oil (Oyl), 24, 86, 92, 99, 166, 226. See also Acorns, Bear, Pigeon
Ointment, from tulip tree buds, 100–1
Old age, Indian veneration of, 43
Old Town Creek (Bath Creek), xxii
Old wife, duck, 141, 151, 156
Olives, 99
Onion, 83–84, 104
Operations performed by Indians, 229. See also Medicine, Surgery
O'Possum (Possum), 31, 33, 125–26, 182, 195
Oranges, 11
Oratory of Indian leaders, 187
Orchards, 88, 93, 104, 125, 271. See also Fruit
Oroonoke tobacco, 175. See Tobacco
Ornaments, Indian, 44–45, 192, 200–3. See also Dress of Indians
Osnaburg cloth, 94
Otter, 120, 124–25, 210
Owl, 141, 149
Oxen, 87, 93
Oxeye, 141, 149
Oxford University, xvii
Oyster, and oyster banks, 16–17, 89, 126, 156, 164–65, 218; shells for lime, 89, 217

P

Pails, 103
Paint, xiii, 24, 42, 271
Palatines, xx, xxiv, xxvi–xxvii, xxx, xxxiv, xlii–xliii, 268–69
Paleontology, xliii
Palisades (Palisados), 55, 107
Palmetto, 108
Pamlico Indians, 226, 242
Pamlico precinct, xxiv
Pamlico (Pampticough) River and Sound, xiv, xvii, xli, xl, 66–67, 71, 104, 267–68; region, xxii, xl, 167, 171
Panther, and panther skins, 33, 120, 123, 204
Papaw (Papau) tree and its apples, 111
Paper, 95
Parakeet (Parrakeeto), 74, 79, 196, 140, 145–47
Paralytics, Indian, 231
Parents, role of, in Indian marriages, 192–93
Parliament, xxvi
Parr, Old, Welsh Methusalem, 36
Parsnip, 82
Parsonage house, 9, 171
Partridge, 50, 73, 140, 144, 221
Paschal, Herbert R., Jr., A History of Colonial Bath, xxii, xxiv
Pasquotank (Paspitank, Paspatank) Indians, 200, 242
Pasturage, 75, 86–88, 166, 271
Paths, Indian trading, 23. See also Trade and traders, Trading Path
Patience of Indians, 205–6, 243
Peas, liv, 14, 30, 39, 44, 54, 82, 88, 144, 146, 185
Peace made with Indians, 77–78
Peach, 24, 35, 115–16, 167, 173, 182, 217, 267, 271; bread, 24; loaf, 54
Peak, Indian money, 184, 201, 203, 214, 224
Pear, 114
Pearls, 16
Pearmain apples, 113–14
Pecan (Pecoon) root, 175
Pedee (Yadkin) River. See Reatkin, Sapona
Pelican (Pellican), 16, 141, 154
Pellitory bark, 106, 241. See also Drugs, Medicine

Pelts. *See* Fur, Hides, Skins, Trade and Traders
Pennsylvania, xxiv, liii, 145, 167, 201, 214, 268
Pens for writing, 150
Pepper, 231
Perch (Pearch) 156, 162–63
Periwinkle, shellfish, 156, 165
Perkins, David, an incorporator of Bath, xxii
Perriauger (Perauger), 103
Perry, a drink, 115
Persimmon, and its uses, 109, 180
Pestilential fevers, 135
Pestles, 105, 216
Petiver, James, London apothecary and collector of botanical specimens, xvi, xxx, xli–xliii; Lawson's letters to, 267–73
Pheasant, 140, 141, 152
Philadelphia, 268
Phthisick, 231
Physician, Indian, 18, 24, 115, 222. *See also* Medicine
Physick, xliii, 54, 98, 134, 222, 229, 240, 272. *See also* Drugs, Medicine
Piedmont area, xv
Pigeon, 48, 50–51, 140, 143, 146, 217
Pigging with Indian females, 36
Pigmy beans, 82
Pigs, 81. *See also* Hogs, Swine
Pike, 156, 162, 217
Pimento tree, 96, 110
Pine, 28, 33, 62, 74, 86, 75, 97, 104, 146, 180; bark for houses, 65
Pine (Piny) land, 65, 75, 80
Pins, 100
Pipes, 36, 99
Pistols, 59
Pitch, 11, 86, 88, 104, 166, 176, 188, 207; methods of making, 104
Pitch-pine, for burning at stake, 53
Plagiarisms of Lawson, lii–liv
Plaice, fish, 156, 160
Plaids, 197
Planks, 100, 166. *See also* Boards
Plantain, 83
Plantations, xii, xx, 20, 34, 66, 72, 81, 87–89, 94, 128, 144, 167, 170–71, 195–96, 201, 226, 229, 244–45. *See also* Agriculture
Plant classification system, xli

Plants, xli–xliii, lii, 84, 92, 169, 269–70, 273
Plasterers, 170
Platters, 76
Ploughing, 81
Plover, 79, 140, 145
Plumbstones, xliii
Plums, 111–12, 116, 119
Pocosin (Percoarson, Perkosan), 16, 32, 63, 120, 144. *See* Swamp
Poisons, 205–6, 228, 232–33; Indian practice of poisoning, 233
Poison vine, 107
Pole beans, 82
Polecat, 33, 120, 124, 182
Polecat Creek, xiv
Polishing of stones by Indians, 173
Pollock, Thomas, large North Carolina landholder, xix, xxvii; quoted, xxvii, xxx
Polygamy of Indians, 41
Pomander, 18
Pompions, 83
Ponds, 271
Poor, problem of, in London, xxvi
Pope's Jubilee, xvii
Poplar (tulip) tree, 100
Poppy, 84, 96
Popular party, in colonial North Carolina, xviii
Population, Indian nations and towns, 242–43
Population of North Carolina, xx
Porcelan, Indian bead money, 197, 203
Pork, 25, 33, 58, 70, 88, 93, 100, 101, 103, 121, 166–67, 182, 224
Porpoise, 155, 158, 221
Porter, John, landowner in Bath, xxiv
Port Royal, South Carolina, 11
Portsmouth, England, xlii, 268
Porridge pot, 44
Portugal, 107
Portugal quinces, 115
Possum, 31, 33, 120, 125–26, 182, 195; coition of described, 125
Posts for houses, 101–2
Potato, 82, 122, 182
Poteskeet (Poteskeit) Indians, 242
Pot herbs, 83
Pot marjoram, 83

Pots, 44, 76, 173, 178
Pox, 25, 26, 226, 231; Indian treatment of, 226
Poultry, 81–82, 93, 127
Pounds for taking fish, 218
Powder, xi, 69, 94, 174, 216, 221, 227. *See also* Shot
Practitioners, Indian, 17, 24. *See also* Medicine
Presents for Indians, 240
"Present State of Carolina," by Lawson, 86, 166
Prices, xlii, 18, 70, 78, 87, 93–95, 98
Prickly ash, 107
Priests, Indian, 27, 221
Prim (Privet), 97
Princes-feather, plant, 84, 96
Prisoners of war and their treatment, xxxvi, 10, 53, 174–75, 205–7, 224, 233
Privateers, French, xxvii
Produce and products of North Carolina, 103, 166
Promotional tracts, xl, lii, liv
Proprietary North Carolina, xv
Proprietors of Carolina, 170–71, 224, 249–63
Prostitution, Indian, 190. *See also* Trading girls
Protestants, xxvi, 20
Provisions, 8, 22, 36, 66, 73, 92, 167, 224
Prunes, 271
Public Register of Pamlico Precinct, xxiv
Puddings, Indian, 111
Punishment among Indians, 27, 220, 225. *See also* Scalping, Torture
Pulse, 24, 50, 82, 87, 166, 177, 182, 216, 269. *See also* Beans, Peas
Purges, used by Indians, xlii, 227, 229, 241
Purslane, 83

Q

Quadrupeds, xli
Quail, 7. *See also* Partridge
Quakers, xviii, xxx
Quarries, stone, 24
Queen, Indian, 35; of England, xxxiv
Quiddony, 24, 182, 217
Quince, 114–15; drink, 115

Quiozogon (Quiogozon, Quiogonzon), 189, 219
Quitrent, xx, 170

R

Rabbit, 7, 58, 120–21, 127–28, 182, 200
Raccoon, 16, 23, 120, 126, 182, 200–1; fur, 201
Raccoon Island, xii, 14
Radish, 83
Raft fowl, 141, 153–54. *See also* Duck
Ragoo, 31
Rags, 56
Rails, 99
Raisins, 271
Raleigh, Sir Walter, 68
Randleman, North Carolina, xiv
Ranges for cattle, 34. *See also* Pasturage
Rappahannock River, 106
Raspberry, 110, 117
Rat, 120, 127, 130
Rattle, 62, 178, 223
Rattlesnake, 49, 131, 133–35, 222–23, 228, 232. *See also* Drugs, Medicine
Raven, 140
Ray, John, *Historia Plantarium*, xli–xlii; tracts on Bannister's plants, xli; book of physick, 268
Razor, 39
Reading, Lionel, xx
Realgar, 56
Reatkin River, 60, 62, 64. *See also* Yadkin River
Rebellion, Cary, xviii
Red-back snake, 131, 136
Red-bellied snake, 131, 136
Redbird, 140
Redbud tree, 106
Red cadiz, 47
Red Carolinians, by J. C. Milling, 18
Red cherries, 116
Redhead, waterfowl, 141, 154
Red hickory, 105
Red oak, 99
Red root dock, 84, 201. *See also* Medicine
Redstreak apple, 114
Reeds, 44, 107, 180, 185, 196, 204, 218, 221, 228–29. *See also* Cane
Reed sparrow, 141

Religion, of Indians, 20, 57–58, 80, 169, 219, 243–45. *See also* Spirits, Idols and idolatry, Happy hunting ground

Religious toleration in Carolina, 9, 171

Remedies, 18, 25, 26, 37, 134, 196; for snakebite, 83–84; for colic, 101

Reptiles, xli, 92, 139–40. *See* Snakes

Research Laboratories of The University of North Carolina at Chapel Hill, xiii

Resources. *See* Land, Minerals

Rheumatism, 231

Rhubarb, 83–84

Rice, 81, 141, 166

Rickets, 90, 196

Richbourg, Philip de, French Huguenot minister, 119

Richland County, South Carolina, xii

Rights, Douglas L., *The American Indian in North Carolina*, xii–xiv

Ring-bones, horses, 88

Ring oak, 99

Rings, 201

Ringtail hawk, 140, 143

Rising Sun, Scottish man-of-war, 15

Rivanna River, Virginia, 42

Rivers, xiv–xv, xvii, xxxix, xl, 6, 8, 11, 17, 20–24, 29–30, 32, 34, 38, 46, 48–49, 52–55, 59–60, 62, 66, 68, 70, 72, 75–76, 78–80, 86–87, 89–90, 93, 100–3, 111, 113, 117, 127, 130, 132, 135, 146, 150, 154, 166, 170, 174, 200, 213–14, 216–18, 222, 231, 244, 267–68, 271

Roach, fish, 156, 163

Roads, xxxi–xxxii, 9, 21, 55, 214. *See also* Trading Path

Roanoak, Indian bead money, 197, 68–69, 127, 184, 224

Roanoke Inlet and Sound, 61, 68, 71

Roanoke Island, and colony, 61, 68–69, 127, 184, 225

Roanoke River, liii

Robbery by Indians, 224

Rockahomine meal, 182

Rocket, 83

Rockfish, 156, 217

Rocks, 74. *See also* Marble, Stone and stone houses

Rocky Point, named by Barbadians, 74

Rocky River, xiii, 55, 60

Rods to whip horses, 106

Rome, xvii, 7

Roncommock, Chowan conjurer, 226

Rook, 143

Roots, drugs from, 17, 27, 82, 92, 107, 228, 233, 268. *See also* Drugs, Medicine

Rope, of elm bark, 100

Rope apples, 114

Rose, 84

Rosemary, 83

Rosin, 88, 92, 104, 166, 229; methods of making, 104. *See also* Naval Stores

Rotten wood worm, 131, 139

Rouncival (Rounceval) peas, 82

Royal Society of London, xli, 272

Royal tomb of Indian king, 188. *See also* Tombs

Rue, 84

Rum, 18, 63, 66, 70, 190, 211, 212, 224, 232–33, 240, 270; trade in, 70; law against sale to Indians, 212; Indian craze for, 232

Runner, bird, 154–55

Runner, fish, 156, 165

Rushes, uses for, 42, 78, 182

Rutland, England, 46

Rye, 81, 166

S

Sabbath, not observed by Indians, 240

Saddles, 95

Saf-flower, 96

Saffron, 96

St. Augustine, Florida, xxix, 10

St. Matheo River, xxxix

St. Thomas Parish, 171

Sails, 19

Salad (Sallad), 83, 231

Salisbury, North Carolina, xiii, 42

Salley, A. S., *Narratives of Early Carolina*, 79

Salmon, 159

Salt, 34, 70, 81, 87; fish, 16, 93; licks, 89

Saltpeter, 89

Samphire, 83

Sandbars and sand banks, 14, 17, 68, 93, 97, 102, 106, 111–12, 116, 154, 157

Sand-birds, 141

Sand for glass makers, 89
Sandhills, 108
Sandy Hook, New York, xi, 8
Sanfoin, 120, 170
Santee Indians, 22, 24–25, 27, 30, 66;
  king of, 27
Santee Jack, hunter and guide, xii,
  31, 34
Santee River, xii, 9, 16, 19, 24, 29, 32,
  34
Sapona Indians, 42, 46, 50, 53, 56–57,
  242
Sapona River, xiii, 52–53, 55, 60, 146
Sapona town, 51–52, 55–56
Sarsparilla, 84
Sashes, Indian, 28, 121, 137
Sassafras 27; root and bark in medi-
  cine, 49, 101, 230
Saunders, W. L., Colonial Records of
  North Carolina, xix
Savannah Indians, 48, 174
Savannas, 11, 23, 31, 34–35, 51, 59, 70,
  84, 86, 110, 120, 149, 151
Savine, plant, 97
Savory, 83
Saw mill and saws, 79, 94, 170
Scaldhead, Indian treatment for, 226
Scallop (Skellop), 156, 165
Scalping by Indians, described,
  xxxvi, 10, 177, 207
Scaly-bark oak, 60, 99
Scarification of patients by Indians,
  223, 232. See also Medicine
Scarlet root, Indian use in medicine,
  174
Scarlet trumpet vine, 102
Schoccores Indians, 64, 242
Schroeter, George, map maker, xl
Scientists, xvi
Scilly Islands, England, 7, 165
Scipio, Indian guide, xii, 23–24
Scissors, 39
Scolds, none among Indian women,
  43, 185, 210
Scorpion-lizard, 131, 136
Scotch linen, 94
Scotland, xvi
Scott's Lake, S. C. 24
Screech (Scritch) owl, 141, 149
Scurvy and its treatment by Indians,
  231
Scurvy grass, 83
Seacoast of Carolina, 6, 108

Sea cock, 141, 151
Sea nettle, 153
Sea-pies or curlues, 141, 151
Sea shells, xli; and their use by In-
  dians, 203–4. See also Wampum
Sea snail horns, 156, 165
Sea tench, fish, 156
Sedge and its use by Indians, 42
Seneca Indians, 49–50, 53, 55, 59, 61,
  207, 231
Sensitive (Sensible) plant, 96
Sepulchres of Indians, 52, 188. See
  also Tombs
Serum used by Indians, 223
Servants, 81, 227
Settlements and settlers, xxvi, xl, 70.
  See also Cape Fear, Roanoke Island
Sewee Bay, 14, 16
Sewee Indians, xii, 17, 20, 21, 34
Shad, 66, 72, 78, 155, 156, 160
Shakori Indians, 61
Shallops, 106
Shallots, 83, 104
Shark, 155, 158
Sharp practices of white traders, xxxi
Shavelock, 94
Shearwater, waterfowl, 141, 154
She-bed-fellow, 192
Sheep, 54, 56, 69, 86, 87–88, 98, 271
Sheepshead, fish, 156, 160
Sheldrake, waterfowl, 141
Shellfish, 16, 156–65, 182, 218
Shells, 16, 35, 92, 177, 267; as pen-
  dants, xiii; as pins, xiii; as money,
  177, 203
Shingles for houses, 100, 103
Ships, and shipbuilding, xxvi, 8, 10,
  18–20, 68, 70–71, 74, 75, 94, 99, 103,
  105, 167–68, 272
Ship surgeons, 227
Ship wrecks, 127
Shirts, 200
Shoe makers, 94, 170
Shoes, 126, 197, 200. See also Mocca-
  sins
Shot, 94, 216, 227. See also Ammuni-
  tion, Powder
Shoveler, bird, 141, 152
Shrimp, 156, 165
Shrubs, 85, 92, 96
Sicknesses and treatment of sick, 220,
  222. See also Drugs, Medicine
Sickle peas, 82

Silica, 31
Silk, 11, 86, 92, 166, 200
Silk-grass, 196, 200
Silkworms, 109
Sills for houses, 102, 107
Silver, 214
Silver Hill, North Carolina, xiii
Simlings, 83. *See also* Squashes
Singing of Indians, 45. *See also* Music
Siouan Indians, tribes of, 17, 23–24,
    38–39, 42, 46, 53, 60–61
Sissipahaw Indians, 60, 64
Skate or stingray, 156, 160, 182, 218
Skins and furs, 8, 18, 46, 182, 184,
    204, 206, 211, 217. *See also* Hides,
    Trade and traders
Skerry, 77
Skunks, 124
Slaves, and slave trade, xxx–xxxi,
    10–11, 19, 48, 64, 81, 87, 94, 174–75,
    187–95, 204, 208–12, 217, 225, 227,
    243
Sloane Collection, British Museum,
    267
The Sloane Herbarium, xliii
Sloane Manuscripts, xli–xliii
Sloops and their building, 68, 70, 99,
    103
Smallpox and its treatment by In-
    dians, 17, 34, 135, 231–32
Smelt, 156
Smith, Hannah, Lawson's mistress,
    xiv, xxxvii, 274–75
Smith, Isabella, Lawson's daughter,
    274
Smith, Richard, North Carolina plan-
    ter, xiv, xxxvii, 67, 275
Smiths, 90, 203
Snake root and its use in medicine,
    83–84
Snakes, lii, 84, 127, 131, 133–39,
    142–43, 182, 187, 219, 222, 228, 270
Snares for fishing, Indian, 217
Snipe, 140, 144
Snowbird, 141, 150
Snow Hill, North Carolina, xxxiii
Society for the Propagation of the
    Gospel, letter to, xxvii
Sodomy, not practiced by Indians,
    193
Soil, fertility of, xiv, 11, 32, 37, 38, 45,
    48, 52, 59–60, 63, 68–69, 80, 84, 86,
    167

Soldiers, 25
Sole, 156, 160
Songs, Indian, 178
Sorcerers, Indian, 30. *See also* Con-
    jurers and conjuration
Sores, Indian cures for, 90. *See also*
    Drugs, Medicine
Sorrell or sourwood tree, 83, 104
Sothel, Seth, Governor of Albemarle
    County, 224, 226
Sounds, 68, 70, 93, 164, 168
Soup of Indians, 51
South Carolina, x, xv, xvii, xxxix,
    liii, 8–11, 13, 49, 68, 80, 97, 117,
    128, 168, 174, 189, 211, 243
South sea trade, xliii, 52
Spain, 56, 94
Spaniards, xi, 10, 26, 93, 98, 166,
    172–73, 230, 245
Spanish oak, 99
Spanish mackerel, 155, 158–59
Spanish oysters, 156, 165
Spaniel, Lawson's bitch, 37, 50, 53,
    55, 56
Sparrow, 141, 148
Sparrow hawk, 140, 143
Spavins, horse, 88
Speaker of House, North Carolina
    General Assembly, xviii
Spearmint, 84
Speck, Frank G., anthropologist, 219
Spermaceti whale, 157
Spinach (Spinage), 83
Spinning, and spinning wheels, 105,
    167
Spirits, Indian belief in, 219, 220, 222
Spleen, treatment of, 228
Splints, horse, 88
Spoons, 36, 76, 217
Sports, Indian, 62
Spotswood, Alexander, Governor of
    Virginia, xx; quoted, xxx, xliv
Spotted fever, xxx, 269
Spring, season, 94
Springs, bubbling, xli, 32, 37, 272
Squashes, 83, 182
Squaw (Squah), described, 36
Squirrel, 120, 129–30, 134, 182, 200
Spunk, tinder, 213
Stag Park, named by Barbadians, 74
Stags, 120, 129
State house, of Indian king, 42–43, 46
Staves, 88, 166

Stealing by Indians, 39
Stearns, Raymond, P. xvi, xli–xliv
Stewart, John, of Virginia, trader
    with Indians, 49–50, 63
Stingray, 182
Stockings, 200
Stone, and treatment for it, 167
Stone and stone houses, 2, 24, 31, 32,
    37, 55, 59–60, 63–64, 74, 89, 92, 170,
    231, 271
Stone crab, 156, 164
Stone quarries, 59, 64
Stories and legends of Indians, 26
Stomach-ache, treatment for, 27, 229
Stork, 35, 141, 149–50
Storms along coast, 68, 71–72
Stoves, 44
Stratagems, Indian, 208
Straw, 81
Strawberry, 38, 117; month, 240
Streams, 51. See also Rivers, Creeks
Streets, Charleston, 8; of Tuscaroras,
    65; of New Bern, xxvii-xxix
Stroud, 31
Struma and its treatment, 231
Stuffs, 94
Sturgeon, 156, 162, 182, 217
Succession to kingship, Indian, 205
Sucking fish, 156, 163
Sugar cane and sugar, 70, 81, 110, 111
Sugar Creek, South Carolina, xiii, 49
Sugaree Indians, xiii, 49
Sugar maple, 111
Sugar pear, 114
Suicides of Indians, 211
Sullivan's Island, South Carolina, xii,
    13
Summers in North Carolina, 168
Sun and moon, Indian idea of, 240
Sun fish, 156, 161
Sun flower, 96
Superstitions, Indian, 58, 98, 217–19
Surgery, Indian, 222, 244. See also
    Cures, Medicine
Surveyor General of North Carolina,
    xxi, xviii, xxxii
Surveyors, 134
Swaddle bill duck, 141, 155
Swamps, 16–17, 20–24, 29, 31–33, 35,
    39, 55, 63, 65–66, 73–74, 97–98, 100,
    106, 108, 135–36, 144

Swamp snake, 131, 135–36
Swan, 16, 52, 54, 79, 141, 150
Swan shot, 99
Swallow, bird, 140
Sweat baths and houses, Indian, 48,
    55, 226, 230. See also Medicine
Sweetgum tree, 102
Swellings, Indian treatment of, 230.
    See also Medicine
Swepsonville, North Carolina, xiv
Swift, bird, 140
Swine, 69, 78–79, 87, 99, 121, 123,
    142, 269. See also Hogs
Swiss Land Company, xxvi, 214
Swiss settlers in North Carolina, xxiv,
    xxvi, xxx, liii, 215, 269
Switzerland, lii, 214
Sword fish, 155, 158
Sycamore, 106
Syphilis, Indian treatment of, 25. See
    also Cures, Medicine

                    T
Tables and table making, 102, 105
Tailor (Taylor), 170
Tallow, 70, 88, 129, 166
Talkative women, 43. See also Scolds
Tanners, 170. See also Leather
Tansey, 83
Tapestry, in Indian cabins, 61
Tar, 11, 86, 88, 92, 104, 166, 229;
    methods of making, 104
Tar River, xiv
Taylor fish, 156, 162
Tea, 98. See also Yaupon
Teal, 16, 31, 74, 141, 152
Terrapin (Terebin), 131, 138, 156,
    165, 182
Tettars, Indian treatment of, 36, 90,
    102. See Medicine
Thames River, England, 7, 52
Theater, Indian, 46, 49. See State-
    house
Theft, and thievery of Indians, 47, 64
Thornback, 155, 161
Thornton, John, map maker, xxxix
Thrasher, fish, 155, 157
Thread, 18, 90, 120
Throstle, bird, 141, 149
Thrush, 48, 141, 147
Thyme, 83
Tides, of ocean, 71–72; Cape Fear
    River, 21, 72

Tiger (Tyger), 33, 37, 120, 124

Tiles, 87. *See also* Brick

Timber, and timber trees, 49, 51, 60, 70, 74–76, 80, 88, 98, 101, 166, 271

Time, Indian reckoning of, 240–41

Toadfish, 156, 161

Tobacco, 16, 24, 27, 36, 39, 63, 83, 88, 94, 167, 175–76, 201, 203, 217, 245, 270; tongs, 39; pipes and pipe-clay, 88, 201, 203, 217; fleets, 94; planting, 94; trade in, 167

Todd, V. H., ed., *Christoph Von Graffenried's Account of the Founding of New Bern*, xxvii, xxxiv, xxxvi

Tomahawks and Indian use of, 209

Tombs, Indian, 27, 29, 188. *See also* Sepulchres

Tomtit or oxeye, 141, 149

Tools, for agriculture, xxvi, 94, 175

Toothache, Indian remedy for, 106, 229

Top masts, 103

Topsail Inlet, 68, 72

Tortoise and tortoise shells, 16, 127, 131, 138, 156, 165, 182

Torture, Indian methods, 205

Totero Indians, 53–54, 242

Town Creek, South Carolina, 8

Towns, Indian, xiv, 34, 46, 49, 52, 63, 66, 177, 184, 214, 232–33

Trade and traders, xiii, xxxi, 6, 8, 9–11, 18, 19, 23–24, 35, 43–44, 46, 49–50, 63–64, 70, 87–89, 93–94, 103, 113, 167, 175, 182, 192, 201, 224, 232–33, 244, 271

Trading Ford, on Yadkin River, xiii

Trading girls, Indian, 41, 50, 190, 194–95

Trading Path, xiii, xiv, 60

Transportation, 51–52, 89, 103, 121

Trap-ball, Indian game, 180

Travail of Indian women in pregnancy, 196

Travel and travelers, xv, lii, 34, 213, 220

Treasurer of North Carolina province, xviii

Treatment of wounds, ulcers, 26–27, 30, 100–1, 103, 226–27, 230

Trees, xli, xliii, lii, 16, 24, 28, 32–33, 35, 37, 50, 51, 56, 59, 60, 62, 70, 73–74, 80, 88, 116, 221, 271

Trefoil, 170

Trenchers, how made, 105–6

Trent River, xxvi–xxvii, 90, 127

Tres colores (tricolor) flower, 84, 96

Tribes, Indian, 18, listed, 242. *See also* names of individual tribes

Trimming fruit trees, Indian, method, 119

Tripoli, 31

Trophies, Indian, 203

Tropic (Tropick) bird, 141, 154

Trout, 156, 161, 218

Trulls, in Salisbury Court, England, 45

Trumpet vine, 102

Tryon, Governor William, xviii, xxvi

Tuberculosis. *See* Consumption

Tulip tree, 70, 100, 172–73, 217, 231; juice used to treat gonorrhea, 231

Turkey, 17, 23, 25, 31–34, 51, 59–60, 64, 73–74, 79, 99, 141, 153, 216, 227, 240

Turkey acorns, 145

Turkey buzzard or vulture, 10, 142

Turkey oak, 99, 145

Turkey-Quarters, named by Barbadians, 74

Turnery ware, 106

Turnips, 58, 82, 96

Turpentine, 88, 104, 166, 176; methods of making, 104. *See also* Naval Stores

Turtle, 16, 131, 138

Turtle dove, 140

Tuscarora (Tusceruro, Tuskeruro) Indians, xiv, xxx, xxxiii, 35, 64–66, 165, 175, 195, 207, 220, 221, 224, 225, 232, 242; names of towns and number of people, 242

Tutcock, bird, 141

Tutors in South Carolina, 9

Tyler, M. C., quoted, xv

U

Ulcer, Indian treatment of, 30, 101, 226–27, 230

Unguents, 25

Unionville, town, xiii

Urmstone, Rev. John, quoted, xxxvii

Ushery King, 46

Uwharrie (Heighwaree) River, xiii–xiv, 56–57, 59

V

Valleys, 32, 272
Veal, 11, 33, 88, 121, 133
Vegetables, xli, 26, 48, 57, 85, 95, 139, 166, 230, 267, 229; used as drugs, 229. *See also* individual vegetables
Venereal diseases. *See* Gonorrhea, Syphilis, Pox
Venison, 23, 25, 31, 44, 59, 61, 87, 182; broth, 35, 51, 105
Vermilion paint, used by Indians, 28, 42, 201
Vermin, 23, 30, 54, 84, 104, 123, 143, 150, 216. *See* Bear, Panther, and other wild animals
Vices of Indians, 240. *See also* Drunkenness, Gambling
Victuals, Indian, 63, 81. *See also* Food
Villages, Indian. *See* Towns
Vinegar, 116
Vines, liii, 70, 108, 117–18. *See also* Grapes and grape vines
Violets, 84
Vipers, 131, 138. *See also* Snakes.
Virginia, xiii, xix–xxi, xxvi–xxvii, xxxi–xxxii, xli, xliv, liii, 9, 42, 49–50, 58–61, 63, 68–69, 81, 84, 87, 103, 104, 114, 150, 167, 170, 174, 201, 214, 268–270
Virginia–North Carolina boundary dispute, xix–xxii, xliii
Virginity, *flos virginis*, 41
Virtues of Indians, 240, 244
Visscher, Nicolas, map maker, xl
Vizards, Indian, 44
Vulneraries, 83
Vulture, 140, 142

W

Wainscot, 100, 102
Walking sticks, 105
Wall-fruit, 115
Walnut tree and walnuts, 74, 80, 105, 109
Wampum, 164, 177, 201, 203–4, 206. *See also* Money, Beads
War and war making, xxxvi, 42–43, 92, 177, 201, 208, 233, 241, 244
Ward, Collingwood, xxii
War dances, 177
Warden pear, 114
War paint of Indians, 201

Warships, 8
Washington, North Carolina, xiv
Wasp, 182
Wat-Coosa, Indian chief, 78
Water, drinking, 37, 78
Water ash, 100
Wateree Indians, xii, 37–39, 50, 63
Wateree River, xii, 21, 33
Waterfowl, 52, 141–55, 269. *See also* names of individual birds
Watermelon, 83
Water oak, 100
Water pheasant, 141, 152
Water rat, 120, 127
Water snakes, 127, 131, 135
Water terrapin (terrebin), 138
Waterways. *See* Creeks, Inlets, Rivers
Water witch or ware coot, 141, 155
Wax, 97, 166
Waxhaw (Waxsaw, Wisack) Indians, xii, 39, 42
Weapons of Indians, 44. *See also* Arrows, Bows, Guns
Weasel, 120, 131
Weather, 13, 16, 19, 31, 33, 37, 46, 52, 55, 59–60, 66–67, 78, 93–94, 221, 222, 269
Weavers, 107, 170
Wedges, 94, 170
Weeds, 81
Weeks, S. B., "John Lawson," in S. A. Ashe, ed., *Biographical History of North Carolina*, xv, xviii
Weet bird, 141, 149
Weirs (Wares), fish, 92, 119
Welchman, fish, 162
Welsh Methusalem, 36
West Indies, 9, 11, 88, 167
Whale, whale fishing, and whale products, 93, 155, 157, 166
Wheat, 70, 80, 88, 114, 166, 203. *See also* Grain
Whippoorwill (Whippoo will), 141, 150
Whistlers (Whisslers), 141, 153
White, John, paintings, 27, 179, 181, 183, 186, 191, 198, 199, 202
White cedar, 103
White fish, 156, 163
White grapes, 108
White gum, 102
White iron or ring-oak, 99

Whores, Indian, 40, 47. *See also* Prostitution, Trading girls
Widgeon, 16, 74, 141, 152
Wigs, 94
Wigwams, 180. *See also* Cabins, Houses
Wild bulls, 182
Wildcat, 120, 123–24, 182
Wild geese, 187. *See also* Geese, Fowl
Wild onions, 83
Wild rhubarb, 83
Wild turkey, 153. *See also* Turkey
Will, Lawson's, xxxvii, 274–75
Williamsburg, Virginia, xxi, xliv, xx
Willow, 74, 106
Willow oak, 100
Will willet, bird, 141, 151
Winchester wedding, 47, 190
Window frames and glass, 95, 100
Winds, 21. *See also* Weather
Windsor bean, 82
Wine and wine making, 27, 86, 90, 92, 106, 109, 115, 117, 166, 215
Wings, 201
Winnick Keshuse, Indian name for Christmas, 241
Winston-Salem, North Carolina, xix–xx
Winter in North Carolina, 69, 94, 168, 240, 269
Winter queening apple, 114
Winyaw (Winjaw, Winyan) River, 30, 48
Wisacky (Wisack) Indians, 46. *See also* Waxhaw Indians
Witchcraft, 169. *See also* Conjurers and conjuration
Wives, Indian sale of, 204
Wizard, 30
Woccon Indians, language, 233–39, 242–45; villages, 224
Wolf, 33, 44, 55–56, 73, 124, 189

Women, colonial, 90–91, 167; Indian, 35
Wood and wood products, 90. *See also* Timber
Woodbine, 70, 96
Woodcock, 50, 58, 140, 144
Wood houses, 8
Woodpecker, 141, 147
Woods, 78. *See also* Forests, Timber
Wool and wool products, 88, 90, 167, 197
Words, Indian and English equivalent, 174, 242–45
Work of Indian women, 195
Worms, treatment for, 101
Wormseed, 84
Worm-ships, 103, 168
Wormwood, 83
Wounds, Indian treatment of, 26–27, 103
Wrecks along coast, 157
Wren, 141, 148
Wyersdale, Nathaniel, Bath landowner, xxiv

Y

Yadkin River, xiii, 42, 52–53, 55, 60. *See also* Reatkin, Sapona
Yards, 103, 166
Yarrow, 84
Yaupon, and yaupon tea, 97–98, 229–30
Yawls, 72. *See also* Ships
Yaws (Yawes), 25
Yellow-wing bird, 141, 150
Yew, 97
Yields of wheat, 80. *See also* Corn, Crops
Yorkshire, England, xv, xvi, 38

Z

Zoology, xliii